Charles Pelham Mulvany

The History of the North-West Rebellion of 1885

Comprising a full and impartial account of the origin and progress of the war

Charles Pelham Mulvany

The History of the North-West Rebellion of 1885
Comprising a full and impartial account of the origin and progress of the war

ISBN/EAN: 9783337013301

Printed in Europe, USA, Canada, Australia, Japan

Cover: Foto ©ninafisch / pixelio.de

More available books at **www.hansebooks.com**

Major-General F. Middleton, K. C. B.,
Commander of Canadian Militia.

THE HISTORY

OF THE

NORTH-WEST REBELLION

OF 1885.

COMPRISING A FULL AND IMPARTIAL ACCOUNT OF THE

ORIGIN AND PROGRESS OF THE WAR, OF THE VARIOUS ENGAGE-
MENTS WITH THE INDIANS AND HALF-BREEDS, OF THE
HEROIC DEEDS PERFORMED BY OFFICERS AND
MEN, AND OF TOUCHING SCENES

IN THE

FIELD, THE CAMP, AND THE CABIN;

INCLUDING A HISTORY OF THE

INDIAN TRIBES OF NORTH-WESTERN CANADA,

THEIR NUMBERS, MODES OF LIVING, HABITS, CUSTOMS, RELIGIOUS RITES AND
CEREMONIES, WITH THRILLING NARRATIVES OF CAPTURES, IMPRISON-
MENT, MASSACRES, AND HAIR-BREADTH ESCAPES OF WHITE
SETTLERS, ETC.

BY

CHARLES PELHAM MULVANEY, A.M., M.D.,

*Formerly of No. 1 Company, Queen's Own Rifles, author of "History of the
County of Brant," "History of Liberalism," etc., assisted by a
well-known journalist.*

TWELFTH THOUSAND.

JLLUSTRATED

WITH **PORTRAITS** OF DISTINGUISHED OFFICERS AND MEN, MAPS, DIAGRAMS
AND ENGRAVINGS.

TORONTO, ONT.:
PUBLISHED BY A. H. HOVEY & CO., 10 KING STREET EAST.
1886.

Dedication.

TO THE

OFFICERS AND MEN

OF THE

CANADIAN VOLUNTEERS

THIS BOOK IS DEDICATED

BY THE

AUTHOR AND PUBLISHERS.

LIST OF 63 ILLUSTRATIONS.

	PAGE
Major-General F. D. Middleton, C.B.	Frontispiece.
Lieut.-Col. A. A. Miller, Q.O.R.	19
Louis Riel	25
Fort Carleton	30
Major L. H. N. Crozier	31
Lieut.-Col. A. G. Irvine, N.-W.M.P.	45
Lord Melgund	65
Major Laurence Buchan	66
Lieut.-Col. W. D. Otter	100
Map of Battleford	106
Francis J. Dickens, N.-W.M.P.	116
Plan of Fort Pitt	117
Hon. Edgar Dewdney	119
Piapot, Chief of the South Crees	120
Capt. Charles Swinford	139
Col. W. M. Herchmer, N.-W.M.P.	158
Geo. E. Cooper, Colour-Sergeant	167
Herbert Foulkes (Brigade Bugler); Capt. E. J. Brown 170,	185
Poundmaker	186
Map of "Batoche," "Duck Lake" and "Fish Creek."	195
Capt. James Mason (Grenadiers)	213
Lieut.-Col. Van Straubenzie	222
Lieut. W. C. Fitch	235
Thomas Moor	237
Bugler Gaughan	241
Alexander Watson	242
Franklin Jackes	244
Lieut. A. L. Howard, in Command of Gatling Gun	246
Lieut. A. M. Irving	257
Lieut.-Col. A. T. H. Williams, M.P.	260
Lieut.-Col. H. J. Grasett	262
Major D. H. Allan, Q.O.R.	274
Adjutant J. M. Delamere	287
Gatling Gun (four illustrations) 297, 298, 301,	304
Staff Sergeant Walker	371
Lieut.-Col. W. E. O'Brien, M.P.	375
Gabriel Dumont, (full length portrait)	382
Sir John A. Macdonald	391
General Strange	394
Colonel James McLeod (Stipendiary Magistrate)	396
Father Lecombe	397
Big Bear	399
Map of Frog Lake Massacre and Surroundings; Mr. Dill	402
Lieut.-Col. Bremner and Major Welsh	409
Capt. James Peters	410
Inspector Joseph Howe	411
Capt. C. W. Drury	412
Col. Maunsell, 415; Col. Blaine, 416; Col. Morris	417
Gunner Walter Woodman	421
Christopher Robinson, Q.C., Crown Counsel in Riel's Trial	424
G. W. Burbidge, " " " "	425
F. X. Lemieux, Q.C., Riel's Counsel	426
Charles Fitzpatrick, M.A., 430; Judge Richardson	432

PREFACE.

The building up of a nation is not a mere effort of will on the part of an individual or a people. A people or an individual may have much to do with shaping the destinies of a country, but when the events which constitute the salient points in the history of that country come to be viewed from the somewhat elevated standpoint which he who would write a history must necessarily occupy in order that his vision may have scope sufficient to include everything bearing on the situation, those actors who in the bustle of "history-making" tower in magnitude and importance as primary causes, suddenly dwindle into "temporary agents," "creatures of circumstance," "mere puppets," moved and controlled by some unseen and unknown power, be it Providence, Destiny or Fate. But while the acts of one agent fit into those of another in making a history which so rises in importance and far-reaching effects as to dwarf the men who made its integral parts, we must not forget to hold each man morally responsible for his acts. An over-ruling Power may so control the acts of individuals as to cause good to result where only greed or selfish ambition prompted, but this must not blind us to the moral responsibility of the actors, who must be judged only by the motives which actuated them.

To-day Canada has just shaken herself free from the clutches of Rebellion, which at one time threatened to bring with her her sisters Anarchy and Revolution. Somebody is to blame for all this, and if the reader after scanning the evidence as to the causes of the rebellion chooses to call prominent men by hard names, we cannot help it. It is not our business to call harsh names nor to judge our neighbours. It is ours to state the

PREFACE.

facts as they are to be found, and leave to the people of Canada the exercise of judicial functions in this matter. We shall tell the truth regardless as to whom we shall hit and wholly indifferent as to both the great political parties who jointly control the destinies of this country.

When the arm of Rebellion had been raised and loyal citizens and Mounted Police shot down for striving to vindicate Canadian authority, it was not for us as Canadians to ask whether the rebels had any right on their side or not. Our National integrity had been assailed, our National honour had been threatened, and it only remained for our citizen-soldiers to draw the sword in their defence. How this has been done, and with what glorious results, it is for these pages to tell. What our future may be no one knows, but the immediate result of this rebellion has been that Canada has proved herself abundantly able to take care of herself. Her volunteers and her little handful of regulars have been pitted against a foe, as brave, as adroit, and as experienced in the hardships, perils and horrors of frontier warfare as can be found under the sun, and after meeting with a desperate and stubborn resistance our gallant fellows have triumphed brilliantly; but it is a costly and blood-bought victory. The mighty unseen force that makes history has pushed us one stage further on in our National development, and it is fitting that some land mark should be fixed to note our progress.

With such materials as are now available, and with a fairly accurate and comprehensive knowledge of the North-West to help us, we shall try faithfully, fearlessly and conscientiously to mark this important stride that has just been made in our National history.

THE AUTHOR.

CONTENTS.

CHAPTER.		PAGE.
I.	To Arms—The Call and the Response	17
II.	Prelude to the Insurrection — The Hudson Bay Company—The Indians—The Half-breeds—The Buffalo	20
III.	Louis Riel — His first Insurrection — His Bill of Rights of 1870 and of 1885	25
IV.	The Duck Lake Fight—How the Police and Prince Albert Volunteers Fought and Fell	27
V.	After the Battle—Retreating to Prince Albert—Burying the Dead	44
VI.	The Indian Tribes of Manitoba and the North-West—Their Numbers, Condition, etc.	50
VII.	Sketches of the Lives of General Middleton and Staff—Lord Melgund and Major Buchan	63
VIII.	Canada's Soldiers to the Front—"Our Boys in the North-West Away."	68
IX.	The War Cloud Bursts on Battleford	75
X.	On Guard at Prince Albert — The Grievances of Settlers—Description of Country	76
XI.	The Siege of Battleford—The Murder of Payne—Flight of Judge Rouleau and Applegarth—Major Walsh gives his Views	80
XII.	The Frog Lake Massacre	89
XIII.	Otter's March to Battleford—Relief of the Besieged Town—Houses Burned and Sacked—The Finding of Payne's Body	100
XIV.	General Middleton's Advance—Waiting for Supplies and Reinforcements	114
XV.	The Fall of Fort Pitt—Gallant Defence by Inspector Dickens—Fort Pitt before its Fall—Big Bear—Dewdney—Pi-a-pot—Big Bear's Prisoners	115
XVI.	The Battle of Fish Creek—The Killed and Wounded—After the Battle—General Middleton's Letter—In Memoriam	126

CONTENTS.

CHAPTER.		PAGE.
XVII.	Battle of Cut Knife Creek—Origin of the Name—Who took Part in it—Colonel Herchmer—The Killed and Wounded	156
XVIII.	Poundmaker—Lord Lorne Visits him.	186
XIX.	Battle of Batoche's Ferry—The Killed and Wounded—Some of the Heroes—Thrilling Incidents—The Man with the Gatling Gun—"Shot Through the Heart"—"Victory at Batoche"	193
XX.	Recollections of Batoche's Ferry—After the Battle—Colonel Williams of the Midland—Who led the Charge?—Description of the Rifle Pits	251
XXI.	The Prisoners and the Vanquished—Half-breed Discipline—Terror and Sufferings of the Rebels—Touching Scenes	271
XXII.	The Gatling Gun Described and Illustrated	299
XXIII.	Poundmaker Heard From—General Middleton's Interview with the Cree Chief Beardy—Riel Captured—His Wonderful Influence—Our Volunteers	307
XXIV.	Prince Albert—Colonel Irvine Explains—A Tribute to the Mounted Police—"The Riders of the Plains"—A Letter from Poundmaker—Journey to Battleford	334
XXV.	At Battleford with Middleton—Life in the Town during Rebellion—Indian Cunning and War Craft—He is not Brave	361
XXVI.	Poundmaker and Middleton—An Interesting Interview	384
XXVII.	General Strange's Column—Colonel McLeod—Father Lecombe—Big Bear Surrenders—The Stories of Mrs. Delaney and Mrs. Gowanlock	394
XXVIII.	Martial Ardour in the Maritime Provinces—Return of the Troops	408
XXIX.	Riel's Trial—Those Engaged in it,—His Execution	423
	The Troops in the Field	437

THE
HISTORY OF THE NORTH-WEST REBELLION.

CHAPTER I.

"TO ARMS!"

AT eleven o'clock on the night of March the 27th the citizens of every city in Canada, from Halifax to Victoria, were startled by the tidings that armed rebellion had broken out in the Prince Albert region of the North-West, that the loyal forces under Major Crozier had been fired upon by rebel Half-breeds, and that two of the Mounted Police and ten Prince Albert Volunteers had been killed, while eleven more of the loyalists had been wounded.

The response of every city in the Dominion was an instantaneous call to arms. It was immediately and universally responded to by the armed youth and manhood of our country. Emerson's noble verses received that night a new illustration:—

> So near is grandeur to our dust,
> So close is God to man,
> When duty whispered low "thou must,"
> The youth replied "I can."

Early on the next morning the peaceful slumbers of the inhabitants of Quebec, Kingston, and Toronto were broken by bugle calls and the unwonted sound of military preparation. At eleven o'clock the night before telegrams had been received from Ottawa to the effect that the fight had taken place, and that the Quebec and Kingston batteries of field artillery, and contingents from the Toronto Queen's Own, Royal Grenadiers, and C Company Infantry (regulars) were to be called out at once for active service. Small rest that night in the usually tranquil streets of the cities of Champlain and Frontenac! Even in ever-busy Toronto, the streets were unusually crowded by uniformed men hurrying to drill shed and armoury, and by officers driving about all through the night to seek out the members of the different companies and warn them of the parade next morning. The Queen's Own were to parade at the drill shed at 9 a.m., the Grenadiers at the armoury at 8 a.m. At the New Fort all was activity; the men, sleepless with excitement, were cleaning arms and accoutrements. At a little table Colonel Miller and Adjutant Delamere sat arranging the details and writing the orders and despatches necessary for such a hasty call to arms. At Quebec, Colonel Cotton had been ordered by telegram to prepare Battery A and one hundred men for immediate departure to the North-West. At Kingston, in the barrack-yard, where stands the last vestige of a bastion of the fort named after the heroic Frontenac, the well-trained little corps of the Field Battery rejoiced at an opportunity of exercising the discipline in which they had been so long practised against the enemies of Canada.

With the morning of Saturday the 28th the general public learned with astonishment the sudden news of the rebellion against Canada. Some rumours then had been afloat for a week previously in the newspapers of disaffection and discontent among the Half-breeds and of meetings held by Riel. But the Half-breeds are *always* discontented; as "Sir John" had said in Parliament, "if you wait for a Half-breed or an Indian to become contented, you may wait till the millennium." But here was bona fide intelligence endorsed by the Federal Government at Ottawa, that a secessionist rebellion against the Canadian Confederation had actually broken out, the first battle had been fought and lost by the loyal forces, and that the scattered settlements were exposed almost undefended to the horrors of Indian warfare.

Such were the rumours which that Saturday the 28th of March made the theme of conversation with excited groups in every city and town, nay, in every backwoods village in Canada. Happy were they who belonged to a volunteer company, even although not at once called on

COLONEL MILLER, Q.O.R.

for service; happiest of all those on whom the lot had fallen to belong to the contingent ordered to the front in the North-West.

In Toronto the volunteers met on parade in busbies, great coats, and leggings, not an available man was absent, all met in the spirit of what Colonel Miller had said the night before: "I don't care who a man is, or what he is doing, but I want every man in the regiment to be under arms and ready!" The Royal Grenadiers showed equal alacrity. With all the struggle was as to who should be accepted as one of the contingent of two hundred and forty men to be drafted out of the two Toronto battalions.

On Sunday the martial excitement continued. Even in douce Sabbath-keeping Toronto, Sunday editions of the *Mail, World, News,* and *Telegram* were published with what purported to be "intelligence" from the seat of war. The churches assumed a martial aspect, the pews ever and anon displaying the scarlet uniform of the Grenadiers, and the dark green of the rifle corps. In many a household sad and excited groups gathered round the gallant soldier boy on whom the lot had fallen to go to the seat of war: excited as they thought of the glory of fighting in the cause of Canada, sad as they felt that this might be the last Sunday they were to pass together. For with all abhorrence for the mischievous alarmists who invariably make the most of such a crisis, there were serious grounds for apprehension. The blow of secession had been struck at the life of our Confederation; the Half-breeds and Indians were dangerous foes; already in the first skirmish defeat had been sustained by a Canadian force, and more life lost than had been lost by Canada in the fighting of 1837, or the Fenian raids of 1866 and 1870.

CHAPTER II.

THE PRELUDE OF INSURRECTION.

THE real course of the events which gave rise to these military preparations was as follows:—

As far back as the summer of 1884, it was known to the Ottawa Government and to those connected with the North-West Territories, that grave dissatisfaction, nay positive disaffection, existed among the Half-breeds.

The Half-breed population had been in process of growth ever since the Hudson's Bay Company received its charter.

This nominally English company was, to a great extent, served by French *coureurs de bois*, officered by Scotchmen. The solitary life of the trading-post in the wilderness, with its sure provision for subsistence, its pension from the Hudson's Bay Company for old age, and its many casual opportunities for gain, were attraction enough to many a canny Scot. The French *coureur de bois*, already half-Indian in blood and temperament, was the best servant the Company could possibly have secured for the fur trade of the sub-Arctic forests.

The Spaniards made the Indians slaves, the British made them freemen, not as yet allowed the franchise, for which savage races are unfit, but protected by law; but the French have intermarried with them and adopted their customs. The result has been a curious intermixture of races.

Captain Butler mentions as a case in point his Half-breed friend Batoche: "His grandfather had been a French-Canadian, his grandmother a Crow squaw; English and Cree had contributed to his descent on the mother's side." —(Butler's *Wild North Land*, p. 46.) The Half-breeds by a very "natural" process of selection chose the handsomest and most vigorous squaws, they also escaped the curse of tribal intermarriage, which more than one factor of a Hudson Bay Company's fort has assured the writer is destined to cause the extinction of the North-West Indian. With the Half-breeds, even with many of Scotch descent, the language, manners and methods of surveying land for farms are French.

So long as the Hudson Bay Company only had to do with the Indians of the Canadian North-West, they were not seriously demoralized. It is quite true that the Company made no attempt to civilize, enlighten or christianize them; while, on the other hand, they were rather inclined to encourage feuds between the Crees and Blackfeet, as both bought ammunition at ruinous prices during these wars, while these dissensions among the tribes rendered anything like a successful attack upon the Company's stores out of the question. Should the Blackfeet threaten, the officers of the Hudson's Bay Company would call to their assistance the Crees; thus it was easy for the great fur traders to retain the balance of power and the friendship of the tribes with a comparatively small force.

As Dakota and Montana began to be opened up for settlement, American traders, who make it their business to keep "on the frontier," pushed their way into British territory and soon began to sell whiskey to the Cree and Blackfeet tribes. Thousands of gallons are estimated to have been sold to the Blackfeet hunters at a price of a pint of whiskey for a buffalo robe! When the Yankee smuggler arrived in a Blackfeet camp the scene of grotesque horror, and damage to life, probably surpassed any spectacle of human degradation brought about by Man's greatest enemy, the "enemy put in the mouth to take away the reason"! The smuggler's appearance with his gaudy canteen gave the signal for the liquor feast. The smuggler roamed triumphant through the camp, selecting everywhere the finest robes at will, and after getting rid of his stock of liquid devilry would immediately drive away to escape the danger of the scene certain to follow. Then began the liquor feast. It lasted sometimes for days. The braves, old and young, drank greedily the undiluted firewater. The women and the young girls drank as eagerly as the men. The young bucks, the vanity and ferocity of their savage natures excited by the strong drink, stalked through camp brandishing hunting knives or parading with careless ostentation revolvers and guns ready to challenge, shoot or stab their best friends. The horrors of this whiskey traffic rendered it necessary that its originators should be driven out of the country as speedily as possible, and for this purpose the North-West Mounted Police force was organized and sent into the country. Of course settlement followed the advent of the police, and with the advance of the settlers the buffalo, the mainstay of the Indian, his strength and his wealth, suddenly left the territory; and then the condition of the Half-breed and the Indian was changed for the worse.

In the old times millions of buffalo roamed the great plains, not only between the North Saskatchewan and the 49th parallel but away north of the great river. In those times it was not a matter of unusual occurrence for an outfit of carts to be compelled to camp for from half-a-day to a day and a-half to allow a herd of buffalo to troop past. At such times one might stand on an eminence and for a belt many miles wide and as far in the direction whence the herd was advancing as the eye could reach, the prairie would be hidden by the vast, black, moving mass. And when such a herd had passed no running fire would leave the prairie more dry, dusty and destitute of grass. It is no wonder that when following the trails of such great bands Capt. Pallissier pronounced many of the best portions of the North-West arid, sterile deserts.

In those days what was to them practically limitless wealth was within the reach of the Indians and Half-breeds and, as might have been expected, they were nearly all improvident. Close upon the advent of anything in the shape of white settlement came the hard times incident to the departure of the buffalo, and it is not to be wondered at that the natives of the North-West, whether Indian or Half-breed, should not look upon the advancement of white immigration with any especial favour. The Half-breeds settled around Qu'Appelle and the Saskatchewan had learned to dread the conditions and methods of land settlement imposed on them from Ottawa. They especially dreaded being compelled to change the location of their farms which had been surveyed on the old French methods of delimitation, for square blocks according to the new survey. With or without reason, they distrusted Lieut.-Governor Dewdney; they looked with fear and hatred on the clique of land speculators which was so influential with those who controlled the allotment of lands. For these reasons they were thoroughly saturated with disaffection to the Ottawa government.

This was remarked by Colonel Houghton, D.A.G., when, in June, 1884, he visited the Saskatchewan settlements in order to remove the arms and ammunition from Fort Carleton and Prince Albert, a step the unwisdom of which this experienced soldier clearly saw.

The Half-breeds and Indians naturally looked to Louis Riel to secure for them the same privileges which they believed him to have won for the Half-breeds of Manitoba. They knew that Riel had held his own against two successive governments representing the two great parties of Canada. An armed rebellion and a judicial murder had been condoned in the teeth of exasperated public opinion; the French vote had supported Riel through everything, the Half-breeds of Manitoba had received what they most wished for: patents for their farms. Clearly, therefore, Riel was their best leader; they invited him to visit their settlements; during the long winter of 1884–1885 he was assiduously engaged in the work of agitation; all peaceful and constitutional means, he told them in a speech delivered at the Catholic church of Batoche, two days before the rising, had been tried and with no hope of redress: and when at length came the news that England was likely to be engaged in a Russian war, he openly preached rebellion. To comprehend the secret of Riel's all-powerful influence with his compatriots, it may be well to take a brief survey of his career previous to the rising inaugurated in March, 1885.

LOUIS RIEL, FROM A PORTRAIT OF FIVE YEARS AGO.

CHAPTER III.

SKETCH OF LOUIS RIEL

LOUIS RIEL was born at the town of St. Boniface, on the west branch of the Seine River. Riel's father was a white, of pure Scandinavian origin, his mother a Half-breed; he was descended from a very mixed stock of Indians, Half-breeds and Irish whites. He was born in a small log-house, of the most primitive backwoods shanty pattern. It was thatched with straw, was one storey high, and contained but one room. As a boy Riel was known for his activity and bodily strength; he was a skilful hunter and marksman, and at school was already the recognized leader among his schoolmates, among whom he sought to gain influence by every means in his power. In order to effect this he was known frequently to share or give away his dinner to a poorer fellow-student. Like all of French descent, young Riel was deeply attached to his parents. Once a boy, who had some quarrel with him, challenged him to fight. Riel refused unless his father would sanction it. He was eight years old when he first attended school at St. Boniface College, now St. Boniface Town Hall, and at eleven was transferred to the Jesuit College, Montreal. He bore the reputation of being an apt scholar, and learned to read, write and speak English remarkably well.

In 1866, Riel returned to St. Vital, Manitoba, where his parents lived, and where his mother now resides. At St. Vital, Riel lived as a farmer, and sought every means of gaining influence among the Half-breeds of Manitoba, whose minds he inflamed by dwelling on their grievances. This is not the place to recount the events of the rebellion of 1869, in which Riel was chosen leader. In passing, notice may be taken of the many recklessly-false tales set forth as to Riel's career by writers who get up what purport to be "histories," on the plan of the dime novel. One such writer informs his readers that the reason Riel had for the Scott murder was that both were in love with the same girl. As a matter of fact, Riel could never have seen the young lady on whom Scott's affections were placed, who lived, or still lives, in a city of Ontario never visited by Riel.

After the collapse of his first fiasco of revolt, Riel travelled a good deal, both in Canada and the United States. He spent much time in Washington, and at Woonsocket, Rhode Island, at the house of his aunt, Mrs. Joyce, mother of Mr. Joyce, formerly chief of police at St. Boniface. In 1879 he settled for a time in Montana, in the Sun River settlement, where he married a French Half-breed named Marguerite Bellimeure, of Fort Ellice. Riel at this time acted as teacher in an Industrial School. He was very poor, and eked out his means by buffalo-hunting, at which he was expert.

When the North-West Half-breeds asked him to lead them as he had led them in Manitoba, he at first refused, saying that he was an American citizen, and wished to have no more to do with Canadian troubles, but their entreaties prevailed on him to consent.

Riel is a total abstainer, can speak French, English, and four Indian languages. He speaks slowly, deliberately, and with effect. He is strong, of fair stature, square-shouldered, with features of greater mobility and expression than most half-Indians.

At a meeting of the Half-breeds in September, 1884, the following Bill of Rights was adopted, on Riel's suggestion :—

BILL OF RIGHTS OF 1885.*

First, the sub-division into Provinces of the North-West Territories.

---

* It may interest the reader to compare with this the Half-breed Bill of Rights of 1870 :—
 1. The right to elect our own Legislature.
 2. The Legislature to have power to pass all laws local to the Territory over the veto of the Executive, by a two-thirds vote.
 3. No Act of the Dominion Parliament (local to the Territory) to be binding on the people until sanctioned by their representatives.
 4. All sheriffs, magistrates, constables, etc., etc., to be elected by the people ; a free homestead pre-emption law.
 5. A portion of the public lands to be appropriated to the benefit of schools, the building of roads, bridges, and parish buildings.
 6. A guarantee to connect Winnipeg by rail with the nearest line of railroad—the land grant for such road or roads to be subject to the Legislature of the Territory.
 7. For four years the public expenses of the Territory, civil, military and municipal, to be paid out of the Dominion treasury.
 8. The military to be composed of the people now existing in the Territory.
 9. The French and English languages to be common in the Legislature and Council, and all public documents and Acts of the Legislature to be published in both languages.
 10. That the judge of the Superior Court speak French and English.
 11. Treaties to be concluded and ratified between the Government and several tribes of Indians of this Territory, calculated to insure peace in the future.
 12. That all privileges, customs and usages existing at the time of the transfer be respected.
 13. That these rights be guaranteed by Mr. Macdougall before he be admitted into this Territory.
 14. If he have not the power himself to grant them, he must get an Act of Parliament passed expressly securing us these rights ; and until such Act be obtained he must stay outside the Territory.
 15. That we have a full and fair representation in the Dominion Government.

Second, the Half-breeds to receive the same grants and other advantages as the Manitoba Half-breeds.

Third, patents to be issued at once to the Colonists in possession.

Fourth, the sale of half-a-million acres of Dominion lands, the proceeds to be applied to the establishment in the Half-breed settlements of schools, hospitals and such like institutions, and to the equipment of the poorer Half-breeds with seed grain and implements.

Fifth, the reservation of a hundred townships of swamp land for distribution among the children of Half-breeds during the next 120 years.

Sixth, a grant of at least $1,000 for the maintenance of an institution to be conducted by the nuns in each Half-breed settlement.

Seventh, better provision for the support of the Indians.

It was forwarded to Ottawa, and contemptuously thrown aside. This was a fatal error in policy, which was yet to cost our country a heavy price in blood and treasure. The Half-breeds were doubtless justified in demanding patents for their farms, and it was iniquitous, as well as impolitic, to refuse this simple act of justice. Had the Half-breeds but felt secure that the farms they had by hard work reclaimed from the wilderness would be safe from the clutches of the land-grabber, there would have been no rebellion. The other demands were purely political, and were introduced by Riel himself in order to found an exclusively French Province in the North-West. To grant this would have been to repeat the lamentable error by which England at the Conquest perpetuated the French language, law, and religion, and established an island of mediævalism and of alien race in the midst of the spread of English Canadian civilization.

CHAPTER IV.

THE DUCK LAKE DISASTER.

ALL through the first week of March, insurrectionary movements took place. Stores belonging to the Hudson Bay Company and to the Government were seized, loyal settlers were compelled to surrender their arms and ammunition. The Indians were tampered with, and were observed to leave their reserves.

Riel began the insurrection on March 17. He seized arms and ammunition at the store of John Keer, a merchant settled at "Batoche's Crossing," a small village on the South Saskatchewan, a short distance from Fort Carlton. He also imprisoned Trees, a magistrate, and several loyal Canadians; Keeley, a miller; Nash, Tomkins, Ross, a freighter, and others, in the house of one Cavan, at Batoche. He used the village church of Batoche as a store-house, and afterwards as a prison. The Half-breeds with Riel formed a Council of Twelve, of which Jackson, formerly a druggist from near Wingham, was the only member of pure white race. This man became a convert to Catholicism just before the rising. The Council appointed captains of the Half-breed force, and placed guards on the trail from Clark's Crossing to Batoche, so as to intercept supplies.

The first reports of the insurrection were hardly credited in Ontario and Quebec. So entirely was this the case that, when the *Globe* published an account of Riel's first movements of rebellion, the story was openly ridiculed as a device of party tactics! But on the afternoon of March 23, Sir John Macdonald, in his place in Parliament, confirmed the news of the insurrection, and on Wednesday, March 25, the 90th Regiment of Rifles, under Colonel Naughton, with a portion of the Winnipeg Field Battery, left Winnipeg for Qu'Appelle, *en route* for the neighbourhood of Batoche, where Riel's headquarters were, and where the Cree reserve, under a chief named Beardy, was of doubtful fidelity. He was a small-sized man, but crafty, and had given much trouble already to the authorities.

But on Thursday, the 26th of March, Major Crozier, with a hundred men, set out from Fort Carleton to a village near Duck Lake, in order to secure some provisions and supplies which lay at that place, and in danger, being undefended, of falling into the hands of Riel. Duck

FORT CARLETON, THE HUDSON BAY POST ABANDONED BY COL. IRVINE AND AFTERWARDS BURNT.

Lake, whose name has attained such a sinister import as that of the spot where flowed the first blood shed in the rebellion, is situated thirteen and a-half miles southeast of Fort Carleton, and twelve miles from Gabriel's Crossing, on the South Branch of the Saskatchewan. The village near which the fight took place is called Stobart, after the founder of its first settlement, a member of the firm of Stobart & Eden, of Winnipeg. It consists of nine long one-storey log buildings. It is fronted by an ornamental fence, and at the sides has a common snake fence. There is no stockade, nor any means of defence whatever. It is sometimes called Duck Lake Village, from a long, low, marshy sheet of

THE DUCK LAKE DISASTER. 81

water which extends to the west of it. The Half-breeds had already visited Duck Lake Village, had seized some of the provisions and arms, and threatened the loyal inhabitants.

Crozier had with him, besides his party of Mounted Police, a number of volunteers from Carlton, some of them mounted and others riding in waggons. When they approached the village they saw a body of some fifty

MAJOR CROZIER, N.-W. MOUNTED POLICE.

armed Half-breeds, apparently about to dispute their advance. A parley ensued with Gabriel Dumont, a Half-breed much in Riel's confidence, who was the daring and fiery leader of the rebels. During the parley a shot was fired, as far as the evidence has been obtained, it would seem from the loyalist side, and on Crozier's orders. It seems that he thought the Half-breeds were about to surround him. Some brisk firing ensued on both sides.

The Half-breeds, according to their custom, sought cover behind a number of bushes. Crozier's men did the same, and the combat was maintained for about forty minutes. Crozier, seeing that his men were getting the worst of it, and that the civilians in the sleighs were exposed to danger, gave the order to withdraw. In their retreat the loyalists suffered still more than during the fight. Gabriel Dumont's deadly skill with the rifle encouraged his men. The Half-breeds fired more than one volley, with what good aim the number of the killed as compared with the number wounded is a sufficient proof. The names of the twelve who were killed are as follow: Captain Morton, a farmer from Bruce, Ontario, and an efficient volunteer officer; Wm. Napier, a law student of Prince Albert, late of Edinburgh, Scotland, nephew of Sir Charles Napier (strange that the kinsman of the victor of Meeanee should fall in an obscure skirmish in the wilderness); A. W. R. Merkley, formerly of Ottawa; S. C. Elliott, son of Judge Elliott, of London, Ont.; R. Middleton and D. McKenzie, both natives of Prince Edward Island; Charles Hewitt, of Portage la Prairie; Daniel McPhail, of Prince Albert; Alex. Fisher, a young Englishman; Wm. Baikie, an old Hudson Bay employé; and Joseph Anderson, a loyal Half-breed. The wounded Prince Albert volunteers were Captain Moore, whose leg was broken; Sergeant A. McNabb; and Alex. S. Stewart. But two of the Mounted Police were killed, viz.: Constables T. G. Gibson and Geo. P. Arnold. The wounded Policemen were Inspector Joseph Howe, of St. John, N.B., of the gun detachment, nephew of the once all-powerful Hon. Joseph Howe, the Nova Scotia statesman; Corporal Gilchrist; and Constables M. K. Garrett, J. J. Wood, Sidney F. Gordon, A. M. Smith and A. Miller. This melancholy list contains the names of young men from almost every part of the Dominion: the Maritime Provinces, London, Kingston, Ottawa, and the North-West settlements are represented as well as England, Scotland and Ireland. At this engagement the rebel force numbered two hundred, and their loss was six killed and three wounded.

The party of Half-breeds which fought at Duck Lake was in reality the advance guard of a much larger force with which Riel had intended to attack Fort Carlton. This he did not do, as Colonel Irvine had arrived with a larger force of Mounted Police and sleighs from Swift Current. He had eluded the Half-breeds who had gone to intercept him at the ford of the South Saskatchewan known as Gabriel's Crossing—where the shelving banks covered with trees would have given great advantage to an enemy—by marching to Clark's Crossing instead, and reached Fort Carleton with his force in good condition just after the Duck Lake fight.

ANOTHER ACCOUNT OF THE DUCK LAKE FIGHT.

A gentleman from Prince Albert cognizant of the circumstances preceding and attending the Duck Lake fight, furnishes the following:

It will be recollected that the Half-breeds of Manitoba received a grant of land (240 acres to each), when the North-West was taken over by the Dominion. A number of Half-breeds were living outside of the present boundary of Manitoba, in this and other parts of the North-West Territory at that time, and though many years have passed since the transfer, and frequent petitions have been sent to the Government, they have never yet received the grant of land bestowed on their brethren in Manitoba. Other grievances, such as want of representation in the Dominion Parliament, the number of Government nominees in the North-West Council, the management of the public lands, and the inattention of the Government to petitions and representations on local matters began, among the white settlers as well as the French Half-breeds, to create during the last year or two a good deal of irritation. The great amount of destitution in this district during the past year added keenness to the feelings of dissatisfaction and indignation.

In these circumstances the French Half-breeds sent to Montana a deputation to invite Riel, whose term of outlawry had expired, to visit Prince Albert settlement, and give to the French-speaking population his counsel and aid in obtaining what they desired from the Government. Riel, on his arrival, was gladly received by the French, and even by many of the Canadian settlers. The latter, when taunted about the indecency of countenancing or employing a man who had been denounced as a bandit and a murderer, vindicated their conduct by pointing to the action of the Government. They said Riel had paid the penalty which was thought sufficient for his former crime. Look how the Government neglect to give attention to our wants! Petition after petition is pigeon-holed in an office at Ottawa and receives no further notice. These French people are entitled to their lands; why should they be so long withheld by the Government? We, too, as well as they, are entitled to redress of other grievances. Perhaps, now that Riel is here, the Government may at last condescend to recognize our existence.

At the public meeting which Riel addressed he spoke with great prudence and propriety, urged above all things unity of action, and proposed to seek redress only by constitutional measures. Some of the discontented Indians came even from great distances to visit Riel and his friends, and it was feared that he was tampering with them. A number of the settlers formed a union, and continued for months to act in concert with Riel, whose agitation they regarded as quite loyal and constitutional. After a time Riel began to urge that the Indian title to the North-West had never been extinguished; that it was not with the Hudson's Bay Company, but with the Indians, the Half-breeds, and pioneer white settlers, to whom the country really belonged, that the Government had to deal. It is believed also that he was bent on claiming from the Government indemnity for personal losses, which he had sustained by the confiscation of property once belonging to him in Winnipeg, and which has increased enormously in value since the time of his banishment. It is almost certain that he began to put forth claims such as the white settlers could have no sympathy with, and the Dominion could not for a moment entertain; and unknown to the English-speaking part of the community a secret combination was formed to attempt to enforce their demands by illegal and violent means. Some say that Riel began to use stronger language only with the hope that he might be arrested on insufficient grounds, and thus excite public sympathy on behalf of himself and the movement of which he was the leader. The language used by him at some meetings came to the knowledge of the police and others. The Ministers of the Dominion were informed, it is said, that there was imminent danger of an outbreak, that the Indians—starving, mutinous, and some of them almost desperate—would fall in with Riel and the Half-breeds, and that the plunder and massacre of many of the white settlers at this remote point might be accomplished before assistance could be obtained from below. Prince Albert is separated from the C. P. R. by an almost unbroken and unsettled prairie 250 miles wide. The journey cannot easily be made in less than a week, and an armed force carrying its own supplies would of course take longer time. Riel could in a few hours raise a force of several hundred Half-breeds and an unknown quantity of Indians. The Police force in the district was not very strong and stationed at a most inconvenient point. The white settlers were therefore, if he had preparations made for a rising, really at his mercy.

Major Crozier, commanding the force at Carleton, sent word to Prince Albert that in the case of an actual outbreak he would like to be assured of assistance. A meeting was consequently held on Wednesday, the 18th of March, when, though most felt that the gravity of the situation had been exaggerated, it was determined that a company of volunteers should be formed to be ready for service when called on by the authorities. During the very time when this meeting was held, Riel, at a point some 40 miles off, was proving that the situation was quite as grave as any one could desire. He, followed by a crowd of Half-breeds, seized the store of Walters & Baker, at Batoche, and launched out on that insane and reckless course which has already brought terrible disaster to some, and must bring still more terrible disaster to many more.

It may be well at this point, before sketching the succeeding course of events, to give an idea of the country and the localities afterwards to be referred to in the narrative.

The North and South Branches of the Saskatchewan unite at a point about thirty miles east of Prince Albert, called the Forks of the River. The North Branch from the west approaches the South Branch flowing from the south at a point called "the Elbow," some 150 miles west of the Forks; then the rivers run parallel to each other, but some twenty or thirty miles apart, first in a northerly and then in an easterly direction, to their point of union. About fifty miles from the Elbow, Carleton Fort is situated on the southern bank of the North Branch, and almost opposite to it, on the South Branch, there is a village called Batoche, which is the centre of the French Half-breed settlement. On the road from Batoche to Carleton, about four miles from the former and fifteen from the latter, is another small village, near an Indian reserve, called Duck Lake. The town of Prince Albert, the centre of the English-speaking population, is fifty miles east from Carleton and about forty miles north-east from Batoche, the roads from these two places converging at a point twenty miles from Prince Albert.

At Carleton there are a few Half-breed settlers and only one or two white families. The fort, facing the river to the north but distant from it almost half-a-mile, is enclosed on the south by a semi-circle of hills, which are about two hundred feet high, and less than one hundred yards distant from the fort, and covered on the sides with brush and small trees. It is hardly possible to conceive a worse situation on which to locate a fort, and station a body of armed men. In case of an attack in force not a man would be allowed to show his head outside of the enclosure; and even inside the whole square could be commanded from the hills, except the part under shelter of the buildings on one side. Besides the Police barracks the only building in the fort is the Hudson's Bay store. Your readers may judge of the wisdom which stationed the mass of the police force in such a gravel pit, forty or fifty miles from the settlement which it was meant to protect. Rumour has it that the Dominion Government is guided in making its appointments and arrangements more by private influences than by concern for the safety or benefit of the general community. Passing such subjects, however, I now return to the outbreak of Wednesday, 18th March, at the Village of Batoche. On the afternoon of that day Riel, followed by two or three score of men, entered the shop of Walters & Baker and said: "Well, gentlemen, it has commenced." "What has commenced?" said Mr. Walters. "Oh, this movement for the rights of the country." He then asked for arms and ammunition, and urged that they should be given up quietly, saying: "If we succeed our government will pay you in full, and even if we are defeated you will be indemnified by your own." Mr. Walters refused to give up the powder in his store and reached for a rifle hanging unloaded on the wall. He was immediately seized by a number of men, and, along with his clerk, was made prisoner. The store was then plundered, the Half-breeds clothing themselves with coats, boots, etc., from the store. All the freight as it passed from day to day through Batoche from Troy, was seized. Private parties obtained a receipt for the goods taken from them, but all Government and Hudson's Bay freight was at once confiscated.

Intelligence of the outbreak did not reach Prince Albert until after midnight on Thursday. The telegraph line had been cut, all travel stopped, and the first news came from Major Crozier, at Carleton, to Major Moffat, who was in charge of the few police in Prince Albert. Crozier recommended the enrolment of volunteers, and

urged that as many as possible should be sent to his
assistance. He was able also to report that Colonel Irvine,
with one hundred men and sixty horses, had already
started from Troy for Prince Albert. At the public
meeting hastily summoned to hear these despatches,
it was strongly felt that it would be much better
for Crozier to abandon Carleton, burning what he could
not carry off, and concentrate all the forces in the district
at a point where they could protect the whites. Riel
could also march from Batoche on Prince Albert long
before the force could reach it from Carleton, and could
plunder the place if he chose. It was determined, however, to comply with the request of the Government
officials, and Captain Moore, with forty-seven men, started
for Carleton after midday, and reached it by 10 o'clock
that night. An operator was sent across the prairie by a
circuitous route to Humboldt, seventy miles south of
Batoche, to telegraph to the East for assistance, and also
to urge Colonel Irvine to advance with all haste. On Saturday Walters and his clerk, having been liberated by Riel,
came to Prince Albert. They reported that they had been
as well treated as could be expected amid the confusion
at Batoche, and that Riel held a number of prisoners
there, whom he had seized on different pretexts. In his
conversation he spoke confidently of obtaining possession
of the country, and said that his government would give
one-seventh of the land to the Indians, one-seventh to
the Half-breeds and pioneer whites, a seventh to the
churches and schools, and hold the rest for public purposes. His force was supposed to consist of three hundred Half-breeds and about one hundred and fifty Indians,
armed with guns and rifles. During the next two or
three days, though freight was still being seized as it
arrived at Batoche, the feeling of alarm was gradually
passing away. All sorts of rumours were abroad of
English and French Half-breeds in the different settlements offering their services to Riel, and of his intentions
to attack Carleton and plunder Prince Albert. The arrival
of Irvine with his force was daily expected, and it was

THE DUCK LAKE DISASTER.

confidently hoped that when he and Crozier united, they, with the aid of the volunteers, would scatter the rebels at the first touch, and that Riel and his leading followers would take to flight across the prairie. On Tuesday night Colonel Irvine with his troop, arrived quietly at 9 o'clock and was greeted with rousing cheers as he passed through the town. The Colonel assured representatives of the town who waited on him that he was more concerned about the safety of the whites than about saving the solitary store and rotten fort at Carleton; and that the great purpose of his mission would be kept in view in all his movements.

On the next day he rested his force, as for several days he had been making forced marches, and about twenty of his men were snow blind.

On Thursday, 26th March, he left at 3 a.m. for Carleton, taking with him eighty police and thirty more volunteers from the town. The people of Prince Albert have reason to be congratulated on their courage and public spirit—having thus sent on two occasions about eighty men, the flower of their manhood and strength, to aid the Government forces at a distant point, and leaving their own town and people almost naked to the attack of the enemy.

Col. Irvine reached Carleton on Thursday afternoon just in time to learn the great disaster which had occurred in its neighbourhood. To reach this properly it may be well to return to the departure of the first contingent of volunteers on the previous Friday in compliance with the entreaty of Major Crozier.

Thos. McKay, one of our most influential citizens, had gone up with the company. He and his family are well known and much respected all over the district. On reaching Carleton he went on his own account to Batoche to interview the insurgents and use his influence to restore peace and order without further violence. He went in company with a Mr. Mitchell, the storekeeper at Duck Lake, who had come, bearing a message from Riel to Major Crozier, requiring his surrender. On reaching

Batoche Mr. McKay told every one that the complete overthrow of their movement was only a question of a short time, and that their only hope of safety was to be found in their immediate dispersal, and the surrender of the leaders of the movement, who must be dealt with and punished by the law. Riel, finding that some were confessing that they had been forced reluctantly into the movement, had Mr. McKay brought before his council, charging him with endangering the success of their cause by statements which he could prove to be false. Mr. McKay had assured them that all the white settlers were against them, and that the English Half-breeds would, at the least, remain neutral. Riel proposed to bring forward witnesses to prove the reverse. The council, however, agreed to liberate Mr. McKay, and as he departed an arrangement was made by Mr. Mitchell by which two from Carleton and two from Batoche should meet near Duck Lake to consider the possibility of a settlement. Captain Moore and Mr. McKay met the representatives from Duck Lake, Nolan and Lepine, on the following day. No terms could be made, as the insurgents demanded the surrender of Carleton and of all Crozier's forces, and McKay and Moore demanded the dispersal of the French and that their leaders should be given up.

On Thursday morning, when Col. Irvine was on the way from Prince Albert to Carleton, it was thought advisable to send a party of sixteen police and volunteers with teams to Duck Lake to get supplies from the store, which, as far as known, had not yet been seized by Riel. Mr. McKay again led this party. On approaching a point about two miles from Duck Lake he was met by a force of twenty-five or thirty armed horsemen. Having told for what purpose he had come, he was insolently challenged to go and take the stores if he dared. Prudently declining this, he was asked to surrender his arms and party to the rebels. This, he firmly said, would never be done while they were alive. Then he was challenged to commence firing, his teams were knocked about, and several shots fired over their heads to provoke them. Mr. McKay and his men remained cool, with rifles in hand. At length he proposed that his party should return as they came, and warned the insurgents not to follow them as he could not answer for his men if molested by pursuit. On getting clear of the rebels he sent word by a patrol to Carleton of what had occurred and followed leisurely with his teams. When the news reached Carleton there was great excitement and indignation. It was not supposed that a very large number of Riel's party could be at Duck Lake. It would even seem that some of the Prince Albert party brought pressure to bear upon the commanding officer not to bear the indignity put upon them. Perhaps some thought that the insurgents might be crushed at once, or at least the stores secured with ease. Major Crozier, as we need not wonder, seems to have hesitated to incur the responsibility of attacking, when his commanding officer was, as he well knew, approaching and within a few hours' march. Volunteers, however, were called for, and on the point of starting, when McKay and the teams reached the fort. Again there was a slight hesitation, but finally sixty police and twenty-five volunteers were commanded to start. They took with them the only field-piece in their possession—a seven-pounder of brass, which had seen service with Napier at Magdala.

On arriving at the place where the teams had been stopped in the morning the scouts were again chased in by twenty or thirty horsemen, followed by a body of men on foot constantly increasing in numbers as others came from Duck Lake. Major Crozier halted his troops, and the police spread out to the left and the volunteers to the right of the road. One of the rebels was waving a blanket, and Major Crozier, with the interpreter, went forward to meet him and a few others who were advancing along the road. A short and unsatisfactory conversation took place as to what was wanted by our men and where they were going. At the same time the rebels kept advancing and scattering across the front of our men. The officer and interpreter insisted that they should be kept back, but no heed was paid to the warning. Crozier then retired to his men and told them to commence firing. The rebels had now mostly left the road and were getting under cover among the bluffs or groves in front of our men, and even around their flank. A number made their way into an empty log building to the right of our line, from which they poured a murderous fire on the volunteers. The cannon fired three shots; then, by a sad mistake, a shell was put in before the charge of powder, and the gun became useless until the engagement was over. The rebels' fire was very severe. Our men were in a hollow, while the enemy had good cover and higher ground. The Indians and Half-breeds fired with great coolness, dropping on their blankets and taking sure aim. They were gradually working round the flank of our force and about surrounding it, when orders were given to retreat. A rush was made for the road, the teams were hitched up, the wounded, with the exception of one man, who was not noticed, had already been put in the sleighs, and the force retreated, leaving nine men dead or dying on the field. Five horses, some of them shot, had also to be abandoned. Had our men remained but a little longer the whole force would have been sacrificed. It was almost a miracle that the gunners and their horses were not destroyed and the gun captured. It would seem to ordinary persons a fatal mistake to have taken it so far to the front, where it was under close rifle fire. About a quarter of a mile farther back there was rising ground, from which the gun could have poured its shot on the enemy, while our men could have advanced under the cover of its fire. It does not seem either to have occurred to the commanding officer after retiring out of rifle range to renew the fire from his cannon, and treat the rebels to a few shells to cover his retreat, even if he did not return to recover the dead. Of incidents during the skirmish there is not now time or space to write. Captain Morton, of the volunteers, a man much respected and loved, was shot in the breast.

He told those beside him who offered him aid that they could do nothing for him, but asked them to care for his wife and family. Poor Napier—one of that gallant Scottish family which has given so many heroes to fight for their country—was hit first on the breast, and dropped to his knees. To the next man he said, "I am shot. Tell my father and mother I died like a man." He was afterwards shot through the neck and in the thigh. S. C. Elliot, our most promising lawyer, immediately after helping a wounded man into one of the sleighs, was shot from behind, the bullet which killed him being found in the front of his shirt after his body was brought home. Arnold, one of the Mounted Police, got a bullet through the upper part of his lungs, and said, "I'm shot, but good for them yet." He stooped forward a little, and fired several shots more, was shot again in the body, and then received a third bullet, but was lifted into the sleigh and reached Carleton, where he died next morning. Newith, a volunteer, wounded in the leg, crept down towards the road, but the sleighs had gone. An Indian came up, and began to club him with his gun. He held up his hands to cover his face and head, and was hit four times, and had two of his fingers broken, when a Half-breed noticed the Indian and compelled him to stop. He was carried to Duck Lake two hours after, and his life again threatened by two Indians. Again the Half-breeds protected him. He was liberated on the following Monday, when the dead bodies were brought home. Two of the men were again shot through the head and one stabbed while lying on the field. Both of them, it is believed, must have been at the point of death, if not actually dead. None of the dead were scalped, although until they were brought in, there was great fear that this had been done.

Of the wounded Capt. Moore's leg is shattered below the knee. Gilchrist, a policeman, with broken thigh, has suffered intensely. Inspector Howe, Gordon, and McNab had only flesh wounds. The last mentioned nearly had the artery of his arm severed. In all twelve died, nine of them (all volunteers) on the field, and seven were wounded.

CHAPTER V.

AFTER THE BATTLE.

IT was plain that the defences of Fort Carleton were not such as to make the place tenable against the Half-breeds now well supplied with provisions and ammunition, and full of triumph from their late success. Besides this, it was thought that Beardy, the Cree chief, whose reserve was a few miles from Carleton, was in league with Riel. Carleton was only defended by an old stockade; it was situated close to a high hill which completely commanded it. On the next day, Friday, March 27, therefore, Colonel Irvine marched out of Fort Carleton. Sacks of flour were emptied and scattered around and soaked with coal oil. The same day Sanderson, one of the prisoners in Riel's camp, was sent to Carleton with an offer to surrender the bodies of the dead. He gave up to Colonel Irvine also a letter from Riel to one Scott, near Prince Albert, who was suspected of sympathy with the rising. For some reason he was at first put under arrest, and the offer was not accepted lest it should prove to be a ruse to draw a party into an ambuscade. On Friday night, before the preparations for leaving were quite completed, a fire broke out accidentally in the fort. No effort was made to stay its progress, and on Saturday morning the whole force started for Prince Albert, which was reached at 3 p.m.

Great relief was felt on their arrival. The people of Prince Albert received on Thursday night news of the skirmish and the death of so many of those whom they had sent off full of life, and confident of an easy if not bloodless victory. It was expected that as soon as Irvine and Crozier had united their forces, the movement would collapse at once. Now a serious disaster had occurred, and Riel and his savage forces, flushed with victory, were nearer to us than our own men. The citizens at once set to work to build a barricade of cordwood around the Presbyterian Church and manse grounds, in which the women and children might obtain shelter. Almost every man in town, including three of the ministers, worked with a will, and in less time than could have been supposed, a strong stockade was completed, in most places

LIEUT.-COL. IRVINE, N.-W. MOUNTED POLICE.

eight feet high, and lined within by another pile of wood on which the men could stand. Stores and ice cut from the river were rapidly driven in. A large shed was run up in the enclosure, and a two-storey house across the street, which commanded the square, and would have given protection to the enemy advancing, was pulled down and levelled with the ground. All through Friday no courier came from Colonel Irvine. In the afternoon one of the scouts who had been as far as Carleton the previous night, and held communication with those in the fort, though not with the officers, reported seven nuns from the convent had the novel experience of spending two nights under the roof of a Presbyterian clergyman; that sixteen men were dead and the seventeenth was dying, and that Big Bear, one of the most dangerous of the Indian Chiefs, had crossed the prairie from Battleford with 100 braves on snowshoes, and was then with Riel at Duck Lake. This news confirmed the fears of a large Indian rising with all its attendant horrors. The suspense on that night was very painful. It was expected that the savages would either at once attack Prince Albert or lie in wait for Colonel Irvine and his troops in "The Pines," where the Carleton trail passes for several miles through thick woods, from which the Indians could easily pick off our men as they passed. Not a little vexation and amazement were felt that Irvine had sent no despatch on which reliance could be placed.

The manse, church, and shed were filled with the people of the town. Three women with little babes only two or three days old were carried on mattresses into the manse. The houses near at hand were also filled with people ready to run into the stockade as soon as an alarm should be given. During the night Nolan came in to Prince Albert. He had been a member of Riel's Council, and acted as one of the French representatives at the meeting with Moore and McKay near Duck Lake. He asserted that he had been compelled to join the movement by threats that on refusal he would be put to death, and that after the skirmish he had contrived to make his escape. He reported that all of the French had been at the skirmish or close at hand; and that only four Half-breeds and two Indians were killed. He stated that many were urging Riel to march at once on Prince Albert, and that what was to be expected was an attack by night from the Indians, who would perhaps cross the river and enter the town from the north side. Major Moffat, who was for giving Nolan his liberty, was induced

AFTER THE BATTLE. 47

to keep him under surveillance, and on Col. Irvine's return on the Saturday he was placed in safe-keeping.

Not till 1 p.m. on Saturday was intelligence received of Irvine's march from Carleton. Two hours after the wounded were driven in. It was with thankfulness learned that only twelve were dead and that the wounded had borne the journey very well. Captain Moore, though the splints had been removed from his shattered leg, said he "came down quite comfortably, and had smoked eleven pipes by the way." The force had not been molested in "The Pines," nor was the enemy anywhere seen. The police and volunteers were greeted on their arrival with ringing cheers—the joy and gratitude shaded only by the thought that nine of their brave comrades were still lying dead upon the field, exposed, as far as was then known, to the hot sun by day and the frost at night, and possibly also to beasts of prey.

About 7 p.m., just as people were hoping that all was safe, the scouts and telegraph operator came in from the road that leads to Batoche and reported that a force of Indians was approaching and close at hand. A shot was fired from the stockade, and messengers rushed in all directions to alarm the people, and bring them within the stockade. The church bell was rung; and even in the midst of the alarm there were many who noticed how different is the effect on the soul of the same sound in different circumstances. The bell which had rung out joy and gladness after a wedding, which had filled them with solemn and devout feelings as they went to the house of prayer, seemed now to be pouring out sounds of horror and making the heart quake with alarm.

> "Hear the tolling of the bells!
>   Iron bells!
> What a tale of terror now their turbulency tells—
>   In the silence of the night,
>   How we shudder with affright
> At the melancholy menace of their tone—
> For every sound that floats
> From the rust within their throats
>   Is a groan."

Such a panic many pray to God that they may not ever see again. Women arose from their sick beds and rushed into the enclosure; children snatched up in their nightclothes were carried into the manse in blankets. Another woman with a babe only a few hours old was added to the number of those previously carried in. The minister and others guarded the door, admitting women and children only, and sternly refusing admittance to selfish or timid men and boys. Some sad and one or two amusing scenes might be described. Two or three of the women fainted and the doctor was passed in to attend to the sick. After the first rush was over all behaved very well, keeping quiet as they sat on the floor, and receiving as well as could be expected the assurance that there was no sufficient cause for the alarm. Meanwhile the stockade was lined with police and volunteers in arms ready to receive the enemy. After a time it was discovered that the scouts had been far too hasty in giving the alarm, as they had not actually seen the Indians at all. A few days after, however, it was said that the Indians had been on the march, but coming to the Carleton Road, and noticing the traces of the passage of the police force, they returned to Riel's camp.

On the Sabbath Sanderson and two others went with sleighs to Duck Lake to bring in the dead. They found that Riel had permitted the prisoners whom he held, and some of the French to go out and carry the bodies into the house from which so many had been shot. On Monday at noon they returned, bringing along with the corpses, Newith, the wounded prisoner, whom Riel had liberated. The bodies were laid out in an empty building, and with great thankfulness it was found that none of them had been grossly mutilated by the savages. The nine bodies lying side by side, the faces of two blackened with powder, formed a ghastly spectacle. A few days before they went forth, full of life and spirit, too eager, poor fellows, for the fray, and too contemptuous of their foes, and there now they lay—stiff, discoloured, and silent in death. But they went at the call of duty, and they died on "the field of honour." Loving and gentle hands carried them to different places and prepared their bodies for the burial. Well may the people of Prince Albert cherish their memory with sorrowing affection and solemn pride. Like Him in whom we trust for salvation, though of course in a lower sense, they "laid down their lives for their friends."

On Tuesday, at 2 p.m., the funeral procession started for the Church of England cemetery, where it was thought best to lay the nine together in one common grave. The Prince Albert band led the way playing a funeral march. Then followed the volunteers, a body of police, and the ministers of the town. Next came the coffins, the mourners, and the general public. The Bishop and two of his clergy read the ordinary burial service. There was no sermon nor address, nor allusion to the peculiar circumstances. To some it seemed a pity that the order of the Church should be so rigid as to prevent any more honour being done to these brave men brought in from the field of battle, than would be shown at the burial of a newborn child. The Bishop of Saskatchewan, and the Presbyterian minister, however, both preached funeral sermons appropriate to the circumstances on the following Sabbath.

Thus closes the story of the first act in the great tragedy. The story is a pathetic one, telling as it does of true heroes whose blood was poured out upon the snow, not in the cause of freedom and the defence of their hearths and homes, but in obedience to that stern call of duty that forbids us to argue as to the justice of the cause and only commands us to defend the honour of the old flag, and ask no questions of the cause. By-and-bye somebody may be called to answer for the blood of those gallant fellows who perished nobly with words of defiance and unquenchable bravery on their lips; but for the present we can only shed bitter tears over the untimely flight of spirits, the bravest of the brave.

As might have been expected, the result of the Duck Lake skirmish aroused the Half-breeds to more active rebellion. Everywhere the telegraph wires were cut, and the stores and ammunition plundered. The Mounted Police and what volunteers could be armed held Prince Albert, Battleford, Fort Pitt, Fort Saskatchewan, and Edmonton in the North.

CHAPTER VI

THE INDIANS OF MANITOBA AND THE NORTH-WEST.

THE great problem now to be solved was the extent to which the Indians would assist in the rebellion upon which the Half-breeds had now fairly launched themselves. The following pretty accurate estimate of the force and disposition of the Indians was made at this time by a gentleman well-posted in matters pertaining to the Indians and to the North-West generally. The question has been answered. This estimate of the probabilities is particularly interesting, as it serves to illustrate the nature and extent of our national peril at this time:

There were in Manitoba and the North-West Territories very nearly or quite 34,000 Indians who were under the care of and to a certain extent dependent upon the Canadian Government. They are divided into several great nations, prominent among which are the "Ojibewas," "Crees," "Sioux," and "Blackfeet." Besides these, however, there are many sub-divisions indicating tribal and sectional distinctions rather than those of race and nationality; at least a general similarity of the languages of the various groups would indicate this.

The Ojibewas, very often corrupted into "Chippewas," besides embracing nearly all of the "bush" Indians of Manitoba, are closely allied to the Saulteux of the more open country west of Red River Valley. Their language is in many respects similar to that of the Crees, and intermarriages with the latter are not infrequent. The

Swampies, who occupy the country about the mouth of Red River, and bordering on Lake Winnipeg, are also of this same nation. In the event of any serious troubles among the Indians, it was not probable that the Ojibewas would take any very active part, as most of their bands were located so as to be nearly or quite surrounded by white settlements of considerable magnitude. They are, as a rule, very peaceably inclined, and poorly armed, most of them using old-fashioned Hudson Bay Company shot guns, which, however, will throw bullets of heavy calibre with considerable accuracy. There are very few of the Ojibewas proper to be found west of the Red River Valley, and most of them occupy the bush country east of Red River, though some bands might be found in portions of Northern Manitoba. There were probably of the Ojibewas proper in Manitoba and the extreme west of Ontario about 4,000.

The Saulteux (pronounced "Sotos") were so intermingled with the Crees in the eastern portion of the North-West Territory and the west of Manitoba that it was not easy to ascertain their numbers. There were, however, not less than 2,500 of them. They are for the most part to be found in the regions of Fort Pelly, Fort Ellice, Moose Mountain, Qu'Appelle, and Crooked Lakes. Among the more well-inclined Cree Half-breeds these Saulteux have the reputation of being rather clever, and often very plausible mischief-makers. Some of them are remarkably well off for Indians, and not a few of them are exceedingly ambitious. They are, as a rule, rather intelligent and extremely active and energetic. Their reserves are for the most part well located.

The Crees largely outnumber any other tribe of the North-West, and it is in a great measure owing to the thoroughly pacific disposition of these people that Canadian supremacy has been so easily maintained thus far. It has long been the boast of the Crees that as a nation they have never shed the blood of the white man. In times past they proved themselves capable fighting men, however, in their struggles with the Sioux and Blackfeet, and they think they are still as capable of fighting as they ever were. There is no doubt, however, that they are not nearly so warlike a people as the Blackfeet, and nothing but a real sense of wrong would ever induce them to take up arms against British authority. Of course it is not saying that they are wronged to say that they have experienced a sense of wrong, and it is just here that the great danger lies so far as they are concerned. They were for many generations accustomed to meeting no white men except the agents of the Hudson's Bay Company, and whatever may be said against that great corporation the offence of lying to the Indians can never be laid to their charge. Aside from the moral aspect of the case altogether, it was a part of their business policy to conduct their traffic with the Indians in such a way that the latter would never have the shadow of a cause for doubting the word of any officer or agent of the Company. If an indiscreet trader made a promise to the humblest member of a tribe, that promise was invariably fulfilled, no matter what the cost might be. In the old times an insignificant order of the value of two or three shillings has been sent all the way to the Old Country, *via* York Factory, merely because something not in stock had been promised to an Indian. As the shipments of goods to York Factory were not very frequent, the dark-skinned customer would sometimes have long to wait before receiving what was promised him, but he rested safe in the assurance that it would not be forgotten, and that however long in coming it was sure to come at last, and so he was satisfied. Accustomed to this sort of treatment, it is not surprising that the Cree became the firm friend of the white man. He could rely implicitly on all that was told him, and he came to look upon the white man as well-nigh all-powerful. In this way the Crees were brought up for many generations in a good school, and it is only a pity that they have not always had such an example of thorough truthfulness before them. Inexperienced men, who knew nothing of Indian character, have been brought in contact with them through the agency of the Indian Department, and these people, too often pressed by the exigencies of what they deemed a trying situation, have made promises to them which have not been fulfilled. Promises had been made which could not with propriety be carried out, and too often promises had been made which had been wholly forgotten. These broken promises might seem little things to the men who made and broke them, but they were big things to these simple-minded children of the wilds. Truthfulness was the one virtue which they prized above all others, and knowing nothing of the nature of the resources upon which the Indian Agent or Farm Instructor had to fall back, they supposed them to be unlimited, and therefore regarded the plea of inability no excuse for the non-fulfilment of any promise.

Big Bear, with a band of about five hundred, had always been a troublesome and dangerous man, more fond of hunting buffaloes, whether north or south of the line, than of tilling the soil. His reserve was not definitely located, and it was not known just where he was at that time to be found. He was of the South Crees, but in common with the rest of that branch of the Cree nation, he had been induced to go north. The policy of the Government in taking the South Crees as far as possible from the international boundary, and from the line of railway, was doubtless a good one. In the South they were frequently getting into difficulty with the Indians and Half-breeds south of the line, as well as with the Bloods and Blackfeet of the South-West, and had they remained there the danger of a collision with the railway navvies was always to be feared.

Had the insurgents had the opportunity of choosing their own time for an outbreak, they could not have selected a season more thoroughly opportune for their own purposes. The winter had been a severe one, and, in any event, these improvident Red-men were always worse off in the spring than at any other season of the year. This was the season at which the Agency supplies were most apt to fall short, and the advent of spring weather would soon render transportation a matter of very grave difficulty.

In the immediate vicinity of the outbreak it was to be presumed that there was more to be feared from the Half-breeds than from the Indians, as the majority of the latter had always had the name of being peaceable and well-inclined.

Mis-ta-was-sis (Big Child) was the most powerful chief in the Carleton Agency, and his band only numbered two hundred and twenty-six. He himself was a devout Presbyterian, as were many of his band, and while it was easy to understand that they would not feel inclined to rise in arms against people of their own race, and perhaps in some instances their own relatives, it was not at all probable they would take any part in the outbreak.

Ahtah-ka-koop had a band of one hundred and ninety-six, and what has been said of the band of Mis-ta-was-sis was mainly true of his followers. They were not at all likely to take action for or against the insurgents.

Beardy, on whose reserve the first battle had taken place, was not by any means an amiable Indian. His band numbered something over one hundred and fifty, and, like their chief, they had small respect for the white man or his institutions. Unlike many of the Indians in the Carleton Agency, they were pagans and had no religious instruction of any kind. They managed to raise some grain and roots, but not nearly enough to supply them with the necessaries of life. It was extremely probable, therefore, that Beardy would cast his fortunes in with the rebels, if he had not already done so.

Altogether, however, it was not probable that many of the Indians of the Carleton Agency would take any part in the insurrection, and those who would do so would very probably be actuated more by a desire to obtain food and clothing, than that of avenging real or fancied wrongs. The condition of these unfortunate people was deplorable. Their staple food, muskrats, had become scarce, their crops even on the very limited acreage broken on their reserves were bad, and as early as July, 1884, it was prophesied that their principal dependence for food the following winter would be upon rabbits. The Crees in the Carleton Agency numbered about one thousand six hundred, and as they subsisted chiefly on the products of the chase, they were doubtless fairly armed. They are divided into about a dozen small bands, and were scattered over a very considerable extent of country.

There were at the Battleford Agency, which lies west of the Carleton Agency, upwards of two thousand Crees and some three hundred Stoneys or Assiniboines, and these were divided into about a dozen separate bands. There was none of them in a particularly prosperous condition, though most of their reserves were well located. The most influential chief in this Agency, and perhaps the most influential chief in the Northern Territory, was Poundmaker, a Cree chief, whose individual following was about one hundred and fifty. His reserve was on Battle River, a short distance west of Battleford. He is a particularly fine-looking specimen of his race, being considerably over six feet high, of rather slight build, and singularly erect. He has an intelligent and rather refined looking face, a high, prominent forehead, and a nose of the purely Grecian type, while there is nothing coarse or sensual about the lower portion of his face. His hands are small and delicate in appearance, his fingers being long and tapered. He is accounted an orator among his own people, but has none of the noise and bluster that too often characterize Indian oratory. He speaks slowly and distinctly and in a manner that gives the hearer the idea of suppressed power. His gestures are invariably very graceful, and his manner thoroughly dignified, without the faintest suspicion of pomposity or self-consciousness. He is always solemn and earnest in his utterances, and generally bears himself after the manner of a religious enthusiast who was oppressed with the idea that he had some great mission to accomplish. Though a pagan, he has more than once betrayed a strong inclination to embrace Catholicism. His father was a Cree and his mother a half-sister to the great Blackfoot chief, Crowfoot. His grandmother on the side of his mother was said to have been a Stoney, and this is corroborated by the great chief's peculiar cast of countenance. Poundmaker's career has been in many respects a remarkable one. To use his own language, he often went among the Blackfeet during his boyhood for the purpose of killing their people and stealing their ponies, but when he grew to be a man he conceived the idea of making peace between the Crees and Blackfeet. Crowfoot, his uncle, was then all-powerful in the councils of the latter, but often when he was absent from the camp Poundmaker lay pretending to sleep while he heard the Blackfeet debating whether to kill him or not. Many a night had he lain hour after hour with his right hand grasping his big Remington revolver at full cock under his pillow. After a winter of terror, and several trips from Eagle Hills to Blackfoot Crossing during the following summer, his great object was accomplished, and peace was made between the two great nations of the plains.

As the friend of Crowfoot, the great chief of the Blackfeet, and as one of the most intelligent and influential of the Cree chiefs, Poundmaker could, if he chose, become the most dangerous Indian in the North-West. His influence with Crowfoot had always been extraordinary, and he was universally looked up to and respected by all the Crees of the North. He had trouble with the Indian Department in the winter of 1883-84, and he was not a man to quickly forget an indignity offered to himself or his people. There was not an Indian in the North-West who knew the country better than Poundmaker. In 1881, when Lord Lorne went across the plains, Poundmaker joined the party for the purpose of interpreting the language of the Blackfeet into Cree, as the Cree interpreter accompanying the party did not understand Blackfoot. Johnny Saskatchewan was taken along to act as guide, but between Battleford and the crossing of the Red Deer the Half-breed lost himself, and for the last two days Poundmaker was "guiding the guide." After crossing the Red Deer, Poundmaker took the lead, and travelled in almost an air-line to the Blackfoot Crossing, though there was no trail, and what was even more remarkable, arranged his time-table so that he hit the best grass and water to be had just about camping time on every occasion.

Little Pine had the largest following of any chief in the Battleford district. His band numbered well toward four hundred and fifty, and as he had but recently settled on his reserve, too much dependence was not to be placed upon his loyalty. He had been one of the South Crees, and one of the last to settle on a Northern reserve. His men were well-armed and well-mounted. Lucky Man was an Indian of very much the same style as Little Pine, he taking treaty and going North at the same time. His band numbered about three hundred and fifty, and, like those of Little Pine, his men were well-armed and well-mounted. Like all buffalo hunters, they were experts with both pony and rifle. There were upwards of two thousand Crees in the Battleford Agency, besides some three hundred Stoneys or Assiniboines.

In the Edmonton district there were about a dozen small bands of Crees, and half-a-dozen bands of Assiniboines. Altogether they numbered nearly three thousand. They were, like the other Indians in the North, in a miserably destitute condition, and though disposed to be pacific it was difficult to say what influence the prospect of unlimited food and clothing might have had upon their loyalty.

The Fort Pitt Agency only embraced about seven hundred people, though at one time, during the summer of 1884, Big Bear and his band of five hundred were located there. So far as the Crees properly belonging to Fort Pitt were concerned, there was not much feared from them, or much expected of them. Like all the rest, they were badly off, and would have done a great deal for a liberal supply of food and clothing.

The Crees of Treaty Four were numerous and well armed and equipped; but as they were for the most part pretty well settled on their reserves, and many of them fairly well off for Indians, they were not likely to take part in any uprising unless it should have become general. The only chief in this treaty who was at all likely to become troublesome was Piapot, who with his band of five hundred and fifty was located at Indian Head, near Qu'Appelle. He was known to have no very friendly feeling toward the Indian Department, and particularly towards Lieutenant-Governor Dewdney. He was so near the railway, and as it were almost in the heart of a fairly settled district, it was thought that he would have some difficulty in getting away unobserved. If there should have come anything like a general uprising among the Indians, however, Piapot would without doubt have taken an active part on the side of the Crees, and unfortunately should he have done so, and made anything like a successful stand, it was only too probable that a large portion of the seven thousand in Treaty Four would have joined him.

Those who knew anything of Indian affairs in the North-West were now watching, with a great deal of anxiety, the attitude of the Blackfeet nation in any future crisis. Though not so numerous as the Crees, these people, if roused, could not fail to become far more dangerous. They numbered nearly six thousand, and instead of being scattered about in small bands over a large extent of country, they were compactly placed as follows, according to their tribal distinctions:

Of the Blackfeet proper there were nearly two thousand two hundred at Blackfoot Crossing, on Bow River, some sixty miles from Calgary.

Of the Bloods there were nearly two thousand three hundred on the Blood reserve, near Fort McLeod.

Of the Piegans (another branch of the Blackfeet family) there were over nine hundred on the Piegan reserve, on Old Man's River, a few miles west of Fort McLeod.

Of the Sarcees there were over four hundred on their reserve near Calgary. These people were not of the Blackfeet tribe, but they had for years been under the protection of and had formed a portion of the Blackfeet nation. The legend concerning them is that they were formerly a powerful and very warlike tribe, occupying a portion of the Peace River country. Their turbulent disposition involved them in one war after another, till by their constant fighting, often against superior numbers, they became so reduced that they were no longer able to exist among the fierce and constantly warring tribes of the North-West. Admiring their unquestionable bravery, the Blackfeet nation took them under their protection, since which time, though they have preserved their own customs, language, and traditions, and though they have to a great extent abstained from inter-marriage with the Blackfeet, they have been to all intents and purposes a portion of the Blackfeet nation.

Thus it will be seen that within a radius of some sixty miles these four powerful branches of the Blackfeet nation were concentrated. They were all of them much more fond of war and pillage than of tilling the soil. Of the four tribes forming this great nation the Bloods had always been regarded as the most powerful and dangerous. Besides being the most numerous they were the most warlike, and were provided with Winchester rifles, revolvers, and abundance of ammunition. The Bloods had again and again been accused, and often convicted, of horse-stealing, and the unfortunate Police Constable Greyburn was murdered by a Blood Indian. In fact, this tribe had always enjoyed a most unenviable reputation amongst the ranchmen of the vicinity. What made them still more dangerous was their close proximity to the cattle ranches, and to the extensive supplies of the Indian Department, and those of the local traders at Fort McLeod. They had no conscientious scruples against the robbery of either the white men or of their own people. Neither they nor any of the Blackfeet tribe had ever had much to do with the Hudson Bay Company, and they had, as a consequence, received nothing like the lesson of honesty and good faith impressed upon those whose traffic had been with the Hudson Bay Company. The Bloods were particularly fond of "Counting Coo," and regarded such a prosy and unromantic occupation as farming as quite beneath the dignity of individuals calling themselves men. Nothing but the pressure of circumstances ever compelled them to adopt farming as an occupation, and should they have discovered that there had been a prospect of a general Indian uprising, they would have been very much disappointed if they had not been permitted to play a part in it on one side or the other. They had no affection for the Crees, nor indeed for any tribe outside of the Blackfeet nation; but, at the same time, as they would probably have imagined the white settlers, ranchmen, and traders in their immediate vicinity would have made much better "picking" for them than the Halfbreeds and Crees, it was not improbable that they might have been induced to join the latter, in view of richer plunder. The Bloods were probably the most accomplished horsemen in the North-West, they having had a large number of good ponies of considerable size and speed.

What was true of the Bloods was also true, to a less extent, of the Piegans. They were less numerous, less warlike, than the Bloods; but they were, for all that, sufficiently numerous, powerful, and warlike to have given ground for very serious apprehension in case of a general uprising among the Indians. They, too, were well-armed, and had in their band some four hundred horses.

Though the acknowledged head of the Blackfeet nation, and though under the immediate leadership of Crowfoot, the chief of the Blackfeet, the Blackfeet tribe was scarcely as powerful in the councils of the nation as were the Bloods. They were rich in horses, and were always well supplied with arms and ammunition, and in the use of all these appliances of war and the chase they had always been adepts. That they were less troublesome than the Bloods was probably less attributable to their disposition than to their surroundings. They were in a measure out of the way of settlement, and their reserve was one of the most charming spots in the North-West, if not on this Continent. They were in the valley of that most beautiful of mountain streams, Bow River, and their land was wonderfully rich and productive.

THE INDIANS OF MANITOBA AND NORTH-WEST. 61

They had an unlimited range for their ponies, and thus far had been very liberally rationed by the Government. They had for a few years made very satisfactory progress in farming, but it would not do to place too much dependence on this circumstance. When Lord Lorne was crossing from Battleford to Blackfoot Crossing, Commissioner Dewdney was fondly hoping that the Blackfeet at the Crossing would have made a grand showing from an agricultural point of view, as it was known that they had broken, fenced, and seeded a considerable tract of land; but alas, before the Governor-General arrived the Blackfeet had received the news that a few buffaloes had crossed the line and were coming northward! This news sealed the fate of the growing crops which the Commissioner had hoped to show Lord Lorne with so much pride, for in order to get their ponies into condition for running buffaloes as rapidly as possible, they had thrown down their fences and turned the animals into the fields, and the highly-prized crops presented a sorry picture by the time His Excellency pitched his first camp on the banks of the crystal Bow.

Crowfoot was an Indian of more than ordinary intelligence, and the comparatively good behaviour of the Blackfeet tribe, and indeed that of the whole Blackfeet nation, was largely due to his rational counsel. He had sense enough to see that there was nothing for it but that the Blackfeet should bow to the inevitable, as the Redmen have always been compelled to do in the long run on the advent of the white man. There was no longer game enough in the country to support his people, and the neighbouring tribes were so poor that they were not worth robbing. Should his people have risen against the whites they would always have felt that besides the white men they would have had their old-time enemies, the Crees, to fight; and, taking all these things into consideration, Crowfoot had evidently come to the conclusion that, as there was nothing else for him to do, it only remained for the Blackfeet to settle down and become peaceable farmers. What influence the news of an outbreak in the North-West might have upon him it was hard to tell. It was not improbable that he and his people might want to take part in it, and not impossible that through Poundmaker's influence they might have been inclined to join the insurgents. And in this connection there was another circumstance worth considering. Crowfoot was getting old, and his younger brother-in-law, Yellow Horse, has a great deal of influence with the more youthful members of the tribe, who had as yet no scalps with which to fringe their deer-skin shirts, and no "Coo to count." Yellow Horse, though an active and intelligent Indian of some means, and a particularly fine appearance, had nothing like the intellectual ballast possessed by Crowfoot. Should Crowfoot have heeded his counsel, there could be little doubt that the Blackfeet would have got into trouble in a very short time. Like One Spot of the Bloods, Yellow Horse bore no very choice reputation among the white men who knew him. He was particularly fond of talking of the good old days when the Blackfeet were nearly always on the warpath.

The Sarcees, though few in point of numbers, would have counted for a good deal in case the Blackfeet had gone to war. They were savages of the most degraded and vicious type. They hated farming, were thoroughly warlike, and, like all the Blackfeet nations, had arms, ammunition, and ponies.

Though a formidable tribe in the more recent histories of American wars, it was thought improbable that either the Sioux proper or their near relatives, the Stoneys, would have taken any part against the whites should there have been an Indian uprising in the Canadian North-West. They were scattered about in small bands all the way from Fort Ellice to the Rocky Mountains. There were some few of them in nearly every agency, and they were, as a rule, active and industrious. They had little to do with either the Crees or the Blackfeet, and were perhaps more remarkable for minding their own business than any other Indians of the North-West. White Cap, the Sioux chief, occupied a reserve at Moose

Woods, only a short distance south of Duck Lake. His band consisted of about two hundred and fifty, and it was not long before he allied himself to the rebel cause, though such a course was not expected of him. He and the elder members of his band had fled to Canada from the United States after the Minnesota massacre, and knew quite well that should they become involved in a second war upon the whites they would have nowhere to go for rest and protection in the event of defeat.

CHAPTER VII.

GENERAL MIDDLETON AND STAFF ON THE SCENE.

IT has been mentioned that the 90th Rifles had been ordered from Winnipeg to Qu'Appelle, together with the Winnipeg artillery. They arrived on Sunday, 29th of March, and were established in comfortable barracks at the immigrant quarters, the division which arrived earliest being placed in Fort Qu'Appelle, eighteen miles to the north. General Middleton, Commander-in-Chief of the Canadian Militia, on his arrival at Qu'Appelle, decided that it would be unwise to proceed to the scene of the rebellion with the force on hand, and resolved to await the reinforcements on the point of arrival from the East. This distinguished officer began his military career in 1842, his commission as ensign bearing date December 30 of that year. His first experiences of active service were in South New Zealand, where the insurgent Maoris carried on a fierce guerilla warfare much the same as that of the Indians and Half-breeds in the North-West. He took part in the successful attack which carried the strongly intrenched "pah" of Wauganui. He was next engaged in the suppression of the Santhal rebellion in India, and took a leading part in the desperate, but glorious, struggle of the few British soldiers who faced the terrible storm of the Hindoo Mutiny in 1857-58.

Captain Middleton served as orderly officer to General Franks at the battle of Sultanpore, and took part in the advance on Lucknow. While thus engaged he was A. D. C. to General Luard. He took part in the storming of Bank-i-Houn and the Martinière; Major Middleton was recommended by the general officer under whom he served to Lord Clyde for the Victoria Cross on account of two signal acts of valor in the field. At the Battle of Azemghur, on April 15, 1858, he was ordered to take command of a troop of the Military Train and to charge a dense column of the rebels. Just as the troop, led by Captain Middleton, had swept sword in hand into the midst of the Sepoys, one of the officers, Lieut. Hamilton, fell wounded from his horse. The wound had completely disabled him, and a number of Sepoys rushed forward to cut him to pieces with their tulwars. Captain Middleton at once dismounted, lifted the wounded officer on his own horse and carried him from the field in safety. In the same fight, a private soldier of the troop being unhorsed and disabled by a wound, was saved in the same way by Middleton. The Victoria Cross so well merited by these gallant acts, was never actually bestowed, some red-tapeism as to Captain Middleton's having been then on the staff is supposed to have interfered with the course of justice.

In accordance with the rules for the retirement of officers after a certain term of service, Major Middleton must have been compelled to leave active service in the army with the rank of Lieut.-Colonel, had not his appointment to succeed General Luard last year given him the rank of Major-General. General Middleton is more frank in his courtesy than his predecessor, and infinitely more popular with the Canadian soldier. In face and figure he is the ideal of a military leader, and is, no doubt, one who, if necessary, can use the sword with good effect. Among the most distinguished officers on Gen. Middleton's staff are Lord Melgund and Major Buchan.

Lord Melgund is also Military Secretary to the Governor-General, and is the eldest son of the Earl of Minto.

Born in July, 1845, he was educated at Eton College, at once one of the most aristocratic of the great public schools of England, and one of the best training places for boys to form a manly bearing and strength of character. From Eton he went to Trinity College, Cambridge, where in 1866 he graduated as B.A. He entered the army in 1867, when he received a commission in the

LORD MELGUND.

Scotch Fusilier Guards. From this regiment he retired in 1870, holding the rank of captain. He is a captain and honorary major in the First Roxburghshire Mounted Volunteer Rifles, and, as has been stated, is a captain in the regular army. He has seen service on a considerable scale, having been in 1877 attached to Colonel Lennox, the English military attaché with the Turkish army, and was present at several hard-contested battles. He also served during the war in Afghanistan in 1879, when he served as a volunteer on the staff of Lieut.-General Sir Frederick Roberts, who is considered one of the best tacticians in the British army. In 1881 he accompanied Sir Frederick Roberts to Natal in South Africa as private secretary. He subsequently took an active part in the Egyptian war, and was wounded at Magwar. In 1883 he married Mary Caroline, daughter of the late Hon. Charles Grey, and niece to Earl Grey, K.G.

MAJOR LAWRENCE BUCHAN.

Major Lawrence Buchan is descended from an ancient Scottish family. He was born in Paris, County of Brant, Ontario, and received his education at Upper Canada College, where he evinced a taste for mathematics and the study of military tactics; he studied then at the Military College, where he received a certificate. He then spent several years in New York city, where he engaged in the commission business. Then returning to Toronto, he became a partner in the stock-broking firm of Blake and Alexander. For six years he held the position of resident secretary in Canada for the Scottish Commercial Insurance Company. When he had carried out the winding-up of this Company's affairs in Canada, he went to Brandon and displayed much energy and business talent in promoting the progress and landed estate interests of that city and the surrounding district. When the Manitoba Municipalities Act was introduced, he was appointed Secretary-Treasurer of the Western Judicial District, which position he still retains.

Major Buchan was connected with the Queen's Own Rifles for a period of ten years; he entered it as ensign, and left with the rank of captain. He was much liked in the regiment, being equally a favourite with both officers and men; of the colonel he has always been a close friend. When the present Half-breed rebellion broke out, Major Buchan telegraphed to Ottawa for leave to enlist three companies in Brandon; he proceeded to Winnipeg where he was gazetted major, and served as adjutant on General Middleton's staff. He is a valuable aide, as he has travelled a good deal through the North-West, and is thoroughly acquainted with the country and the people.

General Middleton asked the Government for a force of two thousand men, and Sir John Macdonald obtained from Parliament an additional grant of a million dollars for the expenses of the war.

Meanwhile, the rebels and Indian sympathizers were actively engaged in pillage of all stores, public and private. Riel detained a number of settlers, among others William Mitchel, prisoners in the little wooden church at the village of Stobart, near the scene of the Duck Lake skirmish. A leading settler named John Kerr was arrested by Riel's orders and brought before his executive council of twelve, on a charge of counselling the escape of a telegraph operator from the neighbourhood. Riel on this occasion affected clemency, and told the council that "Kerr was a good fellow." He was released with a caution to abstain from taking part against Riel.

CHAPTER VIII.

OLD CANADA STRIPS FOR THE FIGHT.

MEANWHILE every effort for defence was made at the towns and forts threatened by the insurgents. At Battleford 200 volunteers were enlisted, and a home-guard at Medicine Hat and Calgary, both of which had to fear the Blackfeet Indians in case Riel should succeed in calling them to the war-path by the influence of their chief Crowfoot who, as has been mentioned, was a relation of the Cree chief Poundmaker. Qu'Appelle, which was in the neighbourhood of some Cree lodges, was well defended by both divisions of the 90th Battalion of Winnipeg Rifles and by the Winnipeg Artillery.

The Canadian Pacific Railway Company resolved on organizing a regiment from among their employés for the defence of the property of the railway against attempts of the rebels, and Captain Gaulter, of the Purchasing Department, an experienced volunteer officer, undertook the work of directing this force which was likely to form a valuable aid to the main army.

At Winnipeg the students of the College organized a company of volunteers; and from Ottawa Colonel Scott telegraphed to Winnipeg to old officers of the Red River Expedition to form companies, and if possible a battalion for active service.

In Ontario the preparations for the despatch of troops continued to be pushed on with an alacrity which proved the universal determination of our people to punish the rebels. Colonel Villiers received orders to form a Provisional Regiment to be constituted as follows: —from the 46th Battalion, one company each from Port Hope and Millbrook; from the 57th Battalion at Peterborough, one company; from the 49th Battalion at Belleville, one company; from the 45th Battalion at

Bowmanville, one company; from the 47th Battalion, Portsmouth, one company; these troops to concentrate at Kingston en route for Qu'Appelle, on March 31. At Port Hope Colonel Williams, M.P., in command of the 46th Battalion, made up a battalion for active service with picked men selected from the 45th Battalion of West Durham and Victoria, the 46th East Durham, and 40th Northumberland. At Cobourg Col. Rogers, of the 40th, had in readiness No. 1 Company, Captain H. J. Snelgrove; No. 2 Company, Captain G. Guilet; No. 3 Company, Captain Bonycastle, of Campbellford.

At Toronto the departure of the troops was attended with enthusiastic excitement of which the city has had no experience for the last peaceable and easy-going half-century.

On Friday night (March 27) the orderly sergeants belonging to the Queen's Own and the Royal Grenadiers, were busily engaged in summoning the men of the several companies to the muster early next morning, at which the 500 picked men for the war contingent were to be chosen.

At eight on Saturday morning the streets leading to the drill shed were packed with a dense multitude eager to know who would be selected for the perilous honours of battle. In the drill shed the whole available strength of both the Toronto battalions was mustered, not a man being absent from the post of duty, except a few who were too ill to attend.

By 2 p.m. the officers who had met in the orderly room of the two regiments had selected the men who were to join the war contingent, the selection being made of those who were not only physically fit to endure the campaign, but who were unmarried and had no relations depending on them.

The next day was Toronto's "Soldiers' Sunday." Everywhere the streets and the churches took a martial aspect, the Rifleman's dark green and the scarlet of the Grenadiers shone gaily in the feeble spring sunshine. Sermons bearing on the war and the duties and responsibilities it brought with it were preached in all the churches. In many a home bright eyes grew dim, and anxious prayers were breathed, at the thought of those loved ones who would depart on the morrow to the distant wilderness, to face the perils of savage warfare.

On Monday at noon the Toronto contingent left for the seat of war. Through the densely crowded streets, amid showers of bouquets from ladies in King Street balconies, with all *eclat* of a triumph and the pomp of martial music, Toronto's soldiers held their steady march to the railway station. No mark of public sympathy was wanting. The city had bestowed a free grant of underclothing on each soldier. The rank and intellect and beauty of Toronto was conspicuous among the concourse of fifty thousand who gathered to cheer them as the train moved away.

Mr. C. VanHorn, Vice-President of the Canadian Pacific Railway, had been in Toronto during March 28 and 29, making arrangements for providing comfortable car accommodation for the soldiers. To that great national railway thanks are due from everyone who is loyal to Canada, since it is only owing to the exertions made by that Company and its officers that sure, rapid and healthful means of transit were provided for the troops.

On board the cars all was merry as a marriage bell. Packs and heavy accoutrements were stowed away, lunch was partaken of from the twenty-four hours' supply of cooked provisions which each man had been directed to provide. Then came the singing of patriotic songs and such hymns as "Only an Armour-bearer," jokes from the regimental wit who had been practising sleight-of-hand all the week so as to juggle the rebel bullets. The time passed merrily and they reached Mattawa in time for a hearty breakfast next morning (March 31) at the Pacific Railway's dining hall.

Much exposure to cold and hardship had to be undergone by the Toronto contingent during the journey, especially over the gaps or uncompleted sections of the railway. Every pains was taken by the officials of the railway to provide teams to carry the soldiers over the gaps with as little delay as possible, and flat cars boarded to the height of four feet and spread thickly with hay were provided for the men during night journeys. But the thermometer was 20° to 30° below zero, the roads through the forests were terribly rough and broken by pitch-holes, six feet or more deep, into which the horses stumbled as into a trap. When the march was over there was no shelter but the wind-flapped walls of a canvas tent with floor of hardened snow. On this the men laid down their blankets, but many preferred to sleep on the snow outside near the huge fires which were blazing all night. Few slept; around them lit by the camp fires were the silent aisles of the columned woods; over all as over the homes they had left was spread the steel-blue vault with the diamond stars of a Canadian winter night. With dawn came cheerful sunshine, fresh strength and effort. The coldest and most trying part of the route was crossing the frozen surface of Lake Superior, a terrible ordeal to any but men of unusually strong constitution. As it was many had their faces partially frozen.

However, on April 5, all arrived at Port Arthur in safety, but such was the eager desire to reach the front that Colonel Otter would not allow the Queen's Own to halt even long enough to partake of a hot dinner, which the people of Port Arthur had prepared. A little less haste perhaps might have been good for the health and efficiency of the troops. The Tenth Royals, however, were allowed time to profit by the hospitality of Port Arthur. The Toronto contingent arrived at Winnipeg on the morning of April 7, and at Qu'Appelle, General Middleton's base of operations, on April 9.

In Toronto some of those interested in the fortunes of the Queen's Own were inclined to wish that their advance by the railway to Winnipeg and Qu'Appelle had been pursued with less relentless hurry. Happily, events proved that in this matter Colonel Otter did not overestimate the powers of endurance of the men under his command.

As the march proceeded the good-humour of the men exposed to many privations was the more note-worthy as most of them were accustomed to the refined luxury of a home in which every comfort abounded. Their officers from the first endeared themselves to the men, and made hard tack and harder marching more cheerfully borne by their own cheerful readiness to share equally with the private soldiers every form of privation and exposure. The officials of the Canadian Pacific Railway were unremitting in their efforts to make the march through "the gaps," or uncompleted portions of the road, as easy as possible. Mr. G. H. Middleton, Chief Engineer of the Western Division, specially deserves the gratitude of Canada. No better appointment could have been made by the Directors of the Railway which at that critical time held in its hands the fortunes of the war. Much of the subsequent success of our army was due to his knowledge of the country and sagacious disposition of the materials at his disposal so as to get the troops over the ground in the quickest possible time. Owing to his exertions and those of Mr. Henry Abbott an ample stock of provisions was provided at the gaps, where the men's strength would be most heavily taxed. Mr. Abbott at his camp at Dog Lake (where the first gap began) was in the habit of baking bread for a large number of railway employés. Our men were well supplied with what the Roman poet described as the best of sauces, active work, and the fresh hot rolls turned out in abundance by Mr. Abbott's shanty cook needed no *pate de foie gras* for a relish! Nor were slices of cold boiled pork wanting, broiled or fried in shanty fashion. When possible, sleeping accommodation was provided. Although it was not feasible to do all that was wished to spare the brave boys from exposure and discomfort, Colonel Otter and his officers were indefatigable in seeing after the wants of the men, and it was shown that they fared in every respect no better than the private soldiers. The boys bore everything with cheerful endurance. The wise counsel of their Colonel here prevailed on them to avoid the materials for "Dutch courage," strong drink forming no part of their equipment.

Songs heard often in the entr'acte at the Toronto Grand Opera House re-echoed as they held their march over the winter-stricken forest trail, or the dark-blue ice floor of Lake Superior. Among them the lyrics of the Tyrtæus of the Queen's Own, John A. Fraser, held a leading place in cheering his former comrades.

Many were the curious incidents resulting from their hasty departure from home. One man was telegraphed for the combination of his bank safe. Another man had left his gas burning, and another was paying three cents a day for a Free Library book, which he had forgotten to return when leaving Toronto.

Meanwhile the dear ones left behind waited in anxious suspense. Captious critics haunted the newspaper offices, and men who had no military experience or whose shoulders had never known the weight of a rifle were loudly asserting that "the raw levies" must fail before the experienced savage fighters of the wilderness. Of all the Toronto newspapers the *Globe* and the *World* gave accurate and unsensational intelligence, and the great mass of our people waited in calm reliance on Providence, not without fear of loss of beloved lives, not without hope that the brave youths of Canada would be victorious. The following poem, published in the *Globe* of May 24, describes a scene witnessed by the writer in a Toronto church on one of those anxious Sundays :—

OUR BOYS IN THE NORTH-WEST AWAY.

I saw the sudden tear-drop rise
In sweetest, purest of blue eyes,
When kneeling in the house of prayer
She heard good words of comfort there,
I knew the angels heard her pray
For one in the North-West away.

It was but noon of yesterday
He bade farewell, he marched away !
The rifle bright and bayonet seen
Above the Queen's Own garb of green,
With our five hundred's bold array
He marched for the North-West away.

As farther then, and farther still,
The dim march sounded down the hill,
As file on file, with steady pace,
Within the cars our boys took place,
As rose our farewell cheer to say
"God bless you," as they passed away.

They bore the foodless, dreary march,
The nights that chill, the days that parch,
Through drifted wilds their way they take,
Their pathway is the frozen lake,
Yet buoyant, bright, and bold are they,
Our boys in the North-West away!

They did not fear that dark ravine
Where Half-breed hell-hounds yelped unseen,
With might predestined to prevail
Trod down the gusts of leaden hail,
Victorious in the fight are they,
Our boys in the North-West away.

They could not fail, they knew not fear
When Otter led the charging cheer.
They charged the open, they laid low
With Gatling fire the Red-skin foe,
They felt the rapture of the fray,
Our boys in the North-West away.

God send them safe, and send them soon,
Each Sabbath hour we ask the boon,
Once more to march, once more to meet
The cheering from each singing street,
While proud resolve and daring high
Blend with their notes of victory!

How sweet to grasp each strong right hand
And greet the saviours of the land,
How good to hear the news at last
Of danger gone and peril past,
How proudly prized will then be they,
Our boys from the North-West away!

C. PELHAM MULVANEY, M.D.,
Formerly No. 1 Company, Q.O.R.

CHAPTER IX.

THE WAR CLOUD BURSTS ON BATTLEFORD.

ON the last day of March Winnipeg was horrified by the news that the most dreaded calamity to be feared as an accompaniment of the Half-breed rebellion had fallen upon Battleford. The Indians had risen in large numbers and had taken possession of a portion of the town. The villagers had taken refuge in the Police Fort, but their houses and the greater portion of their effects were at the mercy of the savages. Worn out with want and suffering, embittered with the recollections of their former prosperity, these misguided people were only too willing to listen to any scheme, however absurd and impossible, that promised to give them back the country and the home which they had bartered away to the white man, but for which they had only received in return dependence, want, and shame. They thought they were on the eve of a restoration to the good old days of wealth, comfort, and happiness enjoyed by them before the advent of the white man, and to any one who has known their history for the past ten or fifteen years, it will not be very surprising that they were thus ready to insanely rush upon their own ruin.

The Indians plundered the Hudson Bay Company's store, and when the agent, Mr. McKay, walked out of the barracks and remonstrated with them, several shots were fired at him. An attempt was also made to intercept him on his return to the barracks. Fortunately this failed.

The Battleford barracks were protected by a substantial stockade, and the Mounted Police force therein had arms and ammunition enough to stand a siege. Mr. Applegarth, one of the ten menaced Indian instructors, had for some time suspected that the Indian Department stores under his charge were being plundered. The imminent death of the Chief Red Pheasant served as a pretext for the assembling of a large body of armed men. Applegarth, who had filled the dangerous post of instructor to Red Pheasant's band, narrowly escaped being murdered.

So began the siege of Battleford, destined to be gallantly maintained by the besieged and successfully relieved. All the civilians capable of bearing arms volunteered for service. The Home Guard were on daily drill. Sentries or scouts watched the movements of the skulking foe with incessant vigilance. Meanwhile the Ottawa Government issued the following proclamation for the appointment of a Commission to settle the Half-breed grievances :—

"His Excellency the Governor-General, on the recommendation of the Minister of the Interior, has been pleased to approve of the appointment of the following Commissioners for the purpose of making an enumeration of the Half-breeds resident in the North-West Territories outside of the limits of Manitoba previous to 15th of July, 1870, who would have been entitled to land had they resided in Manitoba previous to the transfer, with a view to an equitable settlement of their claims, viz., William Purvis, Rochefort Street, of the City of London, Esquire, Q.C., Chairman of the Commission; Roger Goulet, of the Town of St. Boniface, Manitoba, Esquire, Dominion Land Surveyor; and Amedee Edmond Forget, of the Town of Regina, N.-W.T., Esquire, Clerk of the NorthWest Council, barrister-at-law."

CHAPTER X.

ON GUARD AT PRINCE ALBERT.

THE town, or fortified post, known as Prince Albert, is situated on the North Branch of the Saskatchewan along a low fertile reach of alluvial deposit. It is on the south bank of the river, along which it extends for ten miles, the lots being arranged according to the old French method of survey, with frontage to the river. It is thirty miles from the Forks of the Saskatchewan, forty-nine from Carleton, forty-five from the scene of the fight at Duck Lake, and about fifty by the shortest trail from Batoche's Crossing, on the South Saskatchewan. The peninsula between the branches of the river is at this point about fifteen miles wide from north to south. The country in the north-eastern part of this peninsula, extending from a point about twelve miles east of Prince Albert, to a point about fifteen miles south-west of the same, and thence north to the Saskatchewan, is a vast sweep of rolling prairie, containing numerous bluffs or small groves of poplar, cotton wood and gray willow. The land is of unexampled fertility, and the country is one of the most thickly settled in the North-West. In many cases extensive agricultural labour-saving machinery is in use. Much capital has been invested, and the English settler who has learned to make his home in this wilderness of wild-flowers, has a residence, farm buildings and a garden that would compare for elegance and comfort with any in the older-settled Provinces, which have outlived the dangers of Indian war. Twelve miles west of Prince Albert a belt of heavily wooded hills extends on either bank of the South Saskatchewan, which renders its passage dangerous in the presence of an ambushed foe.

The population of the town of Prince Albert previous to the siege was seven hundred. Owing to the attempts of the owners of land to "boom" property for purposes of settlement, Prince Albert has grown in three distinct centres or clusters of houses. The strongest of these for purposes of military defence is that to the east, which contains the Hudson Bay Company's store, flour mill and fort, altogether about seventy buildings. There also are the Mounted Police barracks, a plain red brick building of two storeys, and a large saw-mill belonging to Messrs. Moore & Macdonald. In the central part of the town is situated the "Mission property," and a handsome brick built Presbyterian Church, work shops, dwelling houses, and ten or fifteen of those general stores peculiar to pioneer towns in Canada.

Half-a-mile west of this is the third and smallest portion of Prince Albert, comprising McKay's mill, the post and land offices, and several private residences, including the lately founded Commercial College, and the dwelling house of the Anglican bishop of Saskatchewan. The country around this town is sufficiently open to prevent an Indian attack.

The Saskatchewan where it flows by Prince Albert has an average width of a hundred and fifty yards.

There, since the retreat of Colonel Irvine from Fort Carleton, about three hundred and fifty available fighting men were on guard over a post more than any other likely to be made the object of Riel's attack on account of its containing a large quantity of valuable provisions and ammunition. The following letter will give a just idea of the state of public feeling at Prince Albert at the commencement of the war. It is from Wm. Miller, farmer, of Prince Albert, who has been residing there for upwards of ten years, and has not yet received the patent for his land. He writes as follows:—" The grievances of both whites and Half-breeds are neither few nor small. Money is very hard to get hold of. The Government is to blame for a large share of it. We have to depend on a local market. The Indian and police supplies have all been given by private contract to the Hudson Bay Company; that means nearly all the money goes out of the country. It is put into their power to pay us in trade, and they have taken advantage of it to the utmost. I will give an instance or two :—They let 500 cords of wood by private contract to the Hudson Bay Company at $3.50 per cord. I would have liked to have had the job at $2 per cord, and would have done well by it. It did not cost them $1 per cord. Also a contract for hay at $25 per ton, the Hudson Bay Company paying $7 for it, and paying both in trade. I attended a large meeting a few days ago that was held at the South Branch. Some had come there over thirty miles. In their remarks they threatened rebellion. I was asked an opinion. In a few words I asked them to confer with the Government before they went any further. If they take up arms I don't know how they will equip and feed these men. I suppose the most of them would have a gun of some kind. It is said that Riel could gather up 10,000 Indians on this side of the line. A great many here feel very much alarmed, already talking of building fortifications with cordwood. I cannot say I feel much alarmed yet, although there is a danger with Indians. When they get started they don't know when to stop."

Meanwhile at Prince Albert, as at Battleford, the available men were organized for armed defence. The position was made stronger by that best of extemporized outworks, piles of rough cord wood; but the wires were cut by the rebels and little communication could be obtained from the base of Middleton's operations at Qu'Appelle.

In the meantime, by the night of April 7, General Middleton, who had marched from Qu'Appelle that morning, had arrived at a halting place some thirty miles north. The Queen's Own were already camped at Qu'Appelle.

The entire distance, by the route chosen by General Middleton, from Qu'Appelle to the Saskatchewan was about two hundred miles. The first thirty miles of it lay through open undulating stretches of prairie, amid which, at considerable intervals, were sparsely wooded bluffs, but no caves which foes could occupy in the face of the vigilance with which the General pushed forward his scouting parties in front and on the flanks of his main advance. Beyond this was a succession of gravelly and more thickly wooded hills, known as the Touchwood Hills. They bear this name for the reason that, unlike most wooded tracts, especially in the North-West, they have never had their timber cleared by a conflagration. Those versed in forestry are aware that when trees are suffered to decay by the slow process of dry rot, peculiar to densely wooded regions, the product is what used to be known as *touchwood* or tinder. In days before the lucifer match was known, this hilly region was in great demand among the Indians for supplies of this tinder with which, better than the dry leaves described by Virgil, they could catch the sparks latent in the flint-stone.

Beyond the Touchwood Hills extends the great Salt Plain, stretching for thirty-five miles of dreary saline or alkaline morass, where the melted snow was settling into clayey slush mixed with the alkaline mud into which a settler's waggon would sink hub-deep. Here the only trees were willows, aspens, and the sad grey foliage of the poplar. Here there were many points at which it would have been difficult for the most effective scout to discover a skilfully ambushed enemy, who could have hidden behind cover in places rendered inaccessible to our men by the surrounding morass. But here the General and our Canadian army held their march unopposed.

CHAPTER XI.

THE SIEGE OF BATTLEFORD CONTINUES.—MAJOR WALSH GIVES HIS VIEWS.

AS day after day passed the situation at Battleford became more and more desperate. The town, by reason of its distance from the railway, was necessarily isolated from the outer world, while owing to the very imperfect state of the telegraph line only short despatches were received and that at irregular intervals. From these despatches it was evident that the rising in the district was no merely local affair, but that it was part of a very formidable system of insurrection, which even then threatened to sweep the country from the western boundary of Manitoba to the foot of the Rocky Mountains.

Half the sufferings and perils of the many isolated settlers in the North Saskatchewan region during this Indian Rising will never be told, but occasionally an experience comes to the surface, which serves as a sample of what they had to undergo. Here is one of them:

THE SIEGE OF BATTLEFORD CONTINUES.

George E. Applegarth was Farm Instructor to Red Pheasant's band. On the night of Monday, March 30, he was making up his returns with the intention of going to Battleford next day. The Indians of his reserve had professed great friendliness for the whites. Like all Indians, they said that since trouble had risen they might fight, but they would fight on the side of the whites.

Applegarth went to bed about midnight. At 3 o'clock in the morning he heard a tapping at the door. Getting up he went to see what was the matter, when an Indian quickly strode in and closed the door behind him. He told Applegarth that the reserve was rising, and that some of the bucks who had been to Battleford were after him. Almost while he spoke the door burst open and eighteen redskins rushed in. Applegarth thought his time had come, but luckily this was not the war party. They were eighteen in number—six bucks and twelve squaws—and the friendly Indian whispered that their mission was to hold him until the warriors arrived. Applegarth roused his wife and sister-in-law, a little girl about twelve years old, and Indian teacher Cunningham, and told them to dress. He himself slipped out behind, and hitched up his team, while the friendly Indian engaged the attention of the visitors. Like a true woman, the only article of apparel which Mrs. Applegarth took with her as the team drove off, besides the clothes she wore, was her wedding dress. About half-past three in the morning the party of four set out on their race for life to Swift Current, two hundred miles distant. They had got five miles away when the whiffletree broke. Applegarth had to walk two miles back to get a rail to make a new one not of. Then they flew on again, plunging and galloping through snow three feet deep, with the moonlight streaming overhead.

At dawn they saw six Indians in the distance. They had now struck the trail, which they left again to strike into the coulees and elude their pursuers. They drove all day, and towards nightfall caught sight of the Indians again. This time they thought it was all up with them. The Indians were certainly following them, and were possibly waiting till nightfall to kill them. All Applegarth could do was to tell his wife he would ask them to make short work of the business. His wife and the little girl cried a little, but kept up their courage well. They had no arms with them. Before leaving the house Applegarth had been searched by the squaws, and his arms and money taken from him. The only defence the party had against their pursuers was an axe.

At 2 o'clock in the morning of Wednesday, they rested for a couple of hours. The horses were nearly exhausted. But a little before morning they were put together again and driven on. When daylight came there were no Indians in sight. They drove on all Wednesday, and at nightfall took another rest. Applegarth never closed his eyes, however. Sometime after midnight they went on, and on the forenoon of Thursday they came up with Judge Rouleau, who had left Battleford the previous Sunday with his wife and child, Mrs. Rae, wife of the Indian agent, a hired man, the two Parkers, of Battleford, and a man named Foster—eight in all. This brought up the party to twelve persons. When the judge left Battleford there was no trouble, although trouble was apprehended. Applegarth's report hurried up their movements considerably. Thirty miles from Swift Current they were overtaken by Constable Storer and Mr. Smart. Storer had left Battleford on Saturday, and was the bearer of despatches to Colonel Herchmer. The Battleford garrison believed Herchmer was within a day's march of Battleford. Storer had pluckily volunteered to go out and meet him and tell him of the events that had transpired. On his way he met Smart, who was coming in with goods, and the two journeyed south together. They arrived at Swift Current on Monday morning.

The escape of Judge Rouleau and the party of Battleford refugees above alluded to, constitutes an interesting story especially as they were the last white people to see the ill-fated Farm Instructor Payne, who was murdered by his own Indians only a few moments after he had bade them good-bye.

On Monday, March 30, Mr. Rae, the Indian agent, sent a messenger up to one of the reserves to inquire as to the truth of a rumoured uprising of the Indians. Meanwhile some of the people began packing up such articles as they wished to take with them; but they had not time to complete their preparations before the return of the messenger, who reported to Mr. Rae that the Indians were on their way, and were within eight or ten miles of Battleford. Poundmaker, however, stated that they intended no mischief, but only wanted to have a talk with the Indian agent. On account of the shortness of the time, the number of small children, and other difficulties, most of the people gave up their intention of leaving and concluded to go to the barracks, so that the party which started consisted of Judge Rouleau, wife and three small children; Mrs. Dr. Rouleau and two servants; Mrs. Rae and servant; two brothers named Parker, one of whom was ill, and Mr. Berthiaume. The party had three double rigs and one single rig. Mrs. Rae and servant started in the afternoon, and the others at 7.20 in the evening, arriving at the Stoney reserve at 10.30 p.m. Mr. Payne, the instructor, was to furnish a rig, supply hay and oats, and also to send an Indian with the party to take back the rig after reaching the bush forty miles distant. In the morning, however, this Indian failed to appear, and Mr. Payne sent his mother-in-law to insist upon his going. The instructor, by the way, was married to one of the daughters of the chief, a fine-looking and intelligent woman. From Mr. Payne it was learned that the Indians were painting themselves, and evidently preparing to have a dance during the day. The party started between 8 and 9 o'clock a.m. One Indian at length consented to go and bring the team back, and on leaving took his gun and clothing with him. Mr. Berthiaume left at a quarter to 10 o'clock, shaking hands with Mr Payne in a friendly manner as he left, and fifteen minutes afterwards the latter gentleman was shot by his own Indians. After leaving Mr. Payne the party travelled in company with the Indian on the prairie until 11 o'clock, having no suspicion of what had been occurring in the meantime at the reserve; and the next day at about 3 o'clock they reached the bush, forty miles distant from the reserve, from which point the Indian returned with the rig. The horses being very tired, the party rested there until the next morning. As they were then getting ready to start, Mr. Applegarth arrived with his wife and her sister. They had left at 3 o'clock in the morning (Tuesday), having been informed by the brother of the chief that he had just arrived from Battleford where he had seen the Stoneys plundering the place. It appeared that, after killing Payne, they had started for Battleford, and on their way had stopped at Barney Tremont's, about half-way to Battleford; and that they had proceeded to take away his horses and cattle, and on his resisting, had killed him in his own house, and then helped themselves to all they wanted. Mr. Tremont was an unmarried man, and he had been on very friendly terms with the Stoneys. many of whom had worked for him from time to time. It was further learned that, on the same Monday morning before the party left the reserve, some of the Stoneys had gone to the Cree or Red Pheasant reserve to tell them to go down to Battleford, as the day for action had come.

Among the details of the plundering of Battleford, is the statement that some of the chief's squaws were enabled to present quite a stylish appearance as they promenaded in the silk dresses taken from the homes of Mrs. Rouleau, Mrs. Rae, and other ladies. The wife of Rev. Mr. Clarke, who was married last fall, lost her wedding presents of silver, the savages smashing them in front of the house.

Of course, as the news of the rising spread, greatly exaggerated reports got abroad. It was reported that D.

THE SIEGE OF BATLLEFORD CONTINUES. 85

L. Clink, instructor to Moosomin's band, had been murdered, and at one time the impression prevailed that all the instructors, including Mr. Jefferson on Poundmaker's reserve, had been murdered. Subsequently, however, as the facts came to be known, it was found that Moosomin and his people had remained quietly on their reserve during the trouble, while Poundmaker had never manifested a disposition to take the life of a white man as long as he was allowed to remain unmolested on his reserve. Indeed, from all that has as yet come to light the attack on Poundmaker's camp at Cut Knife Hill appears absolutely inexplicable. It is true that he came down to Battleford, but he alleges that he was coming to have a talk with the Indian agent. That he should have fought after the lodges containing his women and children had been fired on is in no way surprising. To any one who knew the great Cree chief, the idea of his permitting the murder of a defenceless white man on his reserve was of course past belief.

During the few days' calm which followed the storm of excitement, aroused by the news of the Indian rising at Battleford, Major Walsh was interviewed with regard to the rebellion, the causes leading up to it and the best method of suppressing it. Among other things he said:

"When the first news of the Half-breed rising was received my opinion was asked as to its result. I replied then that there would not be a shot fired. I was led to this conclusion by two reasons. 1st. I did not believe that the Half-breeds wanted to spill any blood. They felt they had a grievance and desired to make some demonstration which would attract the attention of the Government and the people of Canada, with the hope that it might lead to their redress, but they never anticipated such a serious result as has been developed. I could not and do not now believe that the Half-breeds wanted war. 2nd. I did not think any official of the Government would be so lost to reason as to take the responsibility of bringing on a war and driving the country into such a state of excitement as now exists until every resource in his possession or power was exhausted.

"During the last twelve years there were two officials on the plains who had many an opportunity, by taking advantage of the simplicity of the Half-breeds and Indians, of making a little notoriety for themselves if they had been disposed to do so, at the expense of an Indian war. But diplomacy was used instead of powder. One of these men was Colonel McLeod. To show you the tractable and peaceful disposition of these people, I will, if you have time, relate a little experience I had with them at Fort Walsh in 1876. There were at that time about 2,000 families of Half-breeds and perhaps 3,000 families of Indians in the Cypress and Wood Mountains. These people feeling dissatisfied with what they called the 'Police Law'—the criminal law of Canada—which was introduced into that country by the police in the spring of 1875, met in grand convention forty-five miles east of Fort Walsh and decided that they must appeal against the further enforcement of the law. They appointed a delegation of fifty men to present their views to me. I met the delegation. They claimed that the law was inconsistent with the good government of a people leading a wandering life, and interfered with their domestic and social habits and comforts, and was to them oppressive. And it is easy to understand how a people living as they had been would find the law oppressive. They, in a very humble but determined manner, announced that they had decided to no longer obey the law of the police. I commenced my argument at pleading—I am not ashamed to say pleading—by reading over to the delegation from the statutes of Canada the Acts which governed the country, and which the population of the prairie, white man, Half-breed or Indian, were amenable to, and pointed out the liberty and protection extended to every individual, and the safety given to life and property as compared with the ordinances of the

Prairie Government, which were tyrannical, and took away the liberty not only of the individual, but of families. For three days the discussion continued, and at the end of the third the conference broke up without my being able to convince the delegation that their demands were unreasonable, and they withdrew, announcing their determination to resist the law that up to that day they had strictly but unwillingly obeyed. I went to my quarters thoroughly discouraged and wishing for the assistance of some one with more power of language and more skilled in diplomacy. I felt the fault was mine, and that I failed for want of ability to convince them. Mind you, I was not afraid of any personal harm, but I felt the seriousness of driving these people into hostility and instituting a war on the people of the plains. Besides I had for these people, whom by this time I had got to know well, a feeling of—shall I call it sympathy? it was more than sympathy, it was justice, and led me to desire to conquer with words rather than with arms. I felt that these people meant to do right and were only doing wrong from my want of ability to enlighten them as to what was right. I sent for my interpreter and instructed him to go and call from among the Half-breeds five men whom I had selected as the most intelligent and influential of the delegation. They arrived at midnight. One of these, a namesake of my own, was Vice-President of the Prairie Government. I said to him that so serious was the step they were about to take that I could not allow them to depart without once more appealing to their judgment. I told them that I had been sent among them not to be a master, but a friend, and that my treatment of them had proved this. The Government of Canada had decided that one set of laws (those I had read to them) should govern the whole country. To allow each community to make its own laws would destroy any State or country. I concluded by saying that the law would have to be enforced, even if force had to be used, and that while the Government of Canada wished to be their friends, if they became enemies it would be the fault of the Half-breeds. They retired, saying the delegation would wait on me again. It did the following day, and informed me that our law would be observed, and that their council would be dismissed and their Government abolished. From that day till I left there, a little over a year ago, the Half-breeds were my firm allies, and on two occasions when my force was small, and I had to be a little more than firm with the Indians, they rendered me assistance. In my last disturbance with Sitting Bull at Wood Mountain, two hundred Half-breeds, some of them now with the rebels, as they are called, offered me their services and went so far as to tell the Indians that whenever a dead Red-coat was found there also would be found a dead Half-breed, meaning that they would die fighting with the police. These are the people we are now having trouble with.

"I think a commission should have been sent out long ago, but that it has been neglected so long is no reason why it should not be sent at once. What great credit would it be to Canada to kill a few poor Half-breeds who feel they have been neglected? Don't forget that these people have the hearty sympathy of all the white settlers in their district. Do you suppose if the white settlers had the grievances the Half-breeds have, that they would not have made a disturbance? and in case they did, who is the man in Canada who would cry out against sending a commission to treat with them? These people are not rebels, they are but demanding justice."

CHAPTER XII.

THE FROG LAKE MASSACRE.

NO matter what the cause, no matter what the wrong he may have suffered, he incurs an awful responsibility who incites the Indians to acts of violence and bloodshed. The demon of anarchy and rebellion becomes tenfold more horrible when he possesses the breasts of those rude tribes who have never learned to respect the usages of civilized warfare. The murder of Payne on the Assiniboine reserve near Battleford and that of the ranchman Barney Tremont, were horrifying; but the news of the Frog Lake massacre was by all odds the most blood curdling that came over the wires during the war.

On the 2nd of April the massacre took place under circumstances which will always stamp it as one of the most cruel and treacherous in the annals of Indian warfare. It had been observed that the Indians of the district had been excited and restless, they had complained that they were not being properly fed, and were dissatisfied generally; the crops were short, and as it was not uncommon for them to grumble under almost any circumstances, their uneasiness was not in all probability deemed to furnish reasonable grounds for anything like serious alarm. In view of the fact, however, that insurrection was rife in the country, and that Big Bear, one of the most turbulent and troublesome chiefs of the North-West, had been doing all within his power to make trouble for several months before the rebellion had broken out at Duck Lake, Sub-agent Quinn thought it advisable to act with the utmost caution and at once do all in his power to allay all semblance of trouble.

When the news of the Duck Lake fight reached them, Big Bear's Indians were loud in their professions of friendship, several times visiting the Indian sub-agency at which Thomas T. Quinn was the officer in charge. On April 2 they were in the village, having the usual jokes of the day, and in the evening they visited Quinn's house, still professing great friendship. They remained there till late. An hour before daylight next morning (April 3) they came in a body to Quinn's. Two Indians went up into the bedroom. One of Big Bear's son's, Bad Child, had intended to shoot Quinn as he lay in bed. Quinn was married to a Cree woman, and had one little girl. His brother-in-law followed up-stairs, and prevented the crime by stepping between Bad Child and Quinn's bed. Meantime the Indians below had taken three guns from Quinn's office. Travelling Spirit called out Quinn's Indian name, saying, "Man-Speaking-Sioux, come down." His brother-in-law, Love-Man, told him not to go. Not taking his advice, Quinn went down, and was at once seized and taken over to Farm Instructor Delaney's house. The Indians had been blustering a good deal, but nobody suspected that they had intended foul play.

Before going to Quinn's, the Indians had already taken the Government horses from Quinn's stable, and Love-Man, who was standing up for Quinn, was going to shoot Travelling Spirit in a quarrel about them.

At Delaney's house the Indians continued their threats and held a confab. Then Travelling Spirit went with others to the Hudson's Bay store. Mr. Cameron, the agent, was already up. Bad Child came in first, and said: "Have you any ammunition in the store?"

"Yes, a little," said Mr. Cameron.

"Well," replied Bad Child, "I want you to give it to us. If you don't we will take it."

Mr. Cameron said, "If you are bound to have it I will give it rather than have you clean out the store." Mr. Cameron was the only official on the premises at this time. He went from the dwelling to the store and gave them what powder, ball, and caps were in stock—only a small quantity. A keg of powder and nearly all the ball cartridge had been sent to Fort Pitt from Frog Lake, on the advice of Mr. Cameron and others, after the news of the Duck Lake fight had been received. While Cameron was getting out the stuff for the Indians, they watched him narrowly with their loaded guns all ready.

Big Bear now appeared on the scene. Entering the store he waved his arm round, saying to his braves: "Don't touch anything here in the Company's place. If there is anything you need, ask Mr. Cameron for it." After getting a few things all but two friendly Indians went out. Cameron followed to see what was going to be done, and was ordered by Travelling Spirit to go to Quinn's and had to obey.

Other white men had meanwhile been brought there along with Pritchard, the Half-breed interpreter. The priests, Father Fafard and Father Marchand were there too, and the place was crowded with Indians. Travelling Spirit said:—"I want to know who is the head of the whites in this country. Is it the Governor or the Hudson's Bay Company, or who?"

Quinn said jokingly, "There's a man at Ottawa, Sir John Macdonald, who is at the head of affairs."

The Indians said, "Will you give us beef?"

Quinn asked Delaney if he had any oxen which he could give them to kill. Delaney said he had one or two, and all then left the house. Five Indians took Mr. Cameron back to the store and asked for more goods. One of the Frog Lake Indians, William Gladien, asked Big Bear's party to leave him in charge of the store, "because," said he, "you are always wanting to get something, and there's no use taking Mr. Cameron there." They agreed to this.

Shortly afterwards Travelling Spirit came up to Mr. Cameron and said: "Why don't you go to church? All the other white people are there already." Then he took him to the Roman Catholic Church. As it was Good Friday the priests were holding service. Big Bear and Miserable Man were standing near the door and the others were kneeling while the service was going on. Travelling Spirit entered and remained half-kneeling in the centre of the little church, with his rifle in his hand. He had a war hat on and his face was daubed with yellow paint in mockery. The priests finished the service, and Father Fafard at the close got up and warned the Indians against committing excesses.

The people then went to Delaney's house, while Mr. Cameron went to breakfast, Yellow Bear, a Frog Lake Indian, keeping close to him all the time. After finishing his breakfast Mr. Cameron went to his store. Travelling Spirit again called for him, ordering him to Delaney's. He went next door to the barracks, which the Indians were ransacking. King Bird (Big Bear's young son) came up saying: "Don't stay here."

Yellow Bear then came out of the barracks saying, "I want to get a hat."

Mr. Cameron said, "Come with me." Yellow Bear said, "Bring it here."

Mr. Cameron replied, "Travelling Spirit has ordered me to come here. If he sees me going back he might shoot me."

The Indian said, "Never mind; I will go with you to the store."

On the road they met Travelling Spirit, who asked them where they were going. Yellow Bear said to the store. They went to the store and Yellow Bear got a hat. Miserable Man entered with an order from Quinn, probably the last writing he ever penned. Mr. Cameron has preserved it. It read as follows:

"*Dear Cameron*,—Please give Miserable Man one blanket.—QUINN."

Mr. Cameron said, "I have no blankets."

Miserable Man looked hard at him but said nothing. Yellow Bear spoke, "Don't you see he has no blankets. What are you looking at him for?" "Well," said Miserable Man, "I will take something else," and he took four or five dollar's worth of odds and ends. Just as they finished trading they heard the first shot. Miserable Man turned and rushed out. Cameron heard some one calling "Stop! stop!" This was Big Bear, who was in the Hudson's Bay Company's house talking to Mrs. Simpson, the factor's wife. As Mr. Cameron went out of the store he locked the door, and while he was doing this an Indian ran up and said, "If you speak twice you are a dead man. One man has spoken twice already, and he is dead."

This man, as Mr. Cameron soon learned, was Quinn, who had been standing with Charles Gouin, the Halfbreed carpenter, in front of Pritchard's house. Travelling Spirit had said to Quinn, "You have a hard head; when you say no, you mean no, and stick to it. Now if you love your life you will do as I say, go to our camp."

Quinn said: "Why should I go there?"

"Go," said he.

"Never mind," Quinn said, quietly, "I will stay here."

Travelling Spirit then levelled his gun at Quinn's head, saying, "I tell you go!" and shot him dead. Gouin, who was an American Half-breed, was shot by the Worm immediately after on the road to the Indian camp, a short distance from Pritchard's house.

Mr. Cameron asked Yellow Bear what all this meant. Yellow Bear caught him by the hand and said, "Come this way." Then seeing Mrs. Simpson about to leave her house, he said, "Go with her; don't leave her."

Mr. Cameron walked away with Mrs. Simpson. When they had got a short distance from the house she stopped and called Cameron's attention to the priests, who were standing about a hundred yards away expostulating with some Indians who were loading their guns. Delaney was close by. Suddenly the Indians raised their guns and rushed at Delaney. Father Fafard dashed up and placed himself in front, menacing the Indians, but was overpowered by numbers and thrown down, and Bare Neck shot Delaney, and then, with the other barrel, fired at the priest. Father Fafard and Delaney were badly wounded,

and, as they lay writhing, Man-Who-Wins walked up
and fired at them, killing both. Father Marchand (from
Onion Lake) was meanwhile attempting to keep the
Indians from going after the women. When he saw that
Father Fafard had been killed he attempted to push his
way through the crowd of Indians to reach the body, but
they resisted. He was a wiry man and fought hard.
Travelling Spirit, however, rushed up and shot him in the
chest and head, and he fell dead.

In the rush that followed a moment after this Gowanlock was killed by the Worm. Gilchrist and Dill were
together, and Little Bear—who had previously killed
Williscraft—fired on them. Gilchrist fell immediately,
but Dill was not hurt and started to run. The Indians
chased him on horseback and he was finally killed by Man-Talking-to-Another.

Mr. Cameron was horrified on seeing the killing of
the priests and Delaney. Of course he could do nothing
to save them. He went up and caught Mrs. Simpson by
the arm, thinking she was going to fall from the shock.
They walked on. She kept saying "Go on faster," for
the Indians were all round ; but there was no use in trying to run away. They afterwards learned that had this
been tried Mr. Cameron would have been shot. After
reaching the main camp, a Frog Lake chief named He-Stands-Up-Before-Him and some head men took Mr.
Cameron into a lodge, where they told him they would
see that no harm should befall him. They then went out
and brought in Travelling Spirit, and told him that he
and his band were to let Cameron alone. Travelling
Spirit assured them all, and Cameron himself that he
would. Mrs. Gowanlock was with Mrs. Delaney, having
left her own house three miles away on the first news of
the trouble. The two women were walking to camp
with Mr. Gowanlock and Mr. Delaney, when the two
latter were shot. Gowanlock fell dying in his wife's arms.
The Indians then brought the women to camp. By this
time almost everything in the place had been taken,

THE FROG LAKE MASSACRE. 95

When Mr. Cameron left they broke open the store and raided it. When the two women arrived in camp they were bought by Half-breeds to save them from the Indians. John Pritchard, the interpreter, bought Mrs. Delaney for a horse and $30. Pierre Blondin bought Mrs. Gowanlock for three horses. The two stayed with Pritchard's family. Mr. Simpson, the Hudson's Bay factor, was at Pitt when the massacre occurred, but returning in the evening was taken prisoner. A day or so after this the bodies of the killed were frightfully mutilated and thrown into the empty houses, after having been stripped of valuables. Dancing and feasting went on for days.

When Pitt was attacked only the men went out, returning after the garrison evacuated with the McLeans and others. The intention of the Indians was to go to Battleford and join Poundmaker and then attack the police barracks, so the whole camp moved towards Pitt, taking about ten days. However, they did not go to Pitt, but moved down the river. Several camps were made close together near the place of General Strange's subsequent skirmish, and it was from east of there where a large thirst dance lodge had been put up, that they were hurried by the appearance of our scouts.

The majority of the Indians of Frog Lake, Long Lake, and Onion Lake, and other bands of Wood Crees, were compelled to join Big Bear, though having no desire to take part in the troubles. They helped themselves to a share of the plunder, but they were in a manner obliged to do so in order to live. The Wood Crees did all they could to save the whites, and did not know anything of the intention of Big Bear's party to kill the people at Frog Lake. Some Wood Crees even threatened to shoot Big Bear's men when the murdering began, but they were too few at the time, and would only have been killed themselves. All the whites saved owe their lives to the Half-breeds and Wood Crees.

During their captivity the prisoners were never hungry nor were they closely confined, although everything was taken from them. The two women remained with Pritchard's family and there was absolutely no foundation for the horrible stories about them which were circulated at the time. The McLean family was not separated and although at first Big Bear's party had charge of them, the Wood Crees took them over because they thought they were not used well enough. A party of Crees took Cameron and others and withdrew from Big Bear's band just prior to Strange's skirmish of the 27th of May, thinking that perhaps the Plain Crees would kill the prisoners if any of their number were wounded or killed. Big Bear's band had been wishing to kill the prisoners all along, and were only prevented by the watchfulness of the Metis and Wood Crees, while the women owe their safety entirely to Blondin, Pritchard, and other Half-breeds.

The victims of this frightful massacre, so far as known at present, are as follows:—

T. T. Quinn, Sub-agent, Indian Department; Father Fafard, Father Marchand, John Delaney, Farm Instructor; J. A. Gowanlock, Charles Gouin, William Gilchrist, John Williscraft, John Dill.

Besides these, Mrs. Gowanlock, Mrs. Delaney, James K. Simpson, and several other settlers were made prisoners.

It is, of course, impossible to describe the horror with which this massacre inspired public sentiment throughout Canada. Mr. T. T. Quinn, the Indian Agent, was known as one of the most capable and competent of the employés in the Indian Department in the North-West. He was born in the Red River valley, his father being an Irish trader and his mother a Cree Half-breed. He received a good education at the St. Boniface College. When a mere lad he went down into Minnesota and spent some time in a trader's store, and it was while he was there that the Minnesota massacre occurred. His employer's store was raided and its owner murdered, but in the midst of these scenes of horror an Indian who had taken a liking to young Tom Quinn's bright and handsome face hid him under the counter among some empty salt sacks, and by that means he made his escape from savages who were sparing neither women nor children, no matter how helpless they were. As a young man Mr. Quinn entered the service of the Hudson Bay Company, in which he soon distinguished himself for courage, intelligence, industry, and thorough honesty. He was placed in charge of the Company's post at Malign Portage on the Dawson Route, over which passengers were carried for some three or four years between Port Arthur and Winnipeg, and remained there till trade in that locality was abandoned. He was always very popular with the Indians wherever he went, thoroughly understanding Indian character, and always conducting his business with that frankness and honesty which the aborigines are sure to respect. He spoke the English, French, Cree, Ojibewa, Saulteux, Sioux, and Assiniboine languages with perfect fluency, and could converse intelligently with the Blackfeet, though he did not profess to have mastered their language. He had been in the employ of the Indian Department for some four or five years, serving some time in Battleford under the direction of Mr. Hayter Reed, who was then in charge of that agency. He was subsequently promoted to the Sub-agency at Fort Pitt, and only made Frog Lake the headquarters of the Fort Pitt Agency some time in June, 1884. Mr. Quinn was probably one of the finest physical specimens of humanity to be found in the North-West Territory. Standing six feet two inches high and weighing about one hundred and ninety pounds he had the peculiarily erect and graceful carriage often characteristic of men of unusual strength and agility. Though no stranger would detect evidences of Indian blood in his appearance or manner, his face had just enough of it to make it unlike the face one usually expects to see when a man is described as tall, dark, handsome, and having black moustache, hair, and eyes. He was a thorough frontiersman either for

6

bush or plain. An accomplished horseman and a skilled canoeman, he was thoroughly at home on snowshoes, an experienced traveller with dog trains, and an expert with axe, rifle, shotgun, or revolver. Mr. Quinn, who was a Catholic, laboured in a very quiet and modest, but effective way toward the conversion of the Indians from paganism to Christianity, as from his boyhood he had always taken a deep interest in anything that was calculated to ameliorate the condition of the Indian, no matter to what tribe he might happen to belong. His death was sincerely mourned by many an old frontiersman between Lake Superior and the Rocky Mountains.

Mr. John A. Gowanlock, one of the victims of the Frog Lake massacre, was a brother of Messrs. A. G. and James Gowanlock, proprietors of the *Parkdale Times.* He was a millwright by trade, and first visited the North-West in 1879, when he went out to Rapid City and was engaged in the erection of a grist mill. He afterwards went into business as a storekeeper at Regina and Battleford. In October of 1884 he came home, and while in Ontario married Miss Johnson, daughter of a U. E. Loyalist of that name living at Tintern, Ontario, who accompanied him on his return to the North-West. His friends were unwilling for him to return to the North-West, as he said when at home that he anticipated a disturbance among the Indians; but having been engaged in trading with them for a long time, and always being on the most friendly terms with them, he had no fears. At the time the troubles broke out he, in partnership with Mr. Laurie, son of the editor of the *Saskatchewan Herald,* was engaged in the construction of a grist-mill at Frog Lake, where they had shortly before completed a saw-mill.

The Rev. Father Fafard was born in Berthier, P.Q., where his parents are still living. His earlier education was carried on in Montreal, and completed at L'Assomption College in 1874. Immediately on finishing his college course he went to the North-West, where he was attached to the Battleford Mission included in the diocese of Bishop Grandin, of St. Albert. His duties were those of a Catholic priest, in addition to which he undertook the education of the children of his flock, which consisted of whites, Half-breeds and Indians.

Of the Rev. Father Marchand, comparatively little is known; he was a young priest who came out from France in 1883, and was at once attached to Bishop Grandin's mission, and at the time of his martyrdom was labouring in connection with Father Fafard. Both of these missionaries were Oblat Fathers.

"TRAVELLING SPIRIT,"
The Leader in the Frog Lake Massacre.

LIEUT.-COL. W. D. OTTER.

CHAPTER XIII.

OTTER'S MARCH TO BATTLEFORD.

ON the 12th of April Colonel Otter and staff arrived at Swift Current. The force composing his column numbered five hundred and seventy-five, including two hundred and fifty of the Queen's Own, half of C Company Infantry (regulars), A Battery, Ottawa Foot Guards and fifty Mounted Police under Superintendent Herchmer.

The country through which Colonel Otter's column had to pass in its journey to Battleford is thus described:

The whole distance traversed between Swift Current station on the Canadian Pacific Railway and Battleford was about two hundred miles, or possibly a trifle more. The march to the Saskatchewan was about thirty miles (perhaps thirty-four), and this brought them to the ferry, some distance west of the mouth of Swift Current Creek. The country between the railway and the river is mainly upland prairie, affording smooth, dry footing. The approach to the river is down a steep bank, about four hundred feet high, and at the foot of this spreads a strip of bottom land a mile wide, stretching to the river's bank.

The river itself is about two hundred yards wide. Once across the river there were no bottom lands to cross, but the ascent of the north bank began at once. The slope is a comparatively gradual one, and the bench land on the north side is only about two hundred and fifty feet above the water; little or no difficulty or delay was encountered at that point. Next came a short march of six or seven miles over a beautiful upland prairie which brought the column to a small sweet water lake which was the scene of the first camp north of the river.

There was no wood north of this point, however, and in fact the whole plain up to a point on the line of march north of Eagle Creek, and probably ninety miles or more from the Saskatchewan, is destitute of anything in the shape of timber.

After leaving the lake already alluded to, the trail leads up a long gradual ascent made over gently undulating prairie uplands. Here, as well as in the short march already mentioned, the footing was reasonably dry and firm. Then comes a very sudden, but slight descent into a strange looking valley, with a smooth, level bottom about a mile wide, and covered with a rich loamy soil. This belt or valley, which appears to extend indefinitely on either side of the trail, looks as though it might have been the valley of some ancient river. On the farther, or what appears to have been the north bank, there is a lofty ridge which stands up out of the plain like a huge wall and up this ridge the trail winds through a rugged, rock-bordered, and somewhat tortuous pass. Above this ridge the ascent continues as the march leads still northward over slightly rolling prairie for some twenty miles, after which high rolling hills are entered. Here the soil is dry and gravelly, and alkali lakes are numerous, but there are also pools and lakes of sweet water quite sufficient to supply all possible requirements for camping. Though the trail through these hills is always firm and dry, it is very tortuous, while some of the hills rise well towards the dignity of mountains. This rough almost mountainous country continues for about twenty miles, and then the trail leads out into a smoother, though still undulating tract. After traversing about fifteen miles of this last mentioned class of country, a big coulee is reached, which contains an abundant supply of sweet water of an excellent quality. Twelve miles further on there is a strongly saline creek forty or fifty feet wide, easily fordable, and having a fairly good bottom. This creek is not alkaline, but pronouncedly "salt" at all seasons of the year. A little farther on Eagle Hills Creek, which is about eighty-five miles from the South Saskatchewan, is reached. A long and rather steep hill leads down into the valley of this creek from the south, and a strip of flat bottom land a mile in width intervenes between the foot of the hill and the edge of the creek. The creek itself is swift, deep, and narrow at this point.

The ascent out of this valley is a comparatively easy one, and when the benches were reached once more the travelling was unembarrassed by anything formidable in the shape of hills or valleys. About twelve miles further on timber sufficient for fuel was reached, and from this spot until Eagle Hills were reached, the trail lay through clean, open prairie. Just at the point of the hill (twenty miles from Battleford) is the Stoney reserve, and it was here that the boys began to keep a sharp look out for trouble, and their vigilance was nowhere relaxed on the journey over the last twenty miles.

The progress of Colonel Otter's command from the South Saskatchewan Crossing to Battleford was very rapid, the average being something more than thirty miles per day. It is not to be understood, however, that the men marched at that rate, for the fact is that after Saskatchewan Crossing was reached part of the men were able to secure a ride on the waggons for portions of the remainder of the distance. Going over the prairie in this fashion was not at all disagreeable. The weather during the day was comfortably warm, and at night, although the pools of water everywhere met with on the prairie were found each morning covered with a fresh surface of ice, the men got along very nicely under the canvas, and accommodating themselves to their changed circumstances really seemed to be beginning to enjoy the vicissitudes of soldiering. The most trying time was on picket or sentry. Those familiar with the country and the Indian method of warfare had no fear that the column would be attacked before reaching Battleford, except it might be that stragglers from the camp might be picked off or that a picket or sentry would be charged at night. While the column was advancing Colonel Herchmer's detachment of Mounted Police, numbering twenty-five, together with some scouts specially engaged, rode about a mile ahead and the same distance to the right and left, beating into every coulee or clump of poplar where an enemy might be ambushed, thus absolutely preventing the possibility of anything like a surprise. At night the pickets extended from a quarter to half-a-mile on all sides of the camp. All felt, or should have felt, perfectly safe and rested as peacefully as need be. The camp was usually pitched between four and six in the afternoon, and struck about five in the morning. At the Eagle River, about half-way up the trail, the spring waters had carried the bridge away, but materials for the construction of a new one had been brought along, and sent on in advance to prepare a crossing for the column, so that no delay was experienced on this account. Stations were made at distances, in most cases of from thirty to forty miles. A couple of men were placed in each.

Colonel Otter started out with only about ten days' forage, and his provisions also were very much short of the thirty days' rations he had expected to take with him. The difficulty was that there were not sufficient teams to get the whole under way at once. The method adopted was to send back the teams for fresh loads as soon as those they started out with were consumed. They expected to meet other loads coming on from the Crossing, pick them up and return, while the teams, thus relieved, carried the empty waggons back to the Crossing.

Colonel Otter's column presented a very formidable appearance as it wound along the crooked trail over the prairies. Its two hundred teams stretched sometimes over two or three miles, and looked at from any prominent position, was such assuredly as would put dread into the heart of the Indian. The Eagle Hills, where it was expected the enemy would be encountered, if at any place along the line, were reached on Thursday, the 23rd April, about 11 a.m. A halt was made for dinner, and among the men the probabilities of the next few hours were discussed with much interest. The day previous Charlie Ross, one of the best-known and most daring of the Mounted Police scouts, had come across a band of probably a dozen Indians in one of the prairie valleys. They had a buckboard and cart, and were apparently engaged in the very peaceful occupation of slaughtering and dressing a calf. They were certainly surprised by the appearance of the scout who advanced to speak to them. When he was about two hundred yards distant they fired a couple of shots in his direction. He replied, but his rifle burst, and the bullet failed to reach its mark. He thought the accident must have occurred by the muzzle of his rifle having got filled with mud. The Indians made off as fast as they could, and Ross returned and reported the occurrence. A detachment was at once ordered to be ready for pursuit, but the Indians were not again seen. This occurrence aroused some apprehension of trouble when the Hills were reached, although it had been reported that the Indians had deserted their reserve a day or two previously. All through these Hills there was a considerable growth of poplar and underbrush. The ravines were deep, and in some cases precipitous, and the ground rises unevenly to a considerable length. By two o'clock on Thursday afternoon, the column had reached the reserve of Chief Mosquito, of the Stoneys. The scouts hunted it over thoroughly, but were unable to discover traces of a living Indian. All was in supreme disorder, and the log huts in which they had lodged gave evidences of very hasty flight. In one of the tepees a most ghastly spectacle met the eye. A couple of boxes, such as are used for dry-goods, were piled one on top of the other, and on the uppermost a smaller box which had been used for packing soap. The latter was first taken down and looked into. It contained the lifeless body of an Indian child, probably two years of age, placed in a sitting posture. Its little head had been knocked out of shape, evidently by the back of an axe, and the eyes, crushed nearly out of their sockets by the force of the blows from behind, seemed to be glaring out in the wildest horror. It was a most revolting sight, and bore terrible testimony to the fiendish nature of the warring Indian. The second box was looked into, and another object almost equally revolting was to be seen. The corpse of a squaw, probably twenty years of age, with what looked like a bullet hole in the left cheek, was deposited there, also in a sitting posture. About the mouth of the woman was a quantity of clotted blood, and the left hand was raised to the cheek, holding a handkerchief smeared with blood. The boxes were restored to the position in which they were found and the search was continued. It was on this reserve that Indian Instructor Payne was murdered, and it was expected that his body would be found some place in the neighbourhood. Diligent search, however, failed to discover it at this time. A large quantity of flour, potatoes, and bacon was found cached in the bush near by, and as much of this as possible was at once loaded on empty waggons and carried along with the column. Preparations in the way of ploughing and harrowing were already on foot on the reserves for putting in the season's crop, when the Indians went on the war path. The trail through the hills was about six miles in length, and as the column advanced the scouts were kept busy scouring the country on all sides. A number of white people had settled in this fertile region, and were laying the foundation of comfortable homes with plenty of every necessary of life at their doors. Their homes had all been deserted, and were

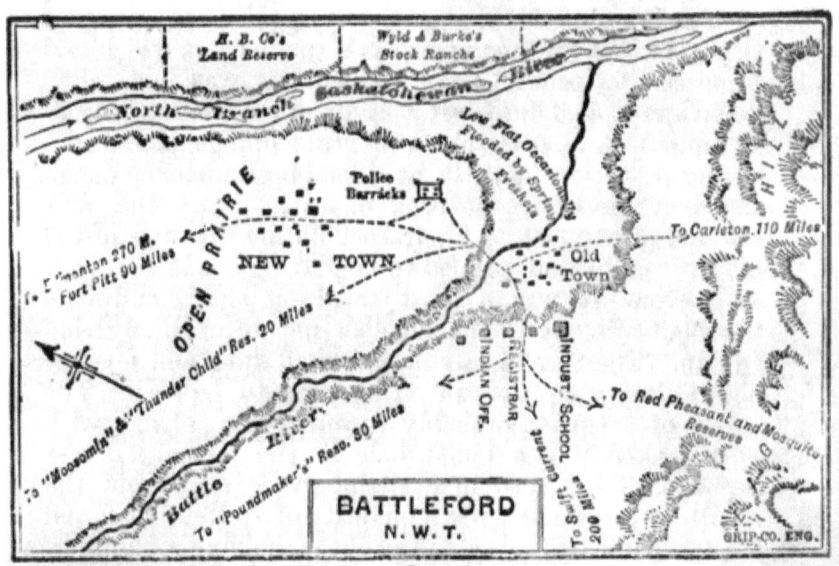

looted by the Indians. No traces of an Indian were found. Seven or eight miles from Battleford the fort and village could be descried from the brow of a high hill, and as the advance of the column came into view of the beleaguered place a hearty cheer was given by the men. Just as the column was winding down the long incline towards old Battleford, and when an intervening hill obscured the town from view, great volumes of black smoke shot up, and for a while it was thought the enemy must have obtained possession of the town and probably the fort as well and, seeing the advance of the forces over the hill, were setting fire to the place previous to deserting it. No news from Battleford had been received by Colonel Otter for some days, and he was, therefore, ignorant of the position of affairs. There was a quarter of an hour of anxious suspense till the troops gained the top of the intervening hill. It was then seen at a distance of probably five miles that a building on the south side of Battle River in the old town was on fire. That it was the work of the Indians was apparent; but it was a relief to find that the fort and new town were still holding out. The column was halted on a plain about three miles from the river, the teams corralled, and the tents pitched for the night. Scarcely had the sun set, sinking as it seemed into the great plain beyond Battleford, than the sky was lit up by another building ablaze in the old town. From a prominence near the camp, with the aid of a good glass, the Indians could be seen dancing about the fire in fiendish delight over the ruin they were making. Charlie Ross, the police scout, accompanied by several others, left the camp at sundown to reconnoitre the position and numbers of the Indians. Just before he and his companions slipped away into the dark underbrush, Colonel Herchmer said, "Take care of yourself, Ross, but if you get a chance to shoot don't forget to do it." "Yes," replied Ross, in a tone that left no doubt of his intention. The party had not gone for more than an hour before firing was heard in the direction of the town, and Colonel Herchmer ordered out a detachment of a dozen Mounted Police to go to the scouts' assistance. Ross and his companions had scattered themselves as they approached the position of the Indians, and crept up to within a very short distance of them. Ross himself got into a dense undergrowth where he lay watching the Indians' antics. So far as he could determine there were about eighty of them, all with horses ready to mount. As Ross lay among the shrubbery he was startled by a cough within a few yards of him, and became aware of the presence of an Indian. The latter no doubt took Ross to be one of his own people, and Ross was not averse that he should hold that opinion under such circumstances. Half-a-dozen Indians presently rose up all around him and went to their horses a short distance away. Ross also moved away, and presently came across his companions near the main trail. There they stationed themselves till a dozen mounted Indians rode slowly along. When they were thirty yards past Ross sprang up and called, " Halt." The Indians did not halt, however, but put spurs to their ponies, and the scouts opened fire on them with their revolvers, the only firearms they carried. This was the firing they heard from the camp. The Indians in a few minutes all seemed to have disappeared, as if by magic. They were doubtless in ambush awaiting the advance of those who had fired on them. The Mounted Police squad presently came up and thought it wise that all should return to camp.

The pickets that night doubtless put in an anxious time of it. It was the general impression in camp that the Indians would make an effort to pick off some of the farthest out, but it was otherwise. The sun rose brightly over the scene of the Indians' bonfire, but no Indian was then to be seen. The house that had been burned the previous evening was Judge Rouleau's handsome residence.

Immediately after breakfast the tents were struck and the whole column advanced to the brow of the somewhat steep declivity running down to Battle River. Here the tents were again pitched close beside the Industrial School and only a short distance from the smouldering ruins of Judge Rouleau's residence. The Indians had made a complete wreck of the old town and had exercised almost devilish ingenuity in their methods of destruction. The contents of the Industrial School were thrown about in shapeless confusion, the windows smashed, and the walls battered and polluted. The interior of every unburned house in the old town presented a similar appearance.

There were shut up in the fort something over five hundred men, women, and children, composed of townspeople and all the white people settled in the district. The fort is about two hundred yards square, with a stockade ten feet high. There was an abundance of provisions—enough, it was thought, to last three months. This comprised both the police and Indian supplies. In so small a space it will be readily understood that the people were pretty well crowded, but not uncomfortably so. Numerous tents were pitched in all parts of the enclosure, and the beleaguered people contrived to make themselves tolerably comfortable.

The fort is situated on an elevated plateau, and can be approached only in the open. The new town lies west of the fort, and the Indians had been kept from sacking it by a wholesome dread of the shells which the seven-pounder gun in the barracks was capable of throwing. Up to the day before Colonel Otter's arrival Colonel Morris was in command, with a detachment of twenty-five police. His situation had been unquestionably a difficult one. His first duty, of course, was to see that the fort and the people within it were protected from the enemy; his second to protect as far as possible the property of citizens and settlers in the neighbourhood. He had succeeded in preserving the fort as well as the property of citizens in the new town, and in order to do this he had to exercise constant vigilance. The property of settlers in the outlying district of course easily fell a prey to the Indians, who had sacked all the houses, and burned most of them for twenty-five miles around—that is throughout the whole settlement. But Colonel Morris was very roundly blamed by many of the people for not making a more determined effort to protect the vast stores of the merchants and Hudson Bay Company in the old town. Every day up to the time of Colonel Otter's arrival the Indians could be plainly seen from the fort, about a mile distant, plundering the stores and carrying off the goods and provisions with the horses and vehicles they had appropriated from the settlers; it must indeed have been a galling sight. About one hundred and fifty of the men in the fort repeatedly requested Colonel Morris to be allowed to go out and attempt to drive the enemy off and secure the provisions. This request he refused persistently, and the plundering went on unchecked, except on two occasions when the gun was brought out about half way to the river, and a number of shells thrown at the enemy. Four of them were killed and the rest dispersed into the woods. On the second day a dozen men of the Home Guards crossed the river, when the Indians fled, and captured a horse and buckboard, the latter loaded with looted goods. It appears the horse was baulky and would not move off with the Indians. In connection with Colonel Morris' refusal to allow a rescue party to leave the fort it must be kept in view that the commanding officer had about as great dread of the enemy within the fort as that without. Many of them were Half-breeds and their loyalty, to say the least of it, questionable. Had they been allowed to get out he did not know what their freedom might have developed. His position, if disaster had followed a compliance with the men's request, would have been a most unenviable one. Another reason for his refusal was that the ice in the river was in such a condition that it might be expected to break up at any moment, and if this had occurred while the men were on the opposite shore, their return would have been next to impossible, and the fort would practically have been left at the mercy of the enemy.

On Wednesday, the day before the arrival of the relief column, one of the most lamentable events of the whole siege occurred in the shooting of poor Frank A. Smart, who was one of the most popular men of the district, and one who seemed to possess the entire confidence of the Indians. But it was a most notable circumstance during this uprising that those men who have been most kind and considerate to the Indians have been those who have first been marked for death.

The situation all through this district was most deplorable. The settlers, of course, had been robbed of everything. Their cattle and horses had been driven away, their houses either burned or sacked, and thus the labour of years had been rendered vain. Those who had toiled amid innumerable hardships to bring themselves and their families into positions of comparative ease, were left homeless and penniless, in an infinitely worse condition than when they first set foot in the country. The seed for which the ground was just being prepared was never sown.

The finding of the body of Payne, the Indian Instructor, on Mosquito's reserve caused something like a sensation in the camp and barracks. It was believed that the Indians had cut it to pieces and disposed of it in that way. Sergeant Langtry was in charge of the fatigue party that made the discovery. The murdered man was lying apparently just as he had fallen, on his face, with his arms stretched out before him, and a number of deep wounds on the back of his head told of the deadly and cowardly nature of the attack. A quantity of straw had been loosely thrown over the corpse, and the wind blowing a portion of this away disclosed the form. In the house which he occupied everything was in confusion. His diary, containing entries up to the night before his death, was discovered. There was no reference to an expected rising, excepting in an entry made three days previous to his death, which showed that Indian Agent Rae had been on the reserve that day, and had had a talk with the Indians and was convinced of their loyalty.

The conduct of Judge Rouleau in deserting the place immediately that the slightest danger showed itself, was very severely commented on by nearly all those in the fort. Ever since cause for fear had manifested itself by the sullen manner of the Indians, Judge Rouleau, it is said, persistently maintained that there was no reason for alarm, and being constituted a censor of all despatches going over the wires, refused to permit any mention of the true condition of affairs to be sent out. Every effort seems to have been made by him to suppress the real condition of affairs, but immediately that matters assumed a gravity that could no longer be gainsaid, he took to horse and "skinned" out of the country. A correspondent in referring to this matter said : " People have stolidly maintained that he did not stop running till he had got to the other side of the big bridge at Ottawa, and that according to the last bulletin of his flight, he had got safely into the Citadel at Quebec, and is now barricaded from the arrows of the enemy by many thicknesses of iron plate. Almost everybody, even his compatriots and personal friends, are thus referring to him."

In referring to the volunteers the same correspondent says:

"No words of mine can sufficiently express the heroic manner in which the Queen's Own regiment has withstood the trials and hardships of the month intervening since their departure from the Union Station, Toronto. There is not a man of them ailing at present, and they take their work and submit to the rigid discipline of active service with a cheerfulness that is in the highest sense creditable. I believe that almost every man in the regiment is roundly disappointed and dissatisfied that an opportunity has so long been denied them to show their merit in the field, and when it comes to that they may be depended on to do their duty. From most of their faces the sun has already removed the outer film of skin, and what remains is tanned a glorious brown. Most of them have perforce allowed their beards to grow, and as they were seen at church parade to-day they presented an appearance vastly different from that they wore on a King Street parade last summer. Until the column arrived here the rations consisted of hard-tack, pork, canned meat, dried apples, beans, and tea, and there was abundance of it, notwithstanding that reports have gone forward to the contrary. Since pitching camp here, fresh beef has been occasionally served, and this change has been hailed with great glee. Whenever a good fat steer is found it is appropriated and slaughtered forthwith, and if the owner is not near by he is settled with as soon as he happens to turn up.

"While making the above remarks about the Queen's Own, the other bodies composing the brigade must not be lost sight of. Company C, of the Toronto Infantry School, half of which are here under Captain Wadmore, are admired by all for their soldierly bearing and handsome appearance in column. Captain Todd's Ottawa Foot Guards are a thoroughly disciplined body of men, and it is only necessary to mention B Battery to provoke plaudits among Canadian militiamen."

Thus the siege of Battleford was raised, and it was thought that the work of Colonel Otter's column was done. How little we know of what is before us. The tragedy of Cut Knife Hill was still to be enacted.

CHAPTER XIV

GENERAL MIDDLETON'S ADVANCE—WAITING FOR SUPPLIES AND REINFORCEMENTS.

WHILE these events were taking place in the West, matters in the eastern portion of the disturbed district were by no means at a stand-still. Recognizing the pressing necessity of doing his utmost to nip the rebellion in the bud, General Middleton was hurrying forward with all possible speed. The provisions for transport service, having been hurriedly made, were of course not particularly efficient nor satisfactory. It too often happens that in emergencies of this kind, people selected in a hurry to fill positions of responsibility and trust, are selected on account of personal popularity, or in acknowledgment of political services rather than because of any especial fitness for the place. The conduct of the campaign in the North-West was not altogether free from blunders of this kind, and it would be too much to expect that it should have been. At the season of the year when the journey from Qu'Appelle to Clark's Crossing had to be undertaken, the grass was not in such a state as to furnish suitable forage for any but native or thoroughly acclimatized horses. In consequence of this supplies for man and beast had to be freighted through. In this way it will be seen that a large proportion of the supplies hauled in were consumed by the horses engaged in the transport service, so that the amount of freighting necessary to keep the force in the field properly supplied was something enormous. With the trails in the worst possible condition, with both horses and teamsters all green at the business, and with, possibly, a very limited aptitude for the work himself, it is not surprising that Mr. Bedson should have made a very sorry job of the transport service. General Middleton was very considerably handicapped in his efforts to push forward by the lack of supplies; his patience was sorely tried at having to wait day after day at Clark's Crossing, knowing well that every day of such inaction was equivalent to giving aid and comfort to the rebel cause. Every day Gabriel Dumont was strengthening his position at Batoche, and still General Middleton was powerless to advance against him. Every day Riel's runners were carrying into Indian camps all over the Territory the news that the white men dared not attack them, and yet, well-knowing this, General Middleton was powerless to advance against him. Finding the transport service via Qu'Appelle would be nearly or quite inadequate to meet the demands of the situation General Middleton determined to open another route for bringing in supplies. The Midland Battalion and a Gatling gun in charge of Lieutenant Howard, an extensive store of supplies, and other necessities for the campaign were started from Saskatchewan Landing near Swift Current to make the long journey down the river by boat.

On the 18th of April, Lord Melgund, with Captain French and Major Boulton with a party of scouts, made a reconnoissance from Middleton's camp and captured three Indians, whom they found hiding in a coulee. One of these was a cousin and two were sons of the Sioux chief, White Cap. Of course they told the old story of being forced into the fight by Riel and the rest of the Half-breeds, but as White Cap and his band manifested a particular fondness for the scalps of white men during the Minnesota massacre, it appears extremely probable that neither he nor his followers required much coaxing to induce them to join Riel.

On the 21st of April the steamer Northcote started from Saskatchewan Landing with the first instalment of the South Saskatchewan branch of the expedition.

On the 22nd a few of Major Boulton's scouts chased two rebels on the west side of the Saskatchewan for some fifteen miles but failed to capture them. They also came upon a small party of rebel scouts with whom they exchanged shots at long range, but nobody was injured.

CHAPTER XVI.

THE FALL OF FORT PITT.

THE events in this tragic history now began to tread close upon the heels of one another. While Colonel Otter was preparing his column for an attack on Poundmaker's reserve, and while General Middleton and his force were impatiently awaiting the hour when they should stand face to face with Gabriel Dumont's Half-breeds, there was, away in the far North-West on the banks of the Great Saskatchewan, far beyond the reach of present assistance, a little band of red-coated prairie troopers, every one of them with as brave a heart as ever beat beneath the scarlet. Their leader was a well-tried soldier whose modest worth, though blazoned by no hireling chroniclers, was well-known to soldier comrades in India, on the rugged mountain slopes of Montana, and in

INSPECTOR FRANCIS J. DICKENS.

every portion of the North-West, from Fort Pelly to Kootenay, and from Edmonton to Wood Mountain. This was Inspector Francis J. Dickens, son of the famous novelist, and though one of the most modest and retiring officers of the North-West Mounted Police, well-known to be one of its coolest and most intrepid soldiers.

THE FALL OF FORT PITT. 117

Under Inspector Dickens, who held Fort Pitt, were twenty-two of the Mounted Police, and it was their charge to protect a little handful of white settlers, and prevent a very considerable store of supplies, arms, and ammunition from falling into the hands of the Indians. Opposed to them was Big Bear, one of the most war-like and powerful chiefs of the North-West. He had under him a force which, in all probability, numbered not less than

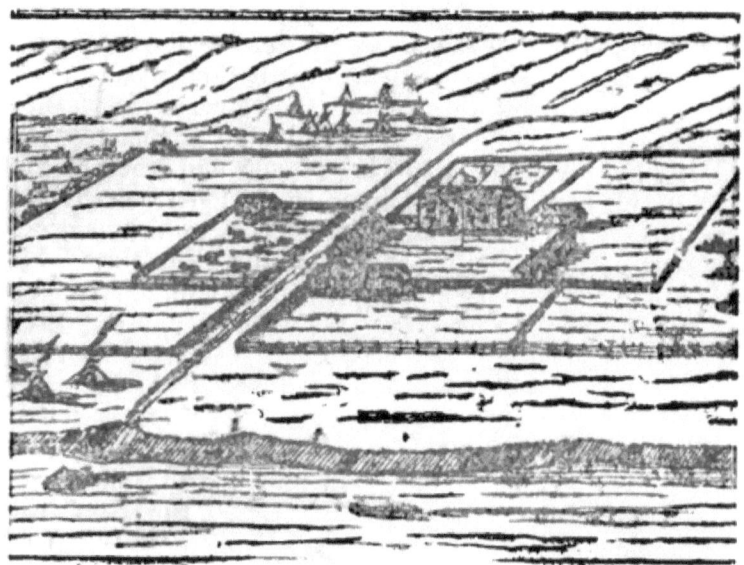

PLAN OF "FORT PITT."

three hundred. Fort Pitt is situated on the north bank of the North Saskatchewan, ninety-eight miles north-west from Battleford, and two hundred and four miles east from Edmonton, by the trail running along the north side of the river. It is situated on a low, rich flat, which lies from twelve to fifteen feet above the river level, and which runs back about half-a-mile to where it meets the high rolling country that stretches away on all sides in the rear of the post. The fort consisted of several log buildings arranged in a hollow square, and was formerly enclosed by a stockade with bastions on the corners, but as this had been removed some years before, it then lay completely unprotected in the midst of some cultivated fields surrounded by common rail fences.

Big Bear, who was besieging Fort Pitt, had been induced by means of much coaxing and many presents to remove from the South, where in his close vicinity to the border line he was continually a cause of anxiety to Fort Pitt, where in the midst of a number of hitherto quiet and peaceful bands of his own nation, and hemmed in on the South by the North Saskatchewan, it was supposed he would settle down and give no further trouble.

Big Bear was the last to take treaty and when he did one of his strongest objections to doing so was that he did not like the idea of hanging as a punishment for murder. It was late in 1882 when Big Bear signed his adhesion to the treaty and expressed his willingness to go on a reserve near Fort Pitt. Whether or not Big Bear was sincere in his professions of loyalty at that time remains to be seen. He had been down in Montana hunting buffaloes all summer in the same region where Riel was at that time said to be doing his best to sow the seeds of discontent and rebellion among both Half-breeds and Indians from north of the border. Big Bear had originally come from Fort Pitt, but in the autumn of 1876 he went South hunting buffaloes, and from that time till after he took treaty about the end of 1882 he remained South making Fort Walsh headquarters for himself and his band. The buffalo hunting was bad even south of the boundary line where he spent the summer, and as early as the latter part of August or beginning of September he sent five of his young men North with a message to his particular friend Piapot. At this time he believed that Piapot was settled on a reserve at Indian Head, and the messengers were instructed to ask Piapot if Lieutenant-Governor Dewdney* had carried out his agreements with the latter fairly and honestly, and if the answer proved to be in the affirmative Piapot was to be requested to signify to the Indian Department that Big Bear was also anxious to take treaty to go upon a reserve. These messengers, however, were met by Piapot before

HON. EDGAR DEWDNEY, LIEUT.-GOV. N.W. TERRITORIES.

they reached Qu'Appelle, and the great chief of the South

---

* Hon. Edgar Dewdney is an Englishman by birth, but with many of his adventurous countrymen found his way to British Columbia during the earlier portion of the gold excitement. Like many others he made and lost more than one handsome competency in that country, but was fortunate enough to finally light on his feet financially. As a representative from British Columbia in the Dominion Parliament he became a man of some importance politically, and on, or soon after, the accession of Sir John Macdonald to power in 1878 he was appointed Indian Commissioner, and on the expiry of Ex-Governor Laird's term in 1881, he was appointed Lieutenant-Governor of the Territory, still retaining his Indian Commissionship.

Crees was in no humour to report favourably to Big Bear's enquiry, as he was then fresh from his famous interview with Lieutenant-Governor Dewdney at Fort Qu'Appelle, in which the latter had been held up by

CHIEF PIAPOT OF THE SOUTH CREES.

Piapot to contempt and scorn. This of course for the time put an end to Big Bear's negotiations with the Indian Department, but as the hunting continued bad Big Bear found his way to Fort Walsh late in the season, and signified his intention of becoming a "Treaty Indian." At this time Mr. Dewdney expressed the opinion that Big Bear had "borne unjustly a bad character," and that if he went North he would "make one of our best chiefs." But after all it took the united efforts of Colonel Irvine of the North-West Mounted Police, Colonel McDonald, Indian Agent for Treaty Four, and Peter Hourie, the Half-breed interpreter, backed by the urgent requests of his own son and son-in-law, to induce Big Bear to consent to take treaty and go North. Piapot and Lucky Man were present when the bargain was finally closed.

Shortly after his arrival at Fort Pitt he attempted to seize the stores at that point, and in order to overawe the small force of police who were stationed there to watch his movements, he not only assumed a very threatening attitude, but used some considerable amount of violence, which fortunately proved of no effect. Subsequently he sent tobacco at different times amongst all the bands in his vicinity, summoning them to pow-wows for the purpose of discussing his old and time-worn grievances, and in short, did all in his power to persuade all within reach of his influence to dig up the hatchet, abandon their reserves, and under his wild, savage, and reckless leadership to demand his rights, and the fulfilment of the promises that had been made him—at the muzzles of their rifles, or at the edge of the scalping-knife. Although this man was getting old, he still retained the active use of a powerful, scheming, and very fertile brain, any deficiency in which was readily supplied by the evil councils of those headmen of his band who were constantly near his person. In addition to this, he was not only very widely known, but was held in high repute by the whole Cree nation as a great chief, whose wise and prudent opinions would carry immense weight in their Great Councils.

The annual dances in which the Indians are accustomed to indulge had always been regarded as a means of connecting them with their heathenish past, and through the labours of the missionaries and Tom Quinn, the Indian Agent, who were among the victims of the Frog Lake massacre, these customs were fast falling into disuse; but with the return of Big Bear the "Thirst Dance" was revived with all its revolting features. These dances take upon themselves the nature of religious ceremonies, and the more enthusiastic of the devotees subject themselves to tortures of the most painful character as a part of the regular programme. The "Thirst Dance" is nearly or quite identical with the Sun Dance of the Sarcees in which the young men make incisions in their backs and passing a cord under the skin allow themselves to be hung up by the loop thus formed, for such a length of time that it would seem incredible to one who had not seen one of these horrible ceremonies.

A fairly accurate estimate of the total number of Indians in the Fort Pitt Agency at this time is as follows:—

Big Bear, with a band of five hundred and twenty, located nowhere in particular, but spending most of his time roaming about between Fort Pitt and Battleford.

See-kas-kootch, with a band of one hundred and seventy-six, located at Onion Lake.

Pay-moo-tay-a-soo, with a band of twenty-eight, located at Onion Lake.

Sweet Grass, with eighteen, at Onion Lake.

Thunder Companion, with five, at Onion Lake.

Wee-mis-ti-coo-seah-wasis, with one hundred and thirteen, at Frog Lake.

O-nes-pow-hay, with seventy-three, at Frog Lake.

Pus-keah-ke-win, with thirty-one, at Frog Lake.

Kee-hee-win, with one hundred and forty-six, at Long Lake.

Chipewagan, with one hundred and twenty, at Cold Lake.

In all about one thousand two hundred.

The following is a detailed list of the Mounted Police left to hold Fort Pitt and its valuable supplies and stores against Big Bear:—

Inspector Dickens, F. J., appointed inspector 4th November, 1874.

Staff-Sergeant Rolph, J. W., engaged 16th September, 1884, at Regina.

Sergeant Martin, J. A., re-engaged 3rd November, 1884, at Battleford.

Corporal Sleigh, R. B., engaged 7th June, 1881, at Fort Walsh.

Constables Anderson, Wm., engaged 10th April, 1882, at Toronto.

Carroll, J. W., engaged 7th June, 1881, at Fort Walsh.

Edmons, H. A., engaged 15th April, 1882, at Toronto.
Hobbs, R., engaged 7th June, 1881, at Fort Walsh.
Ince, R., engaged 18th April, 1882, at Toronto.
Leduc, F., engaged 22nd April, 1882, at Toronto.
Lionais, G., engaged 9th May, 1882, at Winnipeg.
Loasby, C., engaged 12th July, 1883, at Winnipeg.
McDonald, J. A., engaged 29th April, 1882, at Toronto.
Philips, C., engaged 20th April, 1882, at Toronto.
Quigley, J., engaged 8th May, 1882, at Toronto.
Roby, F., re-engaged 9th June, 1884, at Battleford.
Rowley, Geo., engaged 16th October, 1881, at Qu'Appelle.

Robertson, R. H., engaged 4th November, 1882, at Regina.

Rutledge, R., engaged 3rd April, 1882, at Toronto.
Smith, Wm., engaged 29th November, 1882, at Regina.
Tector, John, engaged 10th April, 1882, at Toronto.
Warren, F. F., engaged 23rd July, 1883, at Maple Creek.

Constable Cowan was engaged in Toronto in April, 1882.

The story of the engagement is soon told. Big Bear and his overwhelming force approached a comparatively defenceless fort on the 15th of April, and summoned the whites to surrender. Chief Factor McLean, of the Hudson's Bay Company, went into his camp for the purpose of persuading him, if possible, to abandon his intention of attacking and capturing the fort. Instead of sending him back with terms, however, Big Bear retained McLean as prisoner, and instructed him to communicate with his friends in the fort by letter. Awed by the overwhelming disparity in the relative strength of the opposing parties, Mr. McLean wrote to his family and the other white settlers who were under the protection of the police to surrender themselves to the Indians, and come into the Indian camp, as Big Bear contemplated an almost immediate attack on the fort. Yielding to the Hudson Bay officer's persuasion and their own fears, the settlers, unhappily for themselves, deserted the protection of Inspector Dickens and his gallant little band, and left them as they no doubt supposed to a fate similar to that which had overtaken the unfortunate white settlers at Frog Lake.

Big Bear, however, decided to give the police one chance at least to save their lives at the cost of their honour and what might have been a surrender most disastrous to the loyal cause. The answer of Inspector Dickens and his handful of Mounted Policemen was in keeping with the character which the force has always maintained. They flatly refused to surrender.

Big Bear then offered to allow them to escape provided they would leave their own arms and the arms and supplies under their charge to fall into his hands. This they refused to do, and the attack was made. The fight while it lasted was a hot one. Constable Cowan was killed, and Lansby wounded, and for a time it looked as though the police must succumb, but indomitable British pluck and coolness at last prevailed, and the Indians were driven off, leaving four dead upon the field. Dickens and his force then, destroying everything in the shape of arms, ammunition, and supplies, which they could not take

THE FALL OF FORT PITT. 125

with them, retreated to the river and loading what they required into a York boat made their way down the stream to Battleford. No more heroic fight or successful defence in the face of overwhelming odds illumines the pages of modern history.

The following is the list of the persons held prisoners by Big Bear:

Mr. McLean, Factor, Hudson's Bay Company; Mrs. McLean, Miss McLean, Miss Margaret McLean and Miss McLean, Master Papoman McLean, Master Willie McLean, Master Angus McLean, Master Duncan McLean, Master J. Rose McLean and infant, Mr. Stanley Simpson, Hudson's Bay clerk; Mr. Hodson, Hudson Bay cook; Henry Dufresne, Hudson's Bay Company's servant; Rabisco Smith, Hudson Bay servant, and family of six; Mr. Mann, Instructor, Onion Lake, and family of five; Rev. Mr. and Mrs. Quinney, Episcopal missionary, Onion Lake; Na-co-tan and family, three friendly Indians; three squaws, friendly; Malcolm McDonald, Hudson Bay Company's servant; Penderun and family of six.

Prisoners taken at Frog Lake:—Mrs. John Delaney, Ottawa, instructor's wife; Peter St. Luke, and family of five; Mrs. Gowanlock, Mr. James Simpson and family of three, Hudson Bay agent; Mr. Cameron, Hudson Bay clerk; Otto Dufresne, cook, Indian Department, originally from Montreal, fifty-seven years in employ of Hudson's Bay Company; Pierre, a French-Canadian.

Before the Mounted Police evacuated Fort Pitt, Big Bear sent a letter to Sergeant Martin, a copy of which is as follows:

FORT PITT, April 14, 1885.

Sergeant Martin, N.W.M.P.:

MY DEAR FRIEND,—Since I have met you long ago we have always been good friends, and you have from time to time given me things. That is the reason why that I want to speak kindly to you, so please try to get off from Fort Pitt as soon as you can, and tell your captain that I remember him well. For since the Canadian Government have had me to starve in this country, he sometimes gave me food. I do not forget the last time I visited Pitt, he gave me a good blanket; that is the reason that I want you all out without any bloodshed; we had a talk, I and my men, before we left camp, and we thought the way we are doing now the best. That is to let you off, if you would go, so try and get away before the afternoon, as the young men are all wild and hard to keep in hand.

(Signed) BIG BEAR.

P.S.—You asked me to keep the men in camp last night and I did so, so I want you to get off to-day.

BIG BEAR.

The document in question was written by a white prisoner at the dictation of the old chief

CHAPTER XVI.

THE BATTLE OF FISH CREEK.

THE news of the fall of Fort Pitt and the brilliant and successful retreat of Inspector Dickens, was hardly received and comprehended ere its interest was eclipsed by an event whose importance altogether overshadowed it. Middleton's force was on the move and every day threatened to bring the opposing forces within rifle shot of each other. While no one doubted that our volunteers were as brave as any untrained soldiers that ever shouldered a rifle, there was no overlooking the fact that while they were thoroughly raw so far as active service was concerned, their enemies were for the most part men who were not only inured to all the rigours of the climate and to all sorts of hardships, but who had been under fire again and again, and who were thoroughly versed in everything pertaining to prairie and bush fighting.

THE BATTLE OF FISH CREEK. 127

General Middleton had divided his force into two columns and was advancing down both banks of the South Saskatchewan, determined if possible to preclude the possibility of escape should the rebels decide that it would be better to run than fight.

The force was divided as follows :—

On the left or west bank of the river under the command of Col. Montizambert, with Lord Melgund as Chief of Staff, was the following force :—

French's Scouts	25
Winnipeg Battery	52
Royal Grenadiers	250
Teamsters	80
Total	407

The right column on the east side of the river with Lt.-Col. Houghton as Chief of Staff was composed as follows :

90th Battalion	304
A Battery	120
C Infantry	40
Boulton's Mounted Corps	60
Teamsters	60
Total	584

On the morning of the 24th of April these two columns were advancing down the Saskatchewan about a mile and a-half from the river banks on either side.

In order that the reader may understand the nature of the ground on which the battle took place a few lines of description will be necessary. It must be borne in mind that except in a very limited sense the term "Valley of the South Saskatchewan" is a misnomer. The river runs through the upland prairie in something more like a cañon than a valley. It drains the country through which it runs not by the watershed off slowly sloping banks, but by means of creeks, ravines and coulees, which gather the surface water into their deep narrow channels and fall into the main stream at various angles. Of course each creek or coulee makes a sudden and very deep indentation or break in the river's bank, but between these the banks are usually of about the same level as the surrounding prairie, with only narrow and irregular patches of bottom lands bordering the stream itself. Many of these ravines and coulees which were continually being crossed were lined with stunted poplars, cottonwoods and grey willows; and bluffs or grooves were numerous on the level uplands.

Prior to the fight Dumont with one hundred and twenty-five Half-breeds and Indians had been retreating slowly before General Middleton's right column on the east bank of the river, their scouts keeping them informed of our movements. Dumont appears to have thought of waiting for us to attack him on Thursday night; at least that is the belief of Middleton's scouts who saw some of his mounted men signalling to him all the afternoon on Thursday. However that may be, he lay waiting at the edge of a big coulee near Fish Creek early on Friday morning, his men being snugly stowed away behind boulders, or concealed in the dense everglades of grey willow, birch, and poplar.

When Boulton's scouts first found the enemy, at 9.15 o'clock, they rode back three miles to the main column. Captain Wise, General Middleton's adjutant, at once came up, and ordered the troops to advance. The men gave a loud cheer and then struck out, extending their formation as they neared the edge of the coulee, from which puffs of smoke were already curling up, twenty of Dumont's men, with Winchesters, firing over a natural shelf or parapet protected by big boulders. The column was divided into two wings, the left consisting of B and F Companies of the 90th, with Boulton's mounted corps, and the right of the rest of the 90th, A Battery, and C School of Infantry.

The left wing, F Company leading, came under fire first. As the men were passing by him, General Middleton shouted out:

"Men of the 90th, don't bend your heads. If I had been bending my head I should have had my brains knocked out," he added, touching his cap where a rebel's bullet had pierced it but a moment before.

The men were bending down, partly to avoid the shots and partly because they were running over the uneven, scrubby ground. A, C, and D Companies of the 90th, with A Battery and the School of Infantry, were on the right, the whole force forming a huge half-moon around the mouth of the coulee. The brush was densely thick, and as rain was falling, the smoke hung in clouds a few feet off the muzzles of the rifles.

Here the 90th lost heavily. Ferguson was the first to fall. The bandsmen came up and carried off the injured to the rear, where Dr. Whiteford and other surgeons had extemporized a small camp, the men being laid, some on camp stretchers and some on rude beds of branches and blankets. E company of the 90th, under Captain Whitla, guarded the wounded and the ammunition. General Middleton appeared to be highly pleased with the bearing of the 90th as they pushed on, and repeatedly expressed his admiration. He seemed to think, however, that the men exposed themselves unnecessarily. When they got near the coulee in skirmishing order, they fired while lying prostrate, but some of them, either through nervousness or a desire to get nearer the unseen enemy, kept rising to their feet, and the moment they did so Dumont's men dropped them with bullets or buckshot. The rebels, on the other hand, kept low. They loaded, most of them having powder and shot bags, below the edge of the ravine or behind the thicket, and then popped up for an instant and fired. They had not time to take aim except at the outset, when the troops were advancing.

Meanwhile the right wing had gone into action also. Two guns of A Battery under Captain Peters dashed up at 10.40 o'clock, and at once opened on the coulee. A couple of old barns far back to the right were knocked into splinters at the outset, it being supposed that rebels were concealed there; and three haystacks were bowled over and subsequently set on fire by the shells or the fuses. Attention was then centred on the ravine. At first, however, the battery's fire had no effect, as from the elevation on which the guns stood, the shot went whizzing over it. Dumont had sent thirty men to a small bluff, covered with boulders and scrub, within four hundred and fifty yards of the battery, and these opened a sharp fire. The battery could not fire into this bluff without running the risk of killing some of the 90th, who had worked their way up towards the right of it. Several men of A were struck here. The rebels saw that their sharpshooters were causing confusion in this quarter, and about twenty of them ran clear from the back of the ravine past the fire of C and D Companies to the bluff, and joined their comrades in a rattling fusilade on A. Fortunately only a few of them had Winchesters. A moved forward a little, and soon got the measure of the ravine. The shrapnel screeched in the air, and burst right in among the brush and boulders, smashing the scraggy trees, and tearing up the moss that covered the ground in patches. The rebels at once saw that the game was up in this quarter, though they kept up a bold front and seldom stopped firing except when they were dodging back into new cover. In doing this they rarely exposed themselves, either creeping on all fours or else running a few yards in the shelter of the thicket and then throwing themselves flat on the ground again, bobbing up only when they raised their heads and elbows to fire.

The shrapnel was too much for them, and they began to bolt towards the other side of the ravine, where our left wing was peppering them. This move was the first symptom of weakness they had exhibited, and General

THE BATTLE OF FISH CREEK. 131

Middleton at once took advantage of it and ordered the whole force to close in upon them, his object apparently being to surround them. The rebel commander, however, was not to be caught in that way. Instead of bunching all his force on the left away from the fire of the artillery, he sent only a portion of it there to keep our men busy while the rest tailed off to the north, retiring slowly as our two wings closed on them. Dumont was evidently on the look-out for the appearance of Colonel Montizambert's force from the other side of the river, and in adopting the movement just described, he completely disposed of our chances of cutting him off.

The general advance began at 11.45 a.m., Major Buchan of the 90th leading the right wing and Major Boswell of the same corps the left. When the rebels saw this a number of them rushed forward on the left of the ravine, and the fighting for a time was carried on at close quarters, the enemy not being over sixty yards away. An old log hut and a number of barricades, formed by placing old trees and brushwood between the boulders, enabled them to make it exceedingly warm for our men for a time. At this point several of the 90th were wounded, and General Middleton himself had a narrow escape. Captains Wise and Doucet, of Montreal, the General's adjutants, were wounded about this time. C Infantry behaved remarkably well all through, and bore the brunt of the general advance for some time, the buckshot from the rebels doing much damage. The rebel front was soon driven back, but neither here nor at any other time could their loss be ascertained, though it must have been nearly as large as ours, considering that the artillery had full fling at them for a while. The Indians among them, who were armed with guns, appeared to devote themselves mainly to shooting at our horses. A good many Indians were hit, and every time one of them was struck the others near him raised a loud shout, as if cheering. The troops pressed on gallantly, and the rebel fire slackened and after a time died away, though now and then their front riflemen made a splurge, while the others made their way back. Captain Forrest, of the 90th, headed the advance at this point. Lieutenant Hugh J. Macdonald, (son of Sir John Macdonald), of this company, who had done excellent service all day, kept well up with Forrest, the two being ahead of their men, and coming in for a fair share of attention from the retreating rebels. Macdonald was first reported as killed and then as wounded, but he was not injured, though struck on the shoulder by spent buckshot. Forrest's hat was shot off.

Just before the general advance was ordered General Middleton sent a signal officer to the river to bring over the Grenadiers, who were with the left column, under Colonel Montizambert and Lord Melgund. They had heard the firing of the artillery early in the forenoon, and the Grenadiers, with the Winnipeg Field Battery, had been ordered to the river, skirmishers going in advance, and French's scouts watching the north, where it was supposed another body of the rebels was hovering. The troops had a good five-mile march. They headed for the spot where the artillery firing was loudest, and at noon were at the river bank. General Middleton's messengers at once signalled them to cross, and they came over in a scow. By 1.15 o'clock the Grenadiers had crossed. They were eager to get into action, but by this time Dumont's men were retreating. The Grenadiers, however, were pushed on, and soon joined the 90th and C, their arrival being greeted with tremendous cheering, to which they responded by hoisting their head-gear on their bayonets and cheering in reply.

The rebels now emerged from the woods at the end of a second ravine, behind the one in which they had fought so toughly, and about a mile from the advancing troops. A Battery sent a couple of shells after them, but most of the rebels had their horses tethered behind a clump of trees, and they rode away shouting and defiantly brandishing their guns. This was at 2.30 o'clock.

The infantry could not, of course, follow mounted men, and Boulton's scouts were not numerous enough to

THE BATTLE OF FISH CREEK. 133

attempt a pursuit. The whole force was, therefore, ordered to halt, and at 3.30 it marched back a little to the south of the ravine where the fight began, and close to the river, where dinner was prepared, and the men repaired damages after their hard day's work. The Winnipeg Field Battery arrived from across the river, and, with the Grenadiers, gave the best they had to their gallant comrades of the 90th, A, and C. Camp was pitched here for the night. Just below the camp was the rough field hospital, in charge of Dr. Orton and others, who were busy with the wounded. Nurses were drafted and everything made comfortable for the poor fellows. Rain had fallen from time to time during the day, and about 8 p. m. a heavy storm of rain, hail, and lightning, with terrific thunder, passed over the camp. Double guards were put on, and pickets and vedettes posted everywhere, the General taking the utmost care to protect the troops in case the rebels returned. Nothing was seen or heard of them, however, except when a small mounted party of them approached the outer pickets and cheered.

Dumont was not seen during the fight, but one of our scouts saw him riding off after all was over. His directing hand was plainly seen, however, as nobody else on Riel's side could have arranged the rebel plans or picked the ground so well. The rebel movements appeared to be directed by long, low whistles. General Middleton said it was like the piping of a boatswain. Occasionally they could be heard shouting to each other to "Keep back," "Go on," "This way," "Fire lower," "Fire higher," etc., but during the serious part of the day they fought in grim silence. The rapidity with which some of them loaded their shot-guns with the old-fashioned powder-horns and paper wadding was truly marvellous. A few of them who had Winchesters ran from one part of the ravine to the other, strengthening their line as circumstances directed. General Middleton says they are finer skirmishers and bush-fighters than he ever imagined them to be.

A correspondent writing the night after the fight says: —"The buckshot made very ugly and painful wounds,

Old-style leaden balls were also fired with considerable effect. Had the rebels been armed with Sniders they would have wiped us out in short order from the shelter which they occupied."

The following is General Middleton's official report of the engagement :—

To the Hon. A. P. Caron :

> FROM FISH CREEK, twenty-five miles
> north of Clarke's Crossing, N.W.T., April 24.

I have had an affair with the rebels at this spot, on the east bank of the river. My advanced scouts were fired upon from a bluff, but we managed to hold our own till the main body arrived, when I took measures to repel the attack, which was over about 2.30 p.m. We have captured a lot of their ponies, and have three or four apparently Indians and Half-breeds in the corner of a bluff who have done a great deal of mischief, being evidently their best shots; and as I am unwilling to lose more men in trying to take them, I have surrounded the bluff and shall wait until they have expended their ammunition to take them. Lord Melgund joined me as soon as he could from the other side of the river with the 10th Royals and the Winnipeg half battery, but the affair was over before the most part of the left column had crossed, as it is a work of difficulty to cross. I have ordered the rest to follow, and shall march to-morrow with the united force on Batoche's. The troops behaved very well in this their first affair. The killed and wounded are, I deeply regret to say, too numerous. They are as follow :—

KILLED.

Private Hutchinson, No. 1 Company 90th.
Private Ferguson, No. 1 Company 90th.
Private Ennis, No. 4 Company 90th.
Gunner Demanoilly, A Battery.

THE BATTLE OF FISH CREEK. 135

WOUNDED.

Captain Clarke and Lieutenant Swinford, 90th, seriously.

Captain Wise, A.D.C., and Lieutenant Doucett, A.D.C., one in the leg and the other in the arm.

Mounted Infantry—D'Arcy Baker and Lieutenant Bruce, seriously; Captain Gardner, two wounds, not very serious; C. F. King, H. P. Porin, J. Langford.

A Battery—Gunner Asseltine, Gunner Emeye, Acting-Bombardier Taylor, Sergeant-Major McWinney, Driver Harrison, Private P. H. Wilson, E. G. Maunsell, Private C. Ainsworth, very seriously; Walter Woodman.

C School of Infantry—Arthur Watson, very seriously (since dead), R. H. Dunn, H. Jones, Colour-Sergeant R. Cumming, R. Jones.

90th Regiment—Corporal Lethbridge, C Company; Private Kemp, A Company, very seriously; Corporal B. D. Code, C Company; Private Hartop, F Company; Private A. Blackwood, C. Company; Private Canniff, C Company; Private W. W. Mathews, A Company; Private Lovell, F Company.

I do not know what the loss of the enemy was, but I doubt not it was pretty severe, though from their great advantage of position and mode of fighting it might well be less than ours. I shall proceed to-morrow after burying the dead and sending the wounded back to Clarke's Crossing. By moving on this side I lose the telegraph line, but I shall keep up constant communication by Clarke's Crossing if possible. I regret very much the wounding of my two A.D.C.'s. Captain Wise's horse was shot previously to his being wounded.

(Signed) FRED. MIDDLETON,
Major-General commanding the North-West Field Force.

A corrected list of the killed and wounded in this engagement stands as follows:—

KILLED.

Lieutenant Swinford, 90th.
Private Hutchinson, No. 1 Company, 90th.
Private Ferguson, No. 1 Company, 90th.
Private Ennis, No. 4 Company, 90th.
Gunner Demanoilly, A Battery.
Arthur Watson, School of Infantry.
D'Arcy Baker, Mounted Infantry.
Gunner Cook, A Battery.
Wheeler, 90th.
Ainsworth, A Battery.

WOUNDED.

Captain Clarke, 90th.
Captain Wise, A.D.C.
Lieutenant Doucett, A.D.C.
Lieutenant Bruce, M.I.
Captain Gardner, M.I.
Private C. F. King, M.I.
Private H. P. Porin, M.I.
Private J. Langford, M.I.
Gunner Asseltine, A Battery.
Gunner Emeye, A Battery.
Bombardier Taylor, A Battery.
Sergeant-Major Mawhinney, A Battery.
Driver Harrison.
Private H. P. Wilson.
Private E. Maunsell.
Private Walter Woodman.
Private R. H. Dunn, School of Infantry.
Private H. Jones, School of Infantry.
Private R. Jones, School of Infantry.
Colour-Sergeant Cummings, School of Infantry.
Corporal Lethbridge, 90th.
Private Kemp.
Corporal Code.
Private Hartop.

Private Blackwood.
Private Canniff.
Private W. W. Matthews.
Private Lovell.
Private Lane, 10th Royals.
Private Wheeling, 10th Royals, knee dislocated.
Private Hislop, 90th.
Private Chambers, 90th.
Corporal Thecker, 90th.
Private Bouchette, 90th.
Private Swan, 90th.
Corporal Brown.

Seen as it was from many points of view, the story of the Battle of Fish Creek can best be brought out by a patchwork of letters written by eye-witnesses from time to time, after the fight. A correspondent who, far more than any other correspondent with either Middleton or Otter, manifested an ability to perform the functions of a war correspondent, writes as follows :—

BATTLEFIELD OF FISH CREEK, twenty miles north of Clarke's Crossing, April 24.—The telegraph has advised you of our fight here, and with the present facilities and in the confusion incident to the battle, with twenty wounded men groaning within twenty feet, and as many more too badly hit to groan as near by, with a scattering spray of fire two hundred yards in front, and the Cree war-whoops rising from the infernal ravine in which the Half-breeds and Reds are hidden, one finds little opportunity for finished composition. The fight commenced at 9.15 a. m., and in the settlement of only a few houses within five miles of last night's camp, the Reds and Indians numbering, by guesswork, three hundred, opened fire on our scouts from clumps of trees, the "mattes" of the Southern plains. The ground is rolling down to the river bank. The stream is a mile and a-half west, and here and there are depressions, but the ravine through which Fish Creek takes its winding course is more than a depression—its depth is fully forty feet and the approaches precipitous. On the abutting banks of the stream itself the rebels have their rifle pits, and the timber in the valley, two hundred yards wide; completely conceals them. Ahead the vibrations of a war-whoop, the flash of a gun, or the quivering of a willow are the only objects for the marksmen. We hope many are killed, and as we can see fully a score of horses dead in the stream or on its edge, probably our hopes are well-founded. But we killed more before the whole body of rebels retired into the ravine or fled incontinently. The heaviest loss to the loyal troops was on our right wing, where a party of half and full bloods at ten o'clock made a determined effort to turn our flank. They were repulsed after a hot fire. The two guns of A Battery got into position early, and got the range of the ravine and of the ground in front of the ravine, but the rebels were too well protected in the deep rifle pits, as we now suppose, to be dislodged. They shoot with great accuracy, and have the advantage of seeing their mark. General Middleton has been on his horse and along the entire line time and time again. He has been a constant mark, and one bullet struck his cap, missing the left temporal bone by about a quarter of an inch. Captain Doucet, Aide-de-Camp, and brother-in-law of the General, had an ugly not dangerous flesh wound in the right arm. Captain Wise, Senior Aide-de-Camp, had two horses killed under him, and finally, while forward with C Company on the edge of the ravine, was shot through the right foot, the ball, a 44-calibre Winchester carbine, flattening like putty against the bone. Everybody has behaved with the greatest gallantry, and would long ago have cleared the ravine at the point of the bayonet, had General Middleton permitted. This, up to now he has not done, declining to sacrifice more lives than are absolutely necessary. Some of the best shots among the rebels are in the bush on our right flank, and thus far the east end of the ravine is not covered by our artillery or skirmishers. Not a movement to escape, however, could be made without a withering volley from our men. Since the courier left for the telegraph station Captain Charley Swinford, of C Company, Ninetieth Battalion, has been mortally wounded, shot through the brain.* The French Count DeManally, cook for our mess, had the top of his head blown off by a charge of buckshot early in the engagement. We all fear that when the battle is ended

CAPT. CHARLES SWINFORD.

we may find a good many more dead and wounded lying, as DeManally does, where they fell, and in no good range

---

*Captain Swinford was a favourite with all who knew him. He was thirty-four years of age, and in 1876 went to Winnipeg from Guelph, Ontario, where he resided with his parents for upwards of twenty years. His birthplace was at Greenwich, England. At the time of the breaking out of the Rebellion he was Assistant Manager of the Freehold Loan and Savings Company for Manitoba.

to be brought in. The troops on the west bank of the river went nearly wild with excitement when the firing commenced, and when the scow came down sixty men of No. 2 Company, Royal Grenadiers, Captain Mason, made a rush for the brush and down the bank. Lord Melgund pulled once more on the bow oar and the crossing was quickly effected. The advance was hurried by a call from General Middleton for more infantry, and in two hours three companies of the Grenadiers were on this side pegging away. The guns of the Winnipeg Field Battery and the rest of the troops from the east side are now being crossed as speedily as possible. As I close to catch the courier, only a dropping shot is heard now and then, and the men are munching biscuit and canned beef. The shells of the artillery set fire to several houses on the right flank, and while they were burning the rebels fired slough grass on the right centre to cover a change of position nearer to our centre.

FISH CREEK, April 25.—Doubtless there will be as many accounts of this engagement, which may almost be dignified as a battle, as there were of that preliminary fight in which Crozier lost more than we did. We are now camped within sight of the river, and nearly a mile in the rear of where the action took place. The dead are resting under the prairie sod; the badly wounded are bearing their pain quietly; those but moderately touched are groaning. Without being hypercritical one can find many faults with the result of the action of yesterday. Though not actually defeated, the force, five times as large as that of the rebels, has retired. The enemy, whom we came so many miles to meet, or the greater portion of them, are in that infernal ravine still. No man on our side knows the locale of their covers. No one except themselves has any idea of the maximum or the minimum of their casualty list. Every man you meet has killed at least two. In plain sight there are but two bodies. General Middleton, with mistaken kindness, did not order a charge through the ravine. Had he done so we would

THE BATTLE OF FISH CREEK.

probably have lost twice the number in killed, but the list of wounded would have been smaller, and the result very different. Ten miles to the north of us a far more difficult field than that of yesterday's fight awaits our advance. The moral effect upon the Indians of the North-West cannot fail to be exceedingly bad. So much for the pessimistic side. Looking on the silver lining, one cannot help complimenting the troops, who fought like veterans, or rather better than veterans, as they exposed themselves time and again when there was no need. They were largely encouraged to this by General Middleton, who rode back and forward, a plain target for the enemy, one which they took frequent advantage of, as a ragged hole in his Astrachan cap will bear evidence. The country in which we fought: To the west runs the river, through the rough, deep-cut banks; further down they are sloping and possible of ascent; thence eastward the country is of a semi-rolling character, studded with clumps of timber varying in area from one-half to ten acres. A mile and a-half from the bank runs Fish Creek, henceforth to be noted in Canadian history as the scene of a fruitless fight. The banks of the creek resemble those of the river, on a reduced scale, but instead of stones the land is of the savanna sort. Of course the creek winds, and very crookedly, and equally of course, the rebels took advantage of one of its most abrupt turnings to make their shelter. In the bank furthest from us, as far as we can judge without seeing, are caves and rifle pits, ensconced in which they were as thoroughly safe from fire as if within the strongest battlements ever erected. To the right and left of the ravine the country is the same as that between the river and battle-ground. So much for the scene of action. It was yesterday morning when the mounted infantry and the scouts first felt the rebels by the token of a couple of shots, followed by a volley, which sent them back in rapid transit. C Company, of Toronto Infantry School, in advance of the 90th, rapidly deployed to the front, taking position in extended order, and firing at the timber from which the first shots had been discovered. Rapidly the fight became general. Our line extended over fully a mile of frontage in less than twenty minutes, the guns taking position first on the left centre and later on the extreme right. A well-directed shell fired the houses of the Half-breeds half-a-mile east by north of the clump of bushes in which they were first found, but beyond the destruction of property no harm was done the enemy. Infantry companies supporting the advance were rapidly deployed, and in a semi-circular fashion surrounded the enemy.

It soon became evident to every one that the Half-breeds and Indians (General Middleton numbers them at one hundred and twenty-five), knowing their advantage of position, were determined to make it very hot for us. Without any reckless display of bravery they were able to make their fire an exceedingly well-directed one. Our artillery found trouble in getting the range of the ravine, which is heavily wooded along the brink, and the caves which the enemy knew of, were ready to receive them. As but natural with volunteer troops, a slight nervousness was displayed at first. This wore off as the shots increased in numbers, and lives were hazarded as recklessly as if they amounted to naught. Captain Peters, with a detachment of A Battery, started from the left centre by permission of General Middleton into the ravines and to the woods opposite the centre proper. Here they came within easy range of the enemy, who returned from the bluffs on the edge of the hill; and here the fighting was the hottest. Meantime our skirmishers advanced and the rebels shied into their covers. The nnie-pounders kept pegging away, and of their moral effect no one can complain. Finding it too hot for him, and losing a number of men (poor Cook still lies in the open, dead), Peters retired to his guns, the rebels by this time occupying the thick brush, rifle pits and bluff caves. From that time until four o'clock in the afternoon it was a case of pot shots. You have seen

THE BATTLE OF FISH CREEK. 143

men shoot at a turkey half buried in the ground, the killer to own the bird. I can think of no better simile for our fight. If good luck served, the marksmen could see the heads and even the shoulders of their opponents, but the best nine times out of ten a flash of the rifle or smoke of the powder was the mark at which they had to aim. Either through forgetfulness or because they had a reserve supply, the rebels left a number of their ponies on the bank of the creek. The fire from the right centre soon disposed of twenty-five or thirty of them. How many of the enemy were killed no one knows, probably a dozen. When the Royal Grenadiers came up from the other side they took an advanced position on the right centre, and although rather too close for comfort, were rewarded by the killing of a couple of red devils. The pair had evidently been sent out to see what chance of escape to the east presented itself. Probably more were sent out than the two who were killed, as at five o'clock the firing from the enemy had almost entirely ceased and there was every indication that not more than a dozen remained in the ravine, the larger part of the force having escaped to the eastward. One would naturally ask why they were not completely surrounded. I cannot answer the question any more than you can why the thirty-five mounted rebels who had a parley with Howie, the interpeter, were allowed to ride to the east out of their rifle pits and jeer at our troops, who were ordered to retire to the camp by the river bank. Neither can I explain why the scouts reported this morning that these same thirty-five were allowed to retire to this ravine. The hospital tents were in the rear of the centre, and the accommodations for the wounded were ample. Every comfort was given to those who were hit, and the doctors were cool and efficient. The dead whom we were able to bring from the field were laid beside one of the hospital tents, and were allowed to remain in plain view. The moral effect of course was bad. Later a tent flag hid the bullets' work. The character of the wounds was twofold. Where the forty-five calibre Winchester had been used the orifice of the hurt was clean cut. At close quarters their shot guns made very jagged and terrible injuries. Duck shot, round ball, pieces of lead, irregular in shape, had been used in loading the guns, and in many instances the probe followed the track of one bullet, while the mortal wound lay in a totally different direction. Almost everybody as the action proceeded advanced to the edge of the ravine, and took a pot shot at the rebels, and many of the wounded have to thank their temerity for their sufferings. Captain Wise, Middleton's aide, after losing two horses, was struck by a ball, which evidently ricochetted from a stone, though they say it was flattened on the bone.

A VOLUNTEER'S LETTER.

Corporal Thos. McMullen, of No. 4 Company, Royal Grenadiers, sent the following letter from Fish Creek under date of April 28, to his father :—

I now take advantage of the little time I have to write, assuring you of my safety, as we fought a battle with Riel's Indians on Friday, and we came out all right. But it was a dreadful fight, as five of the 90th were killed, three of A Battery, Watson, of the School, and two of Boulton's scouts; poor Bob Dunn got shot three times in the arm. We were on the other side of the river when the fight started, and about four miles below the 90th's position. As soon as we heard the cannon firing we fell in and advanced in the following order :—No. 1 Company extended in skirmishing order, No. 2 as support, Nos. 3 and 4 reserve. When about opposite the scene of action we got a command to cross the river, and they had to go to the crossing for the scow. No. 1 crossed first, then No. 4, followed by No. 2; No. 3 being left behind with the Winnipeg Field Battery to guard our supplies. When we (No. 4) arrived at the field No. 1 Company was already extended and advancing in splendid form. As soon as we arrived Tom Mitchell, Fred. Curzon, Joe and Will

Dent, McMurray, and myself were detailed off to join A Battery and we slowly crept up until we came to the edge of the bluff, where the enemy were entrenched in an impregnable position. One of the Battery boys was shot alongside of me, and I saw a Half-breed raise himself to see the result of his shot, and I took very good aim and fired at one hundred yards, but it was hard to tell if he was hit, but no more shots came from his rifle pit. Judge and Joe Dent were in the gully with me, and they are responsible for killing two Indians, but we could not dislodge them, and the whole force retired four hundred yards and encamped with the exception of ourselves, the 10th covering the retreat for 100 yards, where we halted and hid in a swamp, and had to lie (soaking wet as we were, it having rained all the time we were fighting) in three inches of water for one hour, without our overcoats. As soon as it was dark we rose up and had to patrol up and down until half-past twelve at night, when the 90th came out to relieve us, and we retired into the tents just vacated by them. When we retired from the bluff the Half-breeds followed us up, but as soon as we halted in the swamp they stopped, and kept signalling to each other all night. As soon as we commenced to patrol, it started to freeze and snow for the rest of the night. Taking it altogether it was a terrible night. The 90th, the Battery, and particularly C School had about forty-five or fifty wounded, C having no less than fifteen, having been in a regular trap, which accounts for their heavy loss. The troops behaved in grand style, and I think, although we were late in action, through no fault of our own, that Toronto was not disgraced by her "crowd of toughs." No. 4 Company alone offered to charge the position with fixed bayonets, but General Middleton said there were enough good men gone, and he also said to our Colonel, "Well done, Grasett, I did not expect you so soon." We crossed the river in very quick time. There is one thing about our regiment, that our officers are good, especially our Colonel, who since we started has asked no man to do what he would not do himself, and he allowed no officer to impose upon any man. Altogether every man is proud to be under such a man. We don't know when the next fight will take place, but I am sure we shall see some more. The 90th and A Battery went into the bluff on Sunday to recover the bodies of two of their men, and found it deserted by all but the dead. There were two dead Indians which the enemy were afraid to carry off, on account of their proximity to our pickets. The bluff is sloping on all sides and the Indians were all hidden in formidable rifle pits which were swimming in blood, telling us that many a Half-breed or Indian had fallen. The pits rose one upon another and were very neatly contrived, the Indians showing much ingenuity in their construction. We are lying encamped at Fish Creek and will remain here probably some time.

BACK TO THE FATAL RAVINE.

Mr. Johnston, the correspondent already quoted, furnishes the following graphic picture of a visit to the ravine two days after the battle, and finishes with some very sensible conclusions regarding the fight as seen in the light of cool after thoughts, and such facts as had come to light since the fatal day. He says :—Almost every one was prepared to discover that the ravine was empty, but there was ghastliness in its silence. It proved an almost impregnable stronghold. The bank nearest our centre and left and right centres is wooded very heavily (none the less, the Gatling we expect on the steamer from Swift Current would have let daylight through it), and is more precipitous than a gable roof. Our fellows shuddered when they saw how near they had been to the very muzzles of the guns of their opponents snugly lying in rifle-pits dug like steps all the way up the bank. The Half-breeds and Indians could see us unless when prone to earth, but even he who had the hardihood to peer over the brink could see nothing but perhaps the flash of a shot gun or rifle. Their pits were three and sometimes five in a row, forming the finest of coverts. These hastily constructed safety trenches pointed up the hills, and over the edge the Half-breed or Indian could rest his gun and take steady and sure aim. Our fire was always quadruple as heavy as theirs, but we fired at a point of the compass from which the killing bullets came. They saved powder, except at the very opening of the fight, and when they saw a white man they fired, not before. The rifle pits were all along the declivity, and not a few were at the bottom of the gully to the right. Further up the stream horses, and fine ones, lay so thick that we could walk from body to body as if on stepping stones. I counted fifty-two dead animals in the ravine, some of them quite high upon the hill, others lying in the stream, but a larger share at a spot along the creek. Many of the animals had been tied to trees by the owners who charged on foot in the open ground in the early morning of Friday. In the woods in the rear of this equine cemetery was the main camp of the Indian allies, and here they had killed an ox; pieces of which, skewered and stuck in the ground before the fire, we found where their intended eaters had left them. On all sides there were evidences of a hurried retreat, and it now seems probable that the twenty-five jeering Half-breeds who showed themselves late in the evening were not in the ravine at all, but among those who made so determined an attempt to turn our right. Like enough from four p.m. onward not a dozen of the enemy lay in the ravine, and these left as soon as darkness had fallen. Fortunately for them the rain fell heavily all that night, and the darkness was intense so that their escape was easily effected. Although their position as described was almost impregnable, yet they must have passed several evil hours. They took away all their wounded, and of their dead but four remain; one Teton Sioux was shot.

Before he could reach the shelter of the hollow, one Cree, Beardy's son-in-law, was shot through the heart, and held by a tree trunk from falling into the ravine, one Cree on the extreme left, and a Half-breed on the upper flank of the right centre. As stated above, fifty-two horses were killed. In three of the rifle pits deep pools of blood remain, and in others lighter marks of injury. Since we have been in the ravine the general conclusion is that the rebel force numbered nearly three hundred (some of them on the extreme right) and that they had ten to twelve killed and wounded. They were led by Gabriel Dumont, and had they been provisioned with ammunition and arms as plentiful and good as our men, our casualty list, large as it was, would have been trebled. On our side, before the arrival of Mason's company of Royal Grenadiers from the other side of the river, there were about three hundred in action. This includes the Artillery, 90th Infantry, and Boulton's scouts. Probably General Middleton was wise in not allowing a charge, although we all felt that night as if we had been practically defeated. Cook and Wheeler, whose dead bodies we found yesterday in the brush, got to within a few feet of the rebels and were killed instantly. We made a trip through the house in plain sight throughout the fight to the east of the ravine. It is owned by a widow, Marie Tourand, who has four Half-breed rebel sons. The house had been deserted in short order, and soiled plates and knives showed where a hurried breakfast had been taken. A sewing machine was standing near a chest of drawers, which a fuse shell had shattered into atoms. General Middleton strictly forbade any looting on personal account, but a good many provided themselves with one thing or another of interest as a trophy. Most of the horses killed had their saddles and bridles on, and this shows the haste in retreat, since the Half-breeds value such paraphernalia highly, and would not have left them except under stress. In several of the unburned houses of this longitudinal settlement known as that of St. Antoine de Padua, stores taken from the merchandise at Duck Lake were found, and in almost every tent in the

camp you can find a French love letter. The division on
the west side did not get their impediments until late last
night, and the inconvenience almost amounted to suffering. We hadn't any blankets or mess facilities. Not a
change of apparel and the rain poured down all Friday
night. But complaint is not the order of the day, nor is
it likely to be when a groan from the operating table
might intercept a growl, or the provost stop the growler
ere he came too near to those shapeless things under the
canvas yonder. What are we to do? Now, I don't pretend to guess in detail, but Middleton regards the action
as a victory, and is inclined to think we will have no more
serious affairs. Many differ from him in both beliefs,
but it is guess work on the part of everybody. As Friday's fight, if nothing else, put Riel, Dumont, and all his
abettors beyond the pale of pardon, they must fight or
run. Dumont would much prefer the former. In one
rifle-pit I picked up a Snider, a Peabody and a shot gun,
No. 12 shell. The shot gun cartridges had the shot
drawn and a couple of round balls forced in. They did
much damage at short range and made the ugliest sort of
wounds.

MAJOR BUCHAN'S ACCOUNT.

The following is a description of the infantry movements, written by Major Lawrence Buchan, of the 90th :—
The Battle of Fish Creek was peculiar from many points
of view. One of the most striking features of it was that
for the whole time of the engagement the infantry, or
rifles, as the 90th Battalion are called, fought without support or reserve behind them, the whole of their
available force, save about a dozen or so of a guard in the
reserve ammunition train, being extended in the fighting
line. So soon as the first shots were heard in the front
when the enemy opened fire on the scouts, the advance
guard, composed of F Company and a dozen men from
other companies of the 90th were pushed to the front and
extended in the bluffs jutting out, into the side of which

at from two to four hundred yards distance the puffs of smoke, followed by the ring of the passing bullets, alone denoted the presence of the enemy who were concealed from view. A return fire at the fringe of smoke puffs on the outer margin of the plains was at once opened by the 90th men, among whom were a dozen and a-half of sharpshooters armed with the Martini-Henry rifle. Presently a company of the 90th came up in support, but the enemy's fire was so hot and evidently increasing in strength to the left, that the officer in command of the advance guard at once extended this company to the right and brought them into the fighting line. Meanwhile B and C Companies of the 90th were extended in through the brush on the left and came to the front, while the Infantry School was extended in the same manner to the right, finally appearing at the edge of the plain on the right of A Company, and supported by D Company and part of E Company. The enemy had by this time developed a very strong attack against our right at a point where the edge of the ravine in which they were concealed and the bluffs in which the Infantry School were extending came within about sixty yards of each other. It became evident that they intended to get possession of the bluff if possible. By so doing they could readily enfilade our centre and completely outflank us. To checkmate this, Company D, and the portion of Company E which were in support, were at once brought up into the bluff to reinforce the Infantry School, as was also the left half of Company A, the remainder of which was extended further to the right, thus making the bluff spoken of the centre of our right defence with flanking parties on either side, the whole covering a front of about three hundred and fifty yards. At this point a very hot fire was directed by the enemy for about two hours, while our men lay quietly in the scrub, and as the rebels, after a deal of ki-yi-ing and whooping, would rush to the top of the bank and deliver their fire, our men would return it with interest. The enemy failing to dislodge us by their bullets set the prairie grass on fire at the brow of the hill, and as the wind was blowing towards us, the smoke filled our men's eyes, while the enemy had clear sight. Presently the fire reached the scrub, so that our men had to jump the flames and lie down again on the burnt and scorching ground. The casualties in our force were very heavy at this point; three of the 90th were shot dead and over a dozen wounded, as well as three men of the Infantry School. The enemy, finding that the efforts against us were in vain, slackened their fire, when an advance was ordered along the line and creeping forward to the brow of the ravine they were discovered in full retreat to the east. A few parting volleys were sent after them, as our men followed them, and their retreat being reported to the General, he ordered the artillery to shell them, which was shortly done, as they got behind a house about two thousand yards distant. The house was fired by the second shell, and the rebels scattered into the wood to the east.

GENERAL MIDDLETON ON THE SITUATION.

"I think you criticize me wrongly when you say I exposed myself unwisely last Friday," said General Middleton *apropos* of numerous strictures by almost every one. "I couldn't do otherwise," he continued, "I had green troops, and, worse still, green officers—green in the sense that they had never been under fire before. They did well and bravely, but while you can drill a man into a soldier in a few months, it takes years to educate officers in whom a general commanding can have implicit confidence. If I had been in command of regulars, or, possibly, if Lord Melgund had been with me from the first, I would have taken a position in rear of the line of battle, set up my flag, and sent my orders. I would have done this, that is as soon as the troops had been inspired with confidence. I value my life as much as any one can, and it is not necessary to prove my bravery, at least in England where I am known, but it was necessary that I shouldn't dodge. By the way," pointing to his Astrachan cap with a smile, "if I had been ducking when that fellow hit me the bullet would have gone into the top of my head and my quietus made. If I hadn't exposed myself you would all have been scalped. I am in an embarrassing, but not a novel position. We have driven off the enemy, but by this enforced wait we are losing all the fruits of victory, while the enemy are boasting that we are afraid to move, and are given ample time to make further preparations for escape or defence. I know the effect of delay is bad, yet what can I do? Here I am with nearly forty wounded, and the long-expected boat is not even within hail from one hundred miles southward. I can't move the wounded to Saskatoon, for that is two days' march away, and the one day transport to Clark's Crossing by waggon and rough roads may, the doctors say, result fatally in several cases. Send them to Clark's Crossing, and the wounded can't be left without a guard or without ample medical assistance. I can spare neither from my present force. I can no longer trust to the boat, but must order her munitions and stores forward overland. We have a good deal of ammunition, and oats enough for several days. I have no complaints to make of the transport service. It is very effective, and I should not wait one day longer for either. The horses couldn't starve before we attacked Batoche."

The following from a correspondent's letter gives an idea of the feelings with which the troops regarded the enemies against whom they were fighting:—

"The feeling that the Half-breeds have been wronged, that the Government has been criminally negligent in its treatment of their claims, and that the politicians should be held accountable for the whole trouble, grows more deeply rooted and more widely spread. The sight of these comfortable homes and the coupled knowledge that the men who reared them, suffered the rigours of frontier life and fostered a love for the very soil itself, cannot get sufficient title to raise $10 by mortgage on one thousand

THE BATTLE OF FISH CREEK. 153

acres, bring home to every man the reality of the residents' grievances. No one defends the alliance with the Indians, nor do any deny the folly of the insurrection or counsel compromise at this stage of the proceedings, but feelings nearly akin to sympathy find lodgment in many of the bravest breasts. Hostility against Riel is outspoken, because it is believed his have been the unwise and demagogical counsels and measures which have led to hardship and bloodshed. It seems paradoxical, but it is actually probable that the men won't fight any the worse for this sympathy."

It would seem from the following extract that men composing the left column, which was advancing down the west side of the river, were in no very amiable humour at having been practically left out of the Fish Creek fight. It will be seen that it was no fault of theirs they were not earlier on the scene:—

"The left column has probably uttered more oaths than any given body of men of equal number assembled in the last decade, and rivals the army in Flanders. They had been halted during the morning to wait for oats, the teamsters having represented to Colonel Montizambert that they could not move unless their horses were fed. About 9.30 they heard the opening of the artillery. The scouts hurried forward to report, if possible, what was going on beyond the dividing river, but soon they were not needed, as the roar of guns and volley-firing were plainly audible. The Winnipeg Field Battery was quickly sent to the front, Lord Melgund and Colonel Montizambert at their head, and after driving over places which in cooler moments would have been regarded as impassable, the river bank was reached. Two guns were spotted and held ready for the assistance of those on the opposite side. They were not fired, as a mounted aide hurrying to the opposite bank yelled across that Middleton wanted infantry to help him and not artillery. The scow which had been used in the morning to transport oats from the right to the left column was hurried downward. Mason's

Company embarked, while two companies were ordered to follow as quickly as possible. Lord Melgund pulled number one at the bow oar of this deeply sunken scow, sunken by reason of water in her hold, and the crossing was effected in less than fifteen minutes. The bank on the east side had an incline of about sixty degrees, but horses and men climbed it as if stairs had been inserted therein, and soon started for the scene of the action on the double. The advance company reached the ravine, and took position on the right centre before two o'clock, and did good service—not only morally, but actually. The other two companies crossed as speedily as possible, also the other two guns of the Field Battery, with the detachment of A Battery, of Quebec, and by six o'clock all but one company of the Grenadiers of the left column and transport had reached this side of the Saskatchewan. If General Middleton made a mistake in dividing his force it was one into which anybody was liable to fall. That the enemy would make so determined a stand was something which neither he nor anyone else not omniscient could have even guessed at. The rebels have underrated the pluck of those they have been pleased to term "militia soldiery." There is no question whatever but that we will be at them eventually. The men did not get anything to eat from 7 a.m until 7 p.m., if a few pickled pieces of hard tack are excepted. The telegraph operator did not cross to the west side last night, and all the despatches had to be sent to Clark's Crossing—twenty-two miles southward. Incited thereto by their chief, Lieutenant L. Bedson, many of the transport teamsters took a hand in the fight, and a few of the good shots were in the fore front of the affair."

"IN MEMORIAM."

Growing to full manhood now,
With the care lines on our brow,
We, the youngest of the nations,
With no childish lamentations,
Weep, as only strong men weep,
For the noble hearts that sleep,
Pillowed where they fought and bled,
The loved and lost, our glorious dead.

Toil and sorrow come with age,
Manhood's rightful heritage,
Toil shall only make us stronger,
Sorrow make our hearts bear longer
All the sunderings of time;
Honour lays a wreath sublime,—
Deathless glory,—where they bled,
Our loved and lost, our glorious dead.

Wild the prairie grasses wave
O'er each hero's new-made grave,
Time shall write such wrinkles o'er us,
But the future spreads before us,
Glorious in that sunset land;
Nerving every heart and hand,
Comes a brightness none can shed
But the dead, the glorious dead.

Lay them where they fought and fell,
Every heart shall ring their knell,
For the lessons they have taught us,
For the glory they have brought us,
Tho' our hearts are sad and bowed,
Nobleness still makes us proud,
Proud of light their names shall shed
In the roll call of our dead.

> Growing to full manhood now,
> With the care lines on our brow,
> We, the youngest of the nations,
> With no childish lamentations,
> Weep, as only strong men weep,
> For the noble hearts that sleep,
> Where the call of duty led,
> Where the lonely prairies spread.
> Where for us they fought and bled,
> Our loved, our lost, our glorious dead.

CHAPTER XVII.

BATTLE OF CUT KNIFE CREEK.

WHILE the Battle of Fish Creek was still an absorbing topic from Halifax to Victoria, and while Middleton was preparing to advance on the enemy's position at Batoche, Colonel Otter was making ready for taking the aggressive with his column. Though there is no satisfactory evidence that Poundmaker had taken any active part in the rising at Battleford up to this time, it was known that there was a considerable body of Indians besides his own band camped on his reserve, that they had a large band of settlers' cattle feeding near their camp, and that they were living on the fat of the land generally, while Colonel Otter and his men were not faring particularly well at Battleford.

What Colonel Otter expected to accomplish by attacking the great Cree chief on his own reserve is not now, and in all probability never will be, properly understood. Be this as it may the result was far from being satisfactory. In spite of all the despatches to the contrary, when the whole truth became known, it was found that with about three hundred men, one Gatling and two seven-pounders, Colonel Otter surprised Poundmaker,

BATTLE OF CUT KNIFE CREEK.

who had about two hundred and fifty poorly armed Indians and Half-breeds, and that after a sharp contest of some seven hours' duration he was compelled to make a hurried retreat, and that it was mainly owing to Poundmaker's forbearance that the retreating column was not cut to pieces. Of course every one who saw the fight, or thought he saw it, had a different story to tell; but take all the accounts from both sides and weigh them fairly, and the above will be found to be pretty nearly the only conclusion that can be arrived at.

It was not till after dinner on Friday, 1st May, that it became known in the police barracks that Colonel Otter intended moving out that day. The question as to when the expedition would start had been the engrossing subject of speculation ever since the arrival there on the 23rd April. On Tuesday the Colonel announced the corps that had been selected to form the column to proceed to Poundmaker's, but then it was not generally believed that an early start would be made. Scouts had already brought in particulars of the position taken up by the Indians, and Bresaylor, a Half-breed who came to the lines on Wednesday, and was arrested as a suspected spy, gave further information. He said he had been taken prisoner by the Indians, and escaped. The force at Poundmaker's, he said, was not more than three hundred and fifty braves. On the following day, Thursday, Mr. McArthur, a surveyor, of Edmonton, came in to the camp and said that he too had just escaped from the Indians at Poundmaker's. He had left Edmonton unaware of the rising of the Indians, and had walked right into their hands. For the most part he corroborated the Half-breed's story, and the latter then gained more credence. This was the whole of the information that Colonel Otter possessed of the position and strength of the enemy, and as the stories of scouts, Half-breed, and surveyor agreed in the main, there was every reason to believe that it was as nearly correct as possible.

It was past three o'clock on Friday afternoon when the long column of teams, forty in number, with the Mounted Police and scouts under Superintendent Herchmer * and Inspector Neale in advance, moved out of the camp on south side of the Battle River in the direction of Poundmaker's. Following the police came the artillery with

COLONEL HERCHMER.

the Gatling and two seven-pounders, under Major Short Captains Farley and Rutherford, and Lieutenants Pelletier

---

* Superintendent Herchmer, one of the most effective and dashing officers of the North-West Mounted Police, is a native of Kingston, where he had attained to the rank of a volunteer Colonel before leaving for the North-West. As an officer of the North-West Mounted Police he has always been very highly esteemed by his fellow-officers as well as the men under his command. Kind hearted, courteous and brave even to rashness; he is just the sort of man for a leader of red-coated prairie troopers.

and Prower. After them came in succession C Company Infantry School, under Lieutenant Wadmore and Lieutenant Cassels (attached from Q.O.R., during the expedition); Ottawa Foot Guards, under Lieutenant Gray; No. 1 Company, Queen's Own, under Captain Brown, Captain Hughes and Lieutenant Brock; ammunition teams, forage and provision teams, and the Battleford Rifles, under Captain Nash and Lieutenants Marigold and Baker, bringing up the rear.

As the column moved out the men who had been left behind gave a parting cheer, and in a few minutes the intervening woods shut out the sight of the camp ground. Rain was dribbling, but the sky soon cleared. The trail ran through an uneven country, with high hills covered densely with poplar and underbrush on the left and the river on the right in a north-westerly direction. It was just such a tract as the Indian delights most to fight in. Coulees or ravines were crossed in endless succession, and the poplar and underbrush that grew thickly up to the trail in many places was impenetrable for any considerable distance with the eye, and in it might lurk a thousand redskins within fifty yards without being seen, despite all the care and sharpness of the scouts, who scoured the country, wherever it was possible, for half-a-mile on either side. The distance to Poundmaker's was thirty-five miles, and by seven o'clock the column had made half the journey, and halted to await the rising of the moon. The teams were corralled in an open piece of ground surrounded with underbrush at a distance of probably three hundred yards on all sides. Fires were lit, and the men got twenty-four hours' rations of canned corned beef, hard-tack and tea. About the fires they whiled away the time till eleven o'clock, chatting about the chances of surprising the Indians in the morning. They were all unquestionably eager for a brush with them, a fact which was plainly evidenced by the impetuosity with which they set upon the foe in the morning when the engagement began. The clouds had cleared almost entirely from the sky when the moon began to peep over the horizon. But it had grown chilly and the fires were kept blazing brightly for the warmth they gave. At half-past eleven the teams were all harnessed and shortly afterwards strung out in a long column, winding at a quick walk over the trail to Poundmaker's. The men made themselves as comfortable as possible in the waggons, but the rugged nature of the trail made any attempt at sleep futile. The scouts still kept well to their work, for the moon, just beginning to wane in a clear sky, rendered it almost as bright as day. A large number of the men, in order to keep themselves warm, walked alongside the waggons during the night. The trail was running through a more open country, at intervals there being some long stretches of flat, grass-covered land with only here and there a clump of red willow. The glow in the east was observable long before the almanacs ascribed to the sun any intention of rising. At length it rose redly, and just as it tipped the horizon the hollow was reached where the Indians had been encamped according to the reports of the scouts, three days previously. The place gave every indication of having been very recently vacated, and it was thought by many that, learning of our approach, they had hastily retreated. There was strong disappointment expressed, for the boys were anxious for a fight.

The column advanced through this hollow, and the trail then led them through a deep gully several hundred yards wide, densely wooded with poplar and willow underbrush, through which the Cut Knife Creek wound its tortuous course. The creek is probably eight or ten yards wide, two and a-half feet deep, with a swift current. Into this gully the column passed without hesitation. The men knew they were in the heart of the enemy's stronghold, and might expect to come in view of them at any moment. That was just what was wanted. There was not long to wait. Immediately that the column got into the gully the men could see to the left, on the slope

BATTLE OF CUT KNIFE CREEK.

of one of the high, rolling hills that led up from the gully, two or three dozen head of cattle calmly grazing. The Indians were known to have driven away some hundreds of them from the settlers, and it was even thought that in the haste of their flight they had left these behind. The column, as it went through the winding path in the gully, was somewhat straggling. The scouts went along considerably in advance, up a long but not precipitous incline, which carried the trail to the head of the Cut Knife Hill, on the opposite side. While passing through the gully a glimpse could be got of the tops of the Indians' teepees, or wigwams, on the summit of a high hill, removed a considerable distance to the left. There was now no doubt about the presence of the Indians, and the word went along the column, "There they are." One or two mounted Indians also now could be seen on the top of a hill to the left. The creek which had been crossed is called by the Indians Cut Knife Creek, and the hill upon which Colonel Otter made his stand Cut Knife Hill, in commemoration of the defeat by the Crees of the Blackfoot chief Cut Knife and his braves, which took place there.

When the scouts reached the summit of Cut Knife Hill, over which the trail ran, they were seen to draw back and take shelter behind some willows on the brow of the hill. The Mounted Police, Colonel Herchmer leading, came up almost at once, followed by the artillery, C Company, the Guards, and Queen's Own close behind, but the rest of the teams were still well down the incline, and the rear teams with the Battleford Rifles not yet half-way over the gully. The scouts, Mounted Police, and artillery advanced immediately.

In a moment the rattle of rifle shots was heard. The fight had begun by the Indians firing on the police and scouts. Those on the incline could not see the enemy, but their presence was no longer in doubt. The artillery pushed at once to the front, and brought their guns into position. The bulk of the enemy engaged was not more than one hundred and fifty yards away, sheltered in the underbrush of a coulee on the left slope of the hill the attacking force had ascended. The garrison division of B Battery, under Captain Farley and Lieutenants Pelletier and Prower, were instantly extended in skirmishing order on the brow of the hill, and began to reply to the enemy's fire, dropping flat on their faces, only their heads appearing over the crest as marks for the enemy. The police at once took up similar positions, having dismounted and placed their horses in a slight hollow on the incline up which they had come. They were no sooner extended in this position than thirty or forty Indians made a rush up the hill on to the guns. The danger of the position was tremendous. Had they gained that hill-top and captured the guns, they could have dealt certain destruction to the column advancing up the hill. Major Short saw the danger instantly, and called on the men about him to repel the charge. They responded without a moment's hesitation, Major Short, revolver in hand, leading the way. The Indians rattled into them as soon as they appeared on the hill-top. The distance was thirty yards, and some of the more daring Red-skins had got to within half that distance. One of these the Major shot at once. The Indians kept the fire up for two or three rounds, and then retreated pell-mell to their cover. The Indians, as they rushed for the guns, would throw their blankets high over their heads to draw our fire, then dropping down would deliver a volley, and repeat the same tactics every time. Besides the fire of the attacking party, the bullets were whistling in scores from a cover two hundred yards off. Before our men could get back to cover again, Corporal Sleigh, of the Mounted Police, lay dead on the field, Lieutenant Pelletier had been shot through the thigh, and Sergeant Gaffney and Sergeant Ward wounded. Major Short had a close call, with a bullet-hole through his wedge cap. Immediately that the firing was heard by those behind, they rushed up the hill. The order was given to extend in skirmishing order. The

BATTLE OF CUT KNIFE CREEK. 163

men were in line in a moment. The Queen's Own and Ottawa Foot Guards went to the left until the enemy came in view. Dropping down they narrowly escaped a hot volley from the enemy, sent in as soon as they appeared. The main body of C Company were turned to the right, to cut off the fire of the Indians, which was beginning to come in hotly from over a deep ravine that ran only about twenty yards from the trail, and, for a distance, almost parallel with it. The Battleford Rifles had jumped from the teams at once when the firing began, and started on a run up the incline. Most of them were called back to protect the rear teams going up to the slight hollow on the trail, when they were drawn up in a bunch. No sooner had the teams got up than the Indians appeared on the trail in the gully below. Thus, in five minutes after the first shot was fired, Colonel Otter's force was completely surrounded and being fired on from all sides. It was evident he had run into a trap. The situation began to look desperate. On all sides the action was hot. The intention of the enemy was to cut off his retreat, and if possible stampede the horses. The little hollow on the face of the hill into which the teams were drawn, afforded them some protection, but from the rear they could easily be reached if the enemy were advanced a little further than they were up the slope. The artillery occupied the top of the hill furthest advanced. The Gatling gun had opened fire on the enemy first, at a range of about two hundred yards, on the left slope of the hill, into a cluster of brush. The Indians got out of that cover and beat a hasty retreat round to the hill on the other side of the hollow, where they again got an underbrush cover. After the first rush it was impossible to see more than two or three of the Indians at once, so that the Gatling was not so destructive as it would have been under other circumstances. But it was kept going for a time almost continuously, and created a terrific din. The two seven-pounders were placed on either side of the Gatling, at a distance of perhaps fifty yards. The first three shells were put into the teepees on the hill to the right front. They were admirably aimed, and created consternation. The teepees were ripped over, and the people scattered in every direction. Both guns soon were throwing their deadly shells into the cover into which the Indians had retreated after their rush. The range was about one thousand five hundred yards. Wherever a shell fell its effect could be seen by a scattering of the enemy in all directions. The firing on us grew hotter and closer. Volley after volley from friend and foe on all sides, the booming of the cannon, the rapid rattle of the Gatling and the rifles, mingled with the wild whooping of the Indians, made up a furious tumult, of which no description can give an adequate idea. Officers and men were as cool and determined as if the day was already theirs. About an hour after the engagement was begun, the order was passed from Colonel Otter to Captain Nash, of the Battleford Rifles, that the rear must be cleared. The men of the ununiformed company did not wait to hear the order twice. With a loud cheer they dashed down the incline and into the wood of the deep gully, over which the column had crossed. The Indians under cover stood the attack a few moments and then began to fall back. The Battleford boys raced them up the gully to the right, firing whenever an Indian head appeared. It took half an hour to clear the back, and then Lieutenant Marigold turned his men to clear the gully on the other side of the trail. The Indians posted there also gave way and ran back to their former position. It was a grand charge, valorously executed. The rear was entirely cleared of the enemy, and Colonel Otter remained in command of the position. But the Indians were again coming down into the gully into the position on the right side of the trail, from which Captain Nash had previously dislodged them. Charlie Ross, the famous Mounted Police scout, who had been all over the field during the action, saw the position, and stepped into the breach. Calling for volunteers, some of the Queen's Own, C Company, and Ottawa Guards were at his side in an instant, and they started to intercept the Indians' advance. The Reds cleared out at once up the gully and into a ravine, from the covered sides of which a number of them had been firing on the men of C Company, who were replying across the ravine near where the teams were stationed. Ross and his followers pursued them hotly. The Guards could not understand why the enemy they had been watching across the ravine had silenced their fire so suddenly. But the Guards did not know that Ross and his daring followers had got round in the rear of the enemy and were engaged in hot pursuit. Ross immediately cleared up the side of the ravine, and the instant he reached the summit, where the Indians had previously been firing from, the skirmishers of C Company mistook him for one of the enemy, and in an instant a dozen rifles were brought to bear on him. But he had tied a white hankerchief to the muzzle of his rifle and waving it above his head the rifles were lowered. One man standing among the teams raised a rifle and fired at Ross, the bullet providentially going wide. Colonel Otter saw the white flag waved and, not recognizing Ross, standing as he was on the ground only a few minutes before occupied by the enemy, evidently mistook the flag as a signal of truce from the Indians. He walked over to the edge of the ravine as if to parley, but Ross was recognized by this time, and in a moment the red coats of his men came up from behind the hill riding the ponies they had captured.

It was now half-past eight o'clock, and the fight had lasted about three and a-half hours. The cannons and Gatling were belching incessantly, but the trail of one of the seven-pounders shortly gave out; the carriage, rotten with age, fell to pieces, and the gun was silenced. A number of C Company had come over to the left flank, and fell into the skirmishing line up to this time held by the Queen's Own, Guards, Police, and Garrison Artillery. All were lying flat on their faces peeping over the side of the hill and across a hollow into an underbrush on the summit of the opposite hill, where the enemy were keeping up a constant fire at a range of from six hundred to seven hundred and fifty yards. If one of the men unluckily rose up into view a dozen puffs of smoke would come out of the underbrush and he had to drop again instantly to get under cover, while the bullets would whistle fiercely but harmlessly over. This position was held with little change for an hour and a-half. The Indians were constantly playing their old game to draw fire. Up would go a hat on the muzzle of a rifle, or a blanket would be thrown up, and as the men took aim at the decoys the enemy would fire on their uncovered heads. Otter's men "got on to the dodge" at length, and played similar pranks. The enemy were shooting with remarkable accuracy, and it was believed that many Half-breeds were among their number. At ten o'clock the guns had about silenced the fire of the enemy directly in front, but they had worked round to the left near the gully, and were beginning to pour in a dangerous flank fire on the skirmishers on the side of the hill. This had to be stopped. Captain Rutherford directed a shell into the gully. It burst almost over the heads of the Battleford Rifles, who were hotly holding the position to which they had been ordered. The shelling of the gully caused them to fall back, but the word was soon sent along that no more shells would be fired there and they resumed their position. Colonel Otter ordered Captain Brown to send the left half of the Queen's Own to occupy a small hill over which the flank fire was coming. The order was passed to Lieutenant Brock, who was in charge of the left half. The object was to drive the Indians farther back, and the Battleford Rifles going up the gully would prevent them again taking cover there. It was a hazardous venture. About twenty men, some of them Guards and Police, responded to Lieutenant Brock's call to charge for the hill. Away they went on a quick run, ducking down to escape the bullets. Brock, revolver in hand, was leading by half-a-dozen yards. The men in the skirmishing line behind let out a loud cheer as they saw the plucky fellows dashing up the hillside, right into the line of the enemy's bullets over the top. More than half the men dropped flat just as the summit was reached. Brock and the remainder passed right over out of view. A thrill ran through every spectator. The men got over the hill and started down in full view of the Indians a little over a hundred yards away. The men opened fire, Brock with his revolver, but it was useless. The enemy

COLOUR-SERGEANT GEO. E. COOPER.

sent up a withering fire, and the men were forced back again over the top of the hill and dropped into cover, five of them having felt the bullets of the enemy. It was a plucky charge. Lieutenant Brock and his brave followers, Colour-Sergeant Cooper * and Privates Varey and

---

*Colour-Sergeant George E. Cooper is a native of Birmingham, England, and is about thirty-seven years old. He came to Canada about fourteen years ago, and joined the Q. O. R. about seven years ago. He is an engraver by trade. He is of unusually fine physique and is one of the most accomplished amateur leapers in Canada.

Watts of the Queen's Own, and one of the Guards were more or less seriously wounded, and Colour-Sergeant McKill's forehead was grazed by a ball. Colonel Otter forwarded orders that the hill should be held, and they kept it until the final withdrawal, in order to protect the teams on the way out.

The Indians were making a great fight of it, and when chased out of one position resumed the fire in another. Their tenacity is, perhaps, unexampled in Indian fighting. Their losses must have been severe. It looked as if they intended keeping it up all day, and it would have been certain disaster to the force to have been left at night fall in the position into which they had been entrapped, without the assistance of the guns, one of which was now perfectly useless and the other almost so. The only safety was in a retreat, and for this Colonel Otter began to lay his plans. The Scouts, Battleford Rifles, and Captain Rutherford and his men, with one of the seven-pounders, were ordered to proceed through the gully and occupy the high banks on the opposite side, through which the trail ran. This position commanded the whole line of retreat. The order was obeyed in splendid style. In a quarter of an hour they were all in position, the rifles and artillery on a cut bank forty or fifty feet high, and the scouts on the top of a high sandhill. The trail out of the gully passed right between these positions. The teams were the first to descend through the gully, and the Indians then became aware that Otter intended to withdraw. This was shortly after twelve o'clock. At that time the enemy had almost ceased firing, and it is the belief of many who know the Indians pretty well, that they were just on the point of getting away themselves when they saw him leaving. None of the men left their positions on the field till every waggon and horse had safely passed through the gully. Then came the real danger of the situation. The men had to retire down the long incline leading to the gully always with their faces towards the enemy, who were following them

BATTLE OF CUT KNIFE CREEK.

up over the ground they had just left. The firing from both parties was hot, and appeared, from the position of the party who were occupying the hills to protect the retreat, much more deadly than it afterwards turned out to be. But it was a moment of supreme danger. A large body of Indians poured down into the gully a considerable distance up, with the object no doubt of coming up with the men as they were crossing the gully, and cutting them off from the teams and the party on the other side. If this could have been done, the chances would have been in favour of the whole brigade being slaughtered. But the foresight of Colonel Otter had provided against such a chance. From the gun on the bank Captain Rutherford sent a couple of shells directly into the horde of Red-skins, who were coming down the hill over the field where the men had fought all day. When the smoke cleared away again, the Indians were turned right about and going in the opposite direction. The Indians who had got down into the gully further up came on, but the scouts posted on the sand hill kept them in check. After all Otter's men had got down to the bottom land in the gully they were thoroughly covered by the men posted on the bank and came right through leisurely enough.

The whole column immediately took to the waggons and returned to Battleford, arriving at 10 o'clock that night. The Indians did not attempt to follow.

The Queen's Own Rifles ambulance corps worked heroically during the whole day. When there was a call for them to any part of the field their courage carried them even under the enemy's fire to rescue a wounded man. No praise of their work is too great.

One incident of the fight cannot be left unrecorded. Private Acheson, of the Queen's Own, ran out from cover at the time the withdrawal was being made, to recover the body of Private Dodds, of the Battleford Rifles. Private Lloyd, of the Queen's Own, was near him at the time, and Acheson asked him to cover him while he went out. Lloyd did so, and went out to assist Acheson, who had shouldered the dead man. When they were returning Lloyd fell, shot in the back. He was in a stooping position when struck and the bullet, entering the centre of the back, penetrated up to the shoulder, under the blade. When Acheson had deposited the body under cover he at once returned to bring in Lloyd. Colour-Sergeant

BUGLER FOULKES.*

McKell, of the Queen's Own, went out to assist him, and between them they got Lloyd safely away from the enemy.

---

* Herbert Foulkes of "C" Company who was killed in the fight with Poundmaker's band came to this country from England about eight years ago. He worked on farms until last September, when he went to Toronto and took a situation at Oak Hall, where he was a general favourite with the employés. He has no relatives in this country.

BATTLE OF CUT KNIFE CREEK. 171

It was a remarkable exhibition of heroism. The enemy were at moderately close range, and firing incessantly.

Poor Rodgers, of the Foot Guards, was killed instantly while lying in the skirmishing line on the side of the hill. He was speaking to Capt. Hughes, who was lying alongside of him, only a moment before. The ball penetrated his head, and he died without a groan. Following is the list of killed and wounded :—

KILLED.

Brigade Bugler Foulkes, Toronto Infantry School, shot in the breast.

Private John Rodgers, Ottawa Foot Guards, shot through the head.

Private Arthur Dobbs, Battleford Rifles, shot through the breast.

Corporal Sleigh, Mounted Police, shot through the mouth.

Corporal Lowry, Mounted Police, shot through the abdomen (died while being taken back in the waggon).

Bugler Burke, Mounted Police, shot through the body (died on Sunday morning).

Teamster Winder, shot through the head.

Private Osgoode, Ottawa Foot Guards, missing, but known to be killed.

THE WOUNDED.

Sergeant Ward, Mounted Police, wounded in the left part of the lower abdomen.

Sergeant Gaffney, wounded in the left fore-arm.

Corporal Morton, B Battery, wounded in the groin.

Private Reynolds, B Battery, compound fracture of the right arm near the shoulder.

Sergt. Winters, Foot Guards, shot in the cheek.

Lieut. Pelletier, B Battery, (attached from 9th Battalion), shot in thigh near hip—flesh wound.

Colour-Sergt. Cooper, Q.O.R.. shot in the hip—flesh wound.

Private Lloyd, Q.O.R., shot in back, bullet coming out of the point of the shoulder.

Private McQuilkin, Foot Guards, shot in the left side, superficial.

Private C. Varey, Q.O.R., shot in the shoulder.

Private Geo. Watts, Q.O.R., flesh wound in the left leg above the knee, slight.

Bugler Gilbert, Battleford Rifles, shot through the scalp at back of the head.

Brigade Sergeant-Major Spackman, flesh wound in the right arm.

Private J. Fraser, Q.O.R., bruised by a spent bullet in the shin.

ANOTHER ACCOUNT OF THE FIGHT.

Half-an-hour after we marched a dense column of smoke arose from the trail several miles in front. This was answered by another column of smoke further on, and showed how close the enemy had been watching every movement. They were signal fires telling of our approach. We camped about sunset on a fine piece of open prairie, and men and horses received a feed—the last, alas! for some of the brave boys who marched out with us. We waited for the moon to rise, and as soon as it was up the column was again in motion. We travelled all night, passing over some very rough ground, the cavalry and scouts beating every bush for half-a-mile on each side of the trail. At last the grey streaks of dawn appeared on the eastern horizon, and shortly afterwards the now deserted houses on the reserve. Directly in front were hills in which, if the reports of the scouts were to be relied on, were the Indians.

But all was quiet, bright and beautiful. The wild fowl, frightened from their quiet morning nap, flew screeching across the prairie towards some quieter resting place. There was not the first sign of Indians. As we rounded a small bluff on the trail we came upon their deserted camp. The marks of a couple of hundred tepees could be seen on one side. They appeared to have been hastily deserted, as many of the poles still stood as they had first been placed. We hurried on. The Indians were no doubt ignorant of our approach and did not expect us until the afternoon. To get as close to them as possible without being discovered was our aim. Everyone was anxious for the fray, and Colonel Herchmer, who had charge of the scouts and Mounted Police, pushed on swiftly. We were soon at the foot of the hills, and there right in front of us, and not more than a mile distant, was a herd of the stolen cattle quietly feeding on the hill side. But Cut Knife Creek flowed between steep banks at the foot of these hills. Its sides were in places well wooded, while scrub brush extended in patches in every direction. The scouts and police crossed the creek and then, extending from the centre, moved up Cut Knife Hill, a sloping piece of ground of a few hundred yards in extent. I was with the ammunition waggon, and could see everything going on in front. The guns and baggage waggons pushed on after the cavalry. To cross the creek was a somewhat difficult matter. The sides were steep and sandy, and some of the teams stuck fast. The teamsters, in some cases, insisted on watering their horses, and halted half-way across the stream for that purpose. But they were soon anxious enough to push on when the bullets began singing about their ears, as they did a few minutes later. Colonel Otter, Colonel Herchmer, Captain Sears and Inspector Neale were amongst the first to follow the scouts. The guns, under Major Short, were only a few seconds behind when " ping " came a rifle bullet amongst the scouts from the ambushed foe.

The Indians had, therefore, fired the first shot, and all we had to do was to open on them. The guns dashed forward at a gallop, unlimbered and went into action. A shell was thrown amongst the tepees, followed half-a-minute later by another and another. One could hear the enemy scampering through the bushes on every side. There seems to be little doubt that they did not expect us so soon, otherwise we should never have got as far as we did without a volley. At the first shot the members of the different corps sprang from the waggons. In fact some of C Company and the Queen's Own were out before a shot was discharged. They were crossing the creek on a small log that afforded but a slippery footing to one man at a time. I ran down to this primitive bridge and found about thirty of the Queen's Own waiting to cross. They were crowded together and must have had the enemy on two sides of them. But not a shot was fired. A well-directed volley would have dropped out half of them, but, as I said before, I believe the Indians hardly expected us so soon. They may have been afraid to open, not knowing how many were behind. I left this group, for I saw there was little chance of an opportunity to cross, and jumping on a waggon that was just entering the water reached the opposite shore. There the men were streaming up the hill like bees. Off to the left front and just above the cattle (set as a bait for us) was an Indian circling his horse round and round. This signal was taken up by another further along the hill, and even before the first shot was fired the enemy were streaming out of the tepees. Squaws, old men, and boys, or rather children (for boys of fourteen years fight beside their fathers) started on a run for the rear and herded the cattle together. We could see them later on upon a hill a mile or so behind the scene of action, where they watched every movement.

It takes a great deal longer to tell the story of those first few minutes than to act them. The guns had scarcely got into action when a body of Half-breeds rounded a small hillock in front of the guns, and actually made an attempt to carry them. The police and B Battery, however, had just got into position on the left of the guns, and well it was that they were there and answered the summons of Major Short with so much alacrity. The breeds dashed up with a wild war whoop when Major Short, springing to the front, cried "Who'll follow me?"

and rushed at the advancing enemy. His appeal fell upon willing ears. The men sprang to their feet, fired a volley into the breeds, who turned tail when within twenty yards of the guns and sought cover. Here was an opportunity that was not to be missed.

The men were anxious to follow the retreating enemy, but Short called them back. A few seconds sufficed to get the Gatling at work. Its "growl" as the bullets streamed out reminded one more of the explosion of a huge bunch of fire-crackers than anything else. The bushes were fairly mowed down, and how anything in shape of flesh and blood could have lived through that leaden hail is a mystery. A wail went up from the squaws when they saw what had happened, while off to the right the Indians in the scrub gave utterance to that indescribable cry of theirs which is only given when they are in a tight corner. Leaving the Gatling when the further grinding out of bullets would have been of little use, Major Short took his post at the seven-pounders. Shell after shell was sent shrieking through the air, and shell after shell burst amidst the brush where the Indians were concealed. Splintered branches were scattered round, and the ground was ploughed and furrowed by the iron fragments. The Indians appeared to be dismayed, for their fire slackened for a time, and we were beginning to hope that they were having enough of it, when they resumed the attack. Our musketry fire was at first wild, but the men soon got down to actual work. The Indians succeeded for a time in practising one of their old dodges. A blanket rolled about a stick, or a hat raised upon one would be cautiously lifted above the brush. Our men, mistaking it for a man, would rise and fire, and as they did so they made excellent targets for the Indians, who were not slow to avail themselves of this opportunity to pick off a soldier. But the boys soon saw through the ruse, and after one or two had been struck very few shots were fired at dummies.

To the left and right of the guns was the skirmish line, the men being on the reverse slope of the hill and looking down into the coulees or ravines that separated them from another range of hills beyond. Down by the creek the Battleford rifle company was extended on each side of the hill. Here it was that some of the heaviest fighting of the day took place. The teamsters, with their usual desire not to hurry too much, lagged behind, and some of them were still in the creek when the Indians opened upon them. Their fire, however, was so promptly met by the Battleford boys that they were more cautious, and only single shots were fired until after the teams were all well up the hill and under comparatively good cover. Still the rear was somewhat exposed. A resolute body of men might have given an infinite amount of trouble from the brush along the creek there. But Indians are not the best long-range shots in the world, for beyond the point-blank range of their rifles their firing is all guess-work.

Once more were the Battleford boys called upon to show what they could do. The brush had to be cleared and bravely they did it. "Remember Smart," someone shouted as they rose from their cover, and with a wild cheer dashed into the scrub at the ambushed enemy. A volley was fired to "stir them up a bit," as one of the men remarked, then they pushed on, each man getting the best cover he could find. The Indians did not wait. The Half-breeds who were with them did better. One or two turned to fire, but the boys in civilian clothes were pressing them so closely that they did not have time to draw a bead. Their shots flew over the heads of our men, cutting the branches of the brush or flying as spent bullets into the front of our line. It was hot work while it lasted, but a few minutes sufficed to clear the Indians off from the neighborhood of the crossing.

Ross, the scout whom I have already mentioned, was there. He had a brother's death to avenge and anything with a red skin received no mercy from him. He dealt with them in their own fashion. As he was rushing down the ravine he came upon an Indian who seeing he was discovered feigned death. But Ross's quick eye saw through the disguise. Another man might have passed on and received a shot in the back. But he did nothing of the kind, and as he ran past he drew his revolver and like a flash a bullet sped into the red-skin's brain. Down in the coulee and close to the heaviest part of the scrub they came upon four Indian ponies which their owners had left in their hurry to get away from the "pale faces" whose cheer yet rang in their ears. These they captured, Ross recognizing one of them as belonging to Little Poplar. They mounted and were about to ride back to the lines when a shower of bullets whistled past in uncomfortable proximity to their heads. It is unnecessary to say they dismounted. They did it in a hurry and were by no means particular as to which side they dismounted from either. In their civilian dress they had been mistaken for Indians and had drawn our fire upon them. Ross, who had sensibly discarded the feathers from his hat, dashed out waving his handkerchief. "A flag of truce," shouted some one. "Flag of truce?" a dozen cried; "look out, it's an ambush, fire on them." "Why, it's Ross," said a keener-eyed skirmisher, and a few seconds later the boys were back. To say that Ross expressed himself as slightly displeased at their being mistaken for enemies will hardly convey a correct idea of his words.

Now come with me to another part of the field. There is no danger now. The bullets have found their billets, and not so much as the smell of powder remains to mark this as the one of the worst places on that battle-field. But something does remain. The empty cartridge cases strew the ridges where the fringe of fire from our rifles swept the grass away. And here and there you may see a stain upon the ground—not much of course—you would scarcely notice it even if strolling along, yet it is there all the same. "What did it?" do you ask. Well, that

11

question is easily answered. A bullet found its billet there. Some brave fellow exposed himself for an instant, but that instant was sufficient to allow an Indian to cover him with his sight and touch the trigger. "Was he wounded?" Well, that is a curious question to ask. Do you think an Indian from that ridge there would only wound a man if he got his sights on him? No, he didn't wound him; he killed him. His comrade, who was lying alongside, asked him a question. "What's that?" he replied, raising his head. "What's that you ——?" He never finished it. The bullet struck him in the forehead and passed clean through his head, and Private John Rogers, of the Guards, had answered his last roll-call. He died with his face to the foe, as did every one of the noble fellows who fell on that hill-side.

We have reached the ridge I spoke of. It is on the left flank, or rather on the left rear of the guns that have been so steadily speaking with iron voices to the enemy beyond. Here some hard work was done. The Indians again and again tried to carry that ridge. Had they succeeded they would have got at the horses belonging to the baggage waggons, which were corralled under cover of the ridge. At times the bullets fairly rained across it, and whistled a deadly chorus about the ears of the teamsters. One horse was struck, and went down like a log, only to plunge in the harness, however, and frighten the animals standing around. He was quickly unhooked and dragged out of the way. That ridge beyond was where the Indians made what I would call their greatest "blanket display." Every artifice was adopted by them to draw our fire, and, as I have previously stated, it succeeded for a time. But Ross came down the line and warned the boys personally. Then our turn came. Let a white man understand the situation and he can usually outwit an Indian. It was so in this case. Five of the scouts, who occupied a position on the ridge, put up what they called a "job" on the Indians. Four of the five laid their rifles for the brow of the opposite ridge, and waited. Then the fifth sprang to his feet, only to drop like a flash. But the ruse succeeded. Four dark visages were raised behind as many rifles, with the amiable intention of sending as many bullets through the audacious rifleman. His four companions, however, were just waiting for this. The Indians were scarcely up when they fired upon them. Quick as the Indians were, they were not quick enough to escape the leaden compliments that were sent over. Whether they were killed or not it is impossible to say, but for some minutes afterwards a man did not run much risk by looking over the ridge. This was tried twice to my certain knowledge, and how much oftener of course I cannot say.

And now there were signs of the enemy crawling down towards the creek again and on towards the guns. They had to be dislodged, and somebody had to do it. The work was particularly dangerous, for at the first rush our men would have to expose themselves on the ridge to the full fire of those in ambush. "Was there any difficulty in getting volunteers?" you ask. "Had the men to be ordered to go?" No, nothing of the kind. Ross, who had been through there before, and knew just where to go, shouted, "Come on boys," and with a bound he disappeared over the ridge. He had no need to look behind to see if they were following. The boys were there. The way some of C Company and the Mounted Police "went for" for that brush is deserving of every praise. "How many had fallen by this time?" you ask. I cannot tell. Those who were dead had to lie on the field. It made no difference to the poor fellows themselves. They were then but clods of the valley, and it would have been unjust to risk the lives of others to carry them in. Did the wounded suffer much? Were they allowed to lie where they fell until after the action, when it would be perfectly safe to carry them in?" No, sir! Veterans could not have done better than the ambulance corps of the Queen's Own. Fifteen minutes after the first shot was fired a call of "Ambulance," came from the front,

It did not need to be repeated. Sergeant Ward, of the Mounted Police, who was by the guns, was struck in the abdomen. He was the first on the long list of casualties, and as the cry for men to carry him off rose above the musketry rattle the stretcher-bearers dashed forward. In doing so, one of them got a bullet through his forage cap, and another bullet cut his shoulder-strap in two. They soon had the poor fellow on the stretcher, and bore him safely through to the baggage waggons, where Surgeons Strange and Leslie had established a field hospital. Everything that medical skill could do to alleviate his sufferings was done, and he was soon as comfortable as it was possible to make him. Bags of oats were built up to stop any stray bullets that might come that way.

For the time being, therefore, the wounded were safe. After that the call for stretcher-bearers came every now and then from all points of the field. Up by the guns, down in the scrub of the creek, off to the right, and off to the left, one could see the Red Cross men doubling about, or slowly and carefully carrying a wounded comrade down to the hospital. The surgeons were hard at work while the fight lasted, and so were the stretcher-bearers. There were some wonderful escapes. Remember the men had had no breakfast that morning. They had their last meal about nine o'clock on Friday night, and went into action on an empty stomach. At 9.15 hardtack was passed along the line by a couple of police, but few took advantage of making a breakfast under fire. Their time was too fully occupied in looking after the enemy. By half-past nine the fire had slackened off considerably, and for a time it looked as though the enemy had quietly slipped away. But we were mistaken. Up on the hill, away to the left front, was an Indian who had occupied the same position for hours. He was surrounded by a few companions, and seemed to be acting as commander-in-chief. On several occasions some of our men had tried a long shot at him, but their bullets all dropped short. The fellow seemed to be directing their movements by the aid of a small mirror, with which he flashed the sunlight first on one part of the field and then on another. He could see almost the whole of our position, and made the most of it. The Indians fought desperately. Boys of fourteen years of age were seen in the bush blazing away with "trade" guns, while others used bows and arrows. In fact a great many arrows were fired, and some of our men were slightly wounded by them.

At last it seemed as though the ammunition of the Indians was being exhausted, and Colonel Otter decided on making a rush for the tepees and burning the whole encampment. There were just two courses open to him, namely, either to withdraw his troops or make a grand rush for their camp. But here fate settled the question. The trail of one of the seven-pounders broke as the gun was discharged, rendering it, of course, useless. The other was cracked some time before, and had been strengthened by a piece of two-inch oak, which was bolted on the lower side. But the constant firing had loosened this, and every time the gun was discharged it jumped out of the trunnion holes. In fact it was a race between the gun and the gunners. The former jumped back every time it was discharged, and the latter had to follow it and carry it back to its place again. It would have been folly to attempt to destroy the tepees without the guns, and so Colonel Otter decided on withdrawing. At 11 a. m., therefore, the teamsters received orders to hook their horses in and load their waggons. And now came the question most important of all: How were we to get out of the box? We were surrounded by thick scrub on every hand, and the idea of crossing the creek under a cross-fire from the enemy could not be entertained. Colonel Otter therefore ordered Captain Nash to clear the woods in the rear, and this was beautifully accomplished by his company and some of the police scouts, the ubiquitous Ross being, as usual, a prominent figure wherever there was anything particularly dangerous to be accomplished. They did their work magnificently, cutting across the ridge to the right of the waggons, and going right down into the teeth of the enemy. These they drove down the creek, running them nearly half-a-mile through the coulee. A couple of the Red-skins were killed, and two others were known to have secreted themselves along the edge of the creek, and could not be found. They then returned, crossed the creek, and with the scouts, drove the enemy back from that side also. The high sand bluff on the right of the creek was occupied by some of these Battleford men, while the remainder held possession of the wooded height on the opposite side of the trail, the scouts holding the woods further up the creek.

Then, and not till then, did the waggons receive orders to move. The dead were carried in from every part of the field, and that at considerable personal risk to those engaged in the work. The wounded were made as comfortable as possible in the waggons; every bag of oats taken on, and, covered by the fire of the troops lining the ridges, they began to withdraw. The enemy had not the slightest idea of what was taking place. The men covering what was now the rear had orders to keep up a smart musketry fire, and this they carried out to the letter. Not till the Indians saw our teams drawing out on the other side of the creek did it appear to dawn on them that we were about leaving. I firmly believe that when they saw the first teams in the creek they imagined we were about to execute a flank movement to destroy their tepees. But they soon discovered our object, and began pressing our men savagely. The guns were withdrawn, together with the Gatling, which covered the retreat of the first line. These, in turn, were covered by some of the Queen's Own, under Lieutenant Brock, who had been doing good work down near the creek. At last all were over, and one of the guns dashed up at a gallop to the top of the sandbank. The Indians at once made an attempt to cut off our retreat. They came galloping down on both sides under cover of the bushes, but the gun was not long in getting into action, and a well-directed shell dropped in the very midst of them made them hesitate. Another shell fell near the same place, and the Indians scampered under cover, and we saw no more of them.

In the meantime the waggons had drawn off to the deserted camping ground of the Indians, through which we had passed seven long hours before. Then the line was formed, the men got into the waggons, and the column started on its way back to Battleford. The scouts were the last to leave, but on doing so fired the prairie to prevent the Indians from following us. There was a stiff breeze blowing at the time, and the flames getting into the woods made a huge blaze, and kept the enemy from heading us off in the woods, no matter how well disposed they might have been to lay another little surprise for us. After travelling for an hour or so we camped and fed the horses and men. Then the march was resumed, and about ten o'clock on Saturday night we reached Battleford, having within thirty-one hours marched eighty miles and fought for seven hours on one meal and a "hard-tack."

We did not succeed in destroying the Indian village or carrying off the stolen cattle. Instead of two hundred warriors we met between five and six hundred. There are those who say that Big Bear's band was in the fight. Ross claims that one of the ponies captured by him belonged to Little Poplar, and if so Big Bear must have been there. On the other hand, there are those who say that had Big Bear and his band been on hand we should not have got away; that, in fact, it would have been a repetition of the Custer Massacre, and I think this is too true. But, be this as it may, we certainly had our hands quite full. Shortly after the fight began a huge column of smoke rose above the woods across in the direction of the Saskatchewan, and some thought it was a signal from Big Bear to Poundmaker which meant "Hold out, old man, and I'll be along to help you." If so, he did not get in in time. On our way back there were times when the prairie seemed on fire in every direction. On the flats between the Saskatchewan and Battle Rivers the woods were in a blaze, and as night cast its mantle over forest and prairie the red glare of the fires could be seen for miles on our left between the two rivers. On reaching camp the wounded were the first to be cared for, before anything else was done, and they were made as comfortable as circumstances would admit. Next morning (that is Sunday) they were removed to a marquee tent across the river.

On the way down, Lowry, of the Mounted Police, died in the waggons. He was a son of General Lowry, and had been in the force about two years. He was expecting to get a commission in it when his untimely death put an end to his career. Bugler Burke, of the Police, who was wounded in the stomach, died about ten o'clock on Sunday morning. He leaves a wife and six young children.

Our losses were heavy. The ratio of killed to wounded was far beyond the usual proportion. There are generally three or four wounded for each one killed, but with us our dead numbered eight and the wounded only thirteen. This shows what every one of us knows to be a fact, that the Indians fired with the greatest deliberation, and never threw a shot away if they could possibly avoid it. During the first few minutes of the engagement our men fired somewhat recklessly, as I have said before, and several were wounded by unnecessarily exposing themselves. But they very soon discovered their mistake, and after that the practice was better.

Altogether the battle at Cut Knife Creek can hardly be regarded as other than disastrous to the loyal cause. The attack was ill-judged and wholly unnecessary. Battleford was safe and Poundmaker was staying quietly on his reserve. There was no evidence that Poundmaker and his band had up to this time committed or even contemplated any acts of violence, but when he was attacked on his own reserve and his lodges containing his women

BATTLE OF CUT KNIFE CREEK. 185

and children shelled, no one could wonder at his taking up arms to defend them, and it must be admitted that when he and his people were forced to fight they fought gamely from first to last. That Colonel Otter and his column owe their escape from Cut Knife to Poundmaker's forbearance there is now no room to doubt, but Poundmaker and his version of the fight at Cut Knife Creek will form the subject of another chapter.

CAPT. E. T. BROWN,
Of Boulton's Scouts, killed at Batoche.
See page 236.

POUNDMAKER.

CHAPTER XVIII.

POUNDMAKER.

A GENTLEMAN who spent some two years in the North-West, and who knew Poundmaker intimately, furnishes the following sketch of the great Cree warrior and statesman :—

When I learned in the winter of 1883-4 that Poundmaker was making trouble at Battleford I was greatly surprised, for at that time it looked as though the great Cree Chief had been actuated by something like personal animosity, and knowing him as I did I thought it impossible that he could be so much moved by such a motive. When I learned of his connection with the present lamentable outbreak in the North-West I was not at all surprised, for I knew him to be a patriotic lover of his own race and people, ready at any time to lay down his life in their service. Though the effort was a mad one that could only end in disaster to those concerned in it, I can readily understand how Poundmaker may have been drawn into it. Though a man of much more than ordinary intellectual force and keenness of perception, even to prescience, it must be remembered that Poundmaker has had no opportunities for learning what is going on in the busy world south of the Milk River Ridge, east of the South Saskatchewan, and west of the Rocky Mountains. Concerning it his ideas are very hazy. Like others of his race he has a good opinion of human nature generally, and is especially adverse to lying in all its forms. If it be true that Riel told the Indians that he expected plenty of help from the Fenians and American Half-breeds in carrying his rebellion to a successful issue, Poundmaker would be just the man to believe it. Weary with waiting for Mr. Dewdney, as the representative of Canadian authority, to carry out the extravagant promises he has been making to the North Crees, Poundmaker was brought to the conclusion that these promises never would be fulfilled, and that the Government were quite prepared to see the Indians perish from the torments of cold and starvation. Believing this, it was easy for a brave and resolute leader to decide that it was better to die fighting than to starve like a coward, and see his race supplanted by a people whom no promise bound and whom no moral obligation affected in the smallest degree.

When Lord Lorne and his party were travelling from Battleford to Calgary, in September, 1881, the train which left Battleford was decidedly a large and imposing one. A long stage of the journey was before us and a formidable supply of stores for the men and forage for the horses had to be carried. This necessitated an unusually large number of horses, and the presence of each additional horse rendered necessary the carrying of more grain, so that altogether the train was an enormously large one when the number of actual passengers it carried is taken into account. There were many Indians and Half-breeds accompanying us, and it took me some days to learn the names and occupations of the more important of these. I know that the guide was Johnny Saskatchewan, a swarthy, square-shouldered, medium-sized man, wearing a heavy black beard, and looking very much like a French Half-breed, but who did not speak French, and who used to stoutly aver that there was not a drop of French blood in his veins.

We had not been long upon the route to Calgary when the belief became very general that Johnny Saskatchewan had too big a contract on his hands. The train was a big one, and he tried to make as much use of the firewood to be reached *en route* as possible. For a considerable portion of the way there was no trail, and in thus turning aside (for wood and water) from the general direction he wished to take, Johnny Saskatchewan was evidently becoming somewhat confused. Many a time could we see him rein in his blacky-brown " cayuse " on the crest of a great yellow ridge a mile ahead of us, and standing there in sharp relief against the hazy blue of the horizon, horse and rider looked like an equestrian statue of bronze. Whenever Johnny Saskatchewan would thus draw rein a tall, slender figure in a close-fitting black frock coat, and mounted on a slender-looking roan cayuse of something of the same pattern as his rider, would soon hurry out of the train to him. The tall, slender rider of the leggy roan pony would talk and gesticulate with the broad-shouldered guide who rode the brown pony, and at length Johnny would resume his journey, while his prompter would drop back into the train. I soon learned that this tall horseman who was thus "guiding the guide" was no other than the great Cree chief, Poundmaker, and that he was taken with us for the purpose of translating Blackfoot into Cree, which was in turn to be translated from Cree into English by our Cree Half-breed interpreter. I had heard of him as a prominent figure among the North Crees, and indeed among all the Crees, but further than this I knew nothing of the man. I soon found that in our night camps his tent was usually pitched in the same locality as my own, and I was not long in making his acquaintance through Peter Countois, my own guide and interpreter. I was not long in learning that, though singularly solemn and dignified in his manner, Poundmaker was very communicative in all matters pertaining to his own people. Knowing in a general way that my business was that of writing for the public, he appeared to think that much was to be gained by having the characteristics of the Indians in general, and those of the Crees in particular, discussed in my letters.

He told stories of his people, of their traditional loyalty to the British flag; their gentleness to the poor, the suffering, and the unprotected; and their love of the pursuits of peace as opposed to those of war and pillage. Like Piapot and other Cree chiefs, Poundmaker was very proud to say that the Crees had never shed the blood of the white man. He was never given to boasting or "counting coo," and always spoke of war and of the old feuds between the Crees and Blackfeet with a perceptible aversion, as though their recollections made him shudder.

Though Poundmaker's views regarding his own race and people were warped by superstition and Cree or Blackfoot legends and romances, they were surprisingly well balanced, and betrayed a breadth of intellectual grasp that seemed to me incredible as coming from a pagan Indian with no pretensions to intellectual culture of any kind save mental introspection. He always appeared to me to be more anxious to shine as a statesman than as a warrior; but though he never spoke boastfully of his own exploits, I could easily gather, from little facts that cropped up as if by accident in the narration of events in his own career, that he was a man who in the fray must have been absolutely indifferent to personal danger. In speaking of fighting he never appeared to recognize the element of personal danger. Death in battle appeared to him to be a matter of course, a danger always present, but, though ever imminent, never to be considered or regarded.

But talking of wars and bloodshed was not what Poundmaker liked best. He would refer to these as things of the past which he earnestly hoped would never be revived. He was proud of having made peace between the Crees and Blackfeet, prouder of that than of the many incursions he had made into the Blackfoot country, killing their people and taking away their horses. In the latter, though he might have brought glory and wealth to his own people, he still brought misery and want to another people of his own race. Indians should all be as brothers, brothers with those of their own race, and brothers with their friends the white men. War must bring misery and sorrow to some, while peace and industry must bring happiness and enjoyment to all. He would show a sort of contempt for what he would term military greatness. Men who could fight the Blackfeet best in the old times were not all of them "any good" except when at war. "They took no care of their families; they saved nothing, and did not care to work or do anything except fight and steal horses." For such men Poundmaker entertained the greatest contempt. They would never help the Crees to become a wealthy and prosperous people like the white men. Turning to another and to him a much more agreeable subject Poundmaker would ramble on in a soft, low voice, speaking very deliberately and often with closed or half-closed eyes, and pausing at regular intervals, often in the middle of a sentence, to allow the interpreter to translate what he said.

I can almost see him now, while I write, as he used to lie close beside a little handful of glowing embers that could hardly be called a fire, but which was all we cared to indulge in on the great treeless stretches where we hauled our fuel from thirty to fifty miles and flanked our tiny fires with dry buffalo chips. The picture was one not easy to forget. The camp all quiet, the snowy cones of the bell tents bathed in bright moonlight, the yellow prairie grass sparkling with hoar frost, and our little group gathered about the fire listening to the mellow voice of Poundmaker as he lay stretched along the grass, his black blanket wrapped around him below the shoulders, his right elbow resting on the ground and his right hand propping up his head, his fine, classically cut face turned partially toward the sky and thrown a little back from his breast, across which one of his two long shining braids of hair hung like a great black rope, and trailed upon the grass. In that mellow musical voice he would tell us how, after wasting years of his boyhood and youth in raiding the Blackfoot country, killing their people and stealing their ponies, it was proposed that the Crees should make a treaty with their brothers, the white men. He saw that peace was good, and he saw, too, that his people could not well adopt the pursuits of peace, as a treaty with the whites implied, and at the same time carry on a successful warfare against the Blackfeet. He did not wish to see his own people turning to farming, when the Blackfeet might attack them and destroy their homes. He thought that a "whole peace" would be good for the Crees and good for the Blackfeet, and he thought it best that they should make peace between themselves, and then all make a treaty with the Government. To accomplish this end Poundmaker set himself at work, and though he passed through perils in the Blackfeet camp while on this peaceful mission, the thoughts of which (to use his own expression), "still made his body shrink," he never faltered in his purpose till the work had been completed.

On this portion of his career Poundmaker used to delight to dwell, but some of the legends of his own people, especially those having a pretty or sympathetic turn, were favourite themes with him. One day we passed an alkali lake with a small island in the centre. That night he told us that it was Child's Lake that we had passed, and that it received its name many years ago. A good chief had been killed in battle with the Blackfeet, and all his family slaughtered except three little children. A good spirit in the form of a great black dog saved the children, and took refuge with them on this little island. They were beyond the reach of their enemies there, and beyond all harm, danger, and death. They never grew old, but remained the same for all time. To this day they were sometimes seen playing together on this island, and the children never grew any larger for their little faces could just be seen peeping over the big dog's back as he stood in front of them to protect them from danger. Child's Lake is between Battleford and Sounding Lake.

Lord Lorne would at times have Poundmaker in his mess tent after dinner and listen for hours to his Cree legends as well as to his story of how he made peace between the Crees and the Blackfeet. When he had concluded the latter history, Lord Lorne, having listened with the closest attention, and with evident interest from beginning to end, spoke in the kindliest and most encouraging manner to him, telling him that his ambition for the progress of his people in enlightenment and material prosperity was one well worthy of a great chief, and that he hoped he would continue to be in the future as he had been in the past, a peacemaker.

Knowing Poundmaker as I do, I shall watch with considerable interest the development of the story of his connection with the rising in the Battleford district. I shall be particularly anxious to know to what extent he acted on the offensive before his reserve was invaded.

The reader is not yet done with Poundmaker, but it will be preferable to let the events related in this history bring his true character to light in their own time than to make unsupported assertions concerning it just now. We may here state, however, that the story of the Battle of Cut Knife Creek is but half-told. We have heard Colonel Otter's side of the story, but at a later period Poundmaker will have an opportunity of giving his version of the affair. It may be added here, however, that while the first telegraphic reports estimated Poundmaker's force at six hundred and his loss at from sixty to one hundred and twenty-five, the facts were that his force was little if any over two hundred and fifty and his loss was six or seven killed and about as many wounded.

CHAPTER XIX.

THE BATTLE OF BATOCHE'S FERRY.

WE now come to the decisive battle of the rebellion, the engagement which crushed the last hope of the Half-breeds and sent out their leaders Dumont and Riel as hunted fugitives and outcasts.

The events which took place on the South Saskatchewan between the Battles of Fish Creek and Batoche can be briefly summed up. The wounded remained to be cared for and put in a place of safety before the column could move on down the river, but besides this there were other causes why General Middleton could not move on. The steamer *Northcote*, with the Midlanders, with supplies and with the invaluable Gatling, made very slow progress. The journey was a long one, the boat was heavily laden and the water was low. Day after day the boys remained in the neighbourhood of Fish Creek, where, as they afterwards learned, a mere handful of one hundred and twenty-five badly armed rebels had wrought such havoc upon a vastly more numerous force fully supplied with small arms and ammunition, as well as a fair complement of artillery.

During this tedious delay General Middleton gave all sorts of excuses for his inaction. One day it was want of supplies, then he had not a sufficient medical staff to take with him after leaving a suitable force to look after the wounded. Then the excuse was that the wounded could neither be left where they were nor removed up the river to Saskatoon. The truth was that he was afraid to advance on the rebels' position at Batoche until he had been materially re-inforced. He had received a lesson at Fish Creek with regard to the fighting capacity of the Half-breeds, which he was not disposed to disregard. He might talk as he pleased, but there was no possible chance of his risking another reverse such as he had experienced on the 24th of April. He would have the Midland Battalion and the Gatling gun before again attacking the rebels.

Again and again reports were sent out that General Middleton would certainly move at once, but the canny old soldier had no notion of bringing on another fight until he had overwhelming odds on his side.

And it is not quite fair to accuse him of cowardice because he adopted this course. He had a superior force available and would have been to blame had he not used it. What he was blamed for, however, was for not exercising more nerve at Fish Creek, many thinking that prompt and resolute action on his part at the critical moment on that fatal day would have turned the tide and won the day for the loyal troops. Had that battle been won and the rebels routed there would have been no battle at Batoche's Ferry.

On the 5th of May, the *Northcote* arrived at Clark's Crossing, and on the 7th (two days later) General Middleton moved out of his camp at Fish Creek.

In the meantime the commander had conceived the rather ludicrous idea of converting the *Northcote* into a gunboat. She was furnished with clumsy barricades, which were to serve as bulwarks, and, as she had no cannon to contend against, the task of rendering these barricades bullet-proof was not a difficult one. The utter folly of equipping and arming her in the manner described, was seen when she passed down the river and began the fight of May 9. Those on board of her not only failed to accomplish anything, but after barely escaping being caught by the ferry rope and held till

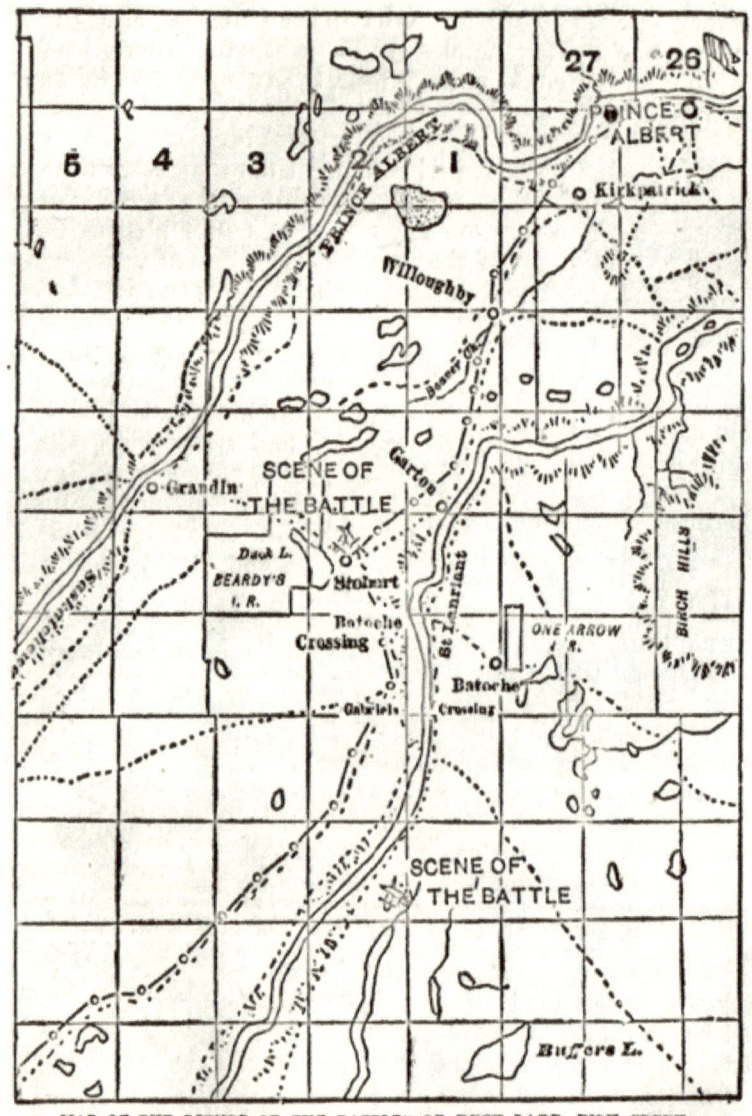

MAP OF THE SCENES OF THE BATTLES OF DUCK LAKE, FISH CREEK, AND BATOCHE.

every one on board could have been massacred or captured, she drifted helplessly down stream where those aboard of her could not even see, to say nothing of taking part in, the battle.

The battle at Batoche's Ferry was scattered over so much ground and covered so much time that it would be extremely difficult to present anything like a complete picture as from one point of view. A better plan will be to give the story of the fight in the words of those who witnessed it. The following is the story of the first day's fighting :—

On leaving the Fish Creek camp on Thursday afternoon we followed the river up to Gabriel Dumont's crossing, which we reached at 6 p.m., camping for the night. Our scouts under Lord Melgund had repeatedly penetrated to Gabriel's, and knew that the woods were clear. Early on Friday morning Dumont's house (on the line between Sections 17 and 20, Township 42, Range 1, west of the third meridian) was visited and found deserted. The troops took out a billiard table and a washing machine and put them on board the *Northcote*, and then fired the house. The scouts then went on to the houses of Vaudal and Poitras on Section 29, right by the river, and fired them. They also attempted to get to Maxime Debois' house, Section 32, but this was unknown ground and they were recalled. Meanwhile the *Northcote*, fitted up as a gunboat, patrolled the river, keeping a sharp lookout on the west bank, where a few rebels had been seen on Thursday. On Friday afternoon the entire force marched from the camp at Gabriel's, following an old road running almost due east. The scouts had reported this route to be safe. It took us out of the dense underbrush fringing the river. It was slow marching. The path was narrow and broken, and on each side lay clumps of poplar and willow, with here and there a swamp. The road brought us to the old trail to Pritchard's Crossing an'. Prince Albert, which further north skirts the base of the Birch Hills. After turning north on this trail for two miles, we camped for the night near one of the numerous alkaline ponds, and not far from the cross-trail leading into the Carrot River settlement. We were then eight miles east and a little south of Batoche's.

The *Northcote*, under Captain Sheets, had been ordered to move slowly down the river. Our plan was to move on Batoche's from the east, while the boat took care of the river to the south of the settlement. The rebel pits began three hundred yards to the east of the church and ran in zig-zag form east and north. There were thirty or forty rows of them, one row partly covering the other and extending in a huge irregular three-quarter circle, embracing in all probably five sections of land, or three thousand two hundred acres, and running at least two miles north-east of Batoche's. The pits, placed from ten to fifty yards from one another, were five feet long, two and a-half feet wide and eighteen inches deep, with a breastwork of earth, rock and boughs a foot high at each end. A man could scoop out one of them in a few minutes. There were from five to twenty-five pits in a row, according to the nature of the ground. Retreat or advance from one row to another was readily accomplished through the scrub and along the rivulet bottoms. The rebels had also prepared excellent cover in the innumerable small bluffs by throwing up breastworks of rock and poplar trees. A number of bluffs and ravines, lying far out, protected the main circle of pits, which was also well guarded in the rear.

One week's sojourn at Fish Creek had enabled General Middleton to procure a great deal of information regarding the lie of the land ; and it was a lucky thing, for the whole district was full of pits and ambuscades. Dumont had turned it into a perfect rabbit-warren.

Friday night was fine but cold. Double pickets were posted, and the scouts were on the alert on every side. The men knew what was before them and few of them slept. We lay formed in a zareba. A Battery and the Gatling men under Lieutenant Howard (of the State

National Guard of Connecticut, and agent for the Gatling factory there), were at their posts all night long. General Middleton issued a general order at 8 p.m., instructing the troops to be on parade at 4 a.m., to breakfast at 4.15, and to be ready to march at 5 sharp, each man carrying 100 rounds of ammunition. The baggage and the armed teamsters were to remain in the zareba camp, and also the few invalided and used-up men, most of them suffering from rheumatism, which of late had played the mischief with our entire force.

At 4 a.m. in this northern latitude there is a good dawn. The men fell in sharp on time, the parade being conducted with as little noise as possible. The rebel scouts had kept track of us, however, from the time we left Fish Creek; and had even fired at our men as we were leaving Dumont's.

At 5.30 we started, going two miles north and east, and then striking the old trail that runs to Batoche's, the junction of the two roads being about nine miles from the settlement. Captain Secretan, of the Transport Corps, was left in charge of the camp, which, as I have said, was left standing. Our march due west was made in the following order:—

Boulton's Scouts	75
Gatling (Captain Howard)	4
Royal Grenadiers	262
90th Battalion	275
Midland Battalion	116
A Battery (two guns)	95
Winnipeg Field Battery (2 guns)	60
French's Scouts (on flanks)	30
Hospital and ammunition waggons.	
Total	917

Nos. 1 and 2 Companies of the Royal Grenadiers headed that regiment. The country on the east side of Batoche's is broken and full of clumps, and

THE BATTLE OF BATOCHE'S FERRY. 199

great caution was exercised. When about four miles from Batoche's, at 7 a.m., we heard the *Northcote* whistling a signal that had been agreed upon, and we at once answered her with a blank shot from a nine-pounder. Batoche's lies on both sides of the river, and the main village is in a basin-shaped depression, with stores on the east side of the river. When about a mile from the east bank, we came in view of the outskirts of the settlement, and the Gatling fired at the first house, but there was nobody there. It was a bright, clear morning, and we could watch operations quite distinctly at first; but later in the day dense clouds of smoke hung over the whole basin. Our scouts now fell back, and A Battery, pushing on ahead, sent a shell through the second house. Some rebels immediately ran out of a ravine behind the house into the bush. The two houses took fire and were soon in ashes. Three hundred yards further on stands the Church of St. Antoine de Padua. A small school house stands near the church, both buildings being about two hundred yards from the high bank of the river. In the rear is a thick wood of poplar, hazel and willow, through which a deep ravine runs. The river makes a long sweep westward and then eastward, leaving Batoche's in a broad peninsula. We moved slowly on, and soon heard heavy firing along the river, the report of the big gun on the *Northcote* being easily distinguishable. The Gatling advanced to within a hundred yards of the school house and church, when a priest opened the door of the latter and waved a handkerchief. General Middleton at once rode up and found five priests and six men who had taken shelter there. They were taken care of, and were extremely thankful for their rescue. The Half-breeds had threatened to kill them all, and would have done so without doubt had not Garnot, one of the rebel leaders, insisted that the church should not be desecrated by murder. No sooner had the priests been saved than the Gatling let fly at the school house from our high elevation, but there was no response. A

Battery now came up, and began shelling the houses on both sides of the river. A dozen women and children were seen rushing out, and our men ceased firing for an instant, General Middleton having given strict injunctions to the force to spare non-combatants as far as possible.

While we were watching these people run off, the rebels suddenly rose from the ravine right in front of us, and opened fire. The guns were ordered to the rear, and the Gatling, which Howard had been working so well, rained down a fusilade, but our position was too high, and the bullets flew over the ravine, and did no harm. This was a ticklish moment, and our men were thrown into some disorder. Howard, however, worked like a Trojan in the thick of it, and kept the rebels from charging us. We should have lost many lives, and probably our guns, but for the Gatling. Meanwhile the first two companies of the Grenadiers advanced to the edge of the wood in rear of the school house, and a little to the right of the spot where we first felt the rebel fire. The rebels detected the movement, and desperate efforts were made to turn our left flank by their men in the bush under the high river bank and on the slope, who fired with great vigour; but they had nothing but shot guns, and their fire fell short. Some rebels with rifles on the other side of the river also took a hand in, but the Gatling silenced them.

It was now 9.45 o'clock. The sharpshooters of the 90th, armed with Martini-Henry rifles, and the dismounted men of A Battery were here brought up and ordered to lie down and fire over the crest of the rising ground into the ravine and the bush on the river. The main body of the 90th was deployed to protect our right centre, which was threatened by another row of rebel riflemen in a ravine, and to support our left centre and left. The heaviest firing was now being done at these points. The Gatling, having done excellent work on the left of the first ravine, was forthwith brought to the rear of the left centre, and was just opening out, when the underbrush in another ravine behind us took fire and spread fiercely. For a time we were surrounded by fires from the sloughs, the smoke of which rolled along the ground like a dense fog. It was a tight place, but the troops never for a moment flinched. They simply looked to their officers, who in turn patiently waited for orders from the chief.

At 11.30 a.m. the order came. It was for the force to move back a little. Our wounded had been placed in the church, but as it was well within the rebel range and the bush fire seemed likely to reach it, they were taken out and carried to the rear near the ammunition waggons. By the time this had been done the rebels had opened at our left flank, and also in rear of our right flank, all the time maintaining their steady fusilade upon our centre and left centre. Here it was thought by some officers that we were about to be surrounded, and they certainly swarmed on all sides, shouting and cheering, as though they thought they had us in a trap. The Winnipeg Battery however, succeeded in planting four shells right in front among their pits, and this kept them off. Evidently, from their experience at Fish Creek, the rebels were well aware when shell was fired. They detected either the report or more probably the word of command, and ensconced themselves in their pits, lying flat on their faces, until the shell burst and the danger was past.

At 1 p.m. we caught sight of a small body of rebels gliding up a ravine on our left, and it was supposed they were moving away. Five minutes later they popped up their heads within one hundred yards of our men and fired a volley with Winchesters. Gunner Phillips of A Battery was killed, and two of the same corps wounded, and the battery with the scouts was compelled to fall back. The fire now slackened until 2 p.m., when half the Midland Battalion was sent up to the ravine last mentioned, with a stretcher in charge of Dr. Codd, of Winnipeg, to get out Phillips' body. They were met with a hot fire, but the Winchester men on the rebel side had gone away to another part of the field, and the rest had only shot guns. The body was secured, none of the Midland men being injured on the trip.

Four scouts were sent back at this time (3 p.m.) to order up some tents and waggons. The firing almost ceased for a time now, and our men lay down while the scouts reconnoitred. At six o'clock the rebels began again, and at 7 p.m. the firing was going on, but it was at long range and no damage was being done.

It was painfully evident that we had not men enough. Owing to their position, one rebel was as good as ten volunteers, just as it was at Fish Creek. The firing on our part had to be done at the puffs of smoke from their guns, or at the spots where we supposed the enemy to be. The terribly broken ground rendered it difficult for the big guns to get into action, and when they did open they could do little with an enemy lying in pits and protected by trees and a heavy underbrush. General Middleton said the men had done remarkably well that day all things considered. Captain Howard was loudly cheered that evening. His Gatling saved us from serious disaster. At 5 p.m. our scouts captured Wm. Brush, a breed, who was hovering near our rear. He said he escaped from Riel three days before. He placed the rebel force at four hundred men, half of whom were Indians. Two hundred of them were on this side and two hundred on the other side of the river. The priests confirmed this. They said the *Northcote* ran down the river that morning under a heavy fire. At 8.30 a.m. our men saw that her smokestack had been knocked down. Bullets had probably smashed the wire bracing. We saw no more of her but about noon she was heard whistling, and then appeared to be going down the stream in the direction of Prince Albert. At 6 o'clock she began whistling as though from up the stream.

Such is the account of the first day's fighting at Batoche, written the same night and in the hurry and excitement of a camp, not only under a dropping fire at long range, but in momentary expectation of an attack from an exultant foe. The following more detailed account, written under more favourable circumstances, will be found interesting and valuable:

It is needless to say the result of Saturday's fight has not been satisfactory to either side, and that the enemy find themselves under fire in their last stronghold is about the greatest satisfaction we can get out of the situation. The day commenced at four o'clock, and by six we were *en route;* the teamsters, under Transport Officer Secretan, being left to guard the camp, every tent standing and all the baggage except haversacks behind. The road was miry in many places, and several ammunition waggons sticking fast delayed rapid advance. When within four miles of Batoche and within site of the opposite bank of the river, the whistle of the *Northcote* was heard, and one of the Winnipeg guns fired a blank cartridge as an answering signal. There seems little doubt that this was a mistake and some other means of communication should have been adopted. The report gave notice to the enemy of our approach, and so far as we know was regarded as an order to advance by the boat. Two miles further on, after passing a Half-breed cemetery, we reached the first evidences of a regular settlement, though isolated houses and Cree cabins (our daily trail lay through one Assoris reserve) were always in sight. All the houses and barns along the road but one were burned as our infantry reached them.

At eight o'clock one of the A (Quebec) Battery guns fired a shell through the upper storey of a house on the right of the road and several rebels hurriedly skedaddled. Very little further on, the Boulton Infantry with Howard and his Gatling being in advance, we came in full view of the much-talked-of Church of Antoine de Padua, a weather-boarded, unpainted structure sixty by thirty or thereabouts, with a two and a-half storey school house similar in materials, fifty feet distant and toward the river. Between the school-house and the church was a camp of Indians, and the scouts retiring,

Howard opened with his Gatling, scattering the enemy, who ran rearward, leaving their breakfasts on the fire. Thirty shots were fired high in the school house, in which were several Half-breed women and children. These waved a flag of truce. A quarter of an hour passed in parley with the priests, from whom it was learned that the enemy numbered about two-hundred Halfbreeds and as many Indians, equally divided by the river; they were absolutely without flour, sugar, and tea, (the latter almost a necessity to them) short of ammunition, especially lead, and many of them dissatisfied with Riel. From the priests we learned that at 8.30 the boat sailed past Batoche's Ferry, the smoke-stack down; and while the talk progressed we heard her whistle from below the Ferry, seemingly a couple of miles away by water. The stream makes a semi-circular curve and thus leaving Batoche's and the church, in a rounded promontory in rear of the opposite landing, at which the ferry scow was moored, was a group of tepees, some of them brilliantly painted. At these and one or two houses beyond, A Battery first fired and then we saw the enemy. They scurried over the hills north-eastward and southward in great haste, women and children being in the majority. Several shells were next fired at the houses beyond Batoche's dwelling, and we were all standing watching the effect as if the enemy had retreated. In moving one of the guns after it was shotted the shell was jammed and several times missed fire. As if the snap of the primer had been a signal, fiendish whoops came from the ravine beneath our feet; the rush of men through the scrub below was heard, and a shower of bullets rushed over our heads. The heavy guns were ordered to retire instanter, and one of them catching in a tree, was held fast for a few minutes. A semi-panic seized most of the onlookers, and they ran backward into a coulee behind. How we all escaped from death or wounds at the first fire no one can tell. But that we all got out eventually all right is due to Captain Howard (the American officer) and his Gatling. Instead of retiring, he advanced and poured in a withering fire. One of the gunners was shot through both legs, but Howard never flinched. He was a target for concealed marksmen, but he turned the crank as coolly as if giving an exhibition. While the artillery had been playing from the crest, A and B Companies of Grenadiers, the advance of the column, had come beyond the church, moving in from the right. When the attack was made from the ravine they were advanced rapidly into the brush and, extended as skirmishers, took position within one hundred and fifty yards of the rifle pits. The sharpshooters of the 90th, armed with Martini-Henrys, were sent forward to the crest to support the Gatling, two companies of the 90th to the left flank and along the river bank, the dismounted detachment of A Battery and French's scouts being sent down the small ravine into which we retreated from the crest. The rest of the Grenadiers formed the centre. The Midlands were in reserve near the church, near which the General and staff took a position, while the remaining companies of the 90th, aided by the Winnipeg Field Battery and dismounted detachments, were deployed on the right centre, right, and right flank. Before very long the enemy came around from the mouth of the main ravine and attacked A Battery and the scouts. Both sides fought persistently, and here Phillips lost his life and Cook was wounded. The scouts being farther down were in a bad place, but Howard discerning it moved his gun farther along the crest and diverted the enemy until the scouts and batterymen got into better position. The rebels had a great deal more ammunition than they were credited with. For hours the falling shots kept up, and about noon the enemy had crawled around, and were trying to turn our left. This they did not succeed in doing, troops being sent to a small cemetery which was on a point of the bluff on our left flank. On the right centre the enemy kept an individual fire, and about one o'clock got on our right flank. Boulton's scouts and the Winnipeg artilleries held them off; but as by this time we could hear the enemy on almost all sides, the fear of a surround grew into prominence in many hearts. We had not heard anything from the steamer for hours, but between one and two her whistle sounded several miles further down stream. That the enemy had not deserted her vicinity was shown by several volleys which followed the sound of the whistle. Again the Indians resorted to their old tactics and fired the brush and grass in front of our right, trusting to the wind to blow the flames into our centre and left. For a time it looked as if the plan would prove successful and the outlying skirmishers had a smoky time of it. The church had been turned into a hospital; but as it was exposed to fire from the enemy and from the burning brush, the wounded were hurriedly made comfortable in waggons, and moved to a place of comparative safety in the rear. About two o'clock one company of the Midlands under Col. Williams was sent into the smaller ravine and down the bluff. to get the body of Phillips. When first wounded he was able to speak, and it was hoped he might be rescued alive. Dr. Alfred Codd, of Winnipeg, gallantly offered to accompany the troops and did so. They got Phillips amid a terrific fire—terrific in continuancy, but fortunately too high. The Gatling again served to distract the enemy. The poor fellow had been first shot (and not mortally) through the shoulder, but when he tried to move it is supposed the enemy made him a target. He was shot through the head. At the same time Phillips was first shot the scouts were having it hot and heavy, and when about to retreat Cook was hit. He called out, " Captain French, my leg is broken. For God's sake, don't leave me here." Under a rattling rain of balls, French stooped, put Cook on his back, and staggered through the brush and up the hill to safety amid the applause of comrades. The act was worth a V. C. Toward three o'clock the fire slackened somewhat, though a head shown by either party was a target for a score of bullets. About this time General Middleton concluded to retire to our present position, which is between five and six hundred yards distant from the church, and immediately sent Boulton's mounted men back to the camp to bring up the transport. He and Melgund had a hurried consultation and the latter started, as we supposed, for the old camp, but really for Ottawa *via* Humboldt. By 6.30 all the troops, except those actually engaged, were in and about the ground, and an advance scout from Boulton reported the transport safe and *en route* on the trot. Hurried breastworks with earth and poplar trees were thrown up on our rear (then thought to be the most exposed portion) and as soon as this was done fires were lighted, and the preparation of supper—such sort as could be hurriedly prepared—started. The Gatling opened to cover the retreat of our advance lines toward camp. Rapidly the transport was driven into a zareba shape, except that the lines formed were double, and the rear was open. The Gatling kept firing quickly (about 3,000 rounds were used during the day), and volleys from both sides turned our attention to the church from which our advanced lines were retreating, covering and being covered by the American gun. Here, as elsewhere, the wonder is that our loss was not heavy. The only reasonable explanations are poor ammunition, poor and hurried marksmanship, greater caution on the part of our forces, and a kind Providence. At last the men withdrew, tired, hungry and angry that the day's work had not proved more successful, and hopeful of at least a short rest. They were doomed to disappointment; the cartridge boxes had scarcely been laid down when they had to be refilled and donned. The rebels, well aware of our retirement, took advantage of their safe route under the brow of the cliff, and rising over the brow fired into the zareba. The 90th and the Grenadiers were sent outside on the run and gallantly repelled the attack, but not before Moor had been killed (he was in the zareba at the time) and five men wounded.

Night came at length, but tired as we were it was scarcely welcome. We were cooped up, and had the extreme satisfaction of furnishing a good mark for potshooters. In the corral were more than six hundred mules and horses, and eighty cattle. Men were busy throwing up hasty entrenchments; teamsters, nervous and frightened, were yelling at equally nervous animals; around the hospital tents the doctors were busy in dressing wounds, probing for bullets, etc. The bullets were whizzing and pinging overhead, and occasionally striking inside. Pleasant prospect for the night, especially when one remembered that a favourite trick among the reds is to stampede the cattle and horses of the enemy. Hoofs would be apt to deal worse wounds than balls, and against affrighted animals, cooped up within a small space, we had absolutely no defence. The anticipations of a mean night were largely realized, though thus far we have escaped a stampede. Few, if any, slept five hours consecutively, and the firing was kept up almost all night. At daylight on Sunday morning our lines were again advanced beyond the night's position, and the scattered shooting recommenced. We had better luck yesterday, and several dead enemies lay in sight of those who shot them. Martin was wounded early in the morning, but no one else until evening. By 9 a.m. the usual question was, "What are we to do? Stay here, advance and take Batoche, or retreat to our camp of Friday last?" Of course General Middleton was the only one who could answer these questions, and he wouldn't for some time. He evidently hadn't made up his mind, and was at first in favour of retiring to the camp nine miles away. Afterwards, however, he decided to remain and fortify, remarking: "I can make this place impregnable, and we can keep pegging away at them. I haven't enough men to charge their position." Teamsters and everybody who could wield pick or shovel were put to work, and by evening the fortifications were in excellent shape. A plan was laid by which, when the Grenadiers retired from the front, they were to do so in a seeming hurry and entice the enemy to show over the bank, where they were to afford good targets for the 90th sharpshooters, who were to relieve the Grenadiers. The plan was carried out, except in one important particular. The 90th opened too soon and gave the game away to the enemy, who did not show over the bank, but fired from the position held throughout the day and from numerous points across the river.

The story of the second day's fighting is told in the following, which takes up the history on Sunday morning:—

After the fight at the southern skirt of the rifle pits on Saturday, we camped for the night in a large cleared space two hundred yards west of the Church of St. Antoine. The rebels on the west side of the river, some two hundred strong, fired one or two volleys across, but their bullets fell short. It was a fine night though somewhat chilly. There is twilight now in these northern latitudes until 9 p.m., and dawn breaks at 3.30 a.m. General Middleton issued an order at 8 p.m. thanking the troops for their efforts during the day, and warning them that there was still a great deal of heavy work before them. Double pickets were posted. The artillery and Gatling men stood beside their guns. The troops were firing off and on for several hours. The smoke from the underbrush fires kindled during the afternoon still hung about the place, and rolled down the river. Now and then we could hear the ki-yi-ki-yi-yi of the Indians in front; on towards midnight many shots were fired; and on the whole we passed a very hard night. Captain Secretan, who had been left behind with armed teamsters in charge of our waggons, seven miles to the east on the Hoodoo trail, sent word at midnight that everything was safe there. This was welcome news, for if Dumont had captured our supply train it would have been all up with us. Secretan's mounted messengers were mistaken by the pickets for Mounted Police, and word went through the camp that Colonel Irvine had come in with a force from Prince Albert. But there was no such luck.

The troops stood to arms sharp at 4 o'clock this (Sunday) morning. There was a film of ice on the water-pails, and the men were weary, stiff, and sore from fatigue, want of sleep, and rheumatism. The rebels had been moving about all night, and the moment we began to stir their advance fired a few shots, and gave a loud cheer, apparently by way of a challenge. The troops were quite cool and collected, though the prospect of another prolonged conflict with this wily enemy was by no means a cheering one. General Middleton had let it be understood, however, that most of the work would be left to the artillery; and at the parade the officers cautioned the men against exposing themselves. A hurried breakfast was made of hard-tack, bacon, and tea, and then a brief delay occurred, the General waiting to hear from the scouts who had gone forward to the outskirts of the bush.

It was a Sunday morning which we are not likely to forget. Dr. Orton and his assistants, aided by a fatigue party, had put up a field hospital in the rear, where Saturday's wounded were lying, soon to be joined by many other gallant sufferers. I walked down there at 5 o'clock. A party had just been detailed to bury Gunner Phillips, of A Battery, killed on the previous afternoon. The grave was being dug, but I learn that he was not buried until this evening, the men having been called into action. The doctors, anticipating another ghastly day's work, were busy in their main tent, getting ready lint bandages and making rude camp beds out of all sorts of material. Dr. Orton said the rebels were now using slugs in their shot guns and even duck shot.

Our artillery moved forward at 5.20, and opened on the ravines where the fighting was done yesterday. Two guns were directed against the houses in the basin-shaped depression along the river. A few rebels lay behind three log shanties just below the river bank, and the artillery soon drove them out. The enemy did not attempt to answer our artillery fire except at times, between shots, when they let fly at the artillery men, who were pretty well covered, however, by skirmishers. Nothing was seen of the *Northcote*. At 8 a.m. skirmishers from the Royal Grenadiers and the 90th were sent a little ahead towards the groves of spruce and poplar north of our position. Howard, with the Gatling, accompanied them, and kept up a rattling fusilade for half-an-hour. The rebels did not fire back, but lay low in their rifle pits. Occasionally two or three of them would jump up and fire and then run, apparently with the view of drawing our men after them; but strict orders had been issued against following them. This game of hide-and-seek lasted a long while, no damage being done on either side. We could not, for prudential reasons, attempt to charge the pits; and, for similar reasons, the rebels refrained from running up against our big guns and Gatling.

The rebel shanties along the river were knocked into splinters by 8.30 a.m., and troops were ordered up to make a dash for the principal houses behind the bluffs. But the men had no sooner formed on the slope than the rebels on the west bank of the river popped up, and began firing, many with Winchesters, at long range. Six or seven volunteers were wounded here, and the men were at once ordered back. This was repeated two or three times during the day.

The fighting during the rest of the day does not admit of detailed description. Our artillery would blaze away for an hour, and then the skirmishers would advance, only to fall back as the rebels, who kept well under cover while shells were flying, suddenly rose in rows in their pits. Neither side gained the slightest advantage. Had Colonel Irvine appeared in the rebel rear we should have had them in a trap. It was rumoured early in the day, two couriers from Prince Albert having come in on Saturday night, that he was on the way; but this was not true.

The big gun firing, advancing, and withdrawing grew quite monotonous, especially as the rebels were a long way off, and out of sight; but it was the only safe game to play. Their pits covered an enormous lot of ground, and being placed at every possible angle, one partly covering another, with easy means of access between them, a charge would expose us to an enfilading and cross fire. Besides this, the ground is rough and broken, with sloughs and ravines and dense underbrush. Under such conditions a bayonet charge would be sheer murder for us. If we had mortars, no doubt we could drive them out of the pits, but the nine-pounders simply wreck the trees over head, while the rebel lies snug in his hole.

The rebel position as well as we can make out is this :— Behind their rows of pits which lie to the front of us, to our right, and then away north in a half-moon, trenches ten or twelve feet wide have been dug, which they will use as their "last ditch." These trenches run north-east and then north-west, a breast work being formed on the inside of each gully with fallen timber and underbrush. Should they be driven out of their advance pits, the rebels will, of course, retreat upon the first row, from that to the second, from there to the third, and so on till the trenches are reached. The priests say they are short of ammunition and have only a few cattle. To-day they certainly practised great economy in firing. Our scouts at first thought that the Half-breeds in the Qu'Appelle valley were supplying them from the west side of the river, but this was a mistake. They appear to be entirely cut off from supplies.

At this hour (6 p.m.) our big guns are firing occasional shots, to which no response is being made by the rebels. Practically, we stand just where we did this morning. The houses north of the church have long since been rendered uninhabitable, and it is evidently the General's intention to send the troops quietly along the river, so as to get on the rebel flank, provided this can be accomplished in the face of the rebels on the west bank. Our casualties have not been very serious. How the rebels have fared we do not know.

General Middleton will not renew the fight in the morning unless attacked, his aim being to starve the rebels out.

The troops behaved splendidly. The General says they are fast becoming veterans. Most of the injured to-day were hit with slugs, which cause jagged and painful flesh-wounds.

CAPT. JAMES MASON, ROYAL GRENADIERS.

Lord Melgund has gone to Ottawa on private business. He came here at first as a spectator, and had arranged to start for England with his family this month. He has rendered us invaluable service.

Reinforcements are expected to-morrow night with a quantity of supplies from the Minnow.

Captain Mason's wound is a painful one, but by no means serious. He led his company with great dash. The wounded are doing well.

General Middleton's headquarters to-night are in the church. We have a strong position here and are quite safe in case of attack.

The *Northcote* has not been heard of since yesterday. She had a number of men on board, among them Lieutenant Hugh J. Macdonald, of the 90th (son of the Premier).

On Sunday night about half-past ten the waggons came up and formed a close corral enclosing about twelve acres with waggons on all sides except one about one hundred yards east of the church. No tents were pitched except two for hospital use. The camp was not formed when the enemy attacked in the front and on both flanks. A heavy skirmish line was sent out and repulsed the attack, but not before hundreds of shots fell in the enclosure. Thomas Moor, C Company, Grenadiers, was shot through the head and killed. Private Stead, A Company, Grenadiers, was shot through the arm, both while in the corral. During the retiring of the advance line of skirmishers from the ravine on Saturday night, Privates Scovel, A Company, and Cantwell, B Company, the first in the arm, the second in the thigh and shoulder, were severely wounded. Private T. Kemp, A Company, 90th, severely wounded in the left eye at the same time. On Sunday morning Private Martin, Royal Grenadiers, while on left front was severely wounded in the shoulder. The total casualties to this date were two killed and eleven wounded, but the list would have been much larger if the enemy had had more ammunition.

A correspondent writing from Batoche on May 11 tells his portion of the story thus :—The rebels let us alone last night. A few scattering shots were fired about daybreak. Shortly after seven we began to make a reconnaissance in force. We had been making reconnaissances over and over again since Saturday, advancing and then withdrawing time after time, not much damage being done on either side. General Middleton had half-led us to think that he intended to remain in our strong positions without carrying on aggressive hostilities until the Half-breeds succumbed to lack of supplies. About 10 a.m., however, it became evident that something more than a mere reconnaissance was on foot. The artillery were ordered to fire vigorously, and the A men worked for all they were worth. The Winnipeg Battery, posted on the top of the slope, sent shells into the houses north of the church and across the river, where a few Indians had gathered threateningly. In the forenoon the Grenadiers, 90th and Midland were fighting in a long line, pressing in upon the rebel pits that protected the houses below the church. The rebels replied to our fire with great energy at first, but at 11 a.m., they had almost ceased firing, probably from want of ammunition. General Middleton had worked round on the rebel rear, and at noon our cannonading increased. Some time before this a message had been brought to him under a flag of truce. The rebel chief threatened to murder his white prisoners if the troops fired on the Half-breed women and children. The General replied that the women and children should be placed in one of the houses and that if this were done the troops would save the house. Riel sent back a vague answer, his object evidently being to bring about delay and get the troops to stop firing for a while. At the time he sent the first message the women and children, as we afterwards learned, were safe, some on the other side of the river and some ten miles up north.

The artillery fire grew hotter and hotter up to 2 p.m., when preparations were begun for a charge upon the first row of rifle pits covering the houses. The Gatling (Howard in charge) delivered a raking fire upon the pits, driving the rebels back. The moment their line of sharpshooters began to waver, General Middleton ordered Colonel Van Straubenzie to lead the troops forward, and a rush was made all along the line. The rebels stoutly contested every pit, but ultimately broke and fled north-east into their other pits, where they now are. The buildings north of the church were at once occupied by the troops and the prisoners saved. The men behaved magnificently, getting over the broken ground amid the rain of buckshot, slugs, and bullets in splendid style, cheering as they charged.

The following is an official despatch from General Middleton:

Hon. A. P. Caron, Ottawa:

BATOCHE'S HOUSE, May 11, }
via CLARK'S CROSSING, May 12. }

Have just made a general attack and carried the whole settlement. The men behaved splendidly. The rebels are in full flight. Sorry to say have not got Riel. While I was reconnoitering this morning, William Astley, one of the prisoners, galloped with a flag of truce and handed me a letter from Riel, which read—

"If you massacre our families I shall massacre the prisoners."

I sent answer that if he would put his women and children in one place and let me know where it was, not a shot should be fired on them. I then returned to camp and pushed on my advance parties, who were heavily fired on. I so pressed on until I saw my chance and ordered a general advance. The men responded nobly, splendidly led by their officers and Col. Van Straubenzie; drove the enemy out of rifle-pit after rifle-pit; forced their way across the plain and seized the horses; and we are now masters of the place, and most of my force will bivouac there. Right in the heat of the action Mr. Astley came back with another missive from Riel, as follows:

"GENERAL,—Your prompt answer to my note shows that I was right mentioning to you the cause of humanity. We will gather our families in one place and as soon as it is done we will let you know. I have, etc.

"LOUIS DAVID (*sic*) RIEL."

On the envelope he had written as follows:

"I do not like war, and if you do not retreat and refuse an interview, the question remains the same concerning the prisoners."

THE BATTLE OF BATOCHE'S FERRY. 217

Our loss, I am afraid, is heavy, but not so heavy as might be expected, as yet. The prisoners are all released and safe in my camp. Among them is Jackson, a white man, who was Riel's secretary, but who is mad and rather dangerous.

(Signed)   FRED. MIDDLETON,
Major-General.

The following accounts will be found more comprehensive than the foregoing, as the writers had an opportunity to put the events together in something like the order in which they occurred.

One correspondent thus tells the story after reaching Prince Albert:—About five o'clock on the morning of the 9th inst. the entire force under the General left their camp of the previous night and moved on Batoche, about eight miles distant. The camp was left standing, that no impediments might interfere with the best fighting being done by every available man. The trail led through an open country until the Indian houses were reached, when it became bluffy, with frequent sloughs, and afforded a safe covering for the enemy from which to pepper our men as they advanced to their four days' fight. Major Boulton's scouts led the advance, and about eight o'clock the *Northcote's* whistle was heard and answered with volleys of blank cartridge from the Winnipeg Field Battery. In another minute the battle of Batoche was begun. No. 1 Company, Royal Grenadiers, was ordered to the front, followed by the remainder of the battalion, and the whole extended in skirmishing order under the fire of the rebels coming from behind the protection of their rifle pits. While this was being done the guns and Gatling were ordered to the front, and the orders were obeyed at a gallop and with cheering. Howard, with his "pet," as cool as a right-down-easter, reached the open at the church and opened his rain-fall of lead upon the Indians with a "Take that, and that, and that, you devils," as if he were sportingly firing into a covey of birds. With each turn of the crank he would repeat his set phrase, until the scene became humorous, and the Indians scattered before the hailstorm of bullets. The guns then came up and occupied a position upon the plateau overlooking the river and Batoche, and shelled the houses to the front. Then it was that poor Mason was shot, a little distance to the right of the church, and Major Dawson rushed back for the surgeon, the bullets whistling with a tish as he left his place for the moment. The guns upon the plateau were noticed to be in danger, and an Indian rush upon them was only averted by the Gatling being run in to their front, and pouring upon the advance the deadly missive with Howard's accompaniment to every turn of the crank: "Take that, and that, and that." The infantry at this period occupied a position somewhat irregular in shape from its following the line of bush in front of the enemy's pits, and the men lay down and opened fire. The right of the column was somewhat thrown back, part of the 90th covering its right flank. The Grenadiers occupied the centre, with one company of the Midland on their left. This was the position the forces maintained for the remainder of the day, under a well directed fire from the enemy, with a more or less irregular fire from our men. At four o'clock Lord Melgund left the field, arriving at Humboldt under the guidance of two scouts the next morning at six. A multitude of causes have been assigned for his sudden departure at such a critical moment in the history of affairs. Camp gossip has it this and that and the other thing. Some whisper that he has had a disagreement with the General. Others, again, allege that his errand away was one for "Regulars," so despondent had the General become at the determined resistance of the rebels. There is little question of the doubtful position of affairs in the General's mind being the true reason, and the entire matter possesses important suggestions of the absolute need of mutual knowledge and confidence between officers and men, so that the former may not incorrectly assume against the latter until they have been given a

THE BATTLE OF BATOCHE'S FERRY. 219

trial. Plucky as was our fire, it seemed to be entirely ineffectual. The rebels seldom, if ever, showed up, being completely sheltered in their pits. About two o'clock the order came to retire, but the movement was immediately perceived by the enemy, as indicated by the brisk fusilade opened upon our men, indicating again that our opponents were quite alive to every movement of the General. As quickly as it was given, therefore, the order was countermanded, and our attack resumed, and kept up unceasingly until dark. It having been decided not to abandon our position, an escort was sent back and a zareba formed about 700 or 800 yards to the rear of our line of skirmishers, upon which the men fell back with the most perfect order and great steadiness worthy of the best form of the oldest campaigners. Darkness overtook the men before they were told off for their positions of the night, but the metal was there, and though under continuous fire no time was lost in forming an outer line of defence with fence rails, bags of oats, bales of hay, and whatever other protection hands could be laid on. All the while rebel bullets came showering into the zareba wounding both man and beast, making the position most unpleasant, the more so as the game of "tit for tat" was impossible and useless, for not a rebel could be seen. In this disagreeable and dangerous state of affairs our men had to snatch their tea—not tea, for fires were not permitted—of hard tack and potted meat, and then their sleep, and truly it was the sleep of the weary, for every man was done up after his all-day fight.

The night passed slowly enough; but too quickly, though, for the men ordered out next morning at five to occupy the position of the previous day. The attempt to do this was made, and made in a truly soldierly spirit, but it failed, for we did not succeed in getting within two hundred yards of our position of the day before. From five in the early morning until sunset the men fought, and fought bravely, lying upon their faces and keeping up a desultory dropping fire upon the enemy's pits, but nothing was gained, and our men were becoming dispirited at the result and longing for the word to charge, which did not come. The Midland copied the tactics of the enemy, and on the left, overlooking the river, dug out rifle pits, and saved a successful flank attack from the enemy in that direction. Thus the day passed wearily enough indeed, and hard-tack and potted meat was again eaten with the relish of exhausted and hungry men. Sleep was less interrupted this night, for the enemy's fire ceased with darkness coming on, perhaps because they failed to come within the same range of our camp as that of the night before. Another day—the third day—and still the same; no advantage seemed to be gained, except that the 90th forced their advance as far as the church, and the Midland, under Colonel Williams, advanced far enough along the river bank on the left side to allow two guns of the Winnipeg Battery to throw a few shells into Batoche, a mile or so distant. Again the men lay down, and fought, being peppered at all the while, and presenting an open target for the rebels. The coolness and indifference of our men was most praiseworthy. Their self-restraint under the unerring fire of the enemy is the surest evidence of the truest discipline in the men. Their one desire was to charge, and the word to charge would not come, so they did their duty as it was given them to do, but with a mental resentment at being made a target for bullets with no means of retaliation. Perhaps it was as well, for their passive submission to the state of affairs goaded the men into fierceness, and when the moment came each man was possessed with the ferocity of rage and revenge. Colonel Van Straubenzie, Colonel Williams, Colonel Grasett, and Captain Hague knew the pulse of the men, and saw that something must be done, and decided upon a charge, weal or woe. Captain Hague pointed out the point of attack, and the next day was settled upon to end this dispiriting fight of three days. On Tuesday the General left the camp about nine in the morning with the Intelligence Corps under Captain

Dennis, and one gun of A Battery and the Gatling, going by the old trail on to the open plateau. His instructions to Colonel Van Straubenzie were that if he engaged the enemy the Grenadiers and Midland should advance at the double. No sound came from the General's direction, and so his orders were not carried out. On his return the troops knew their wishes were to be fulfilled, and the word to double would be given. Dinner and then to work was the order. The key of the position was again pointed out, and a further consultation was held between Van Straubenzie, Williams, Grasett, and Hague. The attack should be made on the left if practicable, and the men had barely reached the position held on the first day when the long-looked-for command: "Break into double, double," came, and was answered with thrilling cheers of satisfaction from the men. Their turn had come—they knew it—they felt it, and with a rush and a cheer they were down on the rebels with the fierceness of Bashi-Bazouks, the Midland on the left, and the Grenadiers in the centre, and the 90th on the right. The advance came sweeping round until but a few minutes saw the line of direction at right angles to the original line of attack. The cheering was that of satisfied and contented men, and the enthusiasm was intense. Nothing could have withstood the pace, the force, and the dogged determination of the men. The cheering attracted the General, and, taking in the situation at a glance, he came on with the Winnipeg Artillery, Gatling, and three companies of the 90th. The guns posted on the plateau shelled the houses, destroying them as if they had been houses of cards. The 90th joined the Grenadiers and prolonged their line of attack upon the right, while the Intelligence Corps and Boulton's scouts were on the extreme right of the 90th. Colonel Williams gained the rifle pits on the left, and took them, following up his success by pushing ahead, having to traverse the greater distance made by the course of the river. The Winnipeg Field Battery played upon the houses across the river, from whence an irregular fire, more or less damaging, had been kept up upon our men from first to last. Captain Ruttan, of the 90th, came up with two companies and reinforced Williams in his hot position, extending from water's edge to plateau. Here two or three men were wounded, but the charge was irresistible, and any resistance ineffectual. The two Helliwells were badly hit when within about two hundred yards of the houses from which the enemy were firing; but their fire seemed less steady, as if they felt the result

LIEUT.-COL. VAN STRAUBENZIE. *

of such an advance as was coming on them. Captain Stewart, No. 2 Company, 90th, was sent back by Colonel Williams to the General, to say that he was determined to charge the houses, and charge them he did. All the while Colonel Van Straubenzie was leading on the column,

---

* No better officer than Colonel Straubenzie could have been chosen to fill so important a position. An old soldier of much and varied experience, he entered the army at an early age, and was appointed to an ensigncy in

hat in hand, waving it and cheering as he went along. The excitement was intense, and nothing could have withstood the enthusiasm of the men. On they came, and in fifteen minutes after the Midland were reinforced they reached the top bank, and were down upon the houses. The first one to come over to us was the small one on the bank, from which the firing was pretty hot, then the log stable opposite to the white store, in the latter of which were Riel's prisoners, pale, slimy, and emaciated with eighteen days of darkness and starvation; then two other stores to the north, and away flew the rebels, fighting as they retreated. Major Hughes, the while, forced round the left flank of the rebels on the sloping bank of the river, and Captain Young, Captain French, and Captain Dennis, with a mixed body of men from the Midland, 90th, and Grenadiers, charged and took Batoche's store and house. Here poor French was killed by a ball from a rebel rifle on the river slope, shot at him as he looked through the upper window. Part of the 90th, Grenadiers, and Midland advanced with Captain Young on past the stores already taken, past the prison-cellar, on to Riel's Council House, at the extreme east of

the famous old 32nd Light Infantry. Not long after his appointment he was called upon to see active service, and, in the ever-memorable Sikh campaign of Lord Gough, our well-known citizen highly distinguished himself. During those trying times for England, Lieutenant Van Straubenzie led the forlorn hope at the seige of Mooltan, and for his pluck and gallantry was specially mentioned in the home despatches. At that time there was no such thing as a Victoria Cross, but had there been the Colonel would no doubt have worn that much-coveted reward on his breast to-day. His wounds were serious, and he was obliged to return to England and serve with the depot of his regiment, where he gradually recovered. Before very long, however, the "war-cry" again sounded, and as a Captain he proceeded to the Crimea on the staff of his brother, Sir Charles Van Straubenzie, who commanded the "Light Brigade." Again the subject of our illustration was favourably mentioned in home despatches. After peace was proclaimed with Russia, the Colonel was once more destined to smell powder, and, from the knowledge the authorities had of his varied and useful services, he was given an important position on the Staff of Sir Hope Grant when the Chinese War broke out. He was at the taking of the Summer Palace, and on that occasion his name was again mentioned in despatches. Colonel Van Straubenzie is much respected, and, looking at his fine soldier-like bearing, there are not many who would imagine that even to-day he is still suffering from his severe wounds of 1849.

Batoche, and secured Riel's papers, and released Jackson, McConnell, and Monkman, who had been imprisoned by Riel for insubordination. The rebels in the meantime had been driven past the line of houses, and pursued by part of the Grenadiers under Grasett, and their centre was driven back with the irresistible force of the Grenadiers, the 90th, and the Mounted Scouts. At four o'clock the charge had proved a grand success, the settlement was captured, and the end had come, the rebels being completely routed. The pursuit was kept up, however, and at 7.30 the last shot was fired. Thus ended a grand and successful charge, begun after dinner, and winning the day, and ending the rebellion at four o'clock in the afternoon.

But during this three days' fighting, where was General Middleton's "navy," the steamer *Northcote*. Let one who was on board tell the story of the "Middleton Navy" before we give any further particulars of the more effective operations of the army on shore.

According to General Middleton's preconcerted plan the *Northcote*, with two heavy laden barges, left Gabriel's at 6 a.m. to-day, and after anchoring a short time so as not to anticipate the arranged time of arrival at Riel's headquarters, reached within one and a-half miles of our destination, where we were to remain until the bombardment of the rebel stronghold by General Middleton was heard, he starting at daybreak from the camping ground reached on the previous day, nine miles east of Batoche's. The rebels, however, materially interfered with the carrying out of these plans by opening fire on the steamer at ten minutes past eight, just after she had got under headway. The first bullet passed through the pilot house. The rebel spies had watched the steamer the previous night on the opposite bank from Gabriel's, and the sentry could hear them shouting, one boastfully singing out to us as he departed: " Now come on, you—!"

This first shot was evidently the signal to the rebels of our boat's approach, and as we rounded the bend a moment or so later we were raked fore and aft by a fierce storm of bullets coming from both banks. From almost every bush rose puffs of smoke, and from every house and tree on the top of the banks came bullets buzzing. The fire was steadily returned by the troops on board, consisting of C Company School of Infantry; and notwithstanding that the rebels were protected by the brush and timber which covers the banks, apparently some injury was inflicted upon them. Volley after volley was fired, and several of the lurking enemy were seen to drop headlong down the sloping banks.

So the fight went on, fierce and hot, as we approached Batoche's.

The pretty little church of St. Antoine de Padua lifted its cross-crowned steeple high above the other buildings, on the eastern bank. A horrifying spectacle met our gaze on the opposite bank. A man, presumably one of Riel's prisoners, was dangling by the neck from a branch of an almost limbless tree—a victim of rebel rage and vindictiveness. Near at hand the rebels, who lined both banks for a couple of miles, were running swiftly and keeping pace with our progress. Several mounted men, evidently leaders, were directing their movements. A few volleys quickly dispersed them to their hiding places, where they fought the customary bush fight. They completely riddled the steamer with bullets, but it was strongly bulwarked on the boiler deck where the soldiers were standing and our casualties were consequently very light.

Just above Batoche's the rapids commence, and a big rock covered with sand juts out into the stream, leaving a narrow channel immediately on the western side, the head of which is at a sharp bend, to round which the boat had to run her nozzle almost on to the bank. It was here the firing became terrifically hot from a favourably located ravine directly in our front in which the rebels were hidden. The rapids were passed safely, notwithstanding that the pilots were totally unacquainted with the river and that the two heavy barges handicapped them in handling the steamer. Fortunately there was no wind to render their duties still more arduous in controlling the boat's movements.

In a few moments the crossing was reached, and in passing it the ferry cable caught the smoke stacks, which came crashing down on the hurricane deck, tearing with them spars and masts. Our misfortune excited loud cheers from the Metis, mingled with fiendish war-whoops from the Indians. The cable, which is strung from the upper banks, was lowered just as we approached it, the intention of the rebels being to corral the steamer and, in the confusion expected to ensue, to capture the boat and massacre its human freight. Very fortunately for us this scheme failed, but only by the merest chance, for had the cable caught in the pilot-house, which it barely missed, the wheelsman, exposed to the enemy's fire, would have been shot down and the steamer rendered utterly helpless. It was successful, however, in cutting off our communication with General Middleton by our code of whistling signals previously arranged upon, the whistle being carried away with the pipes.

Just then the steamer, to avoid two large boulders directly in her course, was allowed to swing around, and floated down stream stern foremost for a while. One barge barely grazed the bank, and the boat would have been boarded by the rebels but for the steady volleys our men poured at them. A withering fire was still maintained from some rifle pits which the enemy had dug at different places, and this was hotly returned until 9 o'clock, when the rebel firing ceased, save a stray shot or two. We had run the gauntlet of their fire for five miles. Many of the enemy's bullets fell short of the mark when we were midstream, shot-guns with common balls being their weapons, although without doubt some had Winchesters and Snider-Enfields. So fast and furious was their fire that it was evident the whole rebel force had gathered here to make a determined stand. As some of the red coats were seen coming up in skirmishing order in the distance, our small force gave three lusty cheers. This was the only glimpse we had of the troops.

Dropping below Batoche's nearly three miles, anchor was cast in midstream, but the steamer, almost unnoticeably, drifted another mile before the anchor firmly caught. The work of repairing damage was begun, and in a short time the smoke stacks, which were reduced in length, were re-erected : but scarcely had this been accomplished before firing disturbed the workmen, who were working behind a barricade of boxes. Afterwards the whistle was repaired—a dangerous task which two men could only be induced to undertake on the promise of a reward of fifty dollars each. The men were driven from this also. Our signals to General Middleton, which had been interrupted altogether since passing Batoche's, were resumed ; but although we could distinctly hear the sound of cannonading no answer to our shrill whistle was given. The scouts evidently could not reach us owing to the presence of ambushed rebels secreted in the bluffs between us and the General's headquarters.

Captain Bedson, Major Smith of C Company, and Captain Wise, A.D.C., held a consultation and decided to return up the river, but the captain peremptorily refused to do so, claiming that not only was it certain death to the pilots, but contrary to the written orders given him by the General. Private William Eccles, of E Company, 90th, who had had some experience in steamboating, volunteered to pilot the steamer up, but after another consultation it was decided not advisable under the circumstances to take advantage of his manly offer. Hence we remain now out of the fight. A number of hostiles are skulking down north. One gave a parting shot to the steamer, hitting McDonald, the ship-carpenter, in the heel, but not inflicting a serious wound. Near by are about fifty Indian ponies quietly grazing, the owners having profited by the experience at Fish Creek, where their horses were slaughtered. Captains Seager and Streets, who piloted the steamer, remained throughout at their posts, and with them was Talbot, the purser, who kept up a steady fire from the pilot-house, which was made a special target of by the rebel marksmen, they being fully aware of the disaster which must overtake us if we were disabled in this vulnerable point. Dozens of bullets had pierced the wheel-house. Seager received one in his coat sleeve, and in the cabin in which I am writing a scene of wild disorder prevails. The skylights are smashed, and the flimsy material of which the upper works were constructed offered no resistance to the enemy's fire, and are punctured here and there with bullets. Later in the run, however, mattresses and bolsters were piled around the sides of the interior, and the place made fully secure.

Captain Wise, who had been unable to take part in the land engagement owing to the wound he received at Fish Creek, remained with Chief Transport Officer Bedson, who was in charge of the boat, in the cabin, and both had several very narrow escapes, the latter having a bullet graze his thigh. His state-room was pierced by seven balls, which he returned with interest. Owen E. Hughes and John Vinen were in a small barricade behind the smoke stacks, which fell over them. Both managed by the skin of their teeth to escape, but after Vinen had entered the cabin and was helping to barricade it, he received a bullet in the thigh. Major Smith, of C Company, was in command of the military, having with him Lieutenant Scott, of the same corps, and Lieutenants Elliott and Gibson, of the Royal Grenadiers. The troops on board implicitly obeyed instructions, while the few civilians rendered excellent service in replenishing cartridges in boxes, and also in handling rifles. Lieutenant Hugh J. Macdonald, although ill with erysipelas in the face, left his bed and took his place in the ranks rifle in hand. The conduct of the men throughout was cool and gallant; though they were not exposed to such constant danger as at Fish Creek, still the bullets whizzed about them in great style, coming through the interstices in the barricade and the openings forward.

THE BATTLE OF BATOCHE'S FERRY.   229

The rebel strength is not known, but from the fury with which they fired, their force must have reached probably four hundred or five hundred, Indians predominating, except at Batoche's, where the Half-breeds had congregated. One man in priest's garb was seen near Batoche's waving his hands as if in despair, and apparently endeavouring to keep the breeds from firing at us, but their bullets poured around him and he disappeared. Some women were also there. In our engagement this morning eight rebels are reported to have been killed and there must have been a large number wounded. Our casualties are trivial. Two besides Macdonald were slightly wounded, Pringle (a son of Judge Pringle, of Cornwall, and a member of the ambulance staff), receiving a flesh wound in the shoulder, and Vinen, of the transport service, a similar injury in the thigh, both early in the fray.

MAY 11, 7 a.m.

The sun heralded another magnificent day yesterday. The men were up the greater part of the night, and breakfasted at 4 a.m. The boiler broke during the night. Between one and two o'clock an alarm sounded, a sentry reporting that he had seen an Indian crawl into one of the barges. The whole boat was aroused but search failed to reveal anything. Almost instantaneously the rebels opened fire on us from the west bank, but the troops, acting under orders, did not answer it. After discharging many shots the enemy dispersed. Sunday passed slowly. We were anxiously awaiting news from Middleton, whose guns could be heard once in a while, but with whom we still had no communication. Several small bands of the enemy were seen during the day moving about on both banks, and one band patiently watched the boat. Shots were exchanged several times, but no damage was done on either side. Another consultation of officers was held an hour ago, and it was decided to render the pilot-house bullet-proof and return up the river nearer Batoche's. This occasioned a delay of several hours, the men being interrupted by firing from the bank. Then one engineer refused to remain at his post, and some of the crew of the boat, who had spent most of the time skulking in the hold, acted in a most cowardly manner. There were two or three exceptions, and these, with Captain Andrews (who with Privates Eccles, Smith, and Wilkes, of the 90th, had been put in charge of the supplies on the barge), and Joe Labelle, telegraph repairer, rendered excellent service. We lay inactive all day, and fuel running short and it being impossible to go up the stream with the barges, it was decided to run down twenty miles to a wood-pile, and then go fifteen miles farther down to the Hudson's Bay ferry, where the steamer *Marquis* is reported to be in waiting, and then return to General Middleton's assistance.

A start was made at 6.30 p.m., but scarcely had the steamer commenced to move than the rebels, who had been hiding, poured in a broadside, the soldiers returning it by volley firing. They followed us for some distance until cut off by the dense woods. We made nine miles, passing many deserted houses, and anchored for the night. Although still in the hostiles' country they had evidently gone south to join Riel at his headquarters and we were not molested. At 6.30 this morning another start was made, but almost immediately the boat ran on a sand bar, and four hours were lost in getting her off. Maxime Lepine's ferry boat, which we had intended destroying, had been taken away in obedience to Riel's orders directing all boats to centre at Batoche's. Obtaining fuel *en route*, we passed Hoodoo and several local Half-breed settlements which were deserted, and reached the Hudson's Bay ferry, twenty-two miles below Batoche's, at 3 p.m., where we were received with loud cheers.

From this it will be seen that General Middleton's navy project did little more than imperil many valuable lives and withdrew from his forces a considerable number of men who were badly needed on Saturday, Sunday and Monday.

The killed and wounded at Batoche were as follow:—

KILLED ON SATURDAY.

A Battery—Gunner Phillips, shot through the head.

WOUNDED ON SATURDAY.

A Battery—Napoleon Charpentier, shot through both legs; Michael Twohey, thigh; W. Fairbanks, thigh; Thomas J. Stout, ribs broken, run over by a gun.

French's Scouts—Cook, left leg broken by ball below the knee; Allen, shot in the knee.

Grenadiers—Capt. Mason, flesh wound in the thigh.

KILLED ON SUNDAY.

Grenadiers—Private Thomas Moor, shot through the head.

90th Battalion—Private Hardisty, shot through the lungs.

WOUNDED ON SUNDAY.

Grenadiers—Adjutant Manly, sole of foot; Private Scovell, No. 3 Company, flesh wound; Private Cantwell, No. 2 Company.

90th Battalion—Private John Kemp, shot through the eye; Private Erickson, in the arm; Private Ralph Barron, in the forearm; Private Stead, No. 2 Company, flesh wound.

KILLED ON MONDAY.

French's Scouts—Captain John French, shot dead while leading his men.

Boulton's Scouts—Captain Brown, shot through the heart.

Grenadiers—Lieutenant Fitch.

Dennis's (Surveyors) Corps—A. W. Kippen.

90th Battalion—Private Fraser, Private Wheeler.

WOUNDED ON MONDAY.

Grenadiers—Major Dawson, slightly in the ankle; Private R. Cook, in the arm; Bugler M. Gaughan, flesh wound in the hand; Private C. Barbour, slight wound in the head; Private J. W. Quigley, flesh wound in the arm; Private J. Marshall, flesh wound in the calf; Private W. Wilson, slight wound behind shoulder.

Midland Battalion—Lieutenant G. E. Laidlaw, R.M.C., attached, slightly; Lieutenant J. Helliwell, 15th Battalion, shoulder; Private Barton, thigh and groin, seriously; Corporal Helliwell, face and arm.

90th Battalion—Sergeant-Major Watson, slightly in the ankle; Sergeant F. R. Jakes, in the hand; Private Alex. Young, flesh wound in the thigh; Corporal J. Gillies, in the leg.

Dennis's Scouts—Lieutenant Garden.

Total killed, 9; total wounded, 30.

The following sketches cannot fail to be of interest:—

A. W. KIPPEN.

Among the arrivals in the city from the North-West were several members of the Dominion Surveyors' Intelligence Corps, who are absent from the scene of the recent disturbance for a short time on leave. The party is composed of Messrs. Walter Beatty, C. Wolff, J. McLean, B. J. Saunders, of the Surveyors; Capt. Clemes, Quartermaster of the Midland Battalion, and Assistant-Surgeon Kinloch. Mr. B. J. Saunders was only a short distance from the spot where his comrade, Mr. A. W. Kippen, met his untimely death. The Surveyors' Corps took an active part in the battle of Batoche. The corps, under command of Capt. J. S. Dennis, of whom Mr. Saunders speaks in the highest terms of praise, joined the loyal forces on the afternoon of the second day of the Batoche fight. Desultory firing was still going on. The corps at once took its place in the trenches, and almost immediately felt the sting of the enemy's lead, Private A. W. Wheeler receiving a ball in his left shoulder. From that time till the capture of the village and the utter rout of the rebels, the corps shared with the boys all the work and the danger of the contest, and is no doubt fully entitled to a full share of the glory and honour that has been and will be accorded to our noble citizen soldiers. On the Tuesday morning, the day of victory, the Surveyors, accompanied by Boulton's scouts, the Gatling gun, and the nine-pounder, proceeded to open the attack that led to such a successful issue. The nine-pounder felt the enemy, and the Surveyors deployed as skirmishers, Mr. A. W. Kippen being in the front. They had just taken up their position, not more than one hundred yards from the rebel rifle pits, and just upon a well-marked surveyor's line, when the fatal bullet found its mark, and Mr. Kippen fell, shot through the head. Death was instantaneous. Dr. Ralston, the surgeon, and Assistant Surgeon Kinloch, quickly secured the body, but the brave surveyor was beyond the reach of their skill. Mr. Saunders speaks of Mr. Kippen as a man of great energy, and brave almost to rashness. He had from the outset manifested an intense desire to take an active part in the struggle, eager to serve his country, and had performed every duty devolving upon him with a will undaunted in the face of gravest dangers. The death-blow came almost in the hour when victory crowned the efforts of the loyal forces.

A. W. Kippen, son of Mr. Kippen, of Perth, Ont., had been for many years one of the most trusted surveyors in the employ of the Hudson Bay Company, and great value was put on his services by Mr. C. J. Brydges, He came to Toronto this winter and entered upon a course of study at the School of Practical Science for the purpose of qualifying himself for a higher position as Government surveyor. While in this city his attractive social qualities and geniality of disposition won him numerous friends. He was extremely fond of athletics, and was one of the most popular members of the Toronto Fencing Club. Shortly before the war broke out he went to Ottawa, and upon hearing of the rebellion volunteered his services as a scout. His knowledge of the North-West was known to be so extensive that his offer was gladly accepted and he was enrolled among Dennis's scouts. It is said he only reached Middleton's camp on Sunday, so that he met his death in the first engagement in which he took part. In his native place, Perth, Mr. Kippen was a great favourite and his loss will be sincerely mourned.

LIEUTENANT FITCH.

Lieut. W. C. Fitch was the only son of Mr. J. C. Fitch, of Fitch & Davidson, wholesale grocers, Yonge Street, Toronto, of which firm deceased was the junior partner. He was born and educated in this city, receiving his primary military training in the Governor-General's Body Guards. A little over a year ago he was appointed lieutenant in the Grenadiers. He immediately afterwards took a course in the Infantry School, obtaining a second-class certificate, upon which he received his commission. Since then he has taken a deep interest in everything pertaining to the welfare of the regiment. He was a member of the Toronto Fencing Club, Royal Canadian Yacht Club, and other athletic organizations of the city, and universally popular among all those who were acquainted with him. No greater tribute could be paid to him than that contained in a letter from Private Hatch, of No. 3 Company, Grenadiers: "Another whom I cannot help mentioning is our commanding officer, Lieutenant Fitch, who, with the amount of work, has a heavy task, but by his kindness and ready help to all members of his company he has the good will of all, and by this alone he has brought the company to what it is— and that is the one which is always there, with everything ready and in good order. I think if we ever return to Toronto he will be a man not soon forgotten by a single member of No. 3 Company." Lieut. Fitch was a cousin of Mr. J. Scriver, M.P. for Huntingdon, P.Q., and a brother of Mrs. Senator Clemow, of Ottawa. Principal King, of Manitoba College, writes of Lieutenant Fitch: "It is twenty-two years since I first saw him, then a winning child of four years of age, the joy and pride of his father and mother. He attended for many years the Gould Street Presbyterian Church; and was a

LIEUTENANT FITCH.

pupil in its Sabbath school. He was all through a gentle and affectionate youth, seldom meeting one without a smile. It is not singular that he was greatly beloved by a wide circle of friends, and that he was an object of special fondness to his parents, who saw in him not only an only son, but one in every way dutiful and affectionate. There have been already many mournful losses in this deplorable and, one can scarcely avoid saying, most unnecessary conflict; there cannot have been many, if indeed any, which will occasion wider and more tender sorrow than this. His parents, old and respected citizens of Toronto, will receive from all who know them the deepest sympathy; but how little can even such sympathy do to relieve the life-long sorrow which must be theirs." The Minister of Militia gave instructions to have the remains of the deceased forwarded to Toronto for interment.

CAPTAIN E. T. BROWN.

Captain E. T. Brown, of Boulton's Horse, who was killed at Batoche's on Monday, was a native of Peterboro'. He was a son of the late Edward Brown, and grandson of Thos. Alex. Stewart, who came to Canada in 1820 and was subsequently a member of the Privy Council of Upper Canada. Captain Brown went to the North-West in 1879 with a surveying party. After the survey was completed he remained in that country. When Boulton's scouts were raised he joined as a sergeant and after the fight at Fish Creek he was promoted to a captaincy. He was about twenty-eight or twenty-nine years old and unmarried. His mother and brother, Mr. Stewart Brown, reside at Goodwood, the family residence, a few miles from Peterboro'.

PRIVATE THOMAS MOOR.

Private Thomas Moor, of No. 3 Company, Grenadiers who was killed on Sunday night, was a son of Mr. Thomas Moor, the well-known representative artisan of 42 Oxford Street, Toronto, and was just eighteen years old the day he left. He was educated in the Public Schools of the city, and had followed the trade of a tinsmith, having been in the employ of Mr. Sawdon, Queen Street, for a number of years. He was a frank, good-natured boy, much loved by all his companions, and an obedient son. When the call was made for volunteers he was very anxious to go, and when he found that he would be allowed to do so clapped his hands and danced with delight.

His parents received the following letter from him on the day before he was killed, dated at Middleton's camp on the 26th of April :—

"DEAR FATHER AND MOTHER.—I received your letter last night and was very glad to hear from home. We

PRIVATE THOMAS MOOR.

left Clark's Crossing on Thursday morning. I was on picket duty Thursday evening, and one of the officers tried to play sharp on me, and he hid in some bushes on my beat. As soon as I saw him I rushed at him with my bayonet and scared him instead of him scaring me. At Clark's Crossing the 10th Royals, the Winnipeg Battery, and Captain French, with fifty scouts, crossed the river and went down one side, and the 90th and A Battery with Major Boulton's scouts went down the other side. On Friday morning the 90th attacked the enemy on the other side. Some of our fellows were down the river a mile getting the mail across and were not armed, so that twelve men, including me, went to their relief. We got the mail across and came back. The 10th had moved on to the scene of action, and we had to bring the waggons along. Two of us were on each waggon with loaded rifles. At last we got up to the 10th and were told to join our respective companies. The battle was raging on the other side. Nos. 1, 2 and 4 Companies were ordered across while No. 3 and the scouts were to stay here and shoot any of the breeds that tried to cross. The breeds were entrenched in the gully. The battle lasted six hours. We were on this side and could hear the shots but could not get across though we would dearly love to have got there. During the battle the General had a shot through his hat, and one of Major Boulton's scouts had his ear shot through and his coat riddled with buckshot. He got through here yesterday, and I saw him. Riel is strongly entrenched, but we will lick him in time. I believe the Fenians are helping him. It was a sad sight to see our men burying the dead yesterday. I cannot tell you half in writing, but will tell you all when I get home.

"Your affectionate Son,

"Tom."

CAPTAIN FRENCH.

Captain John French, who was killed at Batoche's, was an Irishman, formerly a Captain in the Dublin Militia, and a brother of Col. French, the first commissioner of the Mounted Police. In the winter of 1873, the deceased was in Toronto, and having secured a position as inspector on the police went out with the force to the North-West. He served with the force for ten years, when he retired, and turned his attention to farming, taking up land near Qu'Appelle. When the rebellion broke out he organized a corps known as French's Scouts, which he commanded, and whose services were of great benefit to General Middleton. He leaves a widow and several young children, the eldest being a girl of ten. The deceased was a bold and dashing officer, as evinced on Saturday, when amid a shower of bullets he carried away a wounded soldier. His dash into the ravine at Batoche's and his daring attempt to relieve the prisoners when he was shot will keep his memory green. The nearest connection of the deceased in this country since Colonel French's removal to Australia is Mrs. Kenneth Mackenzie, widow of the late senior judge of York County, who is a sister of Colonel French's wife.

H. A. FRASER.

H. A. Fraser was a son of Contractor Fraser, of Winnipeg. He was about twenty-seven years old and married some six months to Miss Speirs, daughter of Alexander Speirs, of that city.

A. O. WHEELER.

A. O. Wheeler was a brother of George Wheeler, killed in the Fish Creek battle, and son of C. H. Wheeler, architect, of Winnipeg.

The wounded are as follow :—

MAJOR DAWSON.

Major G. D. Dawson, of the 10th Royals, who was wounded at Batoche, is an old army officer and experienced soldier. He is an Irishman by birth, having been born in County Carlow, Ireland, in the year 1839. When only sixteen years of age he commenced his military career as an ensign of the 47th Regiment. He was ordered to the Crimea with his regiment, but when his troopship reached Malta news of peace was received and the 47th returned home. Major Dawson continued with his regiment for thirteen years, but left it at Halifax in 1867, retiring with the rank of Lieutenant. He settled down to business in this city and is now chief partner in the well-known firm of G. D. Dawson & Co, 43 Colborne Street, Toronto. When the 10th Royals were re-organized by Col. Grasett, Lieutenant Dawson took an active part in assisting. He was appointed Major at that time, and has ever since taken an active interest in the battalion.

PRIVATE SCOVELL.

Private Alfred Scovell, when in Toronto resided with his mother at 37 Alma Avenue. He has been employed for some time in the law office of Messrs. Cameron & Caswell. Being fond of military life he took a three months' course in the School of Infantry, at the same time retaining his connection with the 10th. His father is at present in Australia.

BUGLER GAUGHAN.

Bugler Gaughan, shot in the hand at Batoche, is a native of Guelph, his parents residing there at present. He was a member of the Wellington Field Battery for some time, and holds a School of Gunnery certificate. In Toronto he has been following his occupation as blacksmith, and when the 10th Royals were called out was one of the first to volunteer for active service.

PRIVATE QUIGLEY.

Private Quigley joined the Grenadiers three years ago, but some months before the outbreak of the rebellion he handed his uniform in. He was among the first to turn up, however, when the call to arms was sounded. Quigley is a stout young fellow of twenty-four years of age. He was employed during the summer working on a farm. He is a single man, but is in reality the only support of his mother, his step-father being in wretched health.

PRIVATE MARSHALL.

Private John Marshall, who is reported as wounded in the calf, was a watch-case maker with R. J. Quigley,

57 Adelaide Street, Toronto. Marshall has been about a year with the Grenadiers. His mother lives at 121 Jarvis Street. He is eighteen years of age, and a strong hardy youth.

BUGLER GAUGHAN.

LIEUTENANT LAIDLAW.

Lieutenant George E. Laidlaw, attached to the Midland Battalion, who is reported slightly wounded, is a son of Mr. George Laidlaw, of 26 Spadina Avenue, Toronto. He is about twenty-five years of age, having been born in Toronto, and educated at Upper Canada College. He passed through the Royal Military College at Kingston, graduating in June, 1882. He afterwards proceeded to British Columbia, where he spent some time on a surveying expedition. When the rebellion broke out he immediately tendered his services to the Government, which were accepted, and he was appointed to a Company under Col. Williams' command.

PRIVATE WATSON.

Private Alexander Watson, F. Co., 90th (Winnipeg) Battalion, who was wounded on the last day of the fight at Batoche, and died the following Saturday, was born in Toronto in 1858, but lived in St. Catharines the greater part of his life till about four years before the rebellion, when he removed to Winnipeg. While in Winnipeg he was in the employ of a contractor and builder, he having

PRIVATE WATSON.

been brought up to that business in St. Catharines. He was the eldest son, but had an elder sister. Personally he was a generous, kind-hearted young man and a great favourite with every one. He was unmarried, but was shortly to have led to the altar a very estimable young lady of Winnipeg.

THE BATTLE OF BATOCHE'S FERRY. 243

PRIVATE COOK.

Private Richard Cook is the son of Mr. Wm. Cook, 137 Hope Street, Toronto. He is about nineteen years of age, and is a shoemaker by trade. He has been a private in the Grenadiers for about a year.

STAFF SERGEANT MITCHELL.

Staff-Sergeant Thomas Mitchell is well-known in militia circles throughout Canada. He is perhaps the most famous shot in the Dominion. He has five times represented his country among the crack shots of the world on the Wimbledon Common. Sergeant Mitchell was slightly wounded in the left eye. He is a member of the firm of Dickie & Mitchell, 142½ King Street West, Toronto. He is a native of Dundee, Scotland. He joined the Grenadiers soon after his arrival in Toronto, five years ago. Besides being a staff-sergeant he is also musketry instructor to the regiment. He has brothers who are also famous as marksmen. One of them, Coulson, is on the field with the 90th Battalion of Winnipeg. Mr. Mitchell is married, and is about thirty-two years of age.

ADJUTANT MANLY.

Adjutant Manly was injured on the sole of the foot. Captain Manly is mathematical master in the Collegiate Institute, Toronto. He is a graduate of University College, and took high honors there. He is an enthusiastic soldier, and has devoted many an hour to the advancement of the Grenadiers. No officer has worked harder or longer for the interests of his crops than has Frederick F. Manly. He is one of the most popular young men about town.

LIEUTENANT HELLIWELL.

Lieut. J. E. Helliwell, wounded at Batoche, belongs to the 15th Battalion, Argyle Light Infantry, of Belleville. His father is rector of Ameliasburg, Ont. Lieutenant Helliwell lives at Belleville, where he is employed in the law firm of Robertson & Thomas. He graduated from Trinity College three years ago.

Corporal E. Helliwell, brother of Lieutenant Helliwell and who was also wounded at Batoche, is a law student from Madoc.

SERGEANT JACKES.

Sergeant Franklin Jackes, of the 90th, is well-known in Toronto, having been for some time book-keeper for

SERGEANT JACKES.

Messrs. Gordon & Co. While in Toronto he was a member of I Company, Queen's Own. About three years ago he removed to Winnipeg, where he has since been engaged in the hardware business. Friends of his reside at Eglinton.

From the foregoing accounts it will be seen that while no one saw the whole of the fighting at Batoche, each man who writes saw something worth recording. The loss on our own side is of course well known as stated already, but the rebel loss is not now, and may never be known. Our people claimed that there were some sixty or seventy killed, but the rebels themselves put their killed at only nine or ten. In the same way Colonel Otter, after his retreat from Cut Knife, thought he had fought against six hundred men and that he had killed from sixty to one hundred and twenty-five of them. When the truth came to be known, however, it was found that he had been defeated by only two hundred and fifty men, and that of these he had killed only six, or at most seven.

The instances of individual heroism were numerous, but there was no more gallant action than that performed by poor Captain French on Saturday, which has been already related.

LIEUTENANT HOWARD.

Lieutenant Howard, who had command of the Gatling gun, distinguished himself on more than one occasion and made himself one of the lions of the day. Whatever his countrymen may think of him as an American fighting against men who were supposed to be struggling for their rights and in behalf of a foreign power, it is certain that Canadians have been very glad to avail themselves of his services and those of his "patent murdering machine." Had it not been for his plucky conduct and the efficiency of his machine on the first day at Batoche, it is not improbable that General Middleton might have found his artillery turned against his own forces, and the slight repulse he received that day turned into a disastrous defeat.

To judge from the "poetic" effusions that have been called forth by this rebellion, Canada must be very easily satisfied as to the quality of her poetry, though she may be more exacting as to quantity. Here is some about Lieutenant Howard that is certainly not any worse than the average:—

LIEUTENANT HOWARD.

THE MAN WITH THE GATLING GUN.

Full many a line of expressions fine
   And of sentiments sweet and grand
Have been penned of "our boys" who, from home's dear
    joys,
   Set out for the North-West land.
We've been told how they've fought for the glory sought,
   We've heard of the deeds they've done;
But it's quite high time for some praise in rhyme
   For the man with the Gatling gun.

Music hath charms, even midst war's alarms,
   To soothe the savage breast;

None can hold a candle to that "music by Handle"
  That lulled Riel's " breeds " to rest,
And they sleep that sleep profound, so deep,
  From which shall awaken none ;
And the lullabies that closed their eyes
  Were sung by the Gatling gun.

All honour's due—and they have it, too—
  To the Grens. and Q. O. R.
They knew no fear but, with British cheer,
  They charged and dispersed afar
The rebel crew ; but 'twixt me and you
  When all is said and done,
A different scene there might have been
  But for Howard and his Gatling gun.

Batoche will long be remembered with a shudder in too many Canadian households. It broke the back of the rebellion, but too many brave hearts are now cold and still that beat high with valour, hope and noble ambition as the *Northcote's* whistle gave the signal that the fight had begun.

Though the Indians under Big Bear continued to offer a stubborn resistance for a time, the Half-breed rebellion as such was crushed, and the hope of the Half-breeds was extinguished when some of their bravest and best lay in the rifle pits that fatal Monday afternoon soaked in their own life blood. We may hate Riel, we may abhor rebellion ; but when time shall have elapsed sufficient to enable us to look at the events of this sad affair with unprejudiced eyes, there is not a Canadian worthy of the name who will not remember with sincere respect and admiration Gabriel Dumont and his valiant little band of compatriots who fought so gallantly in their hopeless cause.

BATOCHE.

"SHOT THROUGH THE HEART."

God guard my darling boy to-night,
   And keep him safe from harm ;
Watch over him in this dread fight,
   Give to his life a charm.
Let every bullet speed him past,
   And turn each blow away ;
From him, my well-loved only son,
   Who meets the foe to-day.

A brave and noble lad is he,
   This one dear son of mine ;
With loyal heart so kind and true
   And full of love divine.
I know he's ready should'st Thou call,
   But spare him, God, I pray,
Let him return to me again,
   My boy not far away !

" O, mother dear," a sad voice speaks,
   And by her side there stands
A girlish form, with tear-dimmed eyes,
   And close locked, restless hands.
"Well, daughter mine, why come you now,
   With face so wist and sad ?
Your loving smiles should cheer and make
   My lone heart warm and glad.

" What say you, child, more news has come,
   A grand victorious fight ;
The Royal Grenadiers this time
   The rebels put to flight.
Thank God for that my prayer was heard,
   And I shall sleep to-night,
With grateful heart and peaceful rest,
   Till comes the morning light,

THE BATTLE OF BATOCHE'S FERRY.

"But why these tears ? Why this distress ?
   I have not heard aright ?
What is it, then ? Come, dear, be brave ;
   Your brother leads the fight.
'Shot through the heart !' Oh, God ! My lad,
   For whom I prayed to Thee ;
My only son, my bonnie boy,
   Will come no more to me !

"'Shot through the heart,' e'en while I prayed
   His form lay still in death,
Not one fond message could he send,
   None caught his dying breath.
The cannon's roar, the clash of arms,
   The crash of ball and shell,
A strangely wild, mad requiem, made
   Where he for country fell !

"Dead, cold and dead, the lonely grave
   Now hides him from my sight ;
Oh ! pitying God, my heart will break !
   Why send on me this blight ?
Why is my home made desolate ?
   My life of joy bereft ?
He was my dearest, only son ;
   I have no other left !

"Forgive me, Lord ! Thy will be done !
   Peace send this aching heart,
That doth rebel o'er this one gone,
   Who was my life's best part.
At rest with Thee ! Oh, blessed light,
   That finds my soul at last !
It brings me patience, comfort now,
   The darkest hour has past."

VICTORY AT BATOCHE.

Victory ! Glorious news comes down
As sudden flash of light from falling star ;
  To God the glory—the renown
To our brave soldiers on the field afar.

Who knowing that with them the breath
Of captives failed, should tardy action be,
  Charged bayonets in the face of death—
Into the pit of hell—and set them free!

While rebel hordes flew, as the dust
Is onward driven by the strong wind's will,
  Batoche has fäll'n, is ours! Our trust,
Our prayers are answered! God is with us still!

The great heart of the nation heaves
With pride in work her sons have done so well,
  And with a smile and sigh she weaves
A wreath of bays and one of *immortelle!*

Baptized with fire, they stood the test;
And earth, in turn, baptized with blood they shed;
  Canada triumphs, but her best
Are not all here—she mourns her gallant dead.

A glorious death was theirs, a bright
Unsullied ending to a cloudless day:
  They sank, as sinks the sun in sea of light;
And in their country's memory live for aye!

But flush of victory pales in pain;
Tears fall for darkened homes where glad tones cease.
  Whose loved that left, come not again—
Heaven give the mourners and the nation—Peace!

LIEUT. A. M. IRVING.

CHAPTER XX.

RECOLLECTIONS OF BATOCHE'S FERRY—AFTER THE BATTLE

ONE of the surveyors thus gives his experiences at Batoche:—Here we are at Batoche, which has, as you know, fallen before us, and we all, from the General to the "grub-rustlers," pose as conquering heroes decked out in our war paint, which in this instance is principally composed of dirt, that has become so much part and parcel of our being that the idea of soap and water is as distasteful as it would be to the dusky braves we have just been shooting at. If you will excuse the dirt, I will try to give you an idea of the movements of the Survey Corps to date.

You will remember that our fifty men were strung out in a line of pickets from Swift Current Creek to Long Lake, a distance of one hundred and thirty miles, to intercept fugitives from Riel's scattered army to more congenial climes. With great forethought was this disposition of our little force made by the General in command before the battle at Fish Creek; but after that encounter with the rebels we were ordered to the front, and on Sunday morning, 3rd May, the messenger reached our headquarters at the Elbow of the South Branch of the Saskatchewan with orders to that effect. To gather in our pickets and supplies was our next move. This being done on Wednesday at noon we "pulled out," as the saying is, and started for here. Our trip was a rapid one, for the orders said "at once," and we reported to the General on Sunday, the 10th, at 3 p.m., having covered the intervening one hundred and forty miles in exactly four days, although encumbered with fifteen days' forage and provisions. We found the little army about half-a-mile east of the church, and rather more than twice that distance from Batoche's Ferry, entrenched within a few yards of the top of the hill which descends steeply to the Saskatchewan, and of all places for entrenchments a ploughed field had been chosen, so you can imagine how nice and clean everything was and is.

The entrenchment in which the troops were placed was made by throwing up sods about four or five feet high, and inside of this, about fifteen or sixteen feet from the breastwork, a second square was made of the transport waggons, placed in such a position that the tongue of one waggon was inside the next one to it, all the baggage and provisions being left in the waggons. Towards the centre of this square another earthwork was thrown up to protect the hospital tents. There were within the encampment the 90th, the 10th Royals, the Midland Battalion, and four nine-pounders, besides horses, mules, cayuses, and horned beasts of all ages, and lastly an instrument known as "Capt. Howard's hurdy-gurdy," otherwise the Gatling gun, which had already played its part and saved two of the nine-pounders from being captured by the enemy. What had been done before our arrival you will read of in the papers before you receive this; but we found that the troops were extended in skirmishing order under cover towards the church exchanging shots with the rebels and gradually driving them back. The enemy were, of course, in possession of Batoche's, and of the slopes surrounding it.

Immediately below the camp the river flows northwesterly for about three-quarters of a mile, when turning sharply it runs almost directly north. At the turn the banks on the easterly side are bold and steep, and clothed with poplar, timber and brush, getting gradually lower as they approach the ferry and village, and again rising and receding as they extend down the river. The approaches to the village were defended by a line of rifle pits along the edge of this bank, as was also the retreat of the rebels across the river should such have been required (as was the case). These pits extended down the river for nearly a mile and a-half north of the ferry, and were strongly constructed and placed at short intervals. Here at the foot of the bank were afterwards found the remains of a Half-breed and Indian encampment in a state of the greatest disorder, showing that they had not looked to the order of their going, but had gone quickly. It was, doubtless, in this camp that the women and children had been placed to be out of the way of stray bullets. A close inspection showed that holes had been scooped out of the hill side and covered over, into which they could crawl and so escape the bursting shells.

The main position of the rebels extended along the edge of a range of hills running northerly from the cemetery and parallel to the river, forming the eastern border of the valley. The sides of these hills are covered with poplar and brush, and broken by ravines. They descend gently to the valley's bottom, leaving an open flat around the village. It was while crossing this open that the greatest number of wounds were received, and it was here Gordon, one of our corps, who had got separated from the main body, and was gallantly charging along with the 90th, was severely wounded in the shoulder. On the right of the village the ground is also open, gradually rising towards the north, while near the hills, and some seven hundred yards in an easterly direction is a rise covered with timber, from which the Gatling did some very effective service.

Independently of the main line of rifle pits along the brow of the hill, pits were dug at every point on the face of the hill that could by any chance become a commanding position. This was especially the case in one ravine immediately behind the eminence spoken of as being occupied by the Gatling, and here after the fight, were found no less than six dead breeds, all of whom were riddled with bullets. Their pits were admirably constructed, and from them a constant fire could be directed upon our men whilst the enemy were completely protected from our rifles. An after inspection showed them to be three or four feet deep with breastworks of earth and logs channelled for the rifles of their defenders, who could sit hidden from view and coolly pot any of our men who showed too much of themselves. Their tactics had in some sort been adopted by the volunteers, but our hastily constructed defences were simply a few sods piled one on top of another, behind which the men lay and fired whenever they could catch sight of the enemy, and very often when they couldn't.

Our survey life as you know accustoms us to various extremes, and after the first half-hour in camp we sat and smoked our pipes and listened to the tales of the older hands, broken every now and then by the crack of a rifle near the church, while an occasional bullet sung over the camp from the enemy's lines. Shortly after our arrival we were uncomfortably awakened to the fact that it was no sham battle going on around us, for Wheeler, one of our corps, sitting in a rifle pit on the river bank, showed rather more of himself than was advisable above the parapet and got a bullet through the shoulder. Fortunately it was only a flesh wound. Towards sundown the firing grew pretty frequent, and we had two horses wounded inside the square and some cattle were also hit, but fortunately no more of our men.

That night all hands slept in the trenches, the lucky ones getting a berth under the waggons and carts. The novelty of the position did not interfere very much with our rest, and we slept the sleep of the just, only growling and grumbling a little when we were awakened to take our turn of "sentry go," two men of the Surveyors being detailed to do this work for an hour at a time.

Next morning we breakfasted somewhere between four and five o'clock, and afterwards got orders to saddle up and go out with the Gatling, Boulton's and French's troops being also told off for the same service. We made a detour to the north and had a skirmish with the enemy on that side of their entrenchments, but the General withdrew us about noon without any loss on our side excepting ammunition. In the afternoon some of the Winnipeg Field Battery went down below the church to shell some houses on the opposite side of the river. The guns were placed side by side about one hundred and fifty yards from the cemetery fence. The house aimed at was about one thousand five hundred yards distant across the Saskatchewan. We always had a sort of an idea that an artilleryman could hit his mark with much greater accuracy than we could with our rifles, for the muzzle of a nine-pounder is not so likely to describe figures in the air as a weapon whose holder feels a strong inclination to duck his head at the whizz of a passing ball. But from what we saw that day we think we could do better. How many shots were fired I do not like to say, but they went all round that house and apparently any where but through it, until we got rather tired of the order : " Common shell, percussion fuse —load." There were a lot of us grouped around the guns all interested in the practice, when a couple of figures were seen to cross the trail some five hundred yards distant in the enemy's lines, and there was an instantaneous scatteration. We who were not encumbered with the dignity of an officer's rank dropped on our faces and a bullet whistled over us. Had the fellows fired before they showed themselves they might have bagged a man or two of any grade from the General down.

The General sauntered up and down with his cane under his arm showing his portly figure most unconcernedly, but many of the officers were not too dignified to stand in line, one behind the other, behind a very small poplar, not large enough to shelter the foremost one.

Then began a rattle of musketry from our side, but what they fired at Heaven only knows, for one couldn't see any signs of the enemy, and the old General as he strutted down to the trail in full view of the hidden marksmen, shouted out: "Keep your fire! What on earth are you firing at?" and then added *sotto voce*: "D——d fools," and walked back to camp, whither the guns follow, and we are left to be potted at if we like.

It was towards sunset when the 90th, who had been out all day, were withdrawn from the pits for the night. As they gradually retired the rebels followed them up. The firing was very heavy, and poor Hardisty was killed.

One or two of our boys, who went down to the pits with them "just to get a whack at the rebels," found it was rather the other way round, as the sun was directly in our eyes and we could not see any of the rebels, whilst they were having nice pot shots at us; but we all got safely back to camp to pass another night in the trenches.

On Tuesday morning we were off again with the Gatling and a gun from the Winnipeg Field Battery to attack the rebels in the same place that we did the day before. We dismounted and leaving our horses under cover of a bluff, moved forward in a skirmishing order up a slight rise in the prairie and through some small poplars. The rebels evidently expected us, for we had only advanced a few yards when they must have caught sight of some of us over the rise, and a volley was fired into our ranks, at the report of which we dropped on our faces in the brush, one of us never to rise again, for poor Kippen fell dead with a rifle bullet in his brain. This was the first man of our corps killed, and we realized more fully that it was no child's play we were in for, but really a fight in which a man's life counts but a very small item. Kippen had not been known to many of us before the affair began, but short though our acquaintance had been, we found him a pleasant and genial companion. We used to chaff him and call him the "Historian," little thinking that his people at home, instead of listening to his amusing accounts of the campaign, would be shocked and saddened by a brief telegram announcing that although no soldier, he had fallen as a soldier should, boldly facing the enemy. I am sure the whole corps, from whose ranks he is missed, can sympathize with his relatives in their far greater sorrow.

The rebels kept a steady fire upon us, and after shelling some bluffs and firing several rounds from the Gatling, we were ordered to retire and return to camp, the enemy putting some bullets very close to us as we mounted.

Just as we had finished munching the bullet-proof discs of that indescribable compound known as Government biscuit that formed our lunch, one of the Midland men on the slope of the hill near the cemetery was hit by a volley from the west side of the river, and the ambulance men going to his relief were also fired upon. This seemed to infuriate the men, and their officers saw that there was no holding them longer. Colonel Williams therefore decided upon charging, and with only two companies of the Midland, he led the way, counting on the 90th and Grenadiers for support. This is what actually took place, but at the time the first inkling we had was hearing the dropping shots of the skirmishers come thicker and thicker: then a cheer rises and a mounted officer dashes into camp. "Fall in, men" is heard everywhere, and the red coats of the 10th, and the black of the 90th move rapidly down the trail, while the rattle of shots has become a steady fire. Everyone is in excitement. Another side dashes up, and out of the enclosure at full speed come the four horses with the Gatling gun, whilst a dozen yards in front, his dark face beaming with delight and the tassel of his touque streaming behind him, rides the American Captain Howard, just spoiling for a fight. We give him a lusty cheer, and in a few moments our troop is ordered to support Boulton's and French's men on the right, and we advance at the double on foot.

Did you ever run a race in top boots and spurs, with a cartridge belt and heavy revolver in it, and clad in a close leather jacket and tight riding breeches? Add to these a hot day and you can imagine how we were handicapped; but we managed to get down and take our place in the line with the scouts on the slope of the hill near the church. Whether we were to support the advance of the uniforms or not we were not sure, but as the dense brush prevented us from seeing our officers, or what the infantry were doing in the valley, we just concluded that we'd clear all the rebels out of the slopes of the hills, and in extended line we started in to do it. Keeping up a heavy fire into the thickets as we advance at the run; catching our spurs and falling headlong; streaming with perspiration; panting with exertion, and swearing with but scant breath, we rush along the hill sides from one ravine to another, our cheers doing more to dislodge the enemy from their pits than the accuracy of our aim. Now and again the boom of a field gun echoes above the rifle shots, while frequently a skir-r-r-r, like the rattle of an alarm clock, tells us that Captain Howard is turning the crank of his "hurdy-gurdy," and in our mind's eye we can see him kneeling behind the Gatling doing two men's work in managing it, and sending a hail of rifle balls over the field, so deadly that one's soul is moved to pity for the unfortunate enemy, and we pump the lever of our Winchester and take a pot at a disappearing Half-breed or so, just to keep him from coming within range of the infernal machine that is rattling out death sentences in so remorseless a style. Now a shout of laughter rises as you take a header into the brush, and then you hear a yell of "Don't shoot that man,—— your eyes, don't shoot that man, he's one of our side," as some dozen rifles cover a scout whose ardour has carried him on in advance of the rest, while the rebel bullets whistle around us, and dropping branches cut by them make us wonder that so few of us are hit. But who is hit no one knows, for in this wild race a man could not find his own brother, and so we press on flushed with success past pit after pit, and the shots of opposing rifles grow thicker and then gradually slacken and die away, and we lie on the slopes gasping for breath, knowing that our share of the work is over, and watch the uniformed men sweeping the rebels before them across the flat at our feet, aiding them as we best can by a fire on the rifle pits that line its further edge some eight hundred yards away. A great deal has been said of the unadvisability of charging with raw recruits, but anyone who saw the advance of our men across the open could not doubt their vim and anxiety to get at the enemy. Of course we were too busy and too well hidden doing our own work to see the beginning of the attack, but we saw enough to convince us that Midlands, Grenadiers, and 90th all struggled for first place in the rush upon the rebels at Batoche's, the rush that drove them from their position, and has struck a blow at the insurrection from which Riel, with all his influence, will never be able to recover.

And then the retire is sounded, and we stroll back to camp, knowing that we can sleep without hearing the now familiar crack of rifle or whizz of a ball, for the rebels are beaten from their stronghold, and Batoche is won.

In endeavouring to settle the much disputed point as to who led the charge, George Ham furnishes the following:

I have received no less than seven telegrams asking me to say which battalion led the famous charge at

Batoche's. My answer is the Midland, Colonel Williams leading them. That gallant officer, with Captain Howard of the Gatling, is the hero of this brigade. The "orders" of the Midland issued the day after the capture of Batoche's read as follows:

"The deeds yesterday performed by the Midland during the battle of Batoche have been such as to call

LIEUT.-COL. A. T. H. WILLIAMS, M.P., MIDLAND BATTALION. *

from all encomiums of the highest order. That flank

---

* Lieut.-Col. A. T. H. Williams, of Penryn Park, Port Hope, was born in 1837, educated at Upper Canada College and Edinburgh University. He was first returned to Parliament at the general election of 1867, when he was sent to the Ontario Legislature. He was re-elected by acclamation at the general election in 1871, and was first elected to the Commons in the 1878 general election, and he was re-elected at the last general election. He is a son of John Tucker Williams, Esq., a commander in the Royal Navy, who sat for Durham in the Canadian Assembly from 1840 to 1848. Colonel Williams distinguished himself at Batoche in such a manner as will cause him to be remembered long after his own and many succeeding generations shall have passed away. He died near Battleford, July 4, 1885.

movement entrusted to us was so rapidly and determinedly made that it is admitted that by it the tide of victory was turned. Amid a shower of lead from the front and left flank, the red line of the Midland pressed steadily on with British cheer and pluck, through the entangled brush on the river slope, until the proper time arrived for the rush across the open prairie front to the houses, the capital of the rebels, a distance of about five hundred yards. The response to this was a noble one, and would have done credit to the most experienced soldiers, as amid a shower of bullets the charge was made and the cheers went up. The Midland had the honour of having been in front of the advance, and the gratitude of the prisoners who were held by the rebels, as they emerged from the cellars of these houses, seemed to be a reward for the noble effort of the day, which was ours.

"The Lieutenant-Colonel commanding has issued commendatory orders to the battalion before this, for pluck shown in enduring hardships, for good order and discipline, and for efforts put forth on the line of march, and now words would fail to convey the deep sense of what is due to the Midland for their steadiness under the fire of a determined and well-entrenched enemy. Nobly have the officers done their duty, and the response of the rank and file to their command under the most trying circumstances has always been a ready and reliable one, as day after day and night after night the thud of the enemy's rifle bullets sounded about our advanced rifle pits. The Lieutenant-Colonel commanding desires to place on record the pride he feels in having had the honour of commanding such soldiers, and to express his thanks to the officers and men for the ready response given under such circumstances to his orders.

"The action yesterday, which has virtually broken the rebellion, will call forth the thanks and gratitude of the country, and none will be more deserving of this than the Midland. While we rejoice over the victory, we cannot forget our wounded comrades whom we leave behind us as we push further on. Let us express our deepest sense of gratitude that none have been dangerously wounded.

"(Signed)   ARTHUR T. H. WILLIAMS,
"Lieutenant-Colonel Commanding
"Midland Battalion."

The Grenadiers and the 90th followed the Midlanders hot-foot at the first dash, and before the first row of the

COLONEL GRASETT, ROYAL GRENADIERS.

rebels had been reached the men of the three corps were pretty evenly mixed up along the line, so it is impossible to say which regiment was actually first into the village. The General divides the honours equally among the three.

The following is an extract from a letter from Colonel Grasett, of the Grenadiers, to a friend :—

AFTER THE BATTLE. 263

In considering the question of this charge it is well to note the numbers and positions of the regiments engaged as well as their names. The Midlands were on the left among the underbrush on the river bank, the Grenadiers occupied the centre opposite the lines of rifle pits in the open; the 90th, when they came up, together with Boulton's scouts, completed the line out towards the right. At the opening of the attack the whole regiment of the Grenadiers, two hundred and fifty men, and fifty men of the Midlands, under Colonel Williams, were the only troops in line, all the remainder of the force being in the zareba. When the charge began, the left of the line, with the two Midland companies at its extremity, swung forward more rapidly than the centre, the charge of the latter being against the pits and key of the position. These carried by a rush, the enemy was thrown into complete disorder, and the whole line, with the reinforcements from the zareba who came up about half-an-hour after the ball had opened, swept forward together into the village, so that representatives of all regiments were side by side.

Apart from their position the Grenadiers were five to one of the Midlands, and upon the greater number fell the greater weight of the charge.

A correspondent furnishes the following admirable story of the fight and the scenes which followed it, and although some of the same sentences occur in this which are given in preceding accounts, for the sake of completeness and continuity, the letter is given as nearly as possible intact:

On Saturday the steamer opened the ball, and called away the attention of the rebels until we were almost upon them. The Grenadiers bore the brunt of the fight, with the 90th in support and the Midlands in reserve, the two batteries of course doing their share. On Sunday we did nothing but lie there, the Midlands on the right, and the Grenadiers on the centre and left. The opposing forces never approached within six hundred yards of each other, unless at sundown, when, retiring to camp with the sun's rays in our eyes, the rebels would crawl up and pick men off. This was of nightly occurrence. Monday was a repetition of the previous day, except that the 90th went out while the Grenadiers stayed in camp. On the last day came the gallant charge and the victory. Ours was the most dismal of all camps. The ploughed earth had turned to dust, to which the earthworks added their clouds. Hundreds of horses and cattle superimposed filthiness ; water was scarce and not fit to drink ; and the area was so limited that it was next to impossible for the troops, unless in the trenches, to lose sight of the dead around the hospital, or to get out of earshot of the groans of the wounded. This camp had been under fire for sixty hours. Bullets were not constant visitors, of course, as our lines were extended during the day, but we were within range all the time, and no one knew the billet of the next stray bullet. Poor Dick Hardisty was dead, and the 90th were mad. So were the Grenadiers, the Midlands and the Artillery. I don't mean to say they were mutinous, but they had nearly reached the limit of suffering. The officers were even more angered than the men since they knew the mettle of the troops. It was tacitly agreed among the field officers (at least each reached the same conclusion) that at the next opportunity the rebels should be charged and driven back no matter what the orders to the contrary from the General commanding might be. Howard (the Connecticut State Guard officer) had begged to take his Gatling forward, to take it apart and put it in the church, to do anything or everything, in short, to secure a victory.

On Tuesday morning all the mounted force except French's scouts, led by General Middleton and supported by Howard and his Gatling, and Drury, with one of the Quebec guns, moved out to the plateau on the east front of Batoche's for a reconnaissance similar to that made the day before. They struck the secluded and protected enemy as usual, and while Drury was throwing shrapnel

AFTER THE BATTLE.

into the brush ahead of him, poor Kippen, of Dennis's scouts, was killed only a few feet from the gun. Presently, and while the skirmishing was going on, a white flag was waved from a house on the flank and John Astley, one of Riel's prisoners, followed by T. W. Jackson, another, came to General Middleton with a note which has appeared in an earlier portion of this volume.

Soon after dinner the Midlands, under Colonel Williams, who had been holding the left on our skirmish line, were reinforced, the Grenadiers, under Grasett, being pushed out on the centre towards the church, and part of the 90th under McKeand sent out on the right, one company being held to assist the larger portion of A Battery and the teamsters in holding the camp, and the rest in readiness to support their comrades if needed. General Middleton, who had ridden forward to the church (our skirmish line having driven the enemy from that vicinity and into the ravine where the trouble commenced on Saturday), then gave the order for a reconnoissance in force, and the men were pushed forward. Soon it was evident that the men and their officers were determined to have more than a reconnoissance. They did not stop nor cease firing though General Middleton cried, "Why in the name of God don't you cease firing?" but kept right on, and in ten minutes the whole line, advancing to the tune of a ringing cheer led by Van Straubenzie and the other colonels, was on the keen run into the ravine. The men had taken the bit in their teeth. Before they got into the bottom of this ravine Astley appeared with another white flag and a message from Riel, in which he said he did not like war, was glad that his former note had received such prompt attention, and asking that the troops cease firing in order that the women and children might be collected. This was altogether "too thin," and General Middleton replied to Riel that he would cease firing when the enemy did, and not before. The roar of the artillery, which had come up at a gallop, leaving one 9-pounder in camp as a protection, was now added to the rattle of the Sniders, Winchesters, and Martinis—the Winnipeg Field Battery opening on the house in which the rebels had hidden, riddling it with shells. A Battery's nine-pounder was also doing good work, while on the right centre the rackety-crash of the Gatling showed that the 90th had Howard's machine-propelled bullets working for them.

In half-an-hour or so the troops had won the key of the position and could take short rests in one or other of the numerous gullies which traverse the place. Then came that saddest of all hails, "Stretcher here!" "Ambulance, quick!" and the hospital badges showed in various portions of the field. There was room for running since our front covered more than a mile and a-quarter, and the advance, on the run, through brush and brake, had winded many a brave fellow, the hot sun adding to the toils of war.

The din now became furious and on went the advance. Panic had seized the enemy now, and it was a case of *sauve qui peut*. One of the Grenadiers bayoneted an Indian who was trying his hardest to get out of a rifle pit. Many of the dead rebels were in their stocking feet, having left their posts so hurriedly that they had not time to don moccasin or shoe, neither of which they wear when on duty in the pits for any length of time. The Village of Batoche's proper, consisting of five houses, and its suburbs of two, were now in plain view and distant but a few hundred yards. Those of the enemy who had not run away were firing from the row of outhouses on the east trail, from a gully in rear of Batoche's handsome two-storey building, and from the hills and brush on the right. One of the Winnipeg guns under Captain Coutlee rushed to the right and shelled the bush in advance, and later Champaigne's house in the rear. It took but a few moments to make the rush to Batoche's new store, and then to Batoche's old store and house; and then the day was won! Not a man was killed while in the open, although several were wounded.

But one of the saddest losses was at Batoche's house. Captain Jack French, tall of form, and his Celtic blood at boiling heat, rushed to its front door facing the south-west, and with a "Come on, boys," ran in and up to the upper storey. He had hardly reached the door when a bullet from the gully toward the ferry pierced his breast below the heart, and he lived long enough only to say, "Don't forget, boys, that I led you here." On Saturday he saved Cook by his personal bravery, snatching him from the very jaws of death. It was a brave act worthy of the Victoria Cross. On Tuesday he led his gallant little band on to his own death.

Colonel Williams, of the Midlands, was close behind French and, with one of the 90th or Grenadiers, kicked in the door of Batoche's, beneath which, in a gloomy hole called a cellar, were the white prisoners. They had broken the fastenings of the trap door which penned them in, but could not lift the stones piled on it, and the troops did this, letting the imprisoned ones free. By this time the fight was practically over, though to our front and across the river came scattering shots. The Indian and Half-breed camp had been carried by a few of the Grenadiers without loss and the inmates had gone in such a hurry that they left their lares and penates and all their paraphernalia of semi-civilized and semi-nomadic life. The 90th was now having about all the fighting there was, and they kept up their well-earned reputation. Major McKeand sprained a tendon while charging, but stayed with his men and supported the Gatling in its deadly work.

As the shadows deepened the steamer *Northcote*, towing and being towed by the *Marquis*, came up stream, and its arrival was received by three rousing cheers, which, re-echoed by the naval brigade, startled the beaten and demoralized Metis who lined the crest of the western bank. The dead were gathered, the wounded cared for, while the helpless women and children flocked in under a white flag and bivouacked in rear of the blacksmith's shop. Entrenchments were thrown up around the houses and the Gatling placed in position fronting down the river, while the rest of the artillery were sent to the camp to protect it against a possible, but not probable, night attack. Quite a number of prisoners were taken, and the rest began to surrender, in batches. The victory was all but complete—Riel and Dumont were not among the slain or captured.

In the morning looting began, and as the General's orders previously issued against it could not be enforced, no interference was made. Some of the men needed articles of underwear, blacking, combs, etc., and these were hurriedly snatched. Guards were of course put on the stores, but the ill-assorted stores somehow or other disappeared. Trunks were ransacked and trophies of the war secured. The rebel state papers were found in the rebel council room, George Fisher's house, an unpretentious log shack, no attempt having been made to secrete them in the hurly-burly of the excitement. An account book was opened showing the transactions of the "Government," and that Dumont was in charge of one wing, and Monkman of the other. The minutes were all in French, of course, and many were moved by Riel himself. One resolution was to the effect that the movement on Duck Lake should be made, showing that the affair was a premeditated one. Other resolutions were in regard to the movement of the rebel forces, which was influenced by the movements of Middleton's force, whose strength, daily advance, supplies and forage, etc., were accurately known. Numerous excerpts from Eastern Canada newspapers, clippings of paragraphs about Riel, the rebels, the Government's course, the strength of the Canadian forces, etc., were also found. French Canadian papers, up to as late a date as May 4, were also found, as were copies of Canadian papers, with articles pointing out the weaknesses of Middleton's forces. One resolution passed on Saturday night, and carried unanimously, was that they should go down stream and complete the destruction of the steamer *Northcote*. A letter of welcome from Monkman to Riel, written to that individual when in Montana, was also discovered.

Batoche's, both on the east and west banks (Batoche proper, on the east, being the most enterprising place north of Fort Qu'Appelle), is a veritable village of rifle pits, strategically located, commanding every available position, and showing that great energy and labour, as well as skill, must have been expended upon them. As a prominent military man remarked, an engineer could profitably take lessons from these untaught Metis of the West. The rebel position (it could not be called lines, for the pits run in all places and in all directions), demonstrated that the plans of defence were admirably conceived and excellently executed. It seemed as if they expected the troops to come along the river bank, and had prepared a ravine, a short distance up stream, to give us a warm reception. Weeks must have been spent in fortifying the place, since every conceivable point of vantage for a radius of a couple of miles was utilized. All their pits were deep, with narrow entrances, which widened at the bottom, thus giving perfect protection. Notched logs, the notches turned downwards, formed a parapet, earth being piled on top, and the notches cleared for loop holes. Lines of sight for the rebel marksmen were cleared in the brush. There were trenches of communication between the pits, arranged *en echelon* on the main road from Humboldt, but fortunately we did not come that way. Not alone in the field had the enemy prepared for a determined stand, but the houses in the village were also ready for an emergency. Even the tents in which some of the rebel warriors lived were not without protection. Almost every one had a rifle pit, and under the cart or waggon—for some of these people have discarded the old-fashioned Red River cart—a parapeted hole was dug for defence. If they had prepared for us at Fish Creek, they had a thousand times more so at Batoche's. It was their last ditch. No trail, no pathway, however insignificant, was left unguarded; no ravine, no gully that was not made a point of attack or defence.

Pointing out to me on the map the rebel lines guarding the main Humboldt trail, Gen. Middleton remarked last night, "They are a veritable Sebastopol." Middleton's detour to the east had evidently led them to believe that he was coming that way but, the steamer coming first, their attention was attracted to the river, as I have described previously, and the force slipped in by another detour to the south, and we had almost reached the church before they heard us, so intent were they on destroying the boat.

But, as it was, they managed to keep our superior force—superior in numbers, in arms, in artillery, in everything—at bay for nearly four days, and then it was only that rousing, ringing cheer and charge that drove them out. It might not have been that alone. Superstition may have had something to do with it. I was told by half-a-dozen Half-breed women that on Tuesday morning Riel had gone over to the west bank, where, after shaking hands with all the people, he told them that the battle would be decided that day. Posing as a prophet (he had previously foretold the darkening of the sun just before the last eclipse, being almanacally informed), he said to them that if the sky darkened they would be beaten. Then the sun was shining bright and clear. In the afternoon dark clouds rolled up, a few drops of rain fell, and the evil omen, influencing the mind of the savage and the semi-savage braves, doubtless helped us materially. This ends my officer friend's account of the battle.

CHAPTER XXI.

THE PRISONERS AND THE VANQUISHED.

I HAD the honour, if it be an honour, of being the first person to place foot on the west bank of the crossing. Early in the morning Alex. Fisher, ferryman, Receiver-General and Acting-Quartermaster of the rebel army and now a prisoner, came over in the ferry scow, under a flag of truce, and surrendered. On the flag was a picture of our Saviour (for a travesty of religion seems to have permeated everything on Riel's side) painted on paper which was sewed on the cloth. He was accompanied by two men. None of them, of course, had voluntarily gone into the fight; but they had been forced into it. Fisher was allowed to go on his parole until 6.30 p.m., when he was put under guard. Accompanied by Geo. Kerr, whose name you have heard before, and Captain Andrews, I crossed the river. Reaching the other side a Half-breed was seen crouching behind a high shelved bank on the side of the ferry trail. We hailed him, but he refused to come out. One of us then spoke in French to him, and a half-scared man walked out. He was Francois Boucher, and after a cordial shake of the hand he said he came from the Mackenzie River. He had been dragged into the trouble.

"Where was Riel?"

"Don't know."

"Which way did he go?"

"Don't know. He was on the other side of the river."

"When did you see him last?"

"Yesterday (Tuesday). Then he went away."

Leaving the old man, we climbed the steep, winding ascent, viewing the admirably-constructed rifle pits which command the river, pits in the brush, pits on the stony lower bank of the river, where the water almost laves them; stones piled up in semicircular form, behind which they could crouch and deal out death and destruction. To the right is a hill, filled with the inevitable pits, and on the top is a white flag, emblem of the surrender. Over the ferryman's house and store to the left flies another white flag, but in the bushes there still float two red flags of the redskins.

In the back-ground was the log building formerly occupied by Walters & Baker as a store, but latterly used as headquarters of the "northern division" of the rebel army. It is an utter wreck, testifying to the destructiveness of the heavy guns which played on it during the fight.

To the left are seen several women and children, tidying up their tents in the woods, and sorrowfully gathering together their scattered goods, and packing them in carts. Caves had been dug—ten, fifteen, twenty feet long—five or six wide, and four or five deep—and these were carefully covered with trees and brush and earth. In these, during the four days' struggle, the families lived, and ate, and slept if they could. After the customary hand-shaking, and being assured of our friendliness, they readily answered questions. Two of them were looking in vain for their husbands who were across the river, they did not know whether dead or alive, but hoped for the best; and laughed with joy at the prospect of peace, and an early return home. Some could only speak Indian, others only French, others again Indian, French, and English. None of them had a good word for Riel. By-and-bye Half-breed men whose suspicions were allayed came riding in unarmed and extended their hands towards us, and cordially grasped ours. All of them were sick of the "troubles"; all of them denounced Riel and Dumont; all of them wanted peace and home. It was curious, though, how unanimous they were in declaring they had been pressed into service. Of over twenty with whom I conversed, not one had joined Riel willingly. To one he had threatened arrest; to another death; to a third the massacre of his wife and children, if he failed to join the insurgents. I asked, "Well, if you were all made to serve, why on earth didn't you rebel against the rebels?" But I did not get any satisfactory answer. If what they said was true, and I am inclined to believe many of them, it only shows that Riel's organized few terrorized the unorganized many. But doubtless some of them lie.

In the afternoon many others came in on ponies, but all unarmed. There were forty or fifty of them, with their families, camped a mile out in the bush. One of them told me his story—several of them did for that matter, but this was a particularly hard one. He said, in answer to my query, that he had no grievance whatever; he lived on an Indian reserve. Riel had taken his cattle, and by threats forced him to join. He stayed two days in the woods during the fight with nothing to eat, and only water to drink. "And now," he said, as he cursed Riel with a good round oath, "here I am, without my cattle, without my horse, not even my gun. No land ready; no seed: nothing but starvation ahead of me. I have no tobacco, no tea, and my family is starving." I suggested that he could be made rich by catching Riel and delivering him up to the authorities, and he told me that they had already been discussing that question on the west bank.

Another's was quite as sad a case. He was a young man, with a crippled wife, who lay sick, terror-stricken, and alone in her gloomy cave while the bullets' ping and the shrapnels' whizz almost deafened her. A bright lad of eighteen, Francois Boucher, the younger, gave me the best description of the fight. He said in English:—

"I was hiding in the bush, and I was pretty scared. I don't like this fighting. When the ship came down the river one man shot hard at it. When it stuck on the ferry rope our men thought everything was smashed

17

and the police all killed (they call the troops police). One man said that he had seen twenty police fall over board dead, and Riel was certain the boat would be his when he wanted it. He thought it was stuck on a sand bar down the river and you were all dead on it. On Sunday night he sent some men down to loot it, but when they got there the boat was gone. They came back and the

MAJOR D. H. ALLAN, Q.O.R.

Indians said that the devil had lifted the big iron (the anchor) up and the boat had gone away."

Then he told me the story of Riel's visit to the west bank the previous evening, his hand-shaking with the people, and his warning about the blackening sky; and about Riel being a second Messiah, and how he imposed upon the people and himself.

A number laid the whole blame of the troubles upon Charley Nolin, who, they allege, was the prime instigator of the uprising, and the one responsible for Riel's advent amongst them; but, they added, he cut connection with them when loud-mouthed agitation gave way to the rifle and the shotgun. He, however, had handed around the little paper badges which they wore on the lappels of their coats, badges with religious devices.

The men were penitent even for their enforced participation in defying the Queen, and only wanted to surrender. A priest came over, and they sent in their guns, nearly one hundred in number. Some of these were fine Winchesters, a Snider or two, a Queen's Own rifle, a Springfield carbine, supposed to have been taken from the Custer battlefield, and shot guns of every description, single and double barrelled, and old flint locks, some almost entirely useless. It seemed almost incredible that, poorly armed as these men were, they managed to pour in such a hot fire on us as they did. But the Metis know how to use a gun, and they always make the best of the weapon they have.

Passing a grove on the way back to the boat, something white suspended to a tree attracted attention. It was a picture of the "Sacred Heart of Jesus," neatly draped with pure white muslin, attached to the card board by those common little tin tags which tobacco smokers know so well. The place was a little sylvan shrine where the terror-stricken women knelt and prayed to God in the very midst of the swirl of life and death.

I asked several who the man was that they had hanged on the Saturday previous. They all denied any knowledge of it. Some said the Indians had put up some feathers in the trees as a decoy for the shots of the police, but I told them feathers did not wear coat and pants. Still they vehemently averred that no one was hanged there. A dozen men in the steamer are prepared to swear that they saw a man dangling in the air. It is strange if so many could have been mistaken.

At Batoche's proper, the village had changed from a battle field to a busy camp. On the right of what would be the main street were the women and children, safely and comfortably living in tents. From these I learned that they at least were glad the war was over. It was the old story: Riel had made their men come. Mrs. Tourand, who lives at Fish Creek, told me that of her husband's six brothers two had been killed, two wounded and one made prisoner. A married sister-in-law sat beside her, venting her grief in tears and lamentations. They had been all hungry, and for over twenty-four hours during the fight had had nothing to eat. None of them were hurt, although a spent ball cut off a piece of one woman's hair, and two innocent little babies were so closely grazed by bullets that a scratch was left on their dusky skins. I asked the women where Riel was. They didn't know. When was he last seen? One contemptuously sneers at the fallen leader: "Bah!" she says, "he is a woman. He stayed all day yesterday with the women and children, and he told the others to go and fight. He calls us women because we can't fight; but he is a woman himself."

As the prisoners were brought up in a waggon, preparatory to being transferred to the steamer, a heart-rending scene ensued. Imagining that they were to be hanged or sent away for ever, wives rushed up and fondly embraced their husbands, and then held up the prattling babes for the father to take a farewell kiss. The little ones laughed and crowed as babies will, but their childish glee was in strange contrast to the tear-stained faces of the women, whose anguish could not be concealed. One touch of nature makes the whole world kin; and those signs of grief from helpless women caused many a battle-stained soldier to turn aside and wipe away a tear. The women were comforted as well as words could comfort, and assurances were given that their husbands would not be harmed unless they were leaders. With grief partly assuaged, the women turned to their tents, their faces

THE PRISONERS AND THE VANQUISHED.

hid in their handkerchiefs. Let us leave them with their sorrow. The fortunes of war are to them a dreadful burden.

Let me tell the plan disclosed in the state papers of the rebels. When we were encamped at McIntosh's, the night before the Fish Creek fight, Gabriel Dumont's designs were to make an attack upon Middleton. In the dead of night, while the camp in fancied security was seeking well-earned repose, the rebel force, five hundred strong, was to steal up, as only these plainsmen can creep upon a foe, overpower the pickets and sentries, and before the men could be aroused, to sweep through the camp like a whirl-wind. In the darkness and confusion success might have followed the daring deed. Our command was divided, as Dumont well knew, by the wide Saskatchewan; communication was cut off between the two columns, the scow being in an inaccessible place; and if the orders given had not been misinterpreted by some stupid brave, the rebels might have boasted of a victory. Fortunately for us, there was a misunderstanding amongst the different divisions of the rebels, some of their strength did not reach the rendezvous in time, some did not come at all, and the surprise was postponed. Little did we know how near to death's door many of us lay that night.

The prisoners released from Batoche's house all bear the deep imprint of the hardships they have undergone during their long imprisonment, their pale, pinched faces and emaciated forms furnishing indisputable proof of sufferings, both bodily and mental. They are easily picked out from among the many civilians about the camp, and it is moving to see the eagerness with which they grasp the hands of some acquaintance one or another may chance to meet. One of them is so overjoyed at being released that he shakes hands with everybody he approaches. Short rations, the close confinement, and the terrible suspense under which they lay, not knowing what moment might be their last, have done their work; and it will take weeks of care before their systems again recover their wonted vigour. One and all agree that but a short time longer and reason must have given way beneath the terrible strain. The prisoners rescued were as follow:—

J. B. Lash, Indian Agent for Carleton district; Wm. Tomkins, agency interpreter; Peter Tomkins, a cousin of the former, and John W. McKeen, telegraph repairers; Harold Ross, deputy sheriff of Prince Albert, and Wm. Astley, D.L.S., who were arrested on a scouting expedition; Edward Woodcock, who had charge of Leesin & Scott's mail station at Hoodoo; A. W. McConnell, one of General Middleton's scouts, and T. E. Jackson, druggist, of Prince Albert, brother of "Crank" Jackson. "Crank" Jackson himself, and Albert Monkman, whose name has obtained unpleasant prominence during the rising, were also found in confinement.

From the prisoners I have gleaned the following particulars of their capture and confinement: Mr. Lash, the agent, accompanied by Mr. Tomkins, his interpreter, were on their way from Carleton to One Arrow's reserve, about five miles from Batoche's, on agency business, on the afternoon of the 18th March. When they were near Batoche's church they were surrounded by a mob of between fifty and sixty armed men, under the leadership of Riel and Gabriel Dumont. Some of the crowd at once unhitched the horses, and Riel informed Mr. Lash that the rebellion had begun, and that he was obliged to detain him and Tomkins as prisoners. They were taken to Batoche's church and kept there until evening when they were taken to Walters & Baker's store on the north side of the river and brought back again the next day. At midnight on the 18th the telegraph wires were cut, the line going "wide open" in the very middle of a telegram of the greatest importance. Peter Tomkins, a cousin of the telegraph operator, undertook to go out and repair the break on the condition that he should be accompanied by a companion. Several men having been asked to go and having declined, J. W. McKeen, the miller in charge of Beaupré's mill at Stobart, or Duck Lake, volunteered. They set out shortly after 1 a.m. on snowshoes, drawing their tools on a flat sleigh, following the line through the bush until near the crossing, where they found the line cut and several poles chopped down. Without a moment's delay they set about repairing the damage, and had just completed their labours, having made three splices, and were gathering up their tools preparatory to the homeward journey, when they were surrounded by between twenty and thirty men who demanded their surrender. One man tapped McKeen on the shoulder and informed him that he was a prisoner. Having no arms they made no resistance, but accompanied their captors to Walters & Baker's store where they were kept over night. Riel was one of the party and was what the Half-breeds called the talking chief, while the redoubtable Dumont was the chief fighting man.

Another couple of the prisoners, Harold E. Ross and W. Astley, were captured on a scouting expedition on the morning of the 26th of March, the day of the battle at Duck Lake. They left Fort Carleton between 11 and 12 o'clock on the night of the 25th, with the view of gaining the high ground in the vicinity of the St. Laurent mission by daylight, in order that they might ascertain if any steps had been taken by the rebels to intercept Commissioner Irvine, who was momentarily expected to arrive at Carleton. A short distance out from the last-named place they met Jerry McKay, who had been scouting on Beardy's reserve, and he told them to be very careful, as that chief did not like people travelling across his reserve. McKay, however, assured them that the journey to Duck Lake was quite safe, Beardy being the only ugly feature of it. This they did not consider of a sufficiently alarming nature to cause them to turn back, and they resumed their journey, travelling leisurely in order that they might arrive at St. Laurent at the appointed time. When they came over the last hill near Duck Lake they were, as they subsequently learned, perceived by the picket from the Indians' houses near the trail. Shortly before this, Astley called Ross's attention to what he thought was a man lighting his pipe, but as the latter had not noticed it they paid no further attention to the matter. As they proceeded down the hill the Half-breeds rode out and down in their rear, the soft snow, which had been falling all evening, completely muffling the footsteps of their pursuers' horses until they were quite upon them.

Hearing a noise behind him, Ross looked back and saw Dumont at the head of about twenty men, with a rifle in his hand. Gabriel at once cried out, "Surrender, you're scouts." Astley did not hear the call, whereupon Ross tapped him on the shoulder and said, "They're on top of us," and wheeled his horse around. Dumont immediately seized him by the foot and ordered him to dismount, which Ross refused to do. The rebel Adjutant-General, as he styled himself in his official documents, then attempted to pull Ross off, upon which the latter endeavoured to draw his revolver. Two Indians got on each side of him, and those on the right pulled his foot from the stirrup, and Dumont succeeded in unhorsing him, and in doing so discovered the revolver, which he demanded. Ross drew it at once, not to give it up, however, but for the purpose of administering a leaden pill to an Indian who had covered him with a gun, at the same time seizing Dumont by the throat with his disengaged hand, to prevent his interference. Feeling something touch his head behind, Ross looked around, and found himself covered by two more guns, seeing which he surrendered. Astley, in the meantime, had endeavoured to escape, but perceiving his comrade was not following, turned back to his assistance, when he also was surrounded and taken. The two unfortunate scouts were conducted to Duck Lake, where they were joined the next morning by their companions in misery.

A number of others were also in confinement, but the majority were only imprisoned for a short time. Those who were placed in Walters & Baker's store for safe-keeping were only kept there during the night of the 18th, and were removed to Batoche's church the next morning, and the next day were removed to the residence of Philippe Garnot, Secretary of the Provisional Government. Among the other prisoners were George Ness, Louis Marion, and Charles Nolin, Half-breeds, who had refused to take up arms; Walters, of Walters & Baker, and J. D. Hanafin, a clerk in their employment; Edward Woodcock, already referred to as captured at Hoodoo, and Thomas Sanderson, of Carrot River, who happened to have camped at that place the night it was plundered. The evening they were removed to Garnot's house a council was held, after which Riel informed the prisoners that Charles Nolin was sentenced to death, and would be shot that night if he did not submit. Riel also told them that the rebellion was gaining strength, and would carry everything before it, and that it was the intention of the Council of Saskatchewan to march on to Carleton in such force that the police would surrender without a shot being fired, and Carleton once disposed of Prince Albert could easily be captured, as there was but a mere handful who did not sympathize with the movement. Marion was also told that he would be "attended to" if he did not submit. Both Nolin and Marion gave in their adherence, but the latter deserted the next day, and Nolin on the day of the Duck Lake engagement. Ness stood out to the last, but was released for some reason unknown to his fellow-prisoners, while Hanafin and Walters were also permitted to go a few days later, as the council decided they would only detain men who were servants of the Dominion Government. On the evening of the 25th March Duck Lake was taken by the rebel army, and the next morning the prisoners were moved over, the upper storey of Mr. Mitchell's house being put into service as a prison. Up to this time they had been reasonably well fed, as their captors had plenty of plunder, and were also freely supplied with tobacco; but they were kept under close surveillance and allowed to talk to no one.

After the fight at Duck Lake, Gabriel Dumont entered the prison and ordered the prisoners to be taken out and shot, but the men in charge refused to obey the order. The Indians were particularly anxious to have revenge, but were restrained mainly through the instrumentality of Monkman. The Provisional Government held a council meeting which lasted through the afternoon of the 26th and the early morning of the 27th, during which they considered the advisability of sending one or two prisoners over to Carleton to see if some terms of settlement could not be agreed upon, and also to invite the police to come over for the dead. It was, however, decided to liberate Sanderson and send him with the message to Major Crozier concerning the removal of the bodies, and this was done, the messenger being furnished with a horse and jumper, and an escort through the lines. After Sanderson left Riel came, when Ross asked for permission for one or two of the prisoners to visit the field of battle and put the bodies in a safe place to protect them from dogs and wolves, to which request consent was given. Wm. Tomkins and Ross went out that evening under a strong escort of Half-breeds and Indians, and placed the dead in a vacant house near by. While this was being done, the Indians said : "We'll shoot the white dogs." "This is a lesson for you," and similar comforting expressions. On Sunday afternoon, March 28, T. E. Jackson, Thos. Sanderson, and Wm. Drain arrived with teams for the dead and left the same night, although Drain was made prisoner for a time and his case was brought before the council; but he was released on explaining that he was present at the fight against his will. Riel learned from them that Carleton had been evacuated, but refused to believe it until he had sent over scouts to reconnoitre. Having satisfied himself on this score the prisoners were moved over on the 31st March to Carleton, under a detachment in charge of Monkman. The accidental fire on the night of the evacuation had only destroyed the hospital and guard room, warehouse, and orderly room.

The Hudson's Bay Company's clerk's quarters were fitted up for a guardroom and the prisoners placed in the upper storey, with a strong guard, Monkman assigning them a man and woman to cook and wait upon them. The afternoon they arrived at Carleton two teams in charge of Charles L'Heureux, of Battleford, were captured on their way from Prince Albert to the latter place. At midnight of the 2nd of April the guards wakened them and ordered them to roll their blankets and prepare to leave. This was done, and all the buildings were set on fire, the evacuating party arriving at Duck Lake at 10 a.m. on the 3rd. The prisoners were at first compelled to walk, but a "kick" was instituted after five miles of the road had been traversed, and they were permitted to ride on sleighs for the remainder of the road. At Duck Lake the buildings were gutted and fired and the march resumed to Batoche's, where they found the ice breaking up and the water running on the side.

The open water was crossed in boats, and the prisoners placed in Baptiste Boyer's house, being guarded by numerous sentries, who were ordered to fire on anyone attempting to escape without calling on him to halt. They were fed on bannocks, boiled beef and tea. The lower storey was occupied by Sioux Indians, who kept up a continuous drumming, thus preventing sleep at night. On 19th April they were put in a cellar and kept all day, the hatch being closed and braced down with an upright post wedged in tightly against the ceiling. In the afternoon the Sioux had a big dance, and made a demand for A. W. McConnell, of Qu'Appelle, who had been captured while carrying despatches to Prince Albert for General Middleton, averring that a man who carried news had no right to live. When the guards refused to give him up, they wanted to go into the room below the one occupied by the victim of their dislike and fire through the ceiling, and it required twenty men to prevent it. Several shots were fired outside, which the poor fellows in the cellar imagined were directed against McConnell, and the effect on their feelings can better be imagined than described. Again when word came that the troops were on the way, the men were confined in the cellar for two days, being fed twice a day on boiled beef and cold water, their gaolers asserting that there was neither flour nor tea. Again on the 23rd April, at 10 a.m., they were ordered down cellar, and the two Tomkinses were tied hand and foot, the remainder having their hands tied behind their backs by order of Delorme, who threatened to shoot any who should get loose. They were not allowed out under any pretext whatever, and did not receive anything to eat until 4 p.m. on the 24th (the day of the Battle of Fish Creek.) On Saturday, the 25th, Monkman brought them out and placed them in their old quarters, where they were allowed to remain until the 4th of May, when they were again put down cellar and kept there until released by the troops on the 12th, with the exception of a few hours on the 7th.

During the four days' fighting stones were piled on the hatchway in lieu of extra guards, as men were required in the rifle pits. They could hear the firing every day, and one day a shell passed through the building. On the 12th Riel opened the hatch and called out, "Astley, Astley, come quick and stop the firing: for if they kill any of our women and children we will massacre all the prisoners." Astley was sent out three times with a flag of truce, the last time getting three bullets through the flag, and another cutting the stick in two on which it was borne. The hole in which the prisoners were confined was only about sixteen feet square and nine feet deep, with neither floors nor walls, and utterly devoid of any means of lighting or ventilation, and in these cramped and unhealthy quarters they were obliged to eat and sleep and take such exercise as its narrow limits would permit. So strict were the restrictions imposed upon them that they were not allowed outside to answer the calls of nature.

When they heard the trampling of feet overhead the most conflicting hopes and fears filled their minds, and the few seconds which elapsed while the stones were being cleared away from the prison doors, were moments of the severest suspense—hopes that the time of rescue had come, fears that Riel or some of his followers had returned to carry out the threat of the morning, and wreak summary vengeance upon them. Imagine if you can the delight and relief which filled their minds when they found that realization had met their hopes instead of their fears. Some of them could scarcely contain themselves for joy, and eagerly shook hands with their rescuers, and then shook hands all around again. But the military had other work to do, and an escort was told off by General Middleton to conduct them to the camp, where they were made as comfortable as could be, and after the fight were congratulated by nearly every man in the force, many of whom felt that an important portion of their duty had been discharged.

Dumont occupied the grand dwelling house of M. L'Etendre *dit* Batoche, who is away from home. The building is pretty badly demoralized, and doubtless the thrifty and discreet Batoche will push a heavy claim against the Government for damages. Riel occupied less pretentious quarters, sometimes in one building, at other times in another, and frequently remaining in camp. Both are married, Dumont being childless, and Riel having two little ones, whom he took with him in his flight. Dumont is said to have lost every dollar and Riel has not a cent at stake in the country, owns not a foot of land, has not even a horse, and possesses only what little money his dupes gave him. The people of Batoche's, however, were not mere men of straw. In one place was found a fat pocket-book with $40 in cash in it, and in another there was $15 of equally good and lawful money.

As has been previously stated, Riel has been posing as the founder of a new religion, the principal feature of which is that he claims to be the Elias referred to by

Jesus Christ as he who must first come to change all things. He calls himself David, and signs his name thus: Louis " David " Riel. The first change he introduced was rebellion against the priests, which he formally did shortly before the Battle of Duck Lake; and as it was a part of his religious teachings that each change should be followed by a victory for the rebel arms, it was with a double gratification that he pointed to the advantage gained at Duck Lake, as the first instalment of the fulfilment of his prophecy. About a fortnight ago he changed the Sunday to Saturday, and contemplated changing the names of all the days of the week, had not the complete extinction of the rebellion interfered with his playing the *role* of Elias any longer. He was very fond of prophesying, but was clever enough to couch his prognostications in the vaguest possible terms. For example, he told his followers that the steamboat should drink water, an expression which may be taken to mean many things. He also told them that troops were coming from the United States to assist them, but when they failed to appear he explained that the Almighty had changed His mind and had ordered him not to seek outside aid as it would redound more to His glory to gain a victory with a small force. But it is needless to go further, as a book could be filled with similar prophecies and explanations for their non-fulfilment or ingenious interpretations to fit passing events. The rebel leader was fond of religious devotion, and spent hours in prayer.

Besides endeavouring to delude his credulous followers into the belief that he was a heaven-born saint sent for their particular benefit, Riel deceived them by keeping information from them. They never knew that General Middleton had issued a proclamation telling them that if they laid down their arms and returned to their homes they would be protected, but their leaders would have to suffer. He carefully kept that back. He also told them that the Americans, fifteen thousand strong, were coming to his assistance; but when some of the Indian prisoners found out last night from our scouts that it was an American who worked the maneton, as they called the Gatling, they lost faith in their leader entirely. Speaking of this gun they said it rained bullets so fast that they could not pop their heads out of the rifle pits to see where to shoot; that is, if they were going to shoot, which most of them contended they were not.

CAPT. J. M. DELAMERE, Q.O.R.

As near as can be ascertained, the rebel strength aggregated four hundred and fifty men, of whom two hundred and fifty are Half-breeds. Mr. Lash, one of Riel's prisoners, calculates the number as about four hundred, his impression of the division of the races being two hundred and fifty Metis and one hundred and fifty Indians. There were, women and children included, over one thousand in camp. The Indians were three bands of

Crees, those of One Arrow, Beardy, and Okamesis; and the band of White Cap, a Sioux, renegades of the Minnesota and Custer massacres, living around Prince Albert. Their provisions were not exhausted, and a large quantity of stores was captured at Batoche's. Beef was plentiful and considerable ammunition was discovered, the powder being of Curtis' English manufacture. Where the Gatling gun had been playing, the trees had been cut by the rebels and Howard's bullets extracted at night and utilized in the next day's fight. The men kept to their pits during the four days' siege of Batoche, night and day, scarcely going in for provisions, and the extremity to which some of them were reduced was evidenced by the mutilated remains of horses and of the dog "Colonel," of the 90th, from which steaks had been cut and eaten. Reinforcements were expected, and an Indian band, some fifty strong, were coming in the day after the fight to help Riel, but were intercepted by the sub lued Half-breeds ten miles away and told to go home for the war was over.

The following is a translation of the rules and regulations of the rebel army, posted on a house, evidently used as a guard room, on the western side. Common foolscap paper is used. The "army" had not indulged in the expensive luxury of printing, but one of the A. D. C.'s had written out the regulations with a blue pencil:—

Regulations which the soldiers should observe to the letter:—

1. The soldiers will rise at 6 a.m.
2. The roll-call will be made at 7.30.
3. They should be respectful to their captains and those other persons who are charged with their supervision and control.
4. They should be obedient and submissive to those who have the authority to command them.
5. They should be active, watchful and careful.
6. They should keep their houses clean and tidy, as also their arms,

7. Every morning their arms should be inspected at 9 o'clock.

8. No soldier will be allowed to leave his company without the permission of his captain.

9. Each captain should look after his company, see to its needs and treat the men impartially.

10. Each soldier should keep the guard which he is called upon to do conscientiously, on account of the very great responsibility which rests upon him.

By order,
GABRIEL DUMONT, Adjutant-General.

St. Antoine, May 2, 1885.

When Walters was released Riel addressed him at some length, telling him that he had been very useful to the movement in supplying goods, which had, of course, been taken without Mr. Walters' consent. "We have taken your goods," said Riel, "but you will not lose by it. We shall fill your store full of goods from the Company," meaning that when the Hudson's Bay Company's stores were robbed they would repay Walters.

Dumont became enraged at one of the priests the other day because the priest refused to carry out some of his commands, and, springing at him, attempted to kill him. A Sioux interfered and saved the priest's life.

The following is a copy of a letter addressed to Mr. Thomas Scott, one of the white agitators at Prince Albert, by the rebel council. It is not dated:—

"To TH. SCOTT, ESQ.

"SIR,—We do not want you to take up arms, if you do not wish to do so. But you could at all events send us delegates to meet ours, in order to consider the conditions upon which it would suit the people to enter the new confederation as a province. Leave the police to fight its own battles; with the help of God we will make them surrender. We will keep them as hostages until we have a fair treaty with the Dominion. In joining us, on the ground that the police has made it a matter of necessity for you, and in leaving the police to its struggles, you will determine the Canadian Government to come and treat with us; and by following that course, we will celebrate in peace and in happiness the 24th of May, otherwise the struggle will continue. The Government will send us reinforcements of police and we will have to call out all the neighbouring Indians and early this spring men will cross the international line, and the final result will perhaps lead us to celebrate the 4th of July instead of the 1st of the same July."

As I write scouts are going out in pursuit of Riel and Dumont, but the latter is not likely to be caught. General Middleton sent and received messages of congratulation to and from Mr. Caron, the Minister of Militia, to-day. In the general orders this morning, after quoting Mr. Caron's message, the General says:—

"With regard to the above message the Major-General has already by word of mouth informed the troops of his appreciation and thanks for their conduct on the 12th instant; but he wishes to put them on record in general orders, and to add that he feels very little, if any, thanks are due to him, as he considers that he owes all the success of that day to the pluck and dash of the officers and the men."

Private Cook was only a few feet from Lieutenant Fitch when that officer fell in the decisive charge of Tuesday, 12th of May, at Batoche's. Cook was himself immediately afterwards struck in the right arm and disabled. The ball entered the muscle above the elbow, and passed upwards, lodging under the skin, where it was easily extracted. His account of the Batoche's skirmishes and final victory and his statements fully bear out the previous accounts of the fixed determination of the Tenth to dislodge the rebels by a charge. In an interview Cook said:—

"On Saturday, Sunday, Monday, and Tuesday we encamped near Batoche's. On Saturday and Sunday the 90th Battalion were in front, and on Monday and Tuesday we were in the front line. In the morning we would advance and extend in skirmishing line and lie down and watch for a chance at the rebels, and return to our original position at night. We had a kraal formed of about two hundred waggons around which we rested, the front rank keeping watch while the rear lines slept. An embankment was thrown up by the teamsters."

"Did the rebels fire on you at night?"

"Yes, they fired on us every night, and many of our men were hit."

"Did you have blankets?"

"Yes, they allowed us two blankets each. We had no tents. In the morning we would advance and watch for a chance at the enemy, and retire in the evening. During the day we would get a couple of hard tack biscuits, and sometimes we had a cup of hot tea. We had no hot food in the evenings, because they did not want to light fires. Each day was like the other, advance in the morning and retire in the evening, until the men were maddened. The rebels were in their rifle pits, and could fire at us without being exposed. All we could see was the puff of smoke. Whenever it would get too hot for them they could retire to a gully."

"Would they be exposed in retiring?"

"No, they could crawl around like cats."

"Had you your great coats on?"

"No, only our tunics."

"You were a good mark to fire at?"

"Yes, we were good targets."

"That was not a comfortable thought?"

"Well, we thought no more of it than sitting here. We had no shelter on the level ground, while the enemy were sheltered. They were so placed, too, that our big guns could not get at them. The shells could not be dropped among them. On Tuesday morning we went out again. The General told us to take our old positions. Instead of that we took the enemy's position before the day was out. During the morning Colonel Van Straubenzie said he would like to go forward. An irregular fire was kept up until afternoon. The Tenth and the Midlands were in the front, and the 90th Battalion behind us. In front was open ground, and further on the bush, in which the rebels had their rifle pits. We did not want to stay lying there any longer seeing our comrades struck down one at a time while we could not strike back. The whole line started forward with a cheer."

"Were you ordered by the General to charge?"

"No; the General did not know we were going to charge. The enemy poured in a hot fire when we started, but I don't think any of our men were hit until we got into the bush. Here many of the men were struck."

"Were you near Lieutenant Fitch when he fell?"

"Yes, I was not three paces from him. We were pushing our way through the bush, which was pretty close, and jumping over the rifle pits, when he was struck in the breast and in the corner of the eye. He fell with a groan, and died immediately without speaking a word. I think he had his revolver in his hand, but not his sword. My heart jumped into my mouth when I saw him fall. I was then struck in the right arm, but did not fall. I was disabled and dropped down, because the bullets were flying thick, and remained there until the men had gone on ahead, when I walked to the rear and had my wound dressed. There were others hit in the bush about the same time. The Ambulance Corps carried Lieutenant Fitch off immediately, and followed the battalion up closely. They picked up and carried away every man as soon as he fell. They wanted to take me off, but I told them to attend to others more severely wounded first. Sergeant Hazleton was in charge of the Ambulance Corps, and they went everywhere and acted splendidly. The big guns did not begin firing until we got into the bush. When our men came to the rifle pits they found rebels who had not had time to get away in some of them."

"Did they offer to surrender?"

"Surrender would not be a bit of use in that crowd. They were bayoneted."

"When did the men halt?"

"They did not stop until the village was captured. Colonel Van Straubenzie and Colonel Grasett were with us, and went everywhere."

"What did the General say of the movement?"

"Oh, he addressed the men in the evening, and told them that they had made him the happiest man in Canada that night. He is a fine man and a gentleman, and could not use us better."

Private Cook spoke in terms of deep regret of the death of Lieutenant Fitch, summing up his expression of gratitude for the kind treatment they had received from the deceased officer in the words, "He could not do enough for us." He shows with much pride the bullet taken from his arm. It is a heavy missile, one and a quarter ounces in weight, and as round as a marble. He intends keeping it.

On the morning of Tuesday, the 12th, some wounded were sent to Saskatoon, and on the next evening he and many others were sent on. After staying there eight or nine days they went to Moose Jaw, one hundred miles by boat, and eighty-five by waggon. The latter part of the journey was pretty hard on the wounded. They then went to Winnipeg, where they remained a day and a night. Of their treatment at this place he does not speak with praise. He speaks very warmly, however, of the conduct of the officers of the steamer on their trip from Port Arthur down. Nothing was too good for them. At Sault Ste. Marie, where they stopped an hour, the American soldiers were very kind to them.

Private William Hughes, No. 3 Company, 90th Battalion, writes the following from Lepine's Crossing under date of 17th May:—

About Batoche's. We camped about six miles out on Friday night, and at 4 on Saturday morning arose, ate a hasty breakfast, and at 6 o'clock resumed our march on Batoche's. The steamer *Northcote* had been fitted up with bullet proof bulwarks, and it was so planned that we were to reach Batoche's at the same time, but she was there about half-an hour ahead of time, and had to run for it, as the fire was too heavy for her to stand long. At last we entered into a very hot fight, lasting all day; but very little advantage was gained on either side. We retired about four hundred yards and threw up fortifications, behind which all lay unmolested until morning. Shortly after daybreak we again went out, or rather I should say the 10th Royals did, and it was they who were in advance on Saturday, too. The General is said to have remarked that the 90th Battalion had done all the fighting at Fish Creek and hence had done our share, so he put the 10th ahead on Saturday and Sunday. That day passed off as the others had done, and again we retired behind our fortifications for the night, lying on a blanket with nothing save the canopy of heaven over us.

On Monday morning we (the 90th) were sent out with the two Midland companies, and drove the rebels back farther than ever and gained possession of their first row of pits and trenches. Colonel Williams asked for permission to let us charge the whole of them, but the General refused, as he thought we could not succeed; so another night and Tuesday forenoon were spent in the trenches; but the boys were almost out of patience and all were terribly angry at losing our nearest and best friends, so we were just in the humour to eat alive anything in the shape of an Indian or Half-breed. Well, about 1 o'clock on Tuesday, the 10th Royals and the Midlands were sent forward as usual to skirmish and had no orders to charge or to do anything else in particular, while the 90th were supporting them. Soon we heard the Midland companies cheering tremendously, and were at once extended into skirmishing line and sent forward

THE PRISONERS AND THE VANQUISHED. 295

on the double to support the 10th. They were then just a little ahead of us, lying down, firing at the red-devils, and with a cheer that was enough to strike terror to a braver man than a Half-breed or an Indian, we all rushed forward on the line of entrenchments and in the face of a fire that no one not there can imagine how severe it was. Cheer after cheer went up and fairly rent the air.

Every one was wild to get at the devils, but when we got within ten or fifteen paces of the pits the breeds and Indians jumped out and ran for their lives, many being shot down, for five lay dead where our company crossed. The fighting line was more than a mile long, and though I could not see any other part but ours it is true that the others did their work well too. I tried to watch Jack's company but could not see for sure, although they are said to have had the hardest of the fight at first, but we were still several hundred yards off the village, so on rushed the whole line, the Midland, the 10th, and the 90th, red and black coats mixed, all firing and cheering tremendously. At last when about three hundred or four hundred yards from the village we were ordered to halt and cease firing because Riel was sending a man with a flag of truce! He came to say something about Riel's wanting to hold a parley; but the General said if M. Riel wanted to talk he must come himself. So again the whole line rushed cheering and firing as before. One part of the line soon came out into the open ground and the firing encountered here was terrible. The bullets flew everywhere, for we were not more than fifty yards in front of some houses, while as the rest of our main line on our immediate right and left had not yet come through the brushwood the rebels blazed at us from three sides. Being fully two hundred yards ahead of our fellows on our right we lay for a few moments puffing and gasping for breath, at the same time picking out as well as we dared the definite location of the enemy in front. While lying here we counted our numbers, and lying side by side were twelve 90th men and one redcoat. He said he was a Midlander, but was several rods away, so I could not recognize him.

As soon as the rest of our line began to come out of the scrub our gang made a dash for a log stable in front and secured it, then for a large building used as a store. One of our boys was at the door before me, but I was second into the house, although all the rest of our crowd were in right afterwards, and Colonel Williams of the Midland Battalion was among them. This was the first house entered in Batoche's. Here beneath the store we found six prisoners in a dungeon, which was reached by means of a trap door. On that trap door was a pole standing upright and cut so as to fit tight from ceiling to floor, besides about fifteen or twenty large stones. We were not long in knocking them down and in lifting that trap, and I tell you it was the happiest moment of my life when we pulled those poor fellows out and were thanked and embraced by them for their liberation. Some of them had not seen daylight for nearly two months, and really the poor fellows looked more like ghosts than living beings. Colonel Williams was the first officer to come up to our part of the village. He then led us from one house to another, but we were not surprised to find them empty.

In the last house we found the body of a nice little girl, about fourteen years old. She had been killed by a shell, and was dressed for burial. So I lifted the poor little thing into the coffin and covered it up and put it away to one side to keep it from being knocked around. As I was doing so Colonel Williams rushed over to me, shouting, "Here is one! Here is one! Give me your rifle!" Mine was leaning against the wall where I put it before lifting the little girl. So he grabbed it up and aimed at a Half-breed's head. The breed was aiming at our fellows about fifty yards off, but my rifle was sighted for four hundred, so the Colonel missed him. The rifle was again loaded up and the sights let down. The breed rolled down the bank. The ball struck him under the

THE PRISONERS AND THE VANQUISHED. 297

left arm and passed clean through him, coming out under the right arm. I got his gun and powder horn. We are not allowed to keep the guns, but I have the powder horn all covered with his blood. Colonel Williams then left me in charge of a small party in one of the houses, and I at once began loop-holing it on the sides facing the river and the rebels. But the breeds did not stand any longer. They ran in all directions. However, we went to work at once, and by dark had the place strongly fortified; but no attack was expected, as the victory was so complete that it will be a miracle if the breeds ever attempt to rebel again.

We spent the next day in taking supplies, etc., from the rebels' houses; and in removing our dead and wounded to the boat which had returned up the river about three hours after the fight was over. Two other companies of the Midland—the Campbellford and the Lifford and Millbrook ones—arrived the day after the fight was over, so were too late for glory.

MUSKET CALIBER, TEN-BARREL GATLING GUN, WITH CARRIAGE AND LIMBER COMPLETE, READY FOR TRANSPORTATION.

CHAPTER XXII.

THE GATLING GUN.

AS the Gatling gun, as well as Lieutenant Howard, the gallant officer who commanded it, played a very important part in this campaign, no apology is necessary for furnishing a full description of this wonderful feature of modern warfare.

It requires no gift of prophecy to predict that machine guns are destined to play an important part in future wars.

They hold the same relation to other arms that the railway bears to the stage-coach; the reaper to the sickle; the sewing machine to the needle, etc.

Of this class of arms, there is none that excels the Gatling gun in originality of design, rapidity of fire, and capabilities as a weapon of warfare.

The main features of the gun may be summed up as follows:—

It has, usually, ten barrels, and ten corresponding locks. In working the gun the barrels and locks revolve together; but, irrespective of this motion, the locks have a forward and backward motion of their own. The forward motion places the cartridges in the chambers of the barrels, and closes the breech at the time of each discharge, while the backward motion extracts the empty cartridge cases after firing.

The gun is loaded and fired only when the barrels are in motion from left to right; that is, while the handle, or crank, is worked forward. When the gun is in action there are always five cartridges going through the process of loading, and five cartridge cases in different stages of being extracted, and these several operations are continuous while the gun is being worked. Thus, as long as the gun is fed with cartridges, the several operations of loading, firing, and extracting are carried on automatically, uniformly, and continuously.

The earlier model Gatling guns had cartridges fed to them by means of feed cases, or by a drum, but recently a new method for supplying the cartridges to the gun has been devised, which is *positive and certain in its action*. In the old methods of supplying ammunition to the gun it was possible for the cartridges to jam in feeding down from the feed cases into the carrier or receiver, but in this newly improved feed, the mechanism never loses control of the cartridges from the time they leave the feed magazine, until they enter the chambers, are loaded, fired, and the empty cases extracted. With this new feed, it is impossible for the gun to fail in its operation, even when it is worked by men unacquainted with its use. This new improvement not only greatly increases the rapidity and certainty of fire, but enables the gun to be fired at the rate of over one thousand two hundred shots per minute, and at all degrees of elevation or depression, which is something no other machine gun can do. By firing the gun at proper elevations, ascertained by means of a quadrant, the bullets discharged from it can be made to fall upon men behind breastworks, or entrenchments, at all distances, from two hundred to three thousand five hundred yards from the gun. This "high angle," or "mortar" fire, adds greatly to the effectiveness of the gun, and will no doubt, prove of inestimable value in future warfare.

Experiments have proved that musket-size balls, fired from a Gatling gun at high angles, strike the ground with sufficient force to penetrate from two to three inches of timber. About one thousand two hundred shots per minute can be fired from the gun, raining down a hailstorm of bullets on the heads of men behind entrenchments, thus making such positions, in a short space of time, untenable. Open breast-works or uncovered entrenchments, would furnish little or no protection to troops, against the fire of this formidable weapon. Trials were made with a Gatling gun, having this improved feed, at Sandy Hook, N.J., by the United States Ordnance Board.

THE GATLING GUN. 301

The following extracts are taken from their report of the trials:

"The objects of the experiments were twofold. First to test the new feed magazine; secondly, to ascertain the effect on targets placed horizontally on the ground, at

THE GATLING GUN, COMMANDED BY LIEUTENANT HOWGATE, READY FOR ACTION.
It fires 1,000 shots per minute—weight of gun 164 pounds.

distances from two hundred to three thousand yards as regards penetration and accuracy."

In speaking of this new feed, the Board say in their report: "The action is, as claimed in the inventor's description, positive and continuous as long as the gun is worked. The substitution of a positive action for one depending upon the carriage of the projectiles to the grooves of the carrier block by means of gravitation modified by friction, is a great improvement. The gun works as well when the feed 'magazine' is horizontal as it does in an inclined or a vertical position. No jamming or interference of any kind occurred during the trials, and the rate of discharge varied uniformly with the revolution of the crank necessarily."

"The penetration from 3,000 to 1,000 yards was through two inches of spruce plank, and from three to five inches into the sand, the projectiles striking point foremost."

The gun used in the trials was 45-inch caliber, with barrels 24 inches in length, and the ammunition used contained a charge of 85 grains of powder, and a bullet weighing 480 grains.

In firing at high elevations, to have the bullets strike the ground at various distances, the following elevations were given the gun: At 200 yards range, the gun was fired at an elevation of $88\frac{1}{2}°$, the bullets so fired remained up in the air 57 seconds from the time they were discharged, until they struck the ground.

At 500 yards range, the gun was given an elevation of 75°.

At 1,000 yards range, the gun was given an elevation of 77°.

At 2,000 yards range, the gun was given an elevation of 66°.

At 2,500 yards range, the gun was given an elevation of 56°.

At 3,000 yards range, the gun was given an elevation of 24° 40'.

At all ranges, when the gun was fired at and below 85° of elevation, the bullets struck point foremost, and retained their rotary motion, as was proven by spiral scratches on them, caused by friction in their passing through the boards.

THE GATLING GUN.

It is evident that an accurate vertical fire from Gatling guns, delivering a storm of bullets descending under a slight angle of arrival, would by grazing the superior crest of parallels erected by besiegers approaching a fortification, or those of ordinary rifle pits or entrenchments, destroy their occupants much more certainly and rapidly than can be done by the shells or case shot fired from mortars or field guns. This "high angle" or mortar fire from a machine gun, opens up a new field in the science of gunnery, and is well worthy of the highest consideration of military and naval men of all nations.

A table of distances and elevations being established for the service of the Gatling gun, all that would be required of the men using it would be to first ascertain the distance at which the enemy was entrenched, and then give the gun the required elevation (by the use of the quadrant) to have the bullets fall within the line of entrenchments of the enemy. The Gatlings could be protected from the direct fire of the enemy by entrenchments or by digging a pit for each gun, so that not even its muzzle would be exposed.

Among the prominent advantages claimed for the Gatling gun, may be enumerated the following: Its adaptation to the purposes of flank defence at both long and short ranges; its peculiar power for the defence of field entrenchments and villages; for protecting roads, defiles, and bridges; for covering the crossing of streams; for silencing field-batteries, or batteries of position; for increasing the infantry fire at the critical moment of a battle; for supporting field batteries, and protecting them against cavalry or infantry charges; for covering the retreat of a repulsed column; and generally the accuracy, continuity, and intensity of its fire, and its economy in men for serving, and animals for transporting it.

It is conceded that small calibre Gatling guns, which use the service musket ammunition, will prove invaluable in naval service when used from top-gallant, forecastle, poop-deck, and tops of ships of war for firing on an enemy's deck at officers and men exposed to view; for firing down from tops upon the roof of turrets; firing into an enemy's ports; and in boat operations against an enemy, either in passing open land-works, or clearing breaches and other exposed places for landing from boats, etc.

The above represents a small-sized Gatling Gun, mounted on a tripod; it can also be mounted on the gunwale of a ship or in the bow of a small launch, etc. It is a very light and effective arm and is recommended for the suppression of riots, etc.

Exhaustive official trials of the gun have been made in many countries, under the supervision of officers of high standing, who have strongly recommended their use, both for land and naval service. The reports of such trials are too extended for a paper of this kind.

Gatling guns have been sold, in greater or less numbers, to most of the governments of the world.

No arms in the world are equal to Gatling guns for night service. They can be placed in a position in the daytime so as to cover any point desired, and as they have no recoil to destroy the accuracy of their aim, an incessant fire can be kept up during the night with the same precision as in daytime.

Lord Charles Beresford, one of the pluckiest officers in the British Army, as he proved himself before Alexandria, wrote as follows of machine guns in the London *Army and Navy Gazette:*

In my opinion, machine-guns, if properly worked, would decide the fate of a campaign, and would be equally useful ashore or afloat. When the Gatling guns were landed at Alexandria, after the bombardment, the effect of their fire upon the wild mob of fanatic incendiaries and looters was quite extraordinary. These guns were not fired at the people, but a little over their heads, as a massacre would have been the result, had the guns been steadily trained on the mob. The rain of bullets, which they heard screaming over their heads, produced a moral effect not easily described. I asked an Egyptian officer, some weeks afterwards, how on earth it was that Arabi, and his nine thousand regular troops, who were within five miles, did not march down upon the town in the first four days after the bombardment, when Arabi knew that Captain Fisher's Naval Brigade, which held the lines, numbered less than four hundred men. The Egyptian officer replied, "That he knew no army which could face machines which 'pumped lead,' and that as all the gates were defended by such machines, as well as having torpedoes under the bridges, such defences could not be faced." This certainly was the case. I believe the Egyptian officer spoke the truth, and that the moral effect produced by the Gatlings on the people in the first landing prevented the army from attacking the diminutive force which held the lines afterwards.

There are several valuable features of the Gatling gun which should not be overlooked; for instance, a ten-barrel Gatling gun fires ten times in one revolution of the group of the barrels. The action of each part is therefore quite deliberate, while collectively the discharges are frequent. Another valuable feature in the Gatling is, that the cartridges are fed into the carrier at the top, and are carried around to the under side of the gun before they are loaded and fired. Thus, it will be seen, the point where the cartridges are fired is far removed from the supply of cartridges used in feeding the gun, so there is no liability of the escape of gas, which may occur by the bursting of the head of a cartridge, and which might communicate with the magazine, causing a dangerous explosion. Most other machine-guns have their magazine, used for feeding cartridges to them, placed in close contact with the firing point, hence the liability of premature and dangerous explosions. Several accidents of this kind have occurred, resulting in death to the operators of such guns.

The Gatling gun is only dangerous to those in its front.

Lord Wolseley, in discussing the subject of machine-guns, has expressed his conviction that the General who, in the next big war, utilizes machine-guns to the best advantage, will have an immense opportunity to gain great fame.

Intelligent men, who have carefully watched and noticed the march of improvement, and the steady development of new ideas, will perceive and acknowledge that the day is not far distant when machine-guns will be extensively employed in warfare; and the nation which is best supplied with them, and which best understands their tactical use, will best preserve the lives of its soldiers and be in the best condition to make favourable treaties, and to preserve the integrity of its own dominions.

CHAPTER XXIII.

POUNDMAKER AGAIN HEARD FROM—RIEL CAPTURED.

BATOCHE was won and the rebellion was practically over, for it only remained for General Strange to catch Big Bear and for General Middleton to relieve Colonel Otter's besieged force at Battleford. This would not take long, but in the meantime Poundmaker, having been forced by the hasty and ill-judged aggressiveness of Colonel Otter to go upon the war path, appeared determined to make his intention known. To this end he left his reserve with a considerable retinue of men, women and children, together with a large herd of live stock and marched east into Eagle Hills. On the very day that Batoche was captured Poundmaker's followers seized upon a large train of supplies, which were being forwarded to Colonel Otter, making prisoners of twenty-one out of some thirty teamsters.

J. Killough, who was employed carrying despatches came into Battleford about noon with information that a waggon train, numbering twenty-one ox teams and about eight horse teams, had been captured by Indians ten miles from here, close by the edge of the woods. Killough met several teamsters galloping towards Swift Current. They told him that early in the morning just as the train was starting from camp, they were attacked by Indians. The teamsters cut the horses loose and escaped. Those who remained were all captured, the onslaught was so sudden. They wanted Killough to return, but he said that the information must be carried to Battleford. Exchanging his pony for a good horse and avoiding the trail, he started. At the place where the attack took place he found two waggons and over a hill two miles distant, he saw the last of the Indians disappearing with the other waggons. He saw no dead bodies. He believes the remainder of the teamsters, ten in number, are prisoners. With the teamsters there were eleven Snider and five other rifles, with ammunition. This train also carried the mail for Battleford which had been waiting two months at Swift Current.

Shortly after Killough's arrival six Mounted Police scouts, including a Half-breed guide named McAllister, under Sergeant Gordon, late of the Queen's Own, came in. They had been scouting, and on rounding a hill were fired into at twenty yards by a large party of mounted Indians and breeds. Constable Elliot, late of the American army, fell at the first fire and staggered into the bushes. Constable Spencer was slightly wounded. The force retreated, the wounded man riding into the ferry where an ambulance came for him a few minutes later. Elliot's horse came in. The Indians pursued the police two miles.

One of the teamsters, after being released by Poundmaker, told the following story: It was Indians who attacked the train. They saw the breeds while driving along the trail, and corralled themselves so as to be in a better position to fight. Shortly afterwards Indians appeared all round, but whenever the teamsters pointed their rifles at them they sought cover. At last Nolin, a Half-breed, rode up and began to parley with them. He said that there were lots of Indians there, and that they were going to have the train. They did not want to kill the teamsters, but if the latter fired a shot they would butcher every one of them. On the other hand, if they gave up their arms and the train they would be allowed to go on to Battleford without further molestation. To this the teamsters consented. But no sooner had they started to walk along the trail towards Battleford than they were pursued by the Indians, who brought them back. On two or three occasions the Indians came howling around their tents, and they expected every minute to be murdered. But as the days wore on and their lives were spared they took heart again. One of the party was a passably good violinist, and while in camp in the evening he would play the fiddle while the others danced to the music. This afforded great amusement to the Indians, who crowded round to see the sport. Then, again, the Half-breed prisoners used to invite them into their tents of an evening. They had an organ with them, and it was no unusual thing for them to spend two or three hours singing together.

A Half-breed who came in with the released teamsters said:

"It was done by the Indians. I tell you those teamsters have the priest and Poundmaker to thank for their lives being spared. If they hadn't been there the Stoneys would have killed the whole outfit."

"Do you know anything regarding Elliot's death?"

"I think he must have fallen from his horse. He got into the woods. Three Crees tried to make him prisoner, and told him if he came out they would not hurt him. But he seemed dazed, and only replied by firing at the man who spoke to him. He kept retreating from bluff to bluff, firing as he went. As he came close to the waggon train, which had been captured a short time before, he was fired on from behind by some Stoneys and killed. I was sorry, and so were we all, for had he given himself up he would have been here now along with the teamsters. Delorme and Poundmaker buried him. That night we camped close by the Stoney reserve. There was a council that night. Poundmaker still wanted to go to the Blackfeet or even to the Rocky Mountains. The Stoneys would not hear of this, and took the council tent. Then Poundmaker went to one side and would have nothing more to say to them. There was nearly a fight that night between the Stoneys and the Crees. But at last Poundmaker consented to go right on to Duck Lake. He said his children were dying for want of food, and if they could get it from Riel it would be well, as they had given up all hope of getting anything from the Indian Agent. I don't believe Poundmaker would have come out had it not been for the Stoneys. He thought he might as well help himself to whatever was going, as well as the Stoneys."

On Friday (May 15) following the taking of Batoche (Monday, May 11), Louis Riel was captured by three scouts, named Armstrong, Diehl, and Howrie, four miles north of Batoche's. Scouts had been out in the morning to scour the country, but these three spread out from the main body, and just as they were coming out of some brush on an unfrequented trail leading to Batoche's, they spied Riel with three companions. He was unarmed, but they carried shot-guns. They at once recognized Riel, and, advancing towards him, hailed him by name. They were then standing near a fence. No effort was made on his part to escape, and after a brief conversation in which they expressed surprise at finding him there, Riel declared that he intended to give himself up. His only fear was that he would be shot by the troops, but he was promised safe escort to the General's quarters. His wife and children were not with him, and he said they were on the west side of the river.

To avoid the main body of the scouts Riel was taken to a coulee near by and hidden, while Diehl went off to corral a horse for him, the other scouts being left with the prisoner. When Diehl returned Riel and Diehl's companions had disappeared, evidently to avoid other scouts. Diehl says Riel was not in the least agitated when arrested, and was willingly made captive. He was assured of a fair trial, which was all he seemed to want.

When he saw the Gatling go down with the scouts at Batoche's, Riel was much alarmed on account of his family.

A correspondent adds the following:—

Riel appears careworn and haggard. He has let his hair and beard grow long. He is dressed in a poorer fashion than most of the breeds captured. While talking to General Middleton, as could be seen from the outside of the tent, his eyes rolled from side to side with the look of a hunted man. He is evidently the most thoroughly frightened man in camp, and in constant fear of violence at the hands of the soldiers. There is no danger of such violence. Riel spent nearly all day on Monday in the woods. At the close of the fight he and Dumont, with their wives and Riel's two children, skipped out on foot, going in a north-westerly direction. Some of the rebels were very bitter against both for leading them into the trouble and then leaving them in the lurch after the fight. The fugitives had no food, and no clothes except what they stood in. Dumont did not want to go, but Riel persuaded him. Dumont fought like a tiger all day Monday. The Half-breed prisoners say he had not slept for a week, working night and day.

Dumont had arranged for Big Bear to strike us in the rear a week ago, but some of the messengers deserted; and the scheme miscarried. Two of the prisoners say Dumont was wounded once on Saturday and twice (slightly) on Monday.

A scout told me last night that he had seen a Half-breed looking for his wife. The breed started to run, when the scouts threatened to shoot. He stopped, and the scout asked him to go to Dumont and tell him to come out unarmed and the scout would meet him, also unarmed, on which the rebel replied: "Dumont says he will never be taken alive." The scout promised protection to Riel until he was handed over to the General, and finally the man consented to this. He said both Riel and Dumont were in a bluff not very far from where they were talking and warned the scout to lie down or he might be shot. The breed left for the bluff and the scout heard them discussing matters. After waiting two and a-half hours and no one coming, the scout returned to the camp. General Middleton took no stock in his story, and said Riel and Dumont were miles away, but it is now evident the story was correct, at least so far as Riel was concerned.

The Half-breeds on the west bank delivered seventy-five stand of arms to-day. Amongst them were several

Winchesters, Sniders, Queen's Own rifles from Battleford, and one Springfield, U.S., carbine, 1873.

The papers belonging to the rebel Government were searched to-day. The minutes show that the Duck Lake fight was a premeditated affair, and that the rebels were thoroughly cognizant of General Middleton's movements from the time we left Qu'Appelle station.

Riel expressed himself to this effect: "I do not think this trouble will be without result, as the complaints of farmers will be regarded with some degree of attention." When told that his books and papers had been captured he said: "I am glad of this, the papers will show that I am not the actual leader of the rebellion. I had been encouraged by people of good standing at and around Prince Albert, who invited me over from Montana." He expresses great anxiety as to whether he will be tried by civil law or court-martial. He seems to have turned out a craven coward, as he spends his time alternately praying and embracing a crucifix.

The truculent Cree chiefs Beardy and Okamesis were also interviewed by General Middleton after the Batoche victory. The following is an interesting account of the interview by Mr. Geo. H. Ham.

The name of Beardy, the troublesome Indian chief, whose reserve is near Duck Lake, has become familiar to Eastern people, not only from the prominent part he has taken in the present trouble, but for his chronic cussedness and continual "kicking" for years past, and general desire to emulate the mule. Beardy, consequently, has gained a reputation for ferocity and boldness, that is, amongst those who don't know him. Those who are acquainted with him, however, say that he is a craven fraud. Be that as it may, he was submissive and cowed enough when he appeared before General Middleton this morning in response to a peremptory demand to come in at once. Beardy is an insignificant looking fellow, with a scattered grayish beard, from which he takes his name, and his chief men are not the typical braves of whom

Fenimore Cooper writes. They all squatted on their haunches, and looked as abject specimens of humanity as one would see in a month's journey. Beardy opened the confab by saying he first meant to speak the truth. He was glad to see so many around him. If his children, who came with him, had done anything amiss he hoped it would be overlooked. He was sorry for what had been done in joining the rebels. As true as he stood there at the present time, he wished to live in peace. He would like to go home and tell his people there was peace. Then he held out his hand and took the General's, shaking it heartily, and said he did so with all his heart, and he asked the General to speak his mind. Continuing, Beardy said he had held out for some time, but his people forced him into the trouble. He had only about forty men in his band.

General Middleton asked, through the interpreter, why his braves joined in the fight against the whites.

Beardy—All children are cowards, and my children were frightened into it.

The General—Did you join yourself?

Beardy—No; I sat still, and told my men to sit still. All my talk was to keep quiet. They mastered me.

The General—Were your intentions good towards the whites?

Beardy (emphatically)—Yes.

The General—When the police marched to Duck Lake, and you knew the Indians and Half-breeds were lying in ambush, why did you not tell them, if you were friendly?

Beardy—I thought I was stopping them enough when I prayed my people to keep still, and telling my head men not to take any white man's life.

The General—Why did you go over to Batoche's?

Beardy—Of course, as I said before, when children are young they are cowards. I was afraid and had to go.

The General—It's very lucky you came here, for if you hadn't I should have sent troops to your reserve and burned everything that's there.

Beardy bowed his head upon hearing this, and hypocritically sniffled :—I suppose it was God who put it in my heart to obey.

The General—If you are not able to command your young braves you are not fit to be chief, and I shall recommend that you be no longer acknowledged as one. It is a matter for consideration if your reserve is not taken away; it all depends upon how you behave yourself. Where is the telegraph wire broken?

Beardy—I cannot say.

The General—Well, I am going to send down a party to repair it, and if one man is fired at I will send a force and destroy everything—not shot merely, but if a man is even fired at.

Beardy bowed assent.

The General then asked if Little Chief, who was one of the first to join the rebels, wanted to say anything.

Beardy whined that they were forced into the trouble; but Okamesis was here and could speak for himself, which he did at some length, first uncovering his head. He said that when staying at his own house word of trouble came, and he hitched his horse and went towards Duck Lake, but his horse became played out. His brother was with him. He saw the priest and the farm instructor (Tompkins), who asked him if he was going to go. He replied that he was, but that his horse was played out and he was unable to go. The instructor said it was better for him to go, and lent him a horse, asking him to find out whether his (Tompkins') son had been taken prisoner or not. He consented to go with the horse, and on arriving saw that the Half-breeds had taken the Duck Lake stores. He saw three Half-breeds and they told him he couldn't go home without seeing their leaders. He said, "Never mind"; but to let his brother go home with the horse, and he would see the rebel leaders. They consented, and he went down where the head men were, and saw that Tompkins was a prisoner. The rebels told him that no one was allowed to go back, and that they would shoot anyone leaving without their knowledge. "I was a coward," he said, as if it were an extenuating fact. "The whole crowd left and went to Duck Lake. I was with them, and we had on a fire and were cooking, when I heard the police were coming. While I was eating I heard shots fired, but I ate on. The shots went on, and I ran to see what was going on. When I got up the ridge the bullets were coming pretty close, so I withdrew and went round by another way. The trail crossed the ridge, and I went there, and heard a shout: 'They are running back!' At the place on the ridge I went to I saw the body of a man; it was my own brother lying dead. I was afraid. From there I saw people lying dead all around. The Half-breeds told me to fetch my family in. I then took horses and went. I brought some families in, and was told to live in the farm instructor's house, which we did. While living at Duck Lake a party went to Carleton. I was not with the first party, but was sent out with the second. We got word from Riel to come back to Duck Lake. Then all broke camp, and went to Batoche's, camping on the river about two miles up on the west side. Word was sent to come, and camp closer. We came a mile nearer. They (the rebels) were not then satisfied, and told us to come nearer still, when we again moved camp, but still they were not satisfied, and ordered us to come right at Crossing (Batoche's). While living here, I heard that a party had gone up the country, and all at once heard big guns, after which the party came back. The next we heard was that there were soldiers coming. When fighting commenced (at Batoche's) I went up to the top of the hill. My sons were with me, watching everything while they were fighting. Every day I did that while the shooting was going on. I had a gun too, but not to kill anyone with, because I am too big a coward to kill anyone. I carried it just for fear. Not for any evil did I do what I did. My intentions were to make a living for my wife and children.

The General—That's enough. It is evident you are not fit for a chief either, armed as you are. You can all go now, but you must give up your medals; they are meant for good men only. There are no presents for you, no tobacco, no tea or meat, no flour for those who are fighting against us.

Beardy sullenly gave up his medals, but it was evident that the severest punishment was the withholding of food. Several clergymen who were present spoke to the General of the hungry condition of the band, but the General was obdurate. The impression was that General Middleton was even too lenient as it was, and that if he had strung Mr. Beardy up by the thumbs he would have been only meting out justice to this wretched old humbug.

A correspondent furnishes the following particulars of Riel's capture and the scenes immediately following it:—

Boulton's men were sent out to scour the country, as reports from different sources came in that the fugitive rebel chieftain was lurking in a bush only a few miles away. Following the scouts were the couriers, viz: Thomas Hourie, Robert Armstrong, and William Diehl, who started out on a similar errand. They soon overtook and passed Boulton's men, and diverging from the trail when nearing Batoche's, came upon four men standing near a fence. One they recognised as Riel—coatless, hatless, and unarmed. His companions were young men and they carried shot guns. The two rode up, and one called Riel by name, and he answered the salutation. They expressed surprise at his being there, and in reply he handed Armstrong a slip of paper—the note which General Middleton had sent him, that if he would give himself up he would be protected and given a fair trial. At the same time he said: "I want to give myself up; but I fear the troops may hurt me." Assurances were given that he would not be harmed, and as Riel had no horse, and the scouts at any moment might come upon them, it was deemed advisable to secrete him in a gully a short distance away, while Diehl corralled an animal for him. While waiting for Diehl to return, the scouts passed near by, and Armstrong and Hourie, fearing they might offer violence to their prisoner, hustled him through the brush, up into a poplar bluff, and on towards camp. In the meantime Deale came back to the spot, but found his companions and their prize had gone. He followed their trail for a while, but surmising that their purpose in making a detour was to avoid the scouts, started for camp, where he reported the gratifying news to the General. It was to be kept a profound secret until Riel had been smuggled in, but somehow or other it leaked out, and in less than five minutes the news went the rounds of the whole camp. Orders were issued to keep the men as busily engaged as possible, so that the arrival of the distinguished personage might not be noticed and any demonstration made. Although keen glances were constantly cast towards the trail it was expected he would reach camp by, at half-past three, before the men were aware of the fact, Hourie and Armstrong had slowly ridden in with a very shabbily dressed Half-breed, who at once dismounted and entered the General's tent.

Riel was safe from harm, if ever harm was intended by the troops. General Middleton held a prolonged conversation with him, and then the seven correspondents sought the opportunity of interviewing the fallen chief. General Middleton shook his head at first and refused, very properly, to allow his prisoner to be catechised by a newspaper man unless Riel was willing. As Riel flatly declined the correspondents missed a sensation.

In the meantime Maxime Lepine, whom I knew well in other times, had come into camp and surrendered, and I visited him. I had known him in other and happier days, and we had a handshake. He asked me if I had seen his brother Ambrose at St. Boniface lately, and I told him I had. Maxime, however, was evidently averse to being interviewed, and asked me to ask the other correspondents not to torture him with questions. He was quite broken down. We had a brief chat, but it was on his family affairs, and of no interest or concern to the public.

Lepine was subsequently taken down to the boat, but on appearing in public one of the released prisoners attempted " to put a head on him," but was frustrated, however, by the guard. Riel in the meantime was kept carefully guarded in the tent adjoining the General's.

Of late on all documents of the rebel council or rebel chieftain has been the word "exovide." When asked what its meaning was he wrote the following:—

"Exovide—From Latin words *ex ovide*: from two Latin words, *ex*, which means from, and *ovide*, ablative of flock. That word I made use of to convey that I was assuming no authority at all, and the advisers of the movement also took that title instead of councillors or representatives, and their purpose in doing so was exactly the same as mine, viz., no assumption of authority. We consider ourselves a part of society, and near us another part of the same society attempted to rule over us improperly, and by false representations and through bad management of public affairs even injuring us greatly. At the same time they were obtaining the ear of the Government; they were turning all the press against us. The situation was leading us simply to annihilation. Without assuming any other authority than that which exists by itself in the condition of our nature, they recurred to the right of self-preservation, and those who agreed to act together in the protection of their existence, threatened in many different ways, took the name of *exovides*, so that having their distinctive titles for the time being, and being known as the men of the movement, when the crisis would be over the reaction would be as slight as possible, for the reason that what would have been undertaken and accomplished under the sound authority of good sense could have no other results than good ones, and consequently the movement prove to be less a disturbance than a remedy to some things which were previously going too far in the wrong.

"Several times, it is true, we made use of the words 'representatives,' 'members of the council,' etc., but we had to do it, until the word *exovides* was understood, and until it would begin to become usual amongst even the men of the movement. So the council itself, not a council but being composed of *exovides*, we have called the *exovidate*.

"I have a mission. So has everybody. For me, I understand my mission in this way:—To bring out practical results."

In Riel's tent last night an officer slept. To him and to others with whom he talked (but he did not talk freely) he expressed high appreciation of the personal qualities of his adjutant-general, Dumont. Riel, however, lays claim to the credit of not only directing the movements of his rabble, but of having conceived the plan of the campaign, and of having designed the rifle pits. He was, according to his own story, the actual as well as the nominal leader of the movement. He said he invariably kept his outer line of pits fully manned and the inner ones sufficiently guarded; but he was always prepared to reinforce the outer pits, if deemed necessary, and to protect and defend any particular point assailed. In Saturday's fight, he admitted, the steamer *Northcote* attracted their attention, and the few remaining in the pits did not wish to commence the attack until the conflict on the river was finished. He denied remaining with the women during the fight on Tuesday as charged by them, and asseverated that when Donald Ross, who killed poor Jack French, was shot, he was behind him, and heard his dying request to have his children brought to him before he passed away to the unknown world. After that he went to the centre, and saw another of his councillors, Ouimet, an old warrior of seventy-five years, lying dead. Thence going to the right centre he saw a number of his followers either dead or wounded, and then, he says, he saw the day was lost. Taking his wife and two daughters he fled to a bluff not three miles from Batoche's, and close to the place where he was captured or, as he insists, where he surrendered.

Of Gabriel Dumont's whereabouts he claims to know nothing. When asked as to the number of his force, at one time he said seven hundred, and at another five hundred, of whom three hundred and forty were Half-breeds. Both statements are obviously incorrect. He probably had five hundred men, but he understates the strength of his Indian allies. At Fish Creek he says he had but one hundred and fifty-four men, and his losses were seven killed, of whom three were Indians. Riel also says that while most of the Indians have gone to their reservations, there are still some unsubdued Half-breeds, rendered desperate by the loss of home, or wife, or family, who may waylay travellers; and he warns people not to go too far from camp unprotected. Indians, too, whose brief career on the war-path has not satiated their taste for blood, will likely make the country a dangerous one to travel through for some time.

After seeing Riel, and conversing with those who have talked with him, I cannot believe that he is altogether sane; he is certainly a "crank," and a cunning crank withal; and it appears to me that, knowing well the impressionable and superstitious nature of the Metis, he has taken advantage of their weakness, and by blasphemously feigning sanctity, has worked upon them in a manner which has made the more ignorant of them his abject slaves.

A courier coming in to-day reports that the Half-breeds are flocking into Batoche's, where their names are taken down by the parish priest, upon which they deliver up their arms and return to their homes. A large number were still there when he passed. In conversation with them they all denounced Riel for leading them into the trouble. They said that they thought they could whip the "police" until that fatal Tuesday afternoon when the charge was made. The charge demoralized them, and they hurriedly left for the protecting banks of the Saskatchewan, down which they fled helter-skelter, and found temporary safety in bluffs a few miles away. They said that Garnot, the secretary of the Riel government, had amongst others delivered himself up, and was strutting about the town. A large number of arms were piled up—weapons of all descriptions, amongst them some Spencer rifles and a bagful of ammunition, old and useless weapons, of course, predominating. They all admitted that they had been thoroughly beaten, and all they were anxious for was peace. They had heard of the capture of Riel, and only regretted that Dumont was not a captive with him. Of Middleton's leniency they spoke in high terms, it being the very reverse of what Riel had led them to believe.

Riel was allowed out of his tent this afternoon for a few minutes, of course escorted by a guard. He had scarcely left the tent when the ubiquitous Captain Peters, of A Battery, who is an amateur photographer of no mean order, had him "taken." Riel looked askance at the "instantaneous" camera, perhaps fearing that it was an infernal machine, but as it didn't go off, he walked back into his tented prison apparently well pleased. Captain Peters, it may be mentioned, is an enthusiast in the photographic art, and has the negatives of both the battles of Fish Creek and Batoche's; the first, it is claimed, ever taken of an action.

The rebel adjutant-general is doubtless safe away in the fastnesses of the Birch hills. He was seen yesterday about thirteen miles from camp, and Boulton's men got within half-a-mile of him, but their horses were pumped out, while he rode Parenteau's fast horse, the fleetest in the North-West, and easily outfooted his pursuers. He carried his trusty rifle, but had no blankets. One person who conversed with him, a Half-breed, who came in to deliver himself up, reports that Dumont told him he merely wanted to see Riel and then he would go away for ever. While scouting for Dumont the scouts discovered that Riel yesterday had breakfasted at Girard's place, and that he secured a chicken to take to his family for dinner, and would probably have returned for supper had not the couriers interfered with his plans.

It appears from what can be learned, that the recalcitrants were not afraid of defeat until Tuesday's gallant charge was made. They imagined they could keep the police at bay, but when the rousing cheer rang out and echoed through the ravines and plains of the bullet-swept battle ground, they became demoralized and fled precipitously, waiting neither for coat nor shoes, and in some instances not even for arms and ammunition. Riel, however, was long before convinced that the day was lost, and early in the morning opened negotiations with General Middleton, through Astley, one of his prisoners, who had frequently warned Riel that he would be beaten when the soldiers came, and had offered his services two weeks previously as a mediator, if one were needed. Riel came to the cellar-prison, and called out to Astley at 8 a.m. His first message to the General regarding the safety of the women and children, and the threat against the prisoners, was merely a pretext to open negotiations. He was then conscious of certain defeat, and paralyzed with fear, and wanted to make the best terms he could. Of these preliminary negotiations his fighting braves were in total ignorance, and they, not knowing what was going on, opened fire while the flag of truce was being borne by Astley. When the answer came back, Dumont was sent for, and he came where Riel was, and what was regarded as a sign of submission was his grasping Astley cordially by the hand and shaking it, the first time he had ever made demonstrations of friendship to any prisoner. Then a hurried consultation was secretly held, and the negotiations were continued to gain time; in the meanwhile a steady fire was being maintained by both forces. The rebel council was convened for the last time, and shortly after that gallant, resistless charge, and that wild cheer I have spoken of, rendered further communication by letter between rebel and loyalist unnecessary. As the boys came bravely on, dismay filled Half-breed and Red-skin, and they fled to the sheltering banks of the Saskatchewan, and then in small bands dispersed to the north-east. At dusk Riel, who had remained all day in fear and trembling with the women, slipped away and was lost in the blackness of the night. Dumont, too, defeated and despondent, hastened away, and in the seclusion of a bluff a few miles away passed the long night with some still faithful adherents.

A CHANGE OF POSITIONS.

It was on the 19th of February, 1869, that Colonel Boulton (who the other day was out scouring the country for Riel) was a prisoner in that person's power, chained and manacled, confined in a cold comfortless cell with nothing to eat but pemmican and water, and under sentence of death. Time has brought around its revenges and the gallant Colonel finds himself now hunting Riel instead of being hunted by him. But he can see, if he looks at the miserable fellow, that he is treated with far more consideration than he accorded his prisoner. No irons manacle his legs, no handcuffs prevent the free use of his arms. Riel is saved that disgrace which many a poor culprit suffers. The Colonel has not yet seen Riel, nor has he any desire to.

As an instance of how serious the rebel losses have been, a little settlement up the river tells a terrible tale. Of six houses, where six families resided, there is now only one man left. Five widows mourn the loss of the breadwinners, and thirty little ones are left fatherless.

I learn that the houses at Fish Creek belonging to the Touronds have been destroyed by fire. Gabriel's has been destroyed, and at Batoche's five houses went up in flames. Those latter belonged to Solomon Veurres, Joseph Caron, S. Gareau, P. Parenteau, and Moise Parenteau. None of the finer buildings were fired, although some were wrecked by shells.

Two merchants have arrived in camp, and opened up "stores." The stores are merely the waggons in which the goods were freighted, with the sky for a roof and the earth for a basement. Prices are not very unreasonable. T. & B. tobacco sells at 35c. a plug; canned oysters, 50c.; syrup, $2 per gallon; canned peaches, 75c.; jam, $1.75 per can; stockings, poor quality, 50c. per pair; and other articles in proportion. A fair trade is done, but not so large as anticipated, many of the boys having supplied themselves free of cost at Batoche's, after the rebels left.

"What are your grievances?" I asked an Indian named Big Star, through an interpreter.

"Don't know."

"Have you any?"

"No."

"Why did you fight?

"Because."

"Because what?"

"Well, they told us we had to. They said the police with big guns were coming up to kill our wives and children, and to take away our lands from us; that Manitou would protect us; that the Americans would help us, and then we would have everything good."

"And what will you do now?"

"Go home if they let me."

"What about Riel?"

"He is a bad man—very bad."

It seemes that at the Fish Creek fight the whole rebel force was engaged, although many left for home early in the day. When they returned at night Dumont boasted that they had defeated the "police," but said they had lost nearly all their ponies. But he added that while he had been victorious in every war he was engaged in he was not so certain about this one. The loss of the ponies was severely felt. They did not expect to fight us at Fish Creek, but were surprised at our sudden arrival. Riel had always maintained that the first encounter would be at Batoche's, and he pointed out the exact trail that the troops would come. "But," he added, "our first shot will kill fifty men."

That Riel possessed a wonderful influence, an influence almost incomprehensible, over the Metis cannot be denied. He is a fluent speaker, almost a born orator, suave, always polite, and very plausible. He is also a born agitator—the son of his father, and when the discontented here sent to Montana for him he came as if conferring a great favour upon them. At this time, however, the Indian blood in the half-castes had not been worked up. There were some wild, turbulent spirits, but the masses had not been aroused. How to raise their enthusiasm, and secure their earnest sympathy and co-operation, was a problem which Riel's fertile brain soon solved. He announced that "a man" was to be baptized in the church—a convert, of course—but that the Orangemen of Prince Albert were determined to prevent the rite being performed. The man was no other than Jackson, a young Ontario fellow who had been prominent amongst the leaders, and who afterwards blossomed out as Riel's private secretary. This presumed interference naturally gave offence to many, and at the appointed day there was a large gathering at the church of St. Antoine de Padua, where Jackson joined Riel's new religion, the authority of the Catholic Church having even at this early period been repudiated by the rebel leader. After the ceremony of Jackson's so-called conversion, Riel addressed the mob, denouncing the priests for "playing into the hands of the Government," and setting himself up as the temporal and spiritual leader of the Metis. Of course, no Orangeman interfered. They had no idea of interfering, nor did they care whether Jackson was baptized or confirmed or buried.

After this there was no lethargy amongst the naturally easy-going Half-breeds. Their red blood was up. They were eager to attend meetings, and Riel was easily enabled to hold them in his power, lead them at his will, and make them do his bidding. Riel gradually claimed divine authority and miraculous gifts, until by some of the Indians he was fairly worshipped as a god. The movement was thus conceived in duplicity, falsehood, and blasphemy; and it is no wonder it came to such a sudden and disastrous termination.

A correspondent writing from Middleton's camp below Batoche on May 18, says:—

I went up to Batoche's yesterday with Major Bedson, chief of the transport service, who took supplies along for the starving families of the homeless recalcitrants. On the way up, he saw the ruins of several houses, buildings belonging to prominent rebels, which had been burned by the passing troops a few days previously. As Batoche's was neared, the bodies of dead cattle and dead ponies were seen strewing the plains, while from every house and every cart floated the white emblem of peace and submission. Past the ingenious rifle pits, past points of vantage prepared for defence, showing weeks of labour in preparations, we rode and reached Batoche's in the early afternoon. Here white flags fly in every direction. Men carry them, they are tied to carts, even little children flaunt little ones in their tiny hands. Asking one of them what is meant, the lad replied:

"It's a sign of peace."

"What peace?" "Oh, there's been war, and my father was shot. But it's all over now. This flag means peace. No more shooting."

"Are you glad?" "Oh, I don't know, but my mother is."

Even Batoche's fine residence, where the rebel commander-in-chief had his quarters, flies its white flag. We visited the school, adjoining the bullet-riddled church of St. Antoine de Padua, where the women and children are congregated. Of the large numbers who were camped here during the battle (for Riel had ordered that everybody, men, women and children, dogs and ponies and cattle, should rendezvous at Batoche's), some had gone home, but there were a score or so remaining. They had tidied the place up, and their little papooses, snugly ensconced in the comfortable moss bags, were decked out in clean linen, and chuckled and crowed in their mothers' arms. It was a far different scene from the Sunday before. Then the bullets whizzed, the Gatling rattled, and the artillery roared, while the mothers and children crouched in caves and tepees, fearing death at every moment. To-day, peace reigns, and freed from the tyranny of the apostate Riel, in whom, true Catholics as they are, they never believed and never trusted, they bore their sufferings unmurmuringly, only asking safety for their duped dear ones, a little to stop the cramp of hunger, and a safe return home. Assurance was given that none but the guilty leaders would be punished, and that they could go home. The waggon loads of flour and bacon and tea told them that the much-abhorred troops which were to massacre them were, after all, kind and generous and humane. The little church was used for a storehouse. It had been utilized for far baser and more sacrilegious purposes during the last month or so. The relief was gratefully received by the poor women. Some of them must have suffered terribly. One woman told me her family had had nothing to eat for four days. Her husband was still in the woods hiding. Another woman was homeless, husbandless and hungry.

The priest, Rev. Father Vegreville, was busily engaged receiving the arms of the submissive rebels, and taking down the names of those surrendering. He had in all eighty names and forty-four weapons. He explained to me that the rebel loss was not so large as at first estimated. It was only sixteen killed, with between twenty and thirty wounded. Previously several persons had reported fifty-one killed and one hundred and seventy-three wounded. When asked to explain the great discrepancy in the figures, the priest said the larger figures had been based upon information obtained by volunteers and others who were not adepts at speaking or understanding the French language. He showed me his official list, and sure enough it totalled up sixteen killed. These have been buried in the little cemetery overlooking the river just opposite the church.

I asked Father Leveque how Riel came to wield such an influence over his flock. He could not tell, but the people were carried away by his oratory. He himself was made prisoner, and when he had defied Riel and loudly protested against his desecrating the church, he found some to openly support him. There were some who were still true to the Church, but they dared not, at least they did not, resist Riel's commands. Riel was clever enough to see that before he could hope to lead the people into rebellion, he would have to depose the priests who were vehemently denouncing the use of force; and he accomplished this by setting himself up as an agent of Heaven. Father Leveque says nobody attended Mass except the women and children, and after a time many of these were compelled to become Rielites. This priest, who is from Old France, went boldly to many of the rebel meetings and denounced Riel at the peril of his life. He warned them that the rising could have only one termination, that the soldiers would overwhelm and disperse them, and that their leader was ruining them; but his words fell on heedless ears, and, sore at heart, he was compelled to leave them to pursue the course they had determined to take. I gathered this from the Half-breed women. Father Leveque himself does not care to talk; he is broken-hearted. He told me, however, that Riel was a coward, and that he had placed him and the other priests and the five sisters from the St. Laurent convent, and some children in that exposed little school-house, midway between the fires of the two opposing forces. It was a diabolical act.

In conversation with Mr. Ness, J.P., who was a prisoner, I learned that Riel told the men not to kill when they could capture people. He was particularly anxious that General Middleton should not be harmed, claiming that he was an old friend and school-mate of his. Mr.

Ness further reports that at Fish Creek the rebels said they had six killed—four Half-breeds and two Indians—and twelve wounded. Riel always held that they should defend Batoche's to the bitter end, and warned them if it were captured their cause was lost. Hence it was that such a determined stand was made here, and such elaborate plans of defence conceived and executed. When the troops did not follow (the rebels had been waiting for them in suspense) Riel inspired new spirit into them by telling them that the police were too frightened to come, and that one whole battalion had been killed, so many that it occupied two days to bury the dead. Thus encouraged, day after day passing and no "police" appearing, they felt certain of victory on their own battle-ground. That implicit confidence remained until the charge was made. Then they sought safety in flight.

Mr. Ness could not learn whether Riel directed the movements of the men at Batoche's or not. He says Riel was not at Fish Creek, although he started for that place with one or two men, but some of the scouts coming in and reporting that thirty or forty "police" were approaching in another direction, a messenger was sent after him and he returned. Mr. Ness says that Riel was invariably the pink of politeness to him and to everyone, and wielded an influence over the people that set the power of the priests at naught.

Mr. Ness is a Catholic, and has always remained true to his Church and to Canada. He was made a prisoner, but after forty-eight hours' confinement was released, after being tried before the council for having given information to the police. He was found guilty, and as a punishment his horse and cutter were confiscated. The Half-breeds were not unfriendly to him, and a sort of communistic rule prevailing amongst them, frequently came into his house and made themselves at home. He says that at first Riel had about five hundred men, but that nearly one hundred or so must have deserted him, which number was probably made up by recruits from the Indian reserves. Mr. Ness was on parole. He could go as far as the church but not to the village. Many opportunities offered for an escape, but hampered with a wife and family, he would not undertake the long trip to the south, preferring to trust his family's lives in rebel hands to facing the bitter winds and terrible storms they might encounter in a winter's journey across the plains.

On the way home we saw two men bearing a white flag coming from a bush. They were unarmed and gave themselves up. One of them was Pierre Vandal, one of the most active men in the rebel ranks; the other Adolphus Nolin, son of Charles Nolin, who is held a prisoner at Prince Albert. They were taken to camp. From what I could glean from them, Vandal had been sent to the Battleford Indians to secure their co-operation in the fight expected to take place at Batoche's. Nolin, who lives at Frog Lake, and claims to have been a prisoner among the Indians, says the object of Riel was to have the Half-breed " prisoners " there released and brought to headquarters. Nolin claims to have escaped. Nolin left the Indians a few miles this side of their reserve in the Eagle Hills, and says he thought they would come to Batoche's. To fight? Well, he admitted that he was coming to help his people. Nolin was engaged in getting out logs at Frog Lake, and was present at the massacre, the details of which have long ago been made public.

Mrs. Delaney and Mrs. Gowanlock, he said, were safe and sound at Johnny Pritchard's, at Frog Lake, he having secured Mrs. Gowanlock's release by giving an Indian two ponies, while Pritchard effected the other lady's by giving one pony.* Nolin says the women were unharmed, although they were naturally very frightened, and remained all one day in the tepee sobbing and crying, not knowing what horrible fate awaited them. At night several Indians came to their place of confinement and

---

* This report afterwards proved to be correct.

demanded an entrance, intending to steal the women's clothes; but they did not accomplish their purpose. Their freedom once purchased, Nolin says, they were not molested, and when he offered them the choice of going to Battleford or remaining with Pritchard at Frog Lake, they decided upon remaining.

Nolin was present at the battle between the Queen's Own and Poundmaker. He says the troops were whipped and compelled to retreat to Battleford, and that they would have been annihilated but for Major Short and Colonel Herchmer, who kept cool throughout. The Indians surprised Colonel Otter at daybreak, and the battle lasted till between one and two o'clock. The Indian loss was four killed and six wounded. The Indians claimed a big victory, and celebrated the event as such. The Indians were about three hundred strong, and had in the ranks some striplings, who were armed with bows and arrows.

Nolin gives an amusing description of the capture of the Battleford supply train, at which he was also present. About two hundred Indians suddenly came upon the train of twenty-nine waggons, when eight of the teamsters "skedaddled," leaving their arms and waggons behind. The other twenty-one surrendered without a shot being fired. The Indians indulged in a regular blow-out, the canned corned beef being a luxury to the half-starved braves. The captured teamsters were not harmed, the Indians with full stomachs becoming good natured. When Nolin last saw them, they were enjoying a dance, one of the teamsters supplying the music with an old fiddle he had with him. Mirth and merriment prevailed, and the dance went on with joy unconfined. As long as the provisions hold out, doubtless the festivities will continue, and after that the teamsters will likely be allowed their freedom. From Nolin's account, it appears that the ramifications of the rebels were more far-reaching than we anticipated, and had they been successful at Batoche's an Indian war, enveloping the whole North-West, would have followed. Defeat, however, has averted such a calamity, and as Nolin tersely put it: "Riel big dam fool."

I dropped into one of the rooms in which Riel had his prisoners confined. It was in the upper storey of Batoche's old store, and comfortable quarters enough. The imprisonment does not seem to have weighed down the prisoners, or interfered with their love of fun. The clean planed wooden partitions bear witness to this. They are covered with caricatures in pencil, and poetry and bills of fare of which is facetiously called "Riel's hotel." One *menu* embraces "bannocks, cowhide, bull's feet, and slough water discoloured with tea;" others are more elaborate if not more tempting. A caricature of Riel's last recruit embellishes the door—an extremely small boy, with an enormous hat and a gun almost as large as himself. Then there were dates, and the signatures of the prisoners, and plain intimations to Monsieur Riel, which indicated that his captives were not in mortal fear of him. In the other prison house, the cellar, the quarters were not so extensive, nor were there any facilities for expressing opinions by pen or pencil.

OUR VOLUNTEERS.

We have cause indeed to glory o'er the fight our boys have won,
O'er the work they have accomplished, o'er deeds that have been done.

Though in peace they have been nurtured, yet, when heard rebellion's cry,
How they rushed to arms determined to conquer or to die.

Canada! such men shall make thee, what we fondly hoped for thee—
A nation great and glorious stretching far from sea to sea!

Lo! methinks the future opens and my words are more than
   true,
Clust'ring cities in their splendour rise where once but forests
   grew;

Vessels heavy with their freightage o'er our boundless waters
   glide;
Railroads netted o'er the country join each mighty ocean's tide;

Prairies long unclaimed, unknown, now are tilled by willing
   hands;
And our sons are sought and honoured by the great of foreign
   lands.

And are those who battled bravely for their country when
   'twas young,
Then to be forgotten by her? No! such names are ever sung!

Names that still are loved and cherished by the loyal and the
   brave;
O'er our fallen shall flowers blossom and dark maples shade
   each grave.

Heroes in the Far West sleeping, brave as those who followed
   Brock,
Gallant as the brave that perished at Quebec's embattled rock;

In a magic maple garland we shall weave each honoured name,
And the future years shall brighten—never dim—your deathless fame.

And may He who orders wisely, soothe the bitter grief of
   those
Whose brave boys in death have fallen where they charged the
   hidden foes.

When the rest come marching homeward, who have fought our
   land to save,
We shall have a fitting welcome to the gallant and the brave.

CHAPTER XXIV.

TO PRINCE ALBERT AND BATTLEFORD.

FROM Batoche General Middleton made his way to Prince Albert. A correspondent writes from that village as follows on the 19th of May :—

At last we reach civilization, and see people who don't fire at us from behind trees or out of rifle pits. The arrival of the troops was a great event in the history of Prince Albert, and the 19th of May will, for many years, be marked as a red letter day. Our reception was an enthusiastic one, the local volunteers, with the citizens and their wives and daughters turning out *en masse* to welcome the boys. The military and local bands played appropriate music, and amidst cheer upon cheer the troops marched in. Colonel Sproat presented the inevitable address of welcome, congratulating the General on his victorious progress through the country, and thanking him for coming to their relief. General Middleton replied briefly, acknowledging the compliment, but modestly accorded all the credit to his officers and men, who, he said, were equal to regulars on the march and on the battlefield. This is a thriving town, the only place of any pretensions we have yet passed through since leaving Fort Qu'Appelle, and, unaccustomed as we were to seeing anything more than a small group of houses in the other "cities," in one's eyes it was magnified till it looked almost as big as Toronto. Of course it isn't, but it contains, with a population of over one thousand, some very fine buildings. There are numerous stores, and the private residences of several of the wealthier residents show signs of culture, taste, and wealth. The town is very prettily situated on the east bank of the North Branch of the Saskatchewan—straggling a length of about five miles. As one genius puts it, "it's seven miles long and fifteen inches wide." Some of the buildings are brick, but the majority are constructed of wood. Another sight brings back remembrances of home—handsomely attired young ladies. Their style of dress may not be according to the latest Paris fashions (you must remember they have been cut off from communication with the outer world for two months), but in neatness and taste the costumes are fit for the sunny side of King Street in Toronto.

The town possesses all the conveniences of Eastern cities, and were it not for the barricaded church and manse, whose cordwood defences make it resemble a gigantic wood-yard, the few rifle pits which had evidently been made by gophers, the numerous red-coated police strolling about, and the port-holes in different buildings one would imagine that he was in a peaceful Ontario town. The place was well garrisoned, and with the means of defence and favourable location, could have withstood any attack that might have been made upon it. There was no lack of provisions, so one naturally wonders what on earth all the scare here was about. I tried to find out, but failed. The several persons I questioned would give me not even the shadow of a reason. One man, who claimed to have been on guard sixteen nights, said that he had not seen the ghost of a rebellious Half-breed or hostile Indian during his term of service, and he had been all through the "siege." Further he did not believe there was an unfriendly person within twenty miles. Time and a rigid investigation, however, will probably bring out facts which cannot now be ascertained. Instead of showing hostility, two chiefs, Iron Bull and Star Blanket (no relation to a namesake in the File Hills), interviewed the General to-day, and professed not only the greatest friendship, but asseverated that they had withstood the blandishments of Riel and the tobacco of other tribes, and remained truly loyal to the Great White Mother, and friendly to the whites. They were glad to see the General, and to be allowed the opportunity of expressing their pleasure at meeting him, and they trusted their friendship would never be broken. Iron Bull, whose Indian name is Mis-ta-was-sis, is the second "biggest Injun" of the Crees in the whole North-West, and wields considerable influence with the Red men. His companion, Ah-tah-kah-koop (Star Blanket), is also a chief of some power. They both came from near Carleton.

The General's exact plan is not yet completed, but from what can be learned the four steamers—*North-West, Alberta, Marquis*, and *Baroness*—will probably take the troops up, and await their visit to the reserve, and then return with them to the mouth of the Saskatchewan, where, after crossing Lake Winnipeg in other steamers, they will take the Canadian Pacific Railway to Port Arthur, and go down the lakes. Should no serious trouble occur at Battleford, in three weeks or a month Toronto should get ready to welcome its gallant volunteers—if not all, at least a large proportion of them. When it does, your citizens will not see band-box soldiers, spick and span, but travel-stained and bronzed veterans, with toggery the worse of wear. As a matter of fact, the Grenadiers are beginning to feel the necessity of a new outfit at once. Many of their unmentionables have seen their best days, and their tunics are soiled and torn. Their headgear also needs replenishing. Fur caps, with which alone many of them are provided, are unseasonable at this time of the year; and their stock of underclothing is also worn out. You will see a pretty ragged regiment walking down King Street some fine day. The health of the whole force is remarkably good. The hardships of a long and tedious march and the bivouac in the battle field, in this clear North-Western air, have not affected them. Were it not for the few wounded we have with us the medical staff would have but little to occupy their time with. Dr. Ryerson tells me he has no sick list now-a-days at all. He speaks in the highest terms of the ambulance corps of the battalion, formed of the buglers and others, which rendered signal service at

Batoche's, bringing in many of the wounded at the peril of their own lives. Of course the ambulance corps of the 90th and the Midlands were equally as efficient, and are deserving of all praise. There was one case of heroism which deserves mention. One of the Grenadiers was seriously wounded at Batoche's and would have bled to death had he been left for any length of time. Colour-Sergeant Curzon, under a shower of rebel bullets, at once knelt down and stopped the hæmorrhage, and carried his wounded comrade to a place of safety, marching coolly away to the music provided by the guns of the enemy.

Now that the march through the fertile country—extending from below Fish Creek on the south to seven miles beyond Lepine's on the north, a distance of about fifty miles—is happily completed, we learn of the narrow escapes and we begin to think of the "what might have been." The rebels have "given away" their plans, and it is learned that the intention of Gabriel Dumont at Fish Creek was to allow the column to pass that terrible ravine, and when descending the slope on the further side to suddenly attack it. Another of the narrow escapes was the intended night attack on the camp at McIntosh's the night before the Fish Creek Battle, when a sudden scoop was to have been made in the early hours of the morning. The rebels, mounted on their fleet little ponies, were to sneak up, and passing the picket, to rush upon the sleeping force, not firing a shot till the tents were reached; and then in the confusion to pour volley after volley into the half-aroused and unprepared soldiery. A third surprise also missed fire. It was to have been made the night before the battle of Batoche's. The steamer *Northcote*, then lying at Gabriel's, was to have been set on fire at night, and those on board shot down as they attempted to escape from the flames. This would have been no difficult job, as there were only forty soldiers on board, and the camp sixteen miles away. Fortunately the merest chance prevented all these disasters. In the first one, there was a misdirection of orders, and all the rebel force to take part in it did not turn up till too late in the night: then our scouts surprised them at Fish Creek, and the Indians, disobeying orders, fired upon them; and the steamer was saved through the stupidity of a scout, who reported that its destruction could be more thoroughly accomplished on the following night. It was a good thing for us that we had the luck on our side. The rebels were no fools. If they had been as well armed as we, and in equal strength, our victory would not have been so complete. I doubt very much if we should have had a victory at all. They are devils incarnate to fight, even with common old shotguns, some of them flint-locks.

There will be many mouths to feed on the South Saskatchewan for the next year or so. From Saskatoon to Pritchard's, some ninety or one hundred miles, there is little if any grain sown this year, and it is too late to put in anything, except perhaps a little barley and potatoes. There is no seed grain. A large proportion of the cattle have been driven off, and the settlers have lost their most invaluable assistants, their ponies. Here and there a household has lost the provider or one of the main-stays; many houses are entirely destroyed; and there is little food or provender in the country. Something must also be done for those loyalists who, owing to the troubles, have been compelled to leave home and neglect their farms; for the merchants and traders whose goods were seized, and who have been brought thus to the verge of ruin. Take the Kerr Brothers, for instance. They were doing well at Duck Lake, when the rebels seized their store and helped themselves to their stock. Since then the firm have been unable to do anything to recover their losses. One of them, George, accompanied the troops and not only furnished important information, but shouldered a rifle and helped to smash Riel. For many a day the terrible effects of this short-lived uprising will be severely felt. The case of those people living in the disaffected district near Prince Albert is a particularly hard one.

They are only now permitted to return to their homes, and as we passed through to-day we saw many houses still deserted and farms untouched, although they petitioned to be allowed to go out from the Prince Albert city of refuge and do their spring work.

On the 21st of May the same correspondent writes as follows:

It is evident that General Middleton will not waste any time in this place, but will push on to Battleford as soon as the means of transportation will permit. The river will be utilized, and, thank goodness, the navigation of the North Branch of the Saskatchewan is not so uncertain as that of the South Branch. The trip should be made in a little less than three days, so that if we leave here to-morrow, as "orders" now state, we should be able to join Otter by Monday at latest. The steamer *North-West*, it is now arranged, will lead the van, and the *Marquis* and other boats will follow immediately after their arrival here. The supply waggons will follow the trail, being escorted by Dennis's Intelligence Corps, and being light will be able to move rapidly. The *North-West*, as I write, is being barricaded, and Captain Sheets is attending to the work himself, not having that confidence in military engineers which one would naturally expect. He had enough of that on the *Northcote*, and proposes to make the *North-West* as nigh bullet-proof as it is possible to make her with the material at hand. All the troops will go up the river, except the Winnipeg Field Battery, which will garrison Prince Albert, and with the Mounted Police and volunteers protect the place against any raid of the Indians, should the Red-skins take it into their head to make one. It is said that the insurgents hereabouts are still saucy. The General's desire is to smash Poundmaker and give his followers a well-deserved drubbing. With the force at hand he should have no difficulty in accomplishing his purpose, provided the turbulent chief can be found or does not surrender. It is said that he has three hundred and thirty braves, and the last we heard of him he was *en route* to Batoche's to help Riel, but as he has had no word of that individual's overthrow, doubtless he will change his tactics and point in some other direction. Riel's runners, who took him the news of the defeat, were to tell him he could not fight the white men with their Gatling maneton and red-coats and "black devils," as the 90th are called by the Indians. It is safe, therefore, to predict an early closing of the campaign, although possibly bodies of troops may be stationed at different points for some time to come.

The necessity for troops is unquestioned, for I fear the prestige of the Mounted Police is lost. Every Half-breed and Indian speaks in contemptuous terms of the force, and has no more dread of it than they have of gophers. I am not saying that the force is not composed of brave and gallant young men, and I know it is at all times prepared to do its duty; but the reverse at Duck Lake, the retreat to Prince Albert, and the two months' masterly inactivity there, the evacuation of Fort Pitt, all have combined to lower the force in the eyes of the savages, with whom prestige is everything. Some of the members of the force unwillingly admit this, while others bewail the unfortunate position in which events have placed them. Whether their prestige and influence can be regained, I will not pretend to say; if it cannot the usefulness of the force is gone. This is said with the full knowledge of the beneficial results which have followed the organization of the police, and the invaluable service it has rendered, and is still rendering, to the country.

I interviewed Colonel Irvine this morning as to his reasons for not venturing out to fight the Indians. When I told him of the reports of his "funking," he expressed the greatest surprise. He had no idea that his conduct would be so misconstrued. He had, he said, given explanations to General Middleton, and he believed they were perfectly satisfactory. The Colonel did not care about being interviewed, in fact he preferred not to be; but finally he gave me a few minutes of his time. He said that he and his *confrères* were thoroughly posted as to the country, and the strength, location, and plans of the insurgents, and he knew that their great aim was to induce him to come out towards Batoche's, where, ambushed in the firs—a long stretch of thick timbers—they could, with their far superior force, have annihilated him and secured arms and ammunition, just what they most needed, and immediately have moved down on Prince Albert, which would have been almost defenceless, as all the arms he could have left there were thirty-five Winchesters and forty shot-guns. At the time he heard that General Middleton was coming with only three hundred and fifty men, he had determined to go to his assistance, although it might result in his force being cut to pieces. However, when a larger force came (over one thousand strong, and he had heard it was one thousand five hundred), he knew it would be folly for him to go out, leaving the only important settlement in the North almost totally undefended; besides, he had no orders to go.

"Why," said the colonel, "whenever it was hinted that the police were going out, women and children raised a terrible cry at the prospects of being left helpless. Although no Indians were seen around, I had no doubt that they were always within striking distance, and that as soon as the police had gone they would have raided the town. You must remember—you can see for yourself—that this long straggling place would require a strong force to defend it, and it required all our strength to patrol the place and scout the country. We had to send forty-two men to guard the stores at Hudson's Bay Crossing on the South Branch, and we kept scouts always out in the direction of the enemy's country. I feel that I have done all that could have been done in the best interests of the country, and I feel certain that General Middleton approved of my course."

From others it was learned that some of the people of Prince Albert were not so truly loyal as they are to-day. Many of them were loud-mouthed sympathizers with Riel at the inception of the troubles, and took a prominent part in his meetings, only cutting the connection when the Metis resorted to arms. One Prince Albert man, whose name for obvious reasons it is better not to make known, told me that he had no doubt that if the troops had suffered a reverse at Batoche's, the number of rebels in the North-West, and particularly in this place, would have wonderfully increased, while the strength of the loyalists would have correspondingly decreased. Immediately across the river, too, is the camping ground of the renegade Sioux, those miscreants who participated in the Minnesota massacre of 1862; and these had suddenly disappeared, leaving only their squaws and old men behind. Some of them had returned two days after the fight at Batoche's. This tribe contributed forty warriors to Riel's strength, and being kept thoroughly informed on the movements of the police would have taken advantage of their absence and returned not with the most friendly intentions. So, after all, perhaps Colonel Irvine has been misjudged and his motives misunderstood or misrepresented: But all the same; mortal injury has been inflicted upon the reputation and usefulness of the police force.

In my last I endeavoured to describe Beardy, the Duck Lake Chief. I have since learned that he emulates Riel in assuming a sanctified personality, and indulges in wonderful dreams which he interprets to his ignorant followers as circumstances may require. He also talks in parables, and up to the other day, aped Louis "David" Riel in every conceivable way. That Beardy is a bad 'un is universally admitted, a cowardly, treacherous, blustering bully, unfriendly to the whites, by whom he had been fed, and ready at all times to keep the country in a disturbed state while he discreetly looks after his own safety. There are, of course, some loyal Indians in the North-West. Several bands of Crees, such as Iron Bull's, and Star Blanket's, who firmly declined all advances from Riel; but from what can be learned had the rebels gained a decided victory, only these and possibly a few more would have remained staunch. Mis-ta-was-sis (Big Child), as has been already stated, is a chief of great influence, and in the old days of intertribal warfare was a renowned warrior, by some called the terror of the plains. He is getting old now, but he keeps his age well. Of small stature, he has fine clear cut features, speaks fluently, and has demonstrated that, having left the war-path years ago, he has become a good Indian.

In the foregoing letter the correspondent has fallen into an error very common to those who visit the North-West for the first time in their lives. People who have suffered for breaking the law (especially whiskey traders) do all they can to prejudice strangers against the Mounted Police. Deserters and "scallawags" of every sort tell heart-rending stories to credulous Eastern editors, but those who have spent any length of time in the North-West, and who have carefully and intelligently studied its institutions will know better than to make any reflections on this admirable force or its officers. Colonel Irvine does not need any certificate of character from newspaper correspondents to induce those who know him best to believe that he is a brave and intrepid soldier, as he has again and again proved himself such since he assumed command of the North-West Mounted Police. As to the reflections upon the force they are too absurd to be worthy of notice. Surely the men could not go to Batoche's without orders, but that they could and would fight when it was their cue to do so Fort Pitt, Cut Knife and Two Lakes amply prove.

A well-informed correspondent writing from Fort McLeod thus referred to the Mounted Police:

In Montana every man travels armed as a measure of personal protection; liquor is sold freely to the Indians, and carried over Indian reservations with impunity. Gambling goes on openly, and the law is everywhere set at naught. Here, though there is only a handful of about three hundred Mounted Police to preserve order in a territory over nine hundred miles long by more than five hundred miles wide, containing a wild, warlike, and semi-starving population of twenty-five thousand Indians and about six thousand scattered settlers and ranchers, of whom a large proportion in the southern district are ex-whiskey traders and refugees from the American laws, the best order prevails. I have travelled over twelve hundred miles through the North-West Territory with horses and waggon; I have camped sometimes alone, and sometimes close to the police camp; I have had no means of locking up anything, and my whole outfit has always been exposed to the depredations of any persons who might be disposed to meddle with it, and yet, with the exception of one blanket, nothing has been stolen from me in the whole journey. Though I have travelled hundred of miles with only my Half-breed guide for company, I have never carried a revolver, and have never kept my shot-gun loaded in my tent. To suppose that such a state of affairs could exist here without the presence of an admirably organized and thoroughly efficient police force would be the wildest nonsense. Whatever may have been the state of the force in the past I do not know from any personal knowledge, but as to its present state under the commissionership of Colonel Irvine, I am certainly in a position to know something, and so far as I am able to judge, I cheerfully testify, not only to the excellent character and soldierly conduct of the officers and men, but to the thorough efficiency of the force, and the invaluable service it is now rendering the Dominion in this territory. I have heard complaints against the force here and elsewhere throughout the territory, but all these complaints have reached me through the medium of deserters, men who have been turned out of the force for bad conduct, and ex-whiskey traders who have suffered in pocket through the suppression of the whiskey traffic by the force. I have talked a good deal, and very freely, with the constables and non-commissioned officers of the force, and without exception I have found them intelligent, thoroughly well-disposed young gentlemen, proud of the standing and character of the force, strongly attached to the Commissioner and the officers in command of their respective posts, and pleased with the country and the mode of life they are called upon to lead. The only semblance of fault-finding that I heard was of the low rate of remuneration (40c. per diem for recruits) and the character of some of the uniforms served out to them, and in these respects I must say that I think there is room for improvement. As to the work the Mounted Police force is performing in the North-West, no one not intimately acquainted with the country can be in a position to judge. The officers and men have, to a very great extent, secured the confidence and good will of the Indians. The Red men are not only afraid to come into forcible contact with the red-coats, but they feel that their best interest lies in assisting the police in the discharge of their duties. They have confidence in the justice of the administration of the police and feel that the Indian rights will be protected as well as those of the white men. Instead of seeking redress for wrongs in the usual Indian way by force or strategy, they complain to the constituted authorities and in all respects recognize the fact that the white man's way of administering justice is better than their own.

Colonel DeWinton speaks of them as a "really wonderful body of men. They always appear to know just what to do in any emergency and proceed at once to do it." Captain Chater, after speaking very highly of the creditable appearance the men were able to make on the shortest notice and the admirable marching and campaigning qualities they had shown, alluded particularly to the feat they had performed in crossing the South Saskatchewan (at Batoche's, with Lord Lorne and escort) in five hours, remarking that he had not known of a regiment in the British army capable of turning out a detachment able to perform a similar feat in the same length of time. He also alluded in the most complimentary terms to the good conduct of the men. Bad language was not heard in the ranks, and when anything was to be done it was done promptly and quietly without any noise or shouting. He thought that the conduct and management of the men reflected the highest credit upon Colonel Herchmer and the non-commissioned officers in charge. Captain Percival, who, like Captain Chater, has seen a good deal of active service within the past few years, also spoke in the highest terms of the officers and men of the Mounted Police, summing up with the remark ; " a most wonderful force ; they combine all the handiness of sailors with the smartness of soldiers."

The following stanzas, written some years ago by a member of the North-West Mounted Police, truthfully and graphically describes the mounted policeman and his mission :—

THE RIDERS OF THE PLAINS.

So wake the prairie echoes with
    The ever welcome sound ;
Ring out the " boot and saddle " till
    Its stirring notes resound.
Our chargers toss their bridled heads,
    And chafe against the reins.
Ring out ! ring out the marching call
    For the Riders of the Plains.

O'er many a league of prairie wild
    Our trackless path must be,
And round it rove the fiercest tribes
    Of Blackfeet and of Cree.
But danger from their savage bands
    A dauntless heart disdains—
'Tis the heart that bears the helmet up,
    Of the Riders of the Plains.

The prairie storms sweep o'er our way,
　　But onward still we go,
To scale the weary mountain range,
　　Descend the valley low.
We face the broad Saskatchewan,
　　Made fierce with heavy rains,
With all his might he cannot check
　　The Riders of the Plains.

We tread the dreaded cactus land,
　　Where, lost to white man's ken,
We startle there the creatures wild
　　With the sight of armed men.
For whereso'er our leader bids
　　The bugle sounds its strains ;
Forward in sections marching go
　　The Riders of the Plains.

The fire king stalks the prairie,
　　And fearful 'tis to see
The rushing wall of flame and smoke
　　Girdling round us rapidly.
'Tis then we shout defiance
　　And mock his fiery chains ;
For safe the cleared circle guards
　　The Riders of the Plains.

For us no cheerful hostelries
　　Their welcome gates unfold ;
No generous board, no downy couch
　　Await our troopers bold.
Beneath the star-lit canopy
　　At eve, when daylight wanes,
There lie these hardy wanderers—
　　The Riders of the Plains.

In want of rest, in want of food,
　　Our courage does not fail,
As day and night we follow hard,
　　The desperado's trail.

His threatened rifle stays us not,
　　He finds no hope remains,
And yields at last a captive to
　　The Riders of the Plains.

We've ta'en the haughty feathered Chief,
　　Whose hands were red with blood,
E'en in the very Council Lodge
　　We seized him as he stood.
Three fearless hearts faced forty braves,
　　And bore the Chief in chains,
Full sixty miles to where were camped
　　The Riders of the Plains.

But that which tries the courage sore,
　　Of horseman and of steed,
Is want of blessed water,
　　Blessed water in our need.
We'll face like men whate'er befalls,
　　Of perils, hardships, pains;
Oh God! deny not water to
　　The Riders of the Plains.

And death who comes alike to all
　　Has visited us here,
Filling our hearts with bitter grief,
　　Our eyes with many a tear.
Five times he drew his fatal bow,
　　His hand no prayer restrains;
Five times his arrows sped among
　　The Riders of the Plains.

Hard by the Old Man River,
　　Where freshest breezes blow,
Five grassy mounds lie side by side,
　　Five riders sleep below.
Neat palings closed the sacred ground,
　　No stranger's step profanes
Their deep repose, and they sleep well
　　These Riders of the Plains.

There is no marble column,
  There is no graven stone
To blazon to a curious world
  The deeds they might have done.
But the prairie flower blows lightly there,
  And creeping wild rose trains
Its wreath of summer beauty o'er
  The Riders of the Plains.

Sleep on, sleep on, proud slumberers
  Who died in this Far West,
No prancing steed will feel your hand,
  No trumpet break your rest.
Sleep on, till the great Archangel
  Shall burst death's mortal chains,
And you hear the great " Reveillé "
  Ye Riders of the Plains.

We bear no lifted banners,
  The soldier's care and pride,
No fluttering flag waves onward
  Our horsemen as they ride.
Our only guide is " duty's " call,
  And well its strength sustains
The dauntless spirits of our men,
  Bold Riders of the Plains.

In England's mighty Empire
  Each man must take his stand ;
Some guard the honoured flag at sea,
  Some bear it well by land ;
'Tis not our part to fight its foes—
  Then what to us remains ?
What duty does our Sovereign give
  Her Riders of the Plains ?

Our mission is to plant the reign
  Of British freedom here,
Restrain the lawless savage,
  And protect the pioneer

And 'tis a proud and daring trust
  To hold these vast domains
With but three hundred mounted men—
  The Riders of the Plains.

And though we win no praise or fame
  In the struggle here alone—
To carry out good British law
  And plant old England's throne;
Yet when our task has been performed,
  And law with order reigns,
The peaceful settler long will bless
  The Riders of the Plains.

RIEL AND THE FENIANS.

Riel asserts that all the talk about Fenian help was merely a blind, but if a letter addressed to him from New York, and intercepted the other day by the police, is not a fictitious one he is open to the charge of mendacity. In the delayed Prince Albert mail were several letters addressed to Riel at Carleton. This particular one was addressed to "General Louis Riel, Carleton," and bore the New York postmark, and was dated 28th March last, shortly after the Duck Lake fight. It was evidently in response to one written by Riel, who had made an offer of some kind or other. The writer was thoroughly posted on North-West affairs and the location of places, and spoke of Humboldt, Clark's Crossing, Carleton, Saskatoon, and other points, and advised Riel to defend Batoche's. Reference was made to sending five hundred men, with guns, ammunition, and hand grenades, which were being manufactured. Allusion was made to different persons, fictitious names, such as "Rock" "Leary," "Sec." being used. The signature was this:—

O —— —— —— ————.

The identity of the writer has, of course, not been established, but he evidently was a *confidante* of Riel's, and his addressing the letter to Carleton indicates a thorough acquaintance with the rebel plans, as it was their intention to capture that place in their first flush of victory.

"Are the people of Prince Albert responsible in any way for this rebellion?" was the question I asked of a leading resident of that town, just before the steamer started for the west.

"They are this far," was the reply. "When Riel first came to the North-West, and was holding meetings throughout the country, they asked him to hold one here. A largely-signed requisition to that effect was presented him, and when he came a large crowd attended and listened to his speech. He was very moderate, of course, and I believe his remarks were applauded, but I don't know, as, being entirely opposed to the movement, I did not attend. However, many white settlers here led Riel to believe that they were heart and soul with him, and he in turn led his people to believe the same thing. I don't suppose these anticipated for one moment that the agitation they then fanned would result in a resort to arms and bloodshed, as it did; but their countenancing it without doubt led Riel to greater lengths than he otherwise would have gone. He counted upon their support."

"And did no one oppose him at the meeting?" I asked.

"Yes, a Mr. Deacon, one of the Wolseley expedition men, rose in the meeting and called Riel a murderer. This somewhat frightened the rebel leader, and he did not hold another meeting here. It also partly deterred some of the white sympathizers with Riel from further following him. It was Riel's boast that the Government owed him money, and that he would make it cost them hundreds of thousands of dollars."

"So you say that Prince Albert is not altogether blameless in the matter?"

"Not blameless in the way I have mentioned. Had the white agitators among us not encouraged Riel by their petitions to him and attendance at his meetings and by supplying him with money, thus misleading him into the belief that the whole white population was at his back, his subsequent action might have been confined to constitutional methods. The agitators here encouraged his campaign among the Half-breeds by every means in their power."

This is the view of a leading Conservative resident of Prince Albert, and a leading Reformer endorses it as correct.

The journey to Battleford from Prince Albert is thus described. The departure was made on May 23:—

Amid loud cheers from the assembled soldiery and townspeople, who lined the banks, the good ship *North-West*, the fleetest in North-Western waters, which is not saying much, steamed out from Prince Albert yesterday morning for Battleford. On board are General Middleton and his staff, the Midland Battalion, under the gallant Colonel Williams, with twenty-three officers and two hundred and thirty-three men; one gun of A Battery, under Captain Drury, with five officers and fifty men; and Colonel Boulton's Mounted Infantry, five officers and sixty men—a total force of three hundred and eighty-two men and eighty-six horses.

The morning was pleasant and full of summer, but in the afternoon the breeze from the west had grown into a strong head-wind, which with the numerous sandbars forming the river's bottom, materially impeded our progress; so much so that Carleton, which it was expected would have been reached before dark, was eight miles ahead of us when the boat went to the bank for the night. The channel in the Saskatchewan changes yearly, and as there is only one pilot on board, who is also captain, and only one engineer, we cannot run at night. However, as it is, only six or seven hours are lost daily. An early start is made at dawn, and (we have long days in these high latitudes) we keep speeding along till darkness prevents further progress, say about nine o'clock at night. This imposes a serious task on Captain Sheets and Louis, the engineer—seventeen or eighteen hours a day—but the captain says that having experienced it almost ever since leaving Swift Current, on the 8th ult., he has become accustomed to the long hours and the hard work of dodging through the intricate channels and avoiding the shifting shoals of the treacherous stream. At Sturgeon River, the wreck of the steamer *Manitoba* is seen, with cabin gone, and hull sunk over her boiler deck. Here it was that she had laid up in winter quarters, but there not being sufficient water she froze to the bottom, and when the ice broke up in the spring it smashed her all to pieces. The *Manitoba*, which formerly plied on the Red River, was built ten years ago, and on her second return trip between Moorhead and Winnipeg was sunk by the opposition steamer *International*. She was raised and afterwards passed into the hands of the Winnipeg and Western line, which, as the railway superseded the river as a means of communication with the East, sent her to the Saskatchewan, where she has since been plying till now, in a lonely and unfrequented spot, she lies a derelict.

This morning Carleton was reached bright and early, and beyond the ruins of the burned fort the forms of men and horses were seen. A couple of longbooted redcoats show us that the place is occupied by Mounted Police, and not hostiles, and a few minutes later a young Indian, a nephew of Poundmaker, and son of one of the biggest scoundrels on the plains, came on board followed by a well-dressed, middle-aged Half-breed named Alexandre Cadian, a gentleman who some years ago was the chief of the Indian tribe at Muskeg Lake, but who of late has been a resident of Duck Lake. With them was Mr. Jefferson, a former farm instructor at Poundmaker's reserve, whose time expired on the 1st April, and who claims he has since been a prisoner of that doughty chief, although it is not clear that he was an involuntary one. Poundmaker's nephew, whose Indian name signifies Blue Horn, was an envoy to General Middleton, and the bearer of the following crafty-worded letter, in Jefferson's handwriting:—

EAGLE HILLS, May 19, 1885.

SIR,—I am camped with my people at the east end of the Eagle Hills, where I am met by the news of the surrender of Riel. No letter came with the news, so that I cannot tell how far it may be true. I send some of my men to you to learn the truth and the terms of peace, and hope you will deal kindly with them. I and my people wish you to send us the terms of peace in writing so that there may be no misunderstanding, from which so much trouble arises. We have twenty-one prisoners, whom we have tried to treat well in every respect. With greeting,

his
POUNDMAKER, +
mark.

To General Middleton, Duck Lake.

To this the General sent the following reply by the bearers, with whom Jefferson also returned:

STEAMER "NORTH-WEST," May 23, 1885.

POUNDMAKER,—I have utterly defeated the Half-breeds and Indians at Batoche's, and have made prisoners of Riel and most of his council. I have made no terms with him, neither will I make terms with you. I have men enough to destroy you and your people, or at least to drive you away to starve, and will do so unless you bring in the teams you took, and yourself and your councillors to meet me with your arms at Battleford on Tuesday, 26th. I am glad to hear that you treated the prisoners well, and have released them.

FRED. MIDDLETON, Major-General.

The story, as learned from the interpreter, was as follows:—Riel had sent his emissary, Alexandre Cadian, with others, to Poundmaker to ask his assistance at Batoche's, should the Government forces meet him there. The day after his arrival, news of the disaster to Riel's men reached Poundmaker, through a friendly Half-breed, with the advice that he should lay down his arms if he wished to avoid having his people killed. Poundmaker did not believe the messenger, and Cadian and others started for Batoche's to ascertain the truth; but after their departure the news was confirmed by couriers sent by Beardy. Poundmaker's nephew had in the meantime been despatched with the letter given above to Prince Albert, where it was thought General Middleton was camped, but finding that he had gone to Carleton followed and overtook him, as stated. Cadian was captured by the Mounted Police, near Duck Lake, and brought to Carleton also. As wired you, he was one of the most prominent in the rebel ranks. His former chieftainship stood him in good stead, and he easily influenced his old braves at Muskeg Lake to go on the warpath. In other ways, especially with the savages, was he an invaluable aid to Riel and the rebel cause. He was sent to Prince Albert, where he will be incarcerated with the other prisoners.

At Carleton we also learned that Gabriel Dumont, with three trusty lieutenants, had been lurking in the Birch Hills, and that but very few of the leaders of the rebellion are now uncaptured. Carleton itself is very prettily located on the bottom land, and immediately in rear rises the tree-covered bench land which almost overlooks it. In front runs the muddy Saskatchewan. There are no buildings except one or two sheds; a neatly painted picket fence, which surrounds the ruins of Lawrence Clarke's house, and the blackened *debris* of the fort itself being all that remains of this former flourishing post. It is so located that it could scarcely be defended against any large number of hostiles, and its destruction was a prudent step. Now that we know that Poundmaker is anxious to submit, further precautions in the way of barricading the boat are abandoned; extra ammunition is put out of sight, and everyone feels that the campaign is nearing its end.

Only Big Bear now remains unsubdued, and, as Colonel Strange is after him, it is thought by persons who are competent to form an opinion that upon the receipt of the news of Riel's overthrow and capture he will follow the example of his more artful fellow-marauder, Poundmaker, and sue for peace. Big Bear has not the influence nor the cunning of Poundmaker, who is credited with having deceived every white man with whom he has come in contact, and that in the most approved fashion. There are, besides Little Poplar, who boasted last fall that the land would be running with blood before long, and who but recently returned from a visit to tribes across the line, and Breaking-through-the-Ice, Lucky Man, lately deposed chief; Curly Head, the Twin Wolverine (Big Bear's eldest son), and the well-named Miserable Being, who threatened Quinn and killed seven of the Frog Lake victims. All of them belong to Big Bear's party. They, with Poundmaker himself, his brother, Yellow Mud, Peachoo, Lean Man, and Grizzly Bear's Head (the two latter Stoneys), will probably be sent as prisoners to Regina when they come in and surrender. They are all bad Indians, and any leniency shown to them would be worse than mistaken kindness, it would be a blunder. With them out of the way the remaining Indians would not be likely to create another disturbance for many a year to come. But if they are not punished, and punished severely, there is every reason to believe that the country will be continually disturbed.

ON THE STEAMER "NORTH-WEST," May 24.

After Carleton is left not a solitary house on either bank is seen, not even an Indian tepee, not a vestige of life is seen, except a few wild fowl, not a sign of civilization. We realize at last, to the full extent, that this is the Great Lone Land. All is eternal silence, broken only by the puffing and wheezing of the steamer. The steep, heavily-timbered banks, on which the dark emerald of the fir contrasts prettily with the lighter green tint of the poplar, become the barriers of a bare, open, rolling prairie, boundless as space itself, whose extent to the vision is only limited by the horizon. Again the timber appears on the banks, poplar only, small-sized, with budding leaves. The river is still tortuous, the islands more numerous, the sandbars more annoying. And so we creep on. Church parade is held in the morning, the General reading the service. Appropriate hymns are rendered, and after the Doxology is sung, "God Save the Queen" rings through the air from a hundred voices. It is the Queen's Birthday. Ours is not a very grand celebration of the event, for it is the Sabbath, but the General tells us we shall right royally celebrate the day to-morrow at Battleford. But in honour of Her Majesty the men tidy up a bit; officers, whose uniforms are travel-stained and begrimed with powder, don their other clothes, the General setting the example. Captain Howard appears in all the pomp and lustre that the regulation blue and gold of the Connecticut State Guard, with red-plumed helmet, can shed. It is a quiet, unostentatious way of observing the day, not what Canadians, at all events, are accustomed to; but however undemonstrative it may be it is none the less loyally observed. A blinding rain-storm sets in early in the morning, the skies only clearing long enough to permit divine service to be held in the sunshine; then the clouds gather again, and it seems as if Jupiter Pluvius had turned on the water and forgotten the combination. Later a strong head-wind, retarding our progress about two miles an hour, drives away the clouds, the sun shines brightly again, and we go on cautiously picking our way past sandbar and shoal.

A canoe bearing a white flag comes down the river, and hails the steamer. It is quickly drawn up alongside, and its occupants climb on board. They are Samuel Ballendine and two other messengers from Colonel Otter, at Battleford, bearing the message which Poundmaker had sent him, a similar one to that sent the General himself. The couriers report having seen a couple of Indians, evidently watching for the boat, a short way up stream, and that they had disappeared as soon as they saw the canoe coming. Poundmaker was camped ten miles back from the Saskatchewan, on the east side, about forty miles from Battleford, and these men say that he has about eight hundred ponies and a number of head of cattle; that he has only about a month's provisions, and, with Indian prodigality, is slaughtering twenty-five, thirty, and forty head a day, while the untouched carcases of fat beeves lie scattered on the plain, killed in sheer wantonness. They also tell us that Poundmaker expects to be able to make another treaty, with all the past forgiven, and that he will be allowed to return to his reserve with even more liberal terms and privileges than he previously enjoyed. He and his men have pillaged the country, driven off the cattle, recklessly destroyed what they could not steal, burned hundreds of houses, massacred unoffending settlers, hopelessly ruined hundreds of people, and now that he sees retribution about to overtake him, this child-like and bland Indian would really like to know, you know, on what terms the little unpleasantness he has created can be condoned. The Stoneys with him, one hundred and sixty strong, and every brave a fierce fighter, will not surrender, but are determined to remain on the war-path.

Ballendine also tells of an Indian named William Lightfoot, who lives near Battleford. He has fifty acres broken, owns numerous ponies and cattle, has a well-furnished house, and is in comfortable circumstances. Noticing his industry and thrifty habits the Indian agents have endeavoured to encourage him in every possible way, and been more than kind to him. Notwithstanding this, he was one of the first to go on the war-path, and one of the most fierce amongst the cruel savages.

This is only one of many instances where the policy of kindness and paternal care which the Canadian Government has exercised in dealing with the Indians has proved to be a failure. It is evident that some new and more rigorous system must be adopted by which the Indians can be more easily and cheaply controlled. Notwithstanding the tens of thousands of dollars annually spent in feeding these wards of the nation, notwithstanding the efforts unceasingly put forth to give them homes and to clothe them, over a thousand of them, without reason, except the insatiable desire for blood and plunder which seems to possess most of them, have gone on the war-path. In fact, one in four of the available Indians north of the track went out fighting against us. So soon as their Half-breed leader is beaten they cringingly supplicate for peace. If it is granted without severe punishment being inflicted, that mistaken leniency will only embolden them to continue their good-for-nothing marauding habits. "What should be done with them?" I asked a gentleman who has spent many years among them, and who, having had considerable experience with them, is fully acquainted with their traits. His prompt reply was: "First, I should punish the leading Half-breed and Indian rebels, commencing with Riel. Then I should reorganize the whole tribal system, abolishing all chiefs and councillors, which has been found to work fairly well where it has been tested already. No more treaty money should be paid to any one found in arms or known to have participated in the recent troubles. All these Indians should be disarmed and their ponies taken away. Force every Indian, whether good or bad, to work; but continue to act faithfully and honestly up to the terms of the treaty with all Indians who were loyal, and did not join Riel. By following these suggestions, my experience of many years teaches me that a better state of affairs will immediately result. The status of the Indian will be raised, and finding himself compelled to either work or starve, fond of grub as he is, he will choose the former. The expense of the service would grow much less annually, and so many being disarmed a feeling of safety from depredations would soon spring up among the settlers. This is a radical change, I know, but after their conduct during the past two months something very radical is needed. Had Riel been victorious at Batoche's, a general Indian uprising would have followed, and although some tribes would perhaps have had no wish to go on the war-path they would have been forced into it. In that case you well know the terrible consequences that would have followed. I shudder to think of them."

My own personal experience, with all the information that can be learned from those well informed on Indian nature and characteristics, leads me to adopt a similar view to that expressed above, and to hope that it will not be many days before it is inaugurated. The sentiment of the people here is pretty well voiced in the following extract from the Saskatchewan *Herald* of May 25 :—

"Five years of pampering and petting have failed to make the Indians see that it was for their good the enormous expenditure was being made. The law of force must be applied to them until they acknowledge its power; for then, and only then, will they become manageable. All treaties have been annulled by this uprising, and in making new conditions the tribal relationship between band and chief should be weakened if not altogether severed, and every Indian made to stand or fall on his individual merits. Whether put on large or small reserves they must be placed there simply as Indians and kept on their limits; and in making them work for their living it will be criminal in the extreme to furnish them with expensive machinery as has hitherto been done, and with the destruction rather than the use of which they have become familiar. They must be made to labour with the plough and the hoe; those were the only things with which thousands of their betters had to begin the world, and that, too, without the addition of rations and free clothing."

Just as the sun begins to sink in the West the steamer draws up to the landing at Battleford. Groups of soldiers and civilians collected along the bank for a mile down stream to greet our coming with cheers, and at the landing there is a large crowd of enthusiastic people whose welcomes are given with a will and as enthusiastically responded to.

CHAPTER XXV.

AT BATTLEFORD.

AT Battleford General Middleton and his men were warmly welcomed. The Royal Grenadiers, though to a certain extent occupying a more humble position in public estimation than the Queen's Own when they left Toronto were now the heroes of the hour. Turn it over as they liked there was nothing but utter defeat and "a retreat on sufferance" to be got out of recollections of the Cut Knife fight, while the Grenadiers were "the heroes of Batoche." More than one of the Queen's Own felt that the disastrous luck of the regiment was following it when they saw the evident pride with which General Middleton regarded "my little devils" as he termed the Grenadiers when they were landing. Of course any one who follows the events of the war knows that only forty of the Queen's Own were at Cut Knife, but the fact that that battle was the only one that brought any of their men under fire during the whole campaign, coupled with the other fact, that Colonel Otter who commanded at Cut Knife had formerly been the commandant of the Queen's Own served to thoroughly identify the regiment with the most disastrous failure of the whole campaign. The following letter from a Battleford correspondent though evidently intended to excuse Colonel Otter, unmistakably shows that the writer was of opinion that he was "rather too light for the place." He begins by giving the following account of the capture of the teamsters:—

About the time we had the engagement at Cut Knife Creek, arms and ammunition were supplied to the teamsters. Colonel Otter also sent an escort to meet the trains on the outskirts of the wood south of here. In the case I am now referring to, however, the police escort had not reached the train. The Indian camp was on the move eastwards, its front and flanks covered with a swarm of mounted braves who scoured every coulée along the line of march. Poundmaker must have thoroughly understood our position and our lack of scouts, for he actually camped with all his women and children within twelve miles of here, and captured the waggon train within about eight. Unfortunately for the teamsters they camped in the woods the previous night; as they were starting next morning they were discovered by the Indians. The latter were not long in arranging their plan of attack. A long slough through which the train had to pass was selected for the surprise. It was heavily wooded on each side of the trail, and offered excellent cover. As the teamsters were urging their horses through the quagmire the Indians jumped on them with a yell. The horses became unmanageable, and before the unfortunate drivers could even grasp their rifles the Indians had captured the outfit. The whole thing was over in a few seconds, and before a single shot could be fired by the whites: in fact they were taken in a trap, and the discharge of a rifle on their part would have meant the massacre of every one of them. As it was they threw up their hands, and we have every reason to believe their lives were spared, the object, of course, being to make better terms with us in case they are cornered at some future time. This is the opinion of Constable Ross and other scouts who have been at the scene of the encounter.

Later on the police escort intended for this train was fired on by the Indians, one man (Elliot) being killed and another wounded. The encounter was a surprise to both parties. The police under Sergeant Gordon noticed a small hill a short distance off the trail which afforded a good position for viewing the surrounding country. The Indian scouts on the opposite side noticed it at the same time, and both rode up. The heads of each appeared above the hill top at the same instant, but the Indians seemed to grasp the situation quicker. They dropped from their horses as if shot, and before the police could even turn round poured in a volley at less than twenty yards. How anyone escaped is a mystery. The police turned and fled. Elliot was thrown from his horse and sought cover in the bushes. A turn in the trail, together with a heavy clump of bushes, saved the police from the second volley that was sent after them, and they escaped. When the police went out a day or two later to look for Elliot's body they found the bushes riddled with bullets. The body was found by them some three or four miles from the place where the attack was made. It is supposed he struggled along and hid himself in the bushes. Then when the Indians left he started off, and seeing the waggon train made for it in the expectation of meeting friends. It was in the hands of the enemy, however, and they ruthlessly murdered him. He was shot through the spine and head, either of which would have proved instantly fatal. Perhaps it was the teamsters or the Catholic priest who is known to be with the Indians who buried him. Be this as it may, our men found the body wrapped in a waggon cover, the hands crossed upon the breast, and buried beneath an inch or two of land.

There is no doubt that Colonel Otter is heavily handicapped for want of scouts. General Middleton has over sixty, General Strange about one hundred and fifty, and Colonel Otter seven. It has unfortunately been impossible to send scouts to him, and therefore the reconnoitering service—by which the commander feels the pulse, so to speak, of his enemy, learns of his movements, and from this draws his conclusions and forms plans to checkmate them—is with us sadly defective. As I said before, Poundmaker must know this, or he never would have ventured within twelve miles of our camp with all his women and children. There are those here who think we missed a golden opportunity to recapture our waggon train and at the same time punish the Indians while they were passing eastward. But here again the question arises, what would we do without a sufficient mounted force to watch their movements and guard against our falling into a similar trap to that laid for us at Cut Knife Hills? No one will deny that whatever advantage we may have gained from time to time during that engagement was in the end of no value to us, simply because we could not follow it up. The same might have happened—in fact was quite likely to happen—had we followed Poundmaker and his braves a second time. It would have been better had we never gone out to Poundmaker's camp, for now the Indians think that we are as glad to withdraw from the encounter as they were. There is little doubt but that since then the Indians have been reinforced, and we would find a more stubborn resistance from them.

To us, however the encounter has proved beneficial in two ways—first, we have come to the conclusion that in bush-fighting an Indian is better than a white man; and, secondly, that the best way to fight him is to adopt his own tactics. I think I may safely say that, taking everything into consideration, we will not attempt to chastise Poundmaker until after the arrival of the General with reinforcements.

Some wonderful stories are told of the skill displayed by the Indians in what for want of a better term I shall call war-craft. Born and reared on the prairie, their whole training through life is craft of one kind or another; to steal unperceived upon the antelope or other animal, and shoot it down in its tracks, is an everyday occurrence with them, and when on the war path the same stealthy cat-like movement stands them in good stead. They are adepts in the art of finding cover and concealing themselves, and can pass almost noiselessly through underbrush that would baffle a white man. Let me here relate an instance that occurred a few days ago.

A man named Dennison, who came into camp saying he had escaped from the Indians, but whose story was not at the time believed, related the following: He said that while in the Indian camp he heard them constantly talking of what was going on round the fort here. A day or two before he escaped from Poundmaker's an Indian whom he knows told how he had just returned from an examination of our stockades. He had crawled up, he said, to within thirty yards of the sentry at the northeastern angle of the stockade and watched him for over an hour. He saw the sentry light his pipe, and walk up and down in a listless sort of way. By-and-bye the sentries starting with number one called out "All's well," but number five (the man he was watching) did not. He evidently did not hear the call. In a few minutes two men with a lantern came out of the stockade and visited number five to see what was wrong. "Had they not come out when they did," said the Indian, "I'd have sent an arrow through him." He was afraid, however, that they were going to examine the neighbouring bushes, and he very sensibly left. The truth of this story was confirmed by looking up the guard report for the night in question, when it was discovered that Private Rose, of the Home Guards, who was number five, did not call out when his turn came. The report further showed that a non-commissioned officer and man took a lantern and went down to his post to see what was wrong. This, no doubt, saved his life.

In this same connection a gentleman resident in Battleford writes under date May 11, as follows:—

Life in Battleford is, to say the least of it, becoming monotonous. Here we are to all intents and purposes prisoners. The farmer cannot venture out to his fields through fear of the lurking foe. No one cares to venture far from the barracks even in daytime, and as soon as the shades of night set in the only persons any distance from the fort are the pickets. These are stationed at various points, some of them being a mile or more from camp. It is not a pleasant duty. Two hours alone on the prairie, with every probability of being watched by an enemy who only requires a favourable opportunity to murder you, is not an inducement to the ordinary mortal to do picket duty. Still it has to be done, and the boys as they go out to their lonely posts think of the bright firesides they have left in far-off Ontario; keep a sharp look out, and are well satisfied when their two hours are completed. The enemy has already begun his usual practice of trying to shoot sentries. A couple of nights ago a picket sentry was fired on near the ferry by someone on the opposite side of the river. Of course he returned the fire, but the chances of hitting a man with a rifle bullet at night are very slim, and the would-be assassin escaped. It was said by some that the man who fired the shot was a teamster, who mistook the sentry for an enemy. If so, perhaps it was the same man who was seen by another picket at what is called " the point " last night. Between midnight and one o'clock this morning a rifle shot was heard at the point, followed an instant later by two or three shots in the line west of the barracks. The guard turned out: the bugles sounded the assembly, and in a minute everyone was astir. For some reason or other, however, the men who should have manned the eastern side of the stockade and the bastion at the south-eastern angle were not in barracks, and it was several minutes before there was a soul in either place. What a determined enemy might have accomplished in that time I will not venture to say. Of course they would ultimately have been wiped out, but once in the fort they could have done an immense amount of damage before the troops outside would have known the first thing about it. This was not the case under our Colonel's (Colonel Morris) *regime*. Every man knew his place, and the minute the assembly sounded everyone was at his post. The troops have relieved us, that is, have relieved our minds to a certain extent, but so far as the fort itself is concerned, it is actually weaker. The sandbags have been taken down, and nothing has ever been done to replace them. But to return to the alarm last night. Everyone turned out, and after a time the bastions and the palisades were manned. For an hour we waited for orders to turn in. At last they came, and we were allowed to sleep in quiet during the remainder of the night. This morning the prints of moccasined feet were discovered on the hillside where the picket said he saw two men the night before, and fired on them. All are anxious for the arrival of the General or reinforcements, and the wiping out of the Indians. Had we had a hundred more men, or had our guns not given out, we would never have had to retire from our position. We were certainly very fortunate to get out as we did. The Indians were too far off to discover what we were doing until it was too late for them to prevent it. Had they succeeded in getting into the brush at the creek in time we would have lost a great many men—some say it would have been a second Custer massacre.

A correspondent, writing from Battleford on May 13, the day upon which Poundmaker captured the waggon train, thus writes:

Since the rebellion broke out Riel has been very anxious to have the public believe that he has had nothing to do with the Indian outbreak. Here are a few facts as related to me by Mr. McKay, who has charge of the Hudson Bay Company's business here. It appears that during March last I-em-e-cease, or The Awkward, Big Bear's son, called on Mr. McKay and told him that Riel had made a private arrangement with his (Awkward's) father at Prince Albert last fall to join in a rising against the whites. They had talked the matter over while in Montana. Riel then arranged with Big Bear that should the former begin a rebellion in Canada the latter was to come over and assist him. I-em-e-cease said that Wandering Spirit, one of Big Bear's councillors and the man who is said to have murdered Quinn at Frog Lake, knows all about the arrangement; also that the Indians west of here had been seen and were ready to rise when Riel gave the word. Riel told his father in his presence that he had made up his mind to come to Canada, and if he did not get what he wanted he would spill Canadian blood—a promise which he has kept to the letter. Riel appears to have had some difficulty in getting Big Bear to join him, and it was not until after several interviews that the Indian promised to join him.

Some time after his last interview with Big Bear, Riel sent a letter written in Cree to the Indians at Frog Lake. This letter stated that he would have a strong force about the time the grass would be long enough to afford good pasturage for their horses. I-em-e-cease offered to get a copy of the letter and show it to Mr. McKay, provided he would say nothing about it to the Indians, and a day or two later I-em-e-cease came to Mr. McKay, and said that the night previous a Half-breed visited their tent, and after asking if he was Big Bear's son, told him to go back to his father's camp and tell him that the trouble had commenced. The wire between Battleford and Edmonton had been cut, and that to Clark's Crossing would be down in a few days. All this, it is needless to say, was only too true. This Half-breed was very anxious to start up country himself, saying that all the Half-breeds had joined Riel, and he was going to tell them that the first blood had been shed.

So much, therefore, for Riel's protestations of innocence regarding the depredations of the Indians.

This is what a correspondent has to say about Battleford as it appeared on General Middleton's arrival:

One can scarcely realize that we are in the midst of an Indian war, a war that can have but one result, but which will cost a wealth of blood and treasure. The Indian is not brave from a white man's point of view. His bravery consists in taking a maximum number of lives with a minimum of risk to himself. In fact they will not attack unless the chances are all in their favour. Poor Smart, as fine a fellow as ever drew breath, was shot in the back; Fremont, the Belgian settler, was shot in the back; Payne was shot in the back, and so on through the long death list. Wherever the victims were taken by surprise it was a bullet from behind that killed them. It would make the heart of a saint ache to visit some of the houses sacked by the Indians. In the house in Old Battleford which belonged to Indian Agent Rae, but now occupied by the officers of the Queen's Own, I saw enough to blot out for ever any friendly feelings I may have had for the "noble Red-man." The devilish ingenuity with which they destroyed everything they could not carry away or did not want, would put the blackest Nihilist to the blush. Explode a charge of dynamite in a gentleman's parlour and the chances are that something will escape.

Turn loose a party of Crees or Stoneys in the same place and dynamite will be double discounted. In the house I spoke of they ripped the feather beds open and saturated their contents with coal oil. The safe containing books and papers was literally hammered to pieces; the shelving and drawers taken out and broken, the papers strewn amongst the feathers. Pictures on the wall were taken down, torn up, and the frames broken. Windows and window sashes were smashed; crockery, vases, stoves, furniture, everything inside and out pulled to pieces. One man, in describing the ruin, said:—"It was just like taking a lady's trunk, packed ready for Saratoga, and pulling both ends two miles apart, with all between them." Not satisfied with breaking the furniture they tore the upholstering to pieces. Carpets were taken from the stores, spread upon the streets, and up and down these the bucks and squaws paraded, in sight almost of the fort on the other side of the river. What flour they did not want was destroyed. In the Government stores they emptied it on the floor, rolled in it, and then, killing dogs, pigs, and chickens, mixed all up together. One man had over $1,000 in bills concealed in a niche between the logs of his house. Even this was discovered. It shows with what completeness every nook and corner was ransacked.

In carting away what provisions they thought necessary every man, woman and child, together with horses, dogs, and even the captured cattle, had to do their share always, excepting the braves, who consider themselves too good to work Bags of flour were strapped on the backs of the cattle, the dogs carried smaller packages, while the squaws, after decking themselves out in whatever finery they could lay their hands on, shouldered sides of bacon or bags of flour, and fell into line. Where they have carted the spoils has not yet been discovered.

Old Battleford on the south side of Battle River, and New Battleford on the north side presented two very different pictures when the troops marched in. Save that the dead animals have been removed from the streets, the appearance is but little changed, even now. On the south side of the river every house is more or less broken up. Those occupied by the troops have been cleaned out and made habitable, but the remainder are about in the condition in which they were left by the last visitors. The Indians did not dare to cross the river. They have a wholesome dread of the Mounted Police, and a perfect horror of the little seven-pounder that has already sent some of their companions to the happy hunting grounds. New Battleford, therefore, was not molested, but the settlers moved into barracks along with those from across the river, taking as much of their stock and household goods with them as possible. Upwards of five hundred and thirty souls have been sheltered in the barracks during the past month, receiving rations. The scene to me was a strange one. Not a month away from the peace and quiet of Ontario, where the settler, no matter how far removed from his neighbour, lies down to rest without the slightest apprehension of danger, the change to the bustle of a military camp is, to say the least, a novel experience. Every man's waist encircled with a belt bristling with cartridges, a rifle in his hand, and a revolver by his side, tells the story. Battleford, that is, the old town, is situated on the south side of the Battle River (see map of Battleford, p. 106), and consisted before its partial destruction by the Indians of about three hundred houses. Government House, which had

AT BATTLEFORD.

recently been turned into an industrial school for Indian children, occupies a commanding position on the plateau above the river. It is a large and commodious three-storey wooden building, and was selected by Colonel

STAFF-SERGEANT WALKER, Q.O.R.

Otter as being best situated for his headquarters. This building has been placed in a state of defence both inside and out. An entrenchment with the necessary flanking defences has been thrown up round it, while inside the windows and doors have been effectively barricaded. It is really too bad that the Indians have no intention of attacking it. If they would only drop down the river some bright moonlight night and rush upon the defences, what a fine thinning out old Poundmaker's braves would get! But there is no hope of their coming, and so the boys must needs go and look for them. The Indians will not attack at night unless they are certain none of their number will be killed. They have a superstition that the man who is killed at night is blind when he goes to the happy hunting grounds, and therefore make their attack either just before dark or at dawn of day. Judge Rouleau's house stood within a stone's throw of Government House, and was a comparatively handsome and well-furnished building. All that remains of it now is a ruined chimney and a few blackened poles and beams. North of a line drawn from Judge Rouleau's to Government House is the camp occupied by the troops, their white tents standing out in bold relief against the dark background of the wood a mile or more in the rear. On the plateau at the north side of the camp is the artillery, their guns commanding the brush and opposite bank of the river. Directly opposite on the north side of Battle River is the fort, distant about fifteen hundred yards from the volunteer camp. A natural glacis slopes up from the river to the palisades, along which it would be almost impossible for a rat to find cover, much less an Indian. A trench has been excavated inside the palisades, which are loop-holed for purposes of defence. Then there is a bastion at the south-eastern angle for a gun which flanks the southern and eastern faces to a certain extent. This is defended, or rather strengthened, by a dry ditch. Inside the palisades the buildings have been placed with a view to flanking each other. They are all bullet-proof, and even if an enemy succeeded in getting inside the palisades he would find himself in a warmer corner than outside. But the barracks are safe. The "untutored savage" of the missionary society is sufficiently tutored to keep at a respectful distance from our defences. He knows enough not to risk his life in a vain attempt to storm them. Could he manage to capture the place by treachery or steal upon the garrison unaware, he would do so. But his chances of success in either way are so slim that he is not likely to attempt it.

Outside the palisades are several houses within close rifle range of the barracks. These would under certain conditions be a source of weakness, as an enemy once in them could find excellent cover. They are at present occupied, but in case of necessity would be deserted, when, if the Indians ventured in, a few rounds from one of the guns would bring the logs about their ears, and they would only be too glad to get out. Between eight hundred and a thousand yards west of the barracks is the town of New Battleford. It consists of about forty houses. There is the Roman Catholic Church, two hotels (western ones, however), a brilliant saloon, two stores, Government telegraph, stores, offices, and stables, post-office, and houses of settlers. All, or nearly all, are substantially built of logs, and could stand a siege from such enemies as Indians. The settlers began to move back into them yesterday, feeling confident that the troops stationed here will be amply sufficient for their protection. Already some of the settlers' tents have been struck, and their owners are once more in their old homes. There are at present about thirty tents of all sizes and shapes pitched within the palisades. Many are heated with camp stoves, and on the whole their occupants are as comfortable as present circumstances will admit. This morning as I strolled through the camp I made a mental memo. of all that came under my notice. At the door of our tent a Half-breed woman was busy washing, while outside the one directly opposite a couple of sun-burnt urchins were pummelling each other over some trifling difference. There are big tents, little tents, medium-sized tents, standing side by side. In some the occupants were preparing the morning meal, while in others they were still in the arms of Morpheus. The police were all active. Some were grooming horses others on guard, while others seemed to have nothing to do but wait for the breakfast bugle to sound.

One very important building is the Indian Department warehouse. This is now occupied by the Home Guard as a barrack and mess room. It is about sixty feet long by thirty broad and built of logs. A huge stove at each end is kept burning all day. This is to do the cooking for the Home Guard, who are quartered there. A long table extends nearly the whole length of the centre of the building, at which the men eat their meals. The walls are loop-holed for musketry fire, while on pegs and beams above hang rifles, saddles, blankets, buffalo skins, spades, axes, hoes, carpenters' tools, and a hundred and one articles that I cannot recollect. Captain Wild, late of Dundas, Ont., is in command. Mr. W. H. Smart, of Quebec, brother of the murdered man, is first lieutenant; J. M. McFarlane, of Quebec, and one of the principal stock raisers here, is second lieutenant; Ronald Macdonald, from near Ottawa, is quarter-master sergeant. This company numbers one hundred and forty men all told. The volunteer company or Battleford Rifles numbers fifty-one officers and men. Captain E. A. Nash, late of the Queen's Own, is in command; Fred. Merigold is first lieutenant, and one of the best known and most popular men in this country. He hails from Woodstock, where he was connected with the militia; L. C. Baker is second lieutenant. He has had considerable experience, having served during the " late unpleasantness " between the North and South and also in western Indian warfare. The police number seventy-one, including the men who were stationed at Fort Pitt. They are under command of Inspector Dickens, a son of the great novelist. Dickens has the name of being one of the bravest men in the country. At Fort Pitt he manned a loophole during the Indian attack and blazed away at them while coolly smoking his pipe. Inspector Norris was in command of the police before the arrival of Dickens, who assumed command, being the superior officer. The arrival of Mr.

Dickens was hailed with delight by everyone within the palisades.

Prior to General Middleton's arrival in Battleford, Poundmaker released his prisoners and sent them to Battleford with a message similar to that which he sent to the General. A correspondent at Battleford thus tells the story in a letter dated May 21st:

LIEUT.-COL. O'BRIEN, M.P.
(In command of York and Simcoe Battalion.)

Scarcely anything within the range of the possible could have caused a more genuine sensation than the arrival in camp at dusk last evening of Father Cochin and the prisoners from Poundmaker's camp, bearing a flag of truce and a letter from the redoubtable chieftain, asking on what terms his surrender would be accepted. Such a surprise was it that many of the officers here believed it to be a ruse to throw us off our guard, and with this belief special instructions were laid on pickets, sentries, and others, on whose vigilance we have to depend to prevent the Indians stealing a march on us in the dark hours, to be particularly watchful that night. As it appears now, we had rightly surmised that Poundmaker was moving eastward to join Riel. It was known that a buckboard and several horsemen had, a day or two previous to Poundmaker's start from the memorable Cut Knife Hill, driven into the Indian camp from the direction of Duck Lake. It was believed by the scouts who discovered this trail that they had come from Riel's camp, and that their errand was to invite the Indians to go to the Half-breeds' aid.

All this was readily enough put down as facts, and the surmises even as to details have been verified in a most singular manner.

The party from Poundmaker's camp, besides Father Cochin, was composed of Charles and Alexander Bremner and daughter, Joseph and John Sayer and daughter, of Bressaylor settlement; Joe Fontaine, the Half-breed scout; L. Coplett, and the following teamsters who were captured in Eagle Hills last week:—Thomas J. McNeice, George McNeice, William McKeown, George Broder, Neil Brodie, Henry Barnes, Joseph Hollands, John Shearer, James Pattee, W. H. Fish, George F. Motion, Charles Sheriff, G. Cooney, Frank Cox, Thomas Hind, Daniel McLean, Frank Westaway, William Parkin, A. W. Freeborn, D. Vigeant. The teamsters all hailed from Regina.

It will be easy to understand the sensation in camp when these people, with the reverend father leading, appeared over the brow of the hill and, advancing to the sentry, asked to be shown to the office of the commandant. The news of their arrival spread with tremendous rapidity throughout the camp, fort, and town, and in a short space of time a large throng had gathered near the officers' quarters to learn what news the strangers brought. The priest and Half-breeds were taken in and their message received by Colonel Otter. The letter brought by Father

Cochin was not permitted to be seen by your correspondent. One of the teamsters, however, claims to have read the letter, and gives the following as being as nearly as possible the words of the communication:

"TO THE COMMANDANT OF THE FORT AT BATTLEFORD:

"SIR,—I and my men are at the foot of the Eagle Hills. Having heard of Riel's surrender, I send you in twenty-one white prisoners, whom I have treated well. I await terms of peace. Please send in writing, so there may be no mistake.

"(Signed)   His
"POUNDMAKER, + mark."

The letter was written by Jefferson, the schoolmaster on Poundmaker's reserve. He is a connection of the chief's, being married to the sister of one of his wives. Most people will admit the letter to be very business-like, and it is quite characteristic of Poundmaker, who has the reputation of being remarkably level-headed for an Indian of the savage kind. He is a born diplomat, I am told by those who know him well, capable of seeing as far into a millstone as most men, and the very embodiment of native dignity. Standing over six feet high, straight as a reed, with a somewhat slender figure and grave aquiline features, he is at once the handsomest and most powerful of the aborigines of the Canadian North-West, and a sample of the very highest type of the North American Indian.

After receiving the letter, Colonel Otter engaged the priest and Half-breeds in conversation for several hours, in order to elicit as much information as possible regarding the Indians' condition, strength, and intentions. The press was not admitted to this informal investigation. The scribes sought out the teamsters who were let loose, and immediately pounced upon by the crowd eager to learn of their adventures. I "corralled" one of the most intelligent of them, and he gave me quite a vivid picture of his experience since the time of his capture.

He said there were thirty-one teams in all, twenty-one of which were ox-teams, in the outfit. They were freighting up general provisions and oats. On Wednesday, 13th instant, they camped at one of the temporary military stations, about thirty miles down the Swift Current. There had been an alarm early in the evening, caused by one of the teamsters declaring he had seen a number of mounted Indians ride over a neighbouring hill. No attack, however, was made during the night, and they started on the way to Battleford at gray dawn on Thursday, 14th. By 9 o'clock they had got into Eagle Hills. When passing through Red Pheasant's reserve (Stoney) the Indians were first seen. Only two or three put in an appearance, and the teamsters, who were armed with eighteen Snider rifles and carbines, felt safe enough if that were all the enemy they had to face. They proceeded unmolested till within ten miles of Battleford, when they suddenly found themselves being surrounded. The men who were driving horses at once cut their teams loose, and mounting started back on the trail as fast as the animals would carry them. Nothing like pursuit of them, except in one case, seems to have been attempted, but the enemy quickly closed around the ox-teams, which had been drawn up into a corral for defensive purposes. Not a shot was fired, and one, a Half-breed, shortly emerged without arms from the wood, and told them if they gave up their loads and arms no harm would be done them, and they would be escorted safely into Battleford. The teamsters were only too glad of such an offer, and immediately threw up their thumbs. About thirty Half-breeds came out of the woods, and, after relieving the men of whatever money and other valuables they had, proceeded to carry out their promises of seeing the teamsters into Battleford. Before they had gone very far, however, about a hundred mounted Stoney Indians came up,

When they saw the prize they howled with delight, and were for shooting the poor teamsters there and then. The Half-breeds protested, saying the Stoneys would have to shoot them too. Then the savages clamoured against sending the prisoners to Battleford, and the captors were forced to let the Indians have their way. It looked bad for the teamsters. The Indians were continually raising their guns to their shoulders and pointing them at the captives as if to shoot, and the teamsters say it required the constant intercessions and threatenings of the Half-breeds to prevent their doing so. They would ride up to the prisoners, however, and prod them to the quick with any sharp instrument they had, spit in their faces, etc., while curvetting around and uttering the most hideous whoops and screeches. The men were put on their waggons and forced to drive their ox-teams to the Indian encampment, about four miles distant, on the edge of the open prairie. On their arrival there was a general outburst of joy. The prisoners were led before the chief, who shortly retired with his council to a teepee a little apart from the general encampment. It was an anxious time for the trembling captives, for they knew that the result of that confabulation was either life or death to them. The Stoney element in the council clamoured strongly for instant death, but Poundmaker and his Crees, as the teamsters say they afterwards learned, were for holding the men as hostages, and this element finally prevailed. Poundmaker came to the men and said they had nothing to fear. If they remained quiet and went along with them all would go well. But if one of them attempted to escape, he said, the whole of them would be shot. "My young men," he said through an interpreter, "want to kill you. If you give them a chance they will do it. I have had great trouble in stopping them. I could scarcely stop them. Thank God for your life; not me." For this message the men were thankful. They were ordered to drive the teams, for the Indians had broken up camp at once. They were afraid the "police," as they call all the soldiers, would come out at once and attack them. They thought the police were aware of the capture, because by this time news had come into their camp of the attack, and the shooting of Constable Elliot a short time previously, and the escape of his companions. The Indians could not move rapidly, however. They had a drove of three or four hundred head of cattle, which had to be driven along. By nightfall they had not made more than ten or twelve miles, and pitched their camp again a short distance east of the point where the Swift Current trail enters the hills. They fully expected an attack that night, and sought out the strongest position they could find, digging rifle pits in a coulee in front of their camp, and sending a large number of scouts to warn them of the approach of the "police." The teamsters were praying that the "police" would not come, for in case of the Indians being routed they believed they would be surely murdered. The night was spent in a teepee set apart for them. They were not, to all appearance, very closely watched, but could not think of attempting an escape on account of the threat made that all would be killed if such an attempt should be thwarted. In the morning a son of Poundmaker called Big Belly, on account of his remarkable obesity, came and asked the men if they were comfortable, or if they wanted anything. One of them intimated they had not enough blankets to keep them warm. The chief's son took off his own blanket (an article of wearing apparel which the Indian always carries with him) and threw it to the complaining teamster, with the remark that he would get them some more. That day the Indians moved eastward about 15 miles, and camped again in a strong position. They regarded an attack from the "police" as a certainty, and threw out about one hundred pickets, some of them four or five miles from the camp. The men had received good treatment. They had plenty to eat. The Indians now had any amount of "grub," and threw it about in their customary improvident fashion. They killed about twenty head of cattle each day, using only those parts most prized by them, the tongue, flank, etc., and leaving the remainder of the carcases to rot on the prairie. Their whole track was littered with food which had been thrown away—biscuits, flour, canned meat, dried apples, tea, and the like. To the best of their reckoning the whole party numbered about eight hundred souls. They had something over three hundred armed and mounted men. The Half-breeds numbered about forty-five, and they camped together, a little apart from the Indians. Their arms were principally Winchesters of the old model, Sniders, and Snider Carbines. Poundmaker's interpreter had already told the teamsters that they were going up to reinforce Riel. Riel had sent down some runners who had told them that the rebels had killed four hundred soldiers and if they could get Poundmaker's help they could drive the white man out of the country altogether. This story was untrue of course, but the teamsters had no means of knowing that and their fears were consequently increased. The treatment they received continued good, and although they were forced to drive the teams, they were otherwise unmolested. Councils were being continually held, however, and they knew at each of them a warm fight was going on regarding the matter of killing the prisoners. The young bucks of the Stoney tribe were determined to have their scalps, and the chief had almost more than he could do to prevent it. At night the turbulent Indians would come about their tent and keep up a very uncomfortable yelling and whooping, meantime going through in mimic fashion, the process of shooting and scalping the unfortunate white men. On Sunday Father Cochin, himself a prisoner, celebrated mass for the benefit of the Half-breeds and those of the Indians in the faith. The teamsters were nearly all Protestants, and the good father, not to see them lacking for spiritual comforts, under such trying circumstances, produced a number of Episcopal Hymn Books, which were on the captured train, and while the teamsters joined in singing some of the more

GABRIEL DUMONT.*

familiar of them, he played an excellent accompaniment for them on the harmonium. Amongst the captured goods

---

* The military leader of the South Branch rising was born forty-five years ago at Edmonton, where his father was employed as a buffalo hunter

were a number of letters for Battleford people, and the files of Toronto papers, for which the troops had been waiting so long and so impatiently. With the papers the squaws amused themselves making head-decorations. Amongst the letters the teamsters say there were a couple from Ottawa to certain Indian Department officials. They were couched in terms denouncing the conduct of the Department here. The communications were made known by the interpreter to Poundmaker, and the wily old chief fell into such convulsions of laughter thereat as threatened quite to destroy his reputation for stoical dignity.

Short marches were made on Monday and Tuesday. On the evening of Tuesday several Half-breeds came into camp, and told of Riel's defeat and capture. At once a council was held, and it was finally decided to take the course of sending in the prisoners, and asking for terms of peace.

---

by the Hudson Bay Company. He is a French Half-breed, well-known for a resolute man and a leader in Indian fighting or buffalo hunting. In the fall of 1880 the family removed to the South Branch, where they took up claims near together—the father and three sons—the permanent settlement there having been started the same season by French Half-breed refugees from Red River. There Dumont's father, now blind, still lives, as well as Gabriel's family. Gabriel put a ferry scow on the South Branch, at his place, which is known as "Gabriel's Crossing." This ferry brought him in a very comfortable revenue, and at the opening of the outbreak he was reported to be well-off. When the fighting commenced he was naturally chosen to be the leader of the rebels, a position for which he proved himself well fitted. In person he is stout and muscular, of middle height and of great strength. His mouth is rather coarse, but the rest of his features are not displeasing. His whiskers are scanty, and his complexion dark. He was always esteemed among his friends as a respectable and honest, as well as brave, man.

CHAPTER XXVI.

POUNDMAKER AND MIDDLETON

ON the 26th of May Poundmaker and several of the chiefs who were supposed to be governed by his council marched into Battleford and formally surrendered themselves. This scene and the interview between Poundmaker and General Middleton which followed constitute one of the most important chapters in the history of Canadian rule in the North-West.

General Middleton sat on a chair with his officers in a little group around him and squatting before him in a long row were the chiefs, with Poundmaker in the centre, and behind gathered the band. Face to face they were, the bearded, firm-faced representatives of the conquering race, and the leaders of the vanishing dark-skinned aborigines. Through his Interpreter the General asked, Is it usual for Indians to go about, pilfering like rats?

Poundmaker—I felt that I had a rope about my neck, and something drawing me all the time.

Middleton—Who raided all the settlers?

Poundmaker—I never collected a party or advised any of the young men to commit robbery.

Middleton—Has a great chief no power?

Poundmaker—I am not sure that I am a chief.

Middleton—Who murdered Payne and Fremont?

Poundmaker—I cannot name them, and I would not tell the great chief a lie.

Middleton—Who raided this place and burned the stores?

Poundmaker—I suppose it might have been other than the Crees. (Poundmaker is Chief of the Crees.)

Middleton—Did you never fight the troops?

Poundmaker—I never thought to fight the white man and all people around Battle River and the Indian Agent (pointing to Reid) can't say different. I always wanted to try and raise from the ground enough to keep my people alive. I said I was no chief, because when I asked for food for my people in my charge it was not given to me.

Middleton—Why did you receive Riel, and promise him two hundred men, as Riel himself told me?

Poundmaker—I never promised to help him. If I had promised I would have sent the men.

Middleton—Tell him (turning directly to the Interpreter) that he's telling a lie. Riel told me that Poundmaker was coming there.

Poundmaker—I can't deny what the General, a great man, says, but I never promised.

Middleton—When Riel told Poundmaker that he had defeated me, Poundmaker consented to come.

Poundmaker—It is very bad that there are no people here to say what I said then. Samuel Trotter, Urbel Delorme, and four others were there, but they have gone home. What I said was: "I don't want to go, because Riel has too little powder and cartridge." That's why I stopped at Cut Knife Creek. When I came this way I was going to Little Devil's Lake, not to Riel.

Middleton—Why did you attack the police and waggons?

Poundmaker—When sleeping quietly they came and fired a cannon on me into my camp; I jumped up and had to defend myself. It frightened me and my children.

Middleton—Poundmaker would never have been attacked if he had not raided and murdered. If the Indians do that they will always be attacked.

Poundmaker remained silent, returning no answer.

Middleton—Poundmaker's men fired first.

Poundmaker—I don't know anything at all about it. I only returned the fire when the camp was fired on by the cannons.

Colonel Otter—The cannons were not up till ten minutes after the firing began.

Poundmaker turned and asked the other Indians if that was so.

24

General Middleton—Poundmaker fired first because he had a bad conscience. He knew he had done wrong, and did not want to be punished. He had been treated very well. He had been greatly honoured by the Queen's daughter (Princess Louise), yet the only reason he gives for not going to help Riel fight the Queen was that he was afraid, because Riel had not much powder. He told Riel he would join him; then, like a squaw, was afraid.

Poundmaker (who was smoking)—I am sorry (puffing smoke), I feel in my heart that I am such a person as I am.

Middleton—Poundmaker opposed the treaty and did all he could to prevent it.

Poundmaker—If I had known then that I was such a great man I would have made them recognize me as such. It was Delorme went for the Half-breed prisoners, and when he went they also went. I'm sorry to have to say so much. I thought when the message came from you we were going to make peace, so I tried hard to come on time. I have given myself up entirely and brought all the guns I had. If I saw any wrong I had done I would not have come.

Middleton—You have been on the war-path since the troubles began, and you and your men have committed murders and kept the country in alarm.

Poundmaker—I have sent word to Big Bear to say that I am giving up my arms to the General.

Middleton—Why did you only come in when Riel was defeated? If you had not done wrong, why did you not come in before?

To the Interpreter—I've told him I did not intend to do any harm. Why mention that so often?

Middleton—His ears are closed, but mine are open. Ask him if he knows about the murders of Payne and Fremont, or any one of the name of Lean Man.

Poundmaker—I know the man; he is an Assiniboine.

Middleton—Did you know that he and his men killed Payne?

Poundmaker— Will I ask him?

Poundmaker here turned to one of the men beside him, who had on a black felt hat with a broad green band around it, who was quietly smoking.

Lean Man, who was thus made to speak for himself, said that he knew nothing about it himself.

Do Indians never talk to one another? asked the General.

Poundmaker—I didn't hear the name of anyone who murdered.

Middleton—He hasn't answered my question.

Lean Man then made a reply in Stoney, which Poundmaker translated into Cree as: I don't know the person who killed Payne.

An Indian with cedar twigs around his head asked the General to allow him to have a bit of talk. (Unnoticed.)

Middleton—The man who killed Payne I consider a murderer. If attacked, men can fight, but I must have the men who committed these two murders.

Poundmaker—That's right, certainly.

Middleton—Now, I'll listen.

An elderly Indian, naked to the waist, with a number of small blue tattoo marks on his body and a circle of yellow paint around his eyes, came forward and asked to shake hands with General Middleton.

Middleton—I do not want to shake hands with a bad man.

Reid, the Interpreter, said that the man who wanted to shake hands was generally a good Indian.

Elderly Indian—God Almighty hears me; this is my country. So when the General come to my country, I want to say a little to him. I don't know anything of anything bad. I vowed to God if anything was wrong I would try to make peace. I wronged nobody.

The General then ordered the rifles to be taken out of the waggons and that they should be driven off.

Elderly Indian (continuing)—I know the great man is strong and can put everything right. I beg of him to put everything right here in our country. Once he has settled things I will go back. I was ashamed to go back to bare earth, where I was (meaning the reserves which had been stripped during the rising). I wanted to go north, but the agent would not let me.

Middleton—If you were so fond of peace why did you go on the war-path?

There was no answer, and here an old squaw tried to quietly intercede with the General for the prisoners.

A thin Indian came forward to where Poundmaker, Old Mosquito, and a few others sat, and said: I'm the same as when the white man first came to this country, meaning that he had made no treaty yet.

The Interpreter broke in on the orator, saying, Come right to the point, and the thin man went on:

There is a God who made us all. We borrow this earth from God. When white man and Indian first met they shook hands; no blood on them until now. I suppose the reason we were put here was to help each other. When I was at Buffalo Lake I heard that Riel had made peace through the country, and the whole country was to be settled. A letter was sent up saying a general was coming up with soldiers to settle everything. This is the reason why I wanted to come and see what settlement they had come to. That was the time they fired at each other. Next night I camped where people were. When I came to the camp, Delorme, Trottier and others said that Riel was making peace and the country was to be settled up all right. They wanted us to go to Duck Lake, and managed to get us along with them, though we didn't want to go. All went, and found young men had captured freighters. We said, "Don't do them any harm," and one man gave me a little tea and sugar belonging to the freighters. That was all. So will you let me shake hands as I have never done any wrong to you?

General Middleton (to Interpreter)—If he has done wrong to any white man he has done it to me. Besides, he was very troublesome, and tried last year to prevent the Indians from taking treaty money.

Thin Indian—I beg that the great man will do what he can so we can live. He is the only white man I'll have to depend on. I have put down arms and everything, and I want him (the General) to tell us how we are to get a living. You are a great man, and if we are to depend on you, let us know as we can tell our people.

Middleton—Is that all?

Breaking-through-the-Ice—I wish my mother to speak now. The Indian pointed out his mother, an old woman with a blue handkerchief on her head.

Middleton—We don't listen to women.

Thin Indian—What's the reason the Queen sends her word here?

Middleton—She has councillors who are men.

Thunder Child—May I say a few words?

Middleton—Yes, if you cut it short.

Thunder Child—I was away at the time the trouble began and didn't know anything was going on. I am so sorry for it all. The reason we were not here before was that last fight made women and children all afraid. Did not know that any of my people made trouble around here. I have never raised a gun against a white man yet only here, and I got so afraid that I didn't use it. I had made a vow not to, and I put the gun down as soon as I remembered it. We are at loss altogether at the question he (the General) puts to us. That's all I have to say, and if he's willing I will shake hands.

Middleton—If I believed you I would, but I will not shake hands with any one who fired on our men.

Thunder Cloud—I didn't fire.

Middleton—Who did then?

Thunder Child—If any one saw me fire let him say so.

Another Indian—Cut Lip—then came forward and squealed out: I would like to say a few words. May I?

Middleton—Yes, but let it be the last.

Cut Lip—Let him—the General—tell us how we are to make a living this summer.

Middleton (standing up)—Tell them they'd better listen to what I am going to say now: After many years

of peace between the white and the red men, when some
bad men, Half-breeds and others, chose to rebel against
the Government, the Indians forgot that peace existed so
long, and a large body rose and joined these other men.
The Indians, even Poundmaker, who had been so well
treated, rose and robbed because they thought the whites
were in difficulties. All around you attacked stores and
killed men and women. You thought that you were
going to have it all your own way, and, instead of saying
"this is the time for showing ourselves grateful to the
white people," you turned on them whenever you got a
chance. This very band (pointing to Poundmaker's)
deliberately went out to join the enemy, and, if they had
beaten us, would have gone on plundering, and would
have committed more murders; and now, when they find
the head rebel Riel, and the Half-breeds, whom they
thought great warriors, beaten, they come in because they
are afraid, and tell all sorts of lies and beg for peace.
They thought the Government hadn't more men, and
thought that the rebels were better fighters, and could lie
in ambush in the bluffs and shoot our men down. Now
we have shown them that it is no use their lying in pits
and behind bluffs, because we can drive them out and kill
them, and they are afraid.

Poundmaker—True.

Middleton (continuing)—Up to this time you Indians
had been in the habit of going to the settlers' houses,
saying you were hungry, begging food, and frightening
women into giving you food. And occasionally you have
even killed men when you have got one alone. Let all
Indians understand that if one white man is killed ten
Indians will suffer for it, and if any disturbance takes
place and the young men think they can go and plunder
they will find themselves much mistaken, for the whole
tribe will be made to suffer. I have more soldiers landing (Poundmaker groans), and more coming up, and if
you (Poundmaker) had not come in I would have hunted
the band down until I had killed everyone if possible,

and if we wish to live at peace, white men with red men, we can't have the red men rising every time trouble occurs and killing small parties, and the sooner you understand that the better. They asked me how they were going to live. Tell them (to the Interpreter) that I am only a soldier and do not know the intention of the

SIR. JOHN A. MACDONALD.
(Leader of the Government.)

Government; but I believe that if they behave well and stay on the reservation they will receive food, will be taught to cultivate the ground, and will be shown how to earn a living. Tell them also that if Big Bear does not come in and do as they have done I will take my troops and go off and attack him. I have received orders from the Government to detain Poundmaker, Yellow Mud,

Blanket, Breaking-through-the-Ice, and Lean Man as prisoners. The rest had better go to the reserves, and for your own sakes you had better give up the men who murdered Payne and Fremont.

Poundmaker—You will find out that. I know nothing about them myself.

Lean Man came forward and said:—God knows I never saw anything to tell. When one was killed I only heard about it while sitting in my tent. Of course when we hear a thing one cannot say it's a fact (meaning it would be mere hearsay evidence). In the morning I heard, "There's a white man killed." Payne (the murdered man) wanted to take the gun from this man. I heard it was Itka, or "One-who-turns-a-blanket-inside-out," that did it.

General Middleton—Tell them they must give up all the flour and goods they have stolen, and they will have rations. They must go to a reserve till the Government decides further.

Another Indian, with an old blanket and a bandaged head, then came forward. It was Itka himself. He said:—I said to Payne, "I want to go hunt, and want grub." Payne said, "I can't give you any." I said: "I am asking quietly; can't you give me any?" "No," Payne said, "I don't want to give you any." "It's only a little for my family while I'm off hunting," I told him, "try and be quick and let me have some so I can go off. You don't seem to listen." Payne said: "I can't let you have any for ten days. I won't give you any." I was talking quietly. He laid hold of me, saying: "Don't you hear me?" He took my gun from me and said he would shoot me. I said, "I don't want my grandchild to die." He said, "We'll both die here." At last by wrestling with him I got my gun back and shot. I have come to give myself up. If you want to cut me up in pieces do so. But I beg you to consider my children.

General Middleton—His statement shall be submitted to the judges at his trial.

Wa-Wanich, a young Indian dude, whose dress was all covered with coloured beads and Indian finery, and with a woman's black straw hat surmounted by a bright green plume for a head dress, stepped forward, and with his arms folded, threw himself on the ground before the General, saying:—I told my people I would give myself up to save them. Five of us came away from the Stoneys' reserve, and we came to the man Fremont who was greasing his waggon. I had a bow and arrow, and the others said: "You shoot him." One Indian from Qu'Appelle said: "You must not do that; why kill a man for nothing?" They said then any one that chooses to fire can. Well, of course, in the fall grass withers— (The dude here degenerated into parables.)

General Middleton (interrupting parable impatiently) —Is this the man that killed Fremont?

Wa-Wanich—Yes, it was me. Of course earth remains the same forever, continued the dude, taking up the parable (which was again interrupted.) Yes, it was me; I must have taken the gun from some other man.

The old woman with a blue kerchief who had begged a hearing, came up and said—Why not listen to me.

We don't have women in our councils. Women's tongues are generally long.

Wife of a Stoney Indian—The Almighty sees; our children and country have been taken.

Poundmaker and the rest of the chiefs round General Middleton, with the two self-confessed murderers, were then led away to prison.

General Middleton—Tell Poundmaker I'll mention he treated the prisoners well.

GENERAL STRANGE.

CHAPTER XXVII.

GENERAL STRANGE'S COLUMN.

WHILE the events described in the preceding chapters were taking place in the eastern and central portion of the Territory, a third column was advancing against the rebellious Indians in the extreme western portion. General Strange, with the 65th Battalion (Montreal) under Col. Ouimet, the 92nd (Winnipeg) under Col. Osborne Smith, a detachment of Mounted Police and scouts under Major Steele, had advanced on Edmonton, and was now engaged in the pursuit of Big Bear, of whom we last heard in connection with the Frog Lake massacre and the fall of Fort Pitt.

The advance to Edmonton was not eventful, as there were no enemies to oppose nor offenders to hunt down in that region. At Edmonton, General Strange found that he had arrived none too soon to put down a very general rising among the Indians, who were becoming very restless.

Before dealing with the doings of General Strange's column it may interest the reader to learn something of the prominent figures who will be remembered as connected, directly or indirectly, with this portion of the history of the troubles in the North-West.

First, then, comes General Strange, whose portrait appears at the beginning of this chapter. The *Army List* says he served in India in 1857-58, and was present in thirteen engagements, was mentioned four times in despatches, and wears a medal and clasp. He represents an old military family of Scotch origin, and in the maternal line of descent can be traced from Charles Martel and Charlemagne through a long line of warriors.

On the evacuation of Quebec in 1871, Colonel Strange was commissioned to form and command the first garrison of Canadian artillery. He established, upon enduring foundations, the schools of gunnery in which so many have been trained for service in different capacities, and the efficiency of the batteries at the front was largely owing to the fact that the Government has adopted the more important recommendations which he, as an inspector of artillery, has seen fit to make. He is a man of marked will power, a disciplinarian, and yet one whose commands are not unkindly enforced.

The Major-General went to Kingston at the time the batteries were transferred in June, 1880. In the spring of 1882 he got his promotion, and soon after left the service. He was chief factor in the organization of the Military Colonization Company, whose ranch is about thirty-five miles from Calgary. His wife and the younger members of the family did not leave for their new home, "Nomoka," until last year. His children numbered six, of whom four are living. Two sons accompanied him to the North-West, Harry Bland Strange and Alexander Wilmot Strange.

Though he took no prominent part in the suppression of the rebellion in the North-West, Colonel James McLeod has long been a very prominent man in the Territory. A successful and popular Commissioner of the North-West Mounted Police, his retirement to his present position as stipendiary magistrate was severely regretted by nearly

COLONEL JAMES M'LEOD.

or quite every officer and member of the North-West Mounted Police. During his lengthy residence in the North-West he has become extremely popular with the Indians, who are always ready to rely implicitly on his word in all matters, whether important or trifling. When a third, or western, column was to be made up, many were of opinion that Colonel McLeod would have command of it; but the Fates or the Government willed differently, and he was left out of their calculations. There is no doubt, however, that it was largely through his influence that the Blackfeet were kept from breaking out, and joining the rebels in the North, who were doubtless counting on their hearty co-operation.

There was another whose influence for good was largely felt by the Blackfeet and their relatives and allies, the

FATHER LECOMBE.

Bloods, the Piegans, and Sarcees. This was the faithful and earnest Oblat missionary, Father Lecombe, who has laboured for many years patiently and faithfully among the Indians and Half-breeds between the west end of Lake Superior and the Rocky Mountains.

General Strange's column was made up as follows:—

Sixty-fifth Battalion, 232; Winnipeg Provisional Battalion (92nd), 307; Strange's Rangers, 50; Mounted Police, 67.

On the 20th of May he left Edmonton with the 65th by boat, the remainder of the command going by trail eastward in search of Big Bear. On the 27th of May, when near Fort Pitt, General Strange had his first engagement. He met the rebels in the immediate vicinity of a large strip of swamp or muskeg. They retreated across this into a strong position, where they were well protected by rocks and under-growth. After engaging them for some hours he was compelled to retreat to Fort Pitt. His loss, however, was not serious, consisting of three wounded. Two days later Major Steele with only seventy mounted police and scouts engaged Big Bear at Two Lakes. They came upon the Indians just as the latter were leaving camp, and a sharp fight ensued. Major Steele found that Big Bear, having some three hundred well armed men, was too strong to be defeated in the first attack which was made upon his front. He executed a clever flank movement however, and advancing upon the Indians with extraordinary impetuosity, drove them out of their position, causing them to retreat slowly up a thickly wooded hill or butte. After fighting from tree to tree and gradually driving the Indians to the top of the hill, Major Steele ordered a charge, and the seventy gallant fellows drove the three hundred redskins from the top of the hill, causing them to retreat in considerable disorder into an almost impassable and impenetrable ravine on the other side. Finding it impossible to pursue them further Major Steele retired, taking his three wounded men with him. The men wounded were Sergeant-Major Fury and the scouts Thomas Fisk and William West. Fury was shot through the lungs; Fisk was hit in the forearm, and West in the knee. All three recovered. The loss of the Indians in this engagement is supposed to have been rather severe. Six dead bodies were found on the battlefield, and it is supposed that others, mortally wounded, were carried off as three more dead were found in Big Bear's camp. Harassed as he was by the resolute and hot pursuit of Major Steele, Big Bear was compelled to give up his prisoners though evidently very loth to do so. Cameron, a Hudson Bay agent, who brought the first particulars of the Frog Lake massacre, was in the first batch of prisoners retaken. Not long after this Mrs. Gowanlock and Mrs. Delaney and two or three Half-breed

BIG BEAR.

families fell into the hands of Major Steele and his men, and last of all, the MacLean family and the remainder of Big Bear's prisoners were brought in by the Wood Crees. It was decided to allow Big Bear to starve in the Far North or surrender to the Mounted Police and other regulars to be left in the country. On July 4, he, with his band, came into Carleton and surrendered to Sergeant Smart of the police. He and his son were taken to Prince

Albert as prisoners of war, and afterwards removed to Regina for trial. His band were disarmed and supplied with provisions at Carleton. This brought the North-West Rebellion to a close. The volunteers started on their return home on the 5th of July, and reached Toronto, where they were received with great enthusiasm, on the 19th, 21st and 23rd of the month. The troops were under orders to return home the day Big Bear was taken, but the news of his capture was almost forgotten and unheeded by them, for they were saddened by the sudden and wholly unexpected loss of one of the bravest and best of their officers, the gallant Colonel A. T. H. Williams, of the Midland Battalion, who died of brain fever while passing down the river by steamer.

The following stories, told by Mrs. Delaney and Mrs. Gowanlock, furnish a graphic history of the experiences of Big Bear's prisoners, which is interesting to the verge of the romantic:—

MRS. DELANEY'S STORY.

Mrs. Delaney tells her pitiful story in the following words:—

"My name is Theresa Delaney. I was married to my husband, John Delaney, on the 27th July, 1882, at Aylmer, in the Province of Quebec, where my mother is now living, and others of my relations. My husband resided, before coming to this country, at Gloucester, in the County of Carleton, Ont., where his father and mother are now living. My husband and I left home on the 1st of August, 1882, and went at once to Frog Lake, N.W.T., where my husband held the position of Indian Instructor. When he first came up here he had five bands of Indians to look after, until a year ago, when the Chippewans where taken from his supervision and given to John Fitzpatrick. A little later Mr. Fitzpatrick was transferred to another jurisdiction, and the Chippewans again came under my husband's care. He then had to look after the Chippewans, Oneepowhayaws, Misstoos, Kooceawsis, and Puskeackeewins, and last year he had to ration Big Bear's tribe. He was so engaged when the outbreak took place. All these Indians were peaceably inclined, and most friendly to us all My husband was much respected, and really beloved by all under his care, and they seemed to be most attached to him. We were therefore greatly astonished at their action towards us; but, after all, it was only Big Bear's following that showed their enmity to us. They, too, pretended to be most friendly, and have often told us that but for my husband they would have starved. The first we knew of the uprising was on the 2nd of April. At five o'clock in the morning, two of Big Bear's tribe came into our house, and told us our horses were stolen by the Half-breeds, and at the same time it was they themselves who had stolen the horses and hidden them. Soon after the arrival of these two Indians some thirty more—all armed, and most of them mounted—came to the house and forced their way in. They took all the arms and ammunition they could find, telling us they were short and wanted all. They required us to go with them, because, they said, they wished to save us from the Breeds. We were taken first to the Agent's (Mr. Quinn), and the Indians also demanded his arms and ammunition, and had a long talk about all keeping together to keep back the Breeds, when they came to take the provisions. I am satisfied now they were not sincere in this, and it was all to deceive us, for there were no Breeds to come. From Quinn's we were taken to the priests' house. The priests were named Father Fafard and Father Marchaud, who were both subsequently killed. We were not at all ill-treated so far, but there was every outward appearance of friendly feeling towards us. When we reached the priests' house mass was going on, the attendants being some Half-breeds who had previously been taken prisoners by the Indians and detained with the priests, in the latters' residence. The Indians would not let the priests finish mass, and ordered them,

25

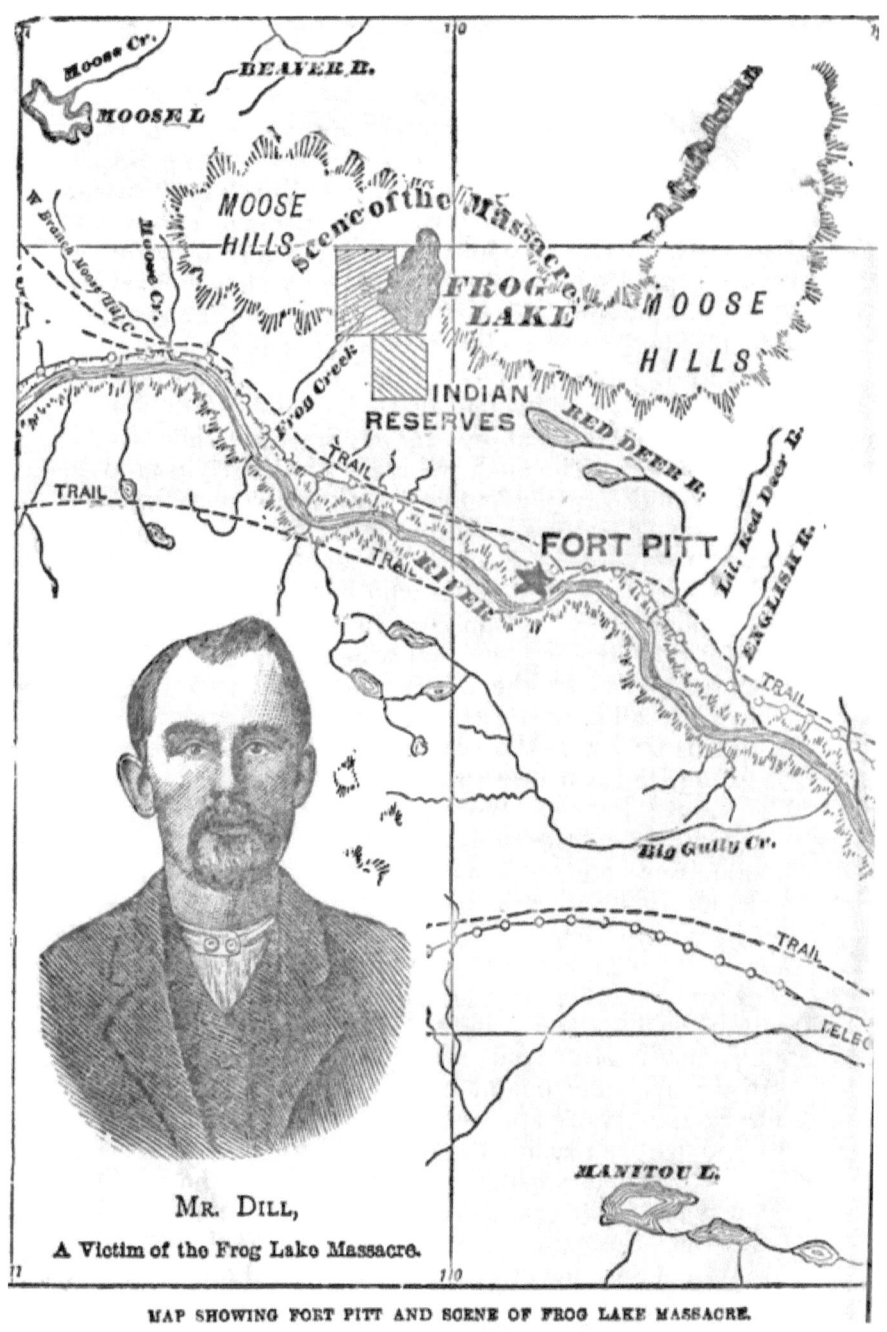

MR. DILL,
A Victim of the Frog Lake Massacre.

MAP SHOWING FORT PITT AND SCENE OF FROG LAKE MASSACRE.

with the Breeds and ourselves, back again to our own house. We were all left for about an hour, the Indians surrounding the house. The priests did not anticipate any danger, supposing that the Indians intended to have a feast of the cattle that had been given them by Mr. Quinn, the Agent. By this time it was about 9.30 in the morning. During our last detention in our house Big Bear came in and told my husband that he was frightened some of his young braves intended shooting the whites, but that he, my husband, would be safe anyway. At this time the only place they had plundered was Mr. Dill's store, which they had gutted; but, while waiting, the Indians told Mr. Cameron, also a prisoner in our house, that they wanted him to accompany them to open the Hudson's Bay store, and Mr. Cameron did so, thus, in my opinion, saving his life. After opening the store, the Indians sent him to their camp, about a mile and a-half away. After securing everything in the latter store, they came to our house, and ordered us all up to the Indian camp. We departed, my husband and I, as well as all others, only taking with us what we had on our backs, not supposing we would be long away. At this time nothing of consequence had been taken from our house. It was not very cold. Before we had gone far from our house the Indians began to shoot down the whites. Mr. Quinn was shot first, though I did not see him shot. All who were killed were behind my husband and me, but I heard several shots fired, and, until otherwise informed, supposed the firing was into the air. At this time, however, Mr. Dill was killed, also Mr. Williscroft, Mr. Gouin, Mr. Gilchrist, and Mr. Gowanlock, the latter of whom I saw fall. Mrs. Gowanlock was beside her husband when he fell, and as he dropped she leaned down over him, putting her face to his, and as two shots had been fired at her husband some supposed she had fallen from the second shot. When I saw Mrs. Gowanlock fall, I saw also some hideous object, an Indian got up in frightful costume, take aim at my husband. Before I could speak, my husband staggered away, but came back and said to me, 'I am shot.' He fell then, and I called the priest and told the latter what had happened. While he was praying with my husband the same hideous Indian fired again, and I thought this shot was meant for me, and I laid my head down upon my husband and waited. It seemed an age; but it was for my poor husband, and he never spoke afterwards. Almost immediately another Indian ran up, and ordered me away. I wanted to stay, but he dragged me off, pulling me along by the arms through the brush and briar and through the creek, where the water reached to my waist. I was put into an Indian tent, and left there until nightfall, without anything offered me to eat, though I could not have eaten anyway. I was not allowed outside of the tent, and so had no opportunity of returning to my dead husband, and have never seen him since. At night time, two Half-breeds, John Pritchard and Adolphus Nolan, came and purchased our release by giving horses to the Indians, the only two horses they had. These Breeds were prisoners also, so that I was virtually still a prisoner with Big Bear; but John Pritchard and all the Breeds were most kind, and I wish to state that I believe both Mrs. Gowanlock and I owe our escape from terrible treatment, and at last massacre, to John Pritchard and other friendly Breeds, prisoners like ourselves. From this time forward we were prisoners for two months all but a day. Every other day we were moved with the entire camp from one place to another. Big Bear's treatment of us would have been cruel in the extreme, but Pritchard saved us from the agony and torture of forced marches through sloughs, brush, and rough land. At this time, accompanying us were Mrs. Gowanlock, and among the Indians were Mr. and Mrs. McLean and their family of five children, Mr. and Mrs. Mann and their family of three children, Mr. and Mrs. Quinney, John Fitzpatrick, and a Frenchman named Pierre. I cannot say how any of these were treated, as I only saw them casually when on the march, but think they were not more ill-treated than I was myself, except that they had all to walk continually, except Mr. McLean and Mrs. Mann, and the very small children. Occasionally an Indian, more humane than the rest, would offer a ride to those who were required to walk; and sometimes John Pritchard would increase his already overladen load by taking some weary one up. Pritchard and all the Breeds walked always, though by making us walk they could have ridden. His two little boys, aged thirteen and fifteen, walked, though their feet became very sore at times, but they never complained, because they knew their walking enabled us to ride. They were noble little fellows. I was terribly stricken down. I seemed demented, and could hardly tell one day what had happened the day before. I went on and on as if in a fearful dream, but seemed conscious all the while of my home at Aylmer, and my longing for it seemed alone to keep me up. I was afraid to ask after my husband, but the Breeds told me later on that they had buried the only four bodies they had been permitted to, my husband's, the two priests', and Mr. Gowanlock's under the church, but as the church was burned the bodies were exposed, and then I asked to have them buried and the Breeds did as I requested. I should have told you that as I was being dragged away from my husband's body I saw the two priests drop. Father Fafard fell first and then Father Marchand. The former was administering to my husband when he fell, and the latter dropped immediately afterwards, as if shot by the same Indian from the second barrel of a gun. During our journey we had plenty to eat, cooking it ourselves. Our direction was backwards and forwards to avoid the police catching us. We were taken from Frog Lake towards Pitt, then back again north for about sixty miles. On a Thursday—a week before we escaped—we had a battle, that is, the battle with General Strange. The women were all left in the woods, but the Indians were entrenched in a ravine, where they had dug rifle pits, as I was informed. This was the first intimation I had of our troops coming. We could plainly hear the firing. We could easily recognize the cannon. The fight began at seven in the morning, and lasted until ten. We could not see any of it, but could hear it. At ten, the police finding they were not strong enough, retreated, and the Indians then fell back into the bush where we were, and from thence back again farther into the bush, all of us having to accompany them. The Breeds at this time were trying to escape, but could not do so, as they were watched too closely. From Thursday Big Bear's men retreated in different bands, and the prisoners got more or less separated, some going with one band, some with another. Mrs. Gowanlock and I were fortunate in yet being left with Pritchard, although we were all still with Big Bear. Mr. and Mrs. McLean and Mr. and Mrs. Mann and their families were still with Big Bear. We kept on moving from Thursday until Monday, each day from early morning till late at night, but I had never to walk, nor had Mrs. Gowanlock. On Sunday night the Indians saw scouts, who they supposed belonged to the police, and they became greatly excited, and in the excitement and heavy fog of Monday morning we got away. Our party that escaped consisted of Mrs. Gowanlock, myself, and five Half-breed families, including John Pritchard and Andre Nowe, the latter of whom had taken the place of Adolphus Nolan, who, on the pretence of acting as scout for the Indians, managed to escape to Prince Albert in the hopes of getting help and assistance. We escaped in carts, and the first day did not go more than two or three miles. We went backwards and forwards through the bush, so as to avoid our trail being discovered, and the next day continued our escape, the men cutting roads through the bush, so as to get along with all our outfit. We travelled on until Wednesday night, tending towards Battleford, and on that night we were overtaken by the police scouts, who had got on to our trail and followed it. They thought our position was not a secure one, and they made us strike camp and go on to a safer place, farther away, about two miles or thereabouts. Here we camped for the night, the scouts remaining with us all the time. On Thursday morning we moved on, reaching Pitt on Friday about ten in the morning, where we were met by Col. Straubenzie and Col. Williams. All came forward to meet us, and at once we were taken on board the *North-West,* where we remained all Saturday and until Sunday morning, when we were transferred to the *Baroness* and reached Battleford Sunday night. We spent some time visiting friends at Regina and Winnipeg, where we were treated very kindly and assisted to make our journey home. Had a pleasant but uneventful trip home, reaching Toronto on July 13th. I desire to express my thanks to Almighty God that He sent with us throughout, such a kind and considerate protector as John Pritchard, and the other Breeds who were with him. There is no telling what abuse we might have been subjected to but for their presence. Frequent attempts were made to reach us by the Indians, but the Half-breeds watched night after night, armed and ready to keep off any attempt to ill-treat us. Four different nights Indians approached our tents, but the determination of our protectors saved us. Terrible as it all was, however, I am grateful that I came through unmolested, and am permitted to return to my home once again unharmed in body and mind."

Mrs. Gowanlock's story is as follows :—

"My name is Mary Theresa Gowanlock. My father and mother are both living. They reside in Ontario, near St. Catharines, where they farm. My husband's name in full was John Alexander Gowanlock. He came from Parkdale. We were married on the 1st of October, 1884, and arrived in Battleford on the 22nd of the same month, going on to Fort Pitt in the December following. From there we went to Frog Lake, where my husband began business as a miller. He had partly erected a grist and saw mill when the rebellion broke out. We knew nothing of the uprising until we got a letter from Mr. Quinn telling us to come to his place, and to go with the others to Fort Pitt, as it was feared Big Bear's Indians would break out, and commit massacres and outrages. We at once left our home, and reached Mrs. Delaney's house, when we were told there was nothing to be feared. We reached Mrs. Delaney's house on Tuesday, and on Thursday morning her house was surrounded. I have heard Mrs. Delaney's experience given to you, and I cannot think of anything differing from what she states."

CHAPTER XXVIII.

MARTIAL ARDOUR IN MARITIME PROVINCES—RETURN OF THE TROOPS.

THE support rendered the loyal cause in this lamentable struggle, though coming mainly from Ontario and Manitoba, as being nearest the seat of trouble, was more or less drawn from nearly every quarter of the Dominion. Quebec contributed the 65th of Montreal, besides "A" Battery from the City of Quebec, while Nova Scotia sent the 66th, which, though not called upon to pass under fire, performed those duties which are infinitely more trying to the discipline of volunteers in a manner which left no room for a doubt as to their soldierly qualities.

New Brunswick too, answered promptly to the call when it was made upon her; but her gallant sons had not reached the field ere the causes which had rendered necessary the calling out of more troops had ceased to exist, and though they had shown a most commendable alacrity in responding to an appeal to their bravery and loyalty, they had not the satisfaction of sharing in the dangers and glories of the battle-field. On the 11th of May they were receiving orders for the front, while on that very day Middleton was dealing a crushing blow to the rebel cause at Batoche.

The Halifax Provisional Battalion, under command of Lieut.-Colonel James J. Bremner, consisting of 168 non-commissioned officers and men of the 66th Battalion "Princess Louise Fusiliers," 100 of the 63rd Battalion Rifles, and 84 of the Halifax Garrison Artillery, with 32 officers, left Halifax under orders for the North-West on Saturday, 11th April, 1885.

MAJOR WELSH. LIEUT.-COL. BREMNER.
(Halifax Battalion.)

Probably never before in the history of Halifax has such excitement been witnessed as on the morning of the battalion leaving, the streets on the line of march and the space in the neighbourhood of the station of the I. C. R. being closely packed with a dense mass of enthusiastic but anxious citizens.

On the previous afternoon four guns from the citadel had given notice that orders had been received for the battalion to proceed to the seat of disturbance. In an incredibly short space of time the battalion mustered at the drill shed with full ranks, when after being inspected the men were dismissed to their homes with orders to assemble early next morning ready to march. At the hour appointed not a man was absent, and many of the men who had not been selected to go were there ready

CAPTAIN JAMES PETERS ("*A*" *Battery*).

in hope that some chance might make it possible for them to go with their comrades.

The journey north of Lake Superior was very trying. The men when in the cars were exposed to rain and cold day and night, with no shelter or means of drying their clothing; and when marching on the ice the water was in many places up to their knees.

THE HALIFAX PROVISIONAL BATTALION.   411

The battalion arrived at Winnipeg on 22nd April, at 5 a.m.

On the 26th April the battalion received orders to march for Swift Current on the following day, but just as it was forming up the order was countermanded. On the 29th the battalion again received orders for the same destination, and marched same day at four p.m. The

INSPECTOR JOSEPH HOWE, N.-W.M.P.

battalion arrived at Swift Current at eight p.m. on the 30th, and next day camped beside the 7th and a portion of the Midland Battalion.

On the 5th May a telegram was received to hold the 63rd contingent of the battalion in readiness to proceed to Maple Creek; but, later in the day, intelligence was received of an apprehended rising of the Blackfeet and other Indians, and that Medicine Hat was in danger of being attacked; the order for the 63rd contingent was countermanded, and the headquarters of the battalion with the 66th contingent was ordered to Medicine Hat, where it arrived next morning early. Encamped on the South Saskatchewan River in company with Stuart's scouts, a body of mounted cow boys (which also had just arrived); and there both remained until the end of the trouble.

CAPTAIN C. W. DRURY, "A" BATTERY.

Shortly after the headquarters of the battalion left Swift Current for Medicine Hat two companies of the 63rd contingent were ordered to Saskatchewan Landing, where they were employed loading scows, forwarding supplies, and assisting in transporting across the river.

One company of the 63rd and the Halifax Garrison Artillery remained at Swift Current whilst it continued to be the base of supplies; and when Moose Jaw afterwards became the base this detachment also removed there, and the two companies from the Landing shortly afterwards joined them. On these two detachments fell the labour of handling and transferring all the supplies going to the front, and furnishing the necessary guards, so that they were kept fully employed, at times of necessity the non-commissioned officers voluntarily doing the fatigue duties of privates. The work was all the more cheerfully performed because the men expected that it was the prelude to being allowed to take part in the fighting at the front, as other corps preceding them had been relieved in due order, but in this they were disappointed. They had, however, the satisfaction to know that they had done their work well, and although it was very different from what they desired they did it without a murmur or complaint.

The headquarters of the battalion left Medicine Hat on the night of the 30th June, and arrived at Moose Jaw early on the 2nd July, the battalion being now re-united entire. After remaining at Moose Jaw a week the battalion was ordered to Winnipeg, where it arrived on the 10th July, and went into camp.

Left Winnipeg on the 16th July for Halifax, and arrived there on the 24th, the entire route being a continued ovation; the kindness of the people of the towns of Manitoba, Ontario and Quebec being beyond description, and which greatly impressed the men of the battalion. The reception at Halifax was most enthusiastic, the whole population apparently having turned out. The battalion was sumptuously entertained by the ladies at the exhibition building, after which it was disbanded by order of the Deputy-Adjutant-General, the men returning to their respective corps.

A better drilled, better disciplined, or braver body of men than the Halifax Battalion was not in the North-West; nor one which would have given a better account of itself if it had had the opportunity.

From the commencement of the rebellion the active militia of the Province of New Brunswick and of St. John, in particular, had taken a deep interest in the stirring events transpiring in the North-West, and many regrets were expressed when it was known that Halifax had been ordered to furnish a battalion for active service, and the doings of that corps were as eagerly watched in St. John as they were in Halifax. On the 7th of April, however, the 62nd St. John Fusiliers were ordered to begin their annual drill, and great care was taken by all officers to have their men perfected in all details in case their services were required; and events were eagerly noted by all ranks from day to day with hopes that the call would soon come for active service. On the evening of the 11th May Lieutenant-Colonel Maunsell, D.A.G., received a telegram from Ottawa ordering out "A" Company, Infantry School Corps, and eight companies of the active militia for immediate service in the North-West. Colonel Blaine, commanding the 62nd Fusiliers, received a despatch at 11 p.m., asking how soon he could have four companies of his battalion ready to march; he answered "in four days, at the very latest": and ready they were, proving that the motto of the corps, "Semper Paratus," was not borne on their colours as a vain boast.

All was soon bustle and activity in St. John and Fredericton, and even in the country districts where the different companies were much scattered. At the first parade of the 62nd, at the drill shed, every man was at his post, with the exception of some few who were away on leave, and great cheering was the result when the orders were read by the Adjutant, though regret was shown by all that only four companies could go. The enthusiasm reached its height on Thursday evening, 14th May, when the four commands of the senior captains were inspected by the Deputy Adjutant-General. The drill shed was literally packed with people, while thousands were awaiting a chance outside for an entrance to view the soldiers. The men looked splendid in review

NEW BRUNSWICK PROVISIONAL BATTALION. 415

order; and a finer or more athletic set of fellows never shouldered a rifle. After being addressed by their Colonel, and ordered to hold themselves in readiness at a moment's notice, the battalion was dismissed. Meanwhile, the officers and men in other parts of the Province were not idle; in Fredericton, the men of the Infantry School Corps were most anxious to be off and were soon

LIEUT.-COL. G. J. MAUNSELL, D.A.G.

ready for the march; the 71st Battalion having been ordered to furnish one company, the men were taken from the City of Fredericton and adjoining parishes, so that each company in the corps would be represented; in Woodstock the same plan was carried out with the 67th Battalion, and many hardy yeomen left their ploughs and took the rifle; nor were the members of the 74th

Battalion idle, their quota of one company being made up of men from Rothesay to Sackville—sturdy farmers who could endure any hardship. A little difficulty was experienced in getting the men of the 73rd Battalion assembled, owing to the great distances the men were from each other; but, in a few days, they also had furnished their quota.

LIEUT.-COL. A. BLAINE.

On the evening of the 16th May, a telegram, received by Colonel Maunsell, ordering him to assemble his men in camp at Sussex and there be joined by two companies of the Prince Edward Island force, the whole to await orders for the route, was quickly communicated to the different commanders. On Sunday, church parades were held at Fredericton and St. John.

At daylight on Monday morning, 18th May, the soldiers of Fredericton were up and preparing for the march; the citizens and friends of all ranks being on the streets to say their farewells. At 6.30 the line of march was taken up, the Infantry School Corps being headed by their own band, while the Fredericton Brass Band

COL. MORRIS, INSPECTOR M. P. AT BATTLEFORD, N.-W. T.
(Formerly of Fredericton, N.B.)—See page 109.

headed the representative company of the 71st Battalion. At 7 o'clock the train steamed out of the station to convey the soldiers to St. John to join their brethren of the 62nd.

The 18th of May is a day always celebrated in St. John, on account of its being the anniversary of the landing of the Loyalists in 1783; but never before was the city so thoroughly aroused as on that day, 1885, which was to see a number of her citizen soldiers leave homes and friends, to join with brother Canadians in suppressing a vile rebellion in the far North-West.

Business was almost suspended, while men, women and children took up vantage-points to see the brave boys of the 62nd march by. At the drill shed all was bustle, but no confusion was visible, every man knew his place; and, at the bugle's call, the four companies were quickly formed, ready to march; and when it became known, at the last moment, that a few men had been rejected by the surgeons, many were the applicants to fill their places, and the captains of companies would have had no difficulty in raising twice the number of men required. At 12 o'clock Colonel Blaine gave the order to march, and, headed by the brass and relief bands of the battalion and every private band in the city, the corps left for the railway station. The streets were lined with people, while cheer after cheer rent the air, and many were the good-byes given and received on the way. So great was the crowd at the railway station that the leading companies could hardly force their way through, and great difficulty was experienced in reaching the train. After many more good-byes, the train slowly steamed from the station, while a farewell cheer went up from 20,000 throats for the citizen soldiers. Sussex was reached in a few hours and tents pitched.*

From the time when this force had been ordered out on the 11th of May till the 18th, events had been succeed-

---

*The following officers and companies being on the ground composing the "New Brunswick Provisional Battalion":—Total force, 408 non-commissioned officers and men, 36 officers. Lieut.-Col. G. J. Maunsell, D.A.G., Commandant; Majors, Lieut.-Col. A. Blaine, 62nd Fusiliers, and Lieut.-Col. E. B. Beer, 74th Battalion; Chaplain, Rev. G. G. Roberts; Adjutant, Capt. McLean, 62nd Fusiliers; Quartermaster, Major Devlin, 62nd Fusiliers; Paymaster, Major McCully, 73rd Battalion; Surgeon, T. C. Brown, M.D., I.S.C.; Asst.-Surgeon, M. L. Macfarland, M.D., 62nd Fusiliers.

Infantry School Corps:—A Company—Captain, Major W. D. Gordon; Lieuts., T. D. R. Hemming and E. V. Wedderburn (attached). B Company—Captain, Lieut. D. D. Young; Lieuts., W. E. Russell (attached) and L. B. Donkin (attached); Sergeants, Colour-Sergt. Walker, Serg. Fowlie, Sergt. Mayne, Sergt. Pulkin, Sergt. Sloan.

ing each other in rapid succession in the North-West. The capture of Batoche on the 12th, followed a few days later by the capture of Riel, and later on the surrender of Poundmaker, cleared the horizon sufficiently to stay further proceedings; and when the close of the Rebellion was assured the New Brunswick Provisional Battalion was not required, and much grumbling was heard when, on the 26th of May, the order to return home was issued, and even then there were further offers to volunteer for three months' service in quelling the Indians; but a soldier must obey, and on that date camp was struck and the different corps returned to their homes, having, however, learned a considerable amount of drill and gained a vast amount of experience during their ten days in camp. The company of the 73rd Battalion, under command of Captain Cameron, and the two companies from Prince Edward Island, composed of the Artillery and 82nd Battalion, did not leave their headquarters and were disbanded at the same time. Each corps and every man was warmly welcomed home again, the general impression being that " every man had done his duty."

Sixty-second St. John Fusiliers :—C Company—Captain, E. T. Sturdee; Lieuts., G. A. Fraser and F. H. J. Ruel; Colour-Sergt., Samuel Jones; Sergts., F. Alward, E. Conley; Corporals, Joseph Watson, F. Allan. D Company—Captain, H. J. A. Godard; Lieuts., C. Y. Gregory and H. H. Godard; Colour-Sergt., J. W. Appleby; Sergts., W. Blaine and D. Conley; Corporals, J. A. Stanton and M. B. H. Henderson. E Company—Captain, John P. Hegan; Lieuts., Geo. F. Thompson and S. B. Lordly; Colour-Sergt, Robert Coleman; Sergts., E. O. Shaughnessy, C. Wilson; Corporals, F. W. James, H. Harrison. F Company—Captain, M. B. Edwards; Lieuts., D. Churchill and J. F. McMillan; Colour-Sergt., W. H. Smith; Sergts., Henry Kerr, James Kennedy; Corporals, H. B. Anderson, Jas. Currie, Edward Nicholls.

G Company *(67th Battalion)*—Captain, Jesse W. Baker, Lieuts., C. R. Carman and F. W. Bourne. H Company *(71st Battalion)*—Captain, W. T. Howe; 1st Lieutenant, Capt. Loggie; 2nd Lieutenant, Lieut. Johnson; Colour-Sergt. Ryan. I Company *(74th Battalion)*—Captain Harper; Lieuts., Capt. McFee, Lieut. F. V. Wedderburn (8th Cavalry); Sergt.-Major Crossman; Sergeants Miller and MacFarland; Corporal, Bliss Manship.

Staff :—Sergt.-Major Mackenzie, I.S.C.; Quartermaster-Sergt., Sergt. Daniel, I.S.C.; Asst. Sergt.-Major, Staff Instructor Sergt. Billman, I.S.C.; Instructors' Staff, Instructors Billman and Sloane, I.S.C.; Orderly Room Clerk, Sergt., Mayne, I.S.C.; Paymaster's Clerk, Sergt. Taylor, 62nd Batt.; Asst. Orderly Room Clerk, Sergt. Shea, I.S.C.

There are few more popular officers in the Dominion than Lieutenant-Colonel Maunsell. He has been over thirty years a soldier. In May, 1855, he was gazetted an ensign in Her Majesty's 15th Regiment. Colonel Maunsell sailed for New Brunswick in January, 1864. An opportunity was offered him to see active service with the Army of the Potomac during the whole of the spring campaign of 1864, during which he was temporarily attached to General Grant's staff. He was gazetted Adjutant-General of Militia of New Brunswick on November 22, 1865. In 1881 he was appointed Deputy Adjutant-General for Military District No. 4, with headquarters at Ottawa, and in 1883 was made Commandant of the Infantry School Corps at Fredericton.

Both the New Brunswick and Halifax Battalions showed unmistakably how thoroughly they were inspired with that loyalty and martial ardour which it is hoped will always actuate Canadian volunteers whenever they may be called upon to face Canada's foes.

Though the volunteers from the Maritime Provinces were not under fire during the struggle, some of the bravest officers and men in the regular arm of the service hailed from our Atlantic seaboard: Captain Peters, of "A" Battery, comes from St. John, N. B., while Captain Drury is also of St. John. Inspector Joseph Howe, of the N.-W M. P., who was wounded at Duck Lake, is also a St. John man and a nephew of the late Hon. Joseph Howe. He was always known to be a brave and gallant soldier, never flinching from duty no matter how perilous it might be. He is a man of whom any province might feel proud. Inspector Howe received a painful though not fatal flesh wound in the leg while fighting gallantly at the Battle of Duck Lake; Gunner Walter Woodman, who is mentioned on page 136 among the wounded at the Battle of Fish Creek, is from Digby, N. S.

THE RETURN OF THE TROOPS.

No description could convey an adequate idea of the enthusiasm with which the volunteers were received on their return from the campaign. They were different looking boys from the neatly-uniformed, clean-looking fellows who went away only a few months before. They were sun-browned and bearded, their uniforms were faded, ragged and dirty. They were veritable veterans, and Canada had good reason to feel proud of them as she did.

GUNNER WALTER WOODMAN.

A grand review was held in Winnipeg in honour of their return. In Toronto, London, Montreal and all the principal cities and towns of the dominion, the streets were fairly ablaze with bunting, while arches and festoons of evergreens made many of the streets look like forest paths through some of Canada's great pineries.

RETURN OF THE VOLUNTEERS.

TORONTO, *July 23rd, 1885.*

Ring out, O bells, ye cannot drown
    The echoing glad hurra,
From thousands' swelling throats that tell
    Our boys come home to-day.

They come from gory battle-fields,
    Brave lads and gallant they;
The city's heart is in the cry,
    Our boys come home to-day.

Beneath the flag so bravely borne
    In many a bloody fray,
Up through the old, familiar streets,
    Our boys come home to-day.

And if through sudden tears our eyes
    See not the glad array,
Each heart-beat tells the joyous tale,
    Our boys come home to-day.

We thought to make a noble show,
    A lordly pageant gay;
But now we only think and feel,
    Our boys came home to-day.

(Not all. Our honoured, gallant dead,
    Again have led the way,
Where rebel bullets sped, their souls
    Went home to God that day.)

Then ring; ye cannot drown, O bells,
    The echoing wild hurra,
From myriad swelling throats that tells,
    Our boys come home to-day.

CHAPTER XXIX.

RIEL'S TRIAL—THOSE ENGAGED IN IT.

LOUIS RIEL was brought to trial at Regina, N.W.T., on July 20. At eleven o'clock the counsel and judge took their seats in the court-room, which was already filled to the doors. Before entering into the particulars of the trial it will be of interest to take a brief glance at the gentlemen who occupied prominent positions in this, the greatest of trials that Canada has ever witnessed.

THE JUDGE.

Lieut.-Colonel Hugh Richardson, Stipendiary Magistrate and legal adviser to the Governor of the North-West Territories, was born in London, England, July, 1826, came to Canada with his parents in 1831, and settled near Toronto, where his father became first Manager of the Bank of Upper Canada. Young Richardson was called to the Bar at Osgoode Hall, Toronto, in November, 1847, went to Woodstock to practise, and was County Attorney of Oxford from 1857 to 1862. In 1876 he was sent to the North-West in the capacity of a stipendiary magistrate, with headquarters at Battleford. After four years' service, on the occasion of the removal of the seat of Government and the retirement of Justice Ryan, Judge Richardson was transferred to Regina, where he has been stationed ever since. Lieut.-Col. Richardson, at Edmonton in 1879, heard the first case of capital punishment ever tried in the Territories, and has altogether tried three capital cases. The first, was that of an Indian who had played the *rôle* of cannibal with regard to his family. The second case was that of the Stevenson brothers, the Regina Half-breeds, who were hanged for the murder of an unoffending man named McCarthy. His third case was that of John Connors, who was hanged the other day at Regina. This was a conviction which had been confirmed on appeal.

COUNSEL FOR THE CROWN.

Christopher Robinson, Q.C. (senior counsel for the Crown), is a brother of the present Lieut.-Governor of

CHRISTOPHER ROBINSON, Q.C.

Ontario, and the third son of the late Sir John Beverley Robinson, Chief Justice of Upper Canada. He is about sixty years of age, though he might, from his appearance, be taken for a considerably younger man. He is one of the leading members of the Bar in Ontario and has several times refused offers of an appointment on the Bench.

D. L. SCOTT, Q.C.

Lieut.-Colonel David L. Scott was born in Brampton, Ont., in 1845. He was called to the Bar of Ontario in 1870, and practised his profession at Orangeville, Ont., until the year 1882, when he removed to the North-West Territories and commenced practice at Regina.

Mr. G. W. Burbidge, Deputy-Minister of Justice, was born at Cornwallis, N.S., in 1847. He was educated at

G. W. BURBIDGE, DEPUTY-MINISTER OF JUSTICE.

Mount Allison Wesleyan College, and was called to the Bar of New Brunswick in 1872, afterwards practising his profession for some years in St. John as a member of the firm of Harrison and Burbidge. In 1882 Mr. Burbidge was appointed Deputy-Minister of Justice. His salary is $4,000 a year, besides which he receives $400 as solicitor to the Indian Department.

B. B. OSLER, Q.C.

Mr. Osler, son of the Rev. H. Bath Osler, was born near the village of Bond Head, York County, in 1840. He took his law and LL.B. courses simultaneously, and was called to the Bar in 1862. He has received the distinction of Queen's Counsel. He is a man of marked personality, and, as many a juryman knows, is possessed of a fund of humour and shrewdness.

COUNSEL FOR THE DEFENCE.

F. X. LEMIEUX, Q.C. (SENIOR COUNSEL FOR RIEL.)

Francis Xavier Lemieux was born at Levis, P.Q., in 1851. He was educated at the Levis College and Quebec Seminary, and was admitted to the Quebec Bar in July, 1872. He was married in 1874 to Miss Plamondon, daughter of Judge Plamondon, of the Superior Court for the District of Arthabaska. He was a candidate for Bouaventure at the Provincial General Elections after the Letellier *coup d'etat*, but was defeated by I. Tarte, editor of *Le Canadien*. He ran again for the Commons in Beauce against Bolduc (now Senator), at the General Elections of 1881, and was again defeated. In 1883, when Hon. T. Paquet, Provincial Secretary, was appointed Sheriff of Quebec, Lemieux was selected as the Liberal candidate for Levis, and after one of the most desperate struggles in Provincial history, was elected to represent that county in the Quebec Assembly by a majority of thirty-eight votes over his Conservative opponent, Jos. Roy, editor of *Le Quotidien*. Mr. Lemieux is a first-class speaker, and has made a number of remarkable orations in the Legislature. His position at the Bar is a leading one, and as a criminal lawyer he has been exceedingly successful.

CHARLES FITZPATRICK.

Charles Fitzpatrick was born at Quebec in 1853. He was educated at Quebec Seminary and graduated at Laval University with the degree of B.A., carrying off also the Dufferin medal. He is now an M.A. He was admitted to the Quebec Bar in 1876. He married Miss Caron, daughter of the late Lieutenant-Governor Caron, and sister of the Militia Minister. He practised his profession for some years as a member of the leading firm of Andrews, Caron, Andrews & Fitzpatrick. He acted as Crown prosecutor at Three Rivers and Quebec under the Joly Government. He represented the Second National Bank of New York in the Eno extradition case. An ardent Liberal in politics.

JAMES N. GREENSHIELDS.

James N. Greenshields, of Montreal, counsel for Riel, was born in Danville, Richmond County, Quebec, and is now about thirty-two years of age. He was educated at St. Francis College in Richmond, where he graduated with the highest honors. He early showed a bent for the law, and after his graduation attended a law course at

McGill University, at which college he won the Elizabeth Torrance Gold Medal in March, 1876, given for the highest aggregate of marks. He was admitted to the Bar in Montreal in January, 1877. Mr. Greenshields is already reported one of the ablest lawyers in Montreal, and is believed to have a brilliant future before him.

After some cross-firing among the counsel as to the jurisdiction of the Court (the objections urged on behalf of the defence being overruled) Riel pleaded "not guilty" to the charge of treason. On being asked if he were ready for trial an adjournment till ten the next morning was asked in order that necessary affidavits might be prepared on which to base a claim for further adjournment. This was granted, and on the morning of July 21st an adjournment of one month was asked in order to enable the defence to bring witnesses from Montana and from Ottawa. The request was not acceded to, but an adjournment of one week was granted.

The trial was resumed on July 28th. Eight witnesses were examined for the Crown. On July 29th, Charles Nolin was examined and swore that Riel's object in raising the rebellion was to get an indemnity of $35,000 from the Government. Riel's counsel put in a plea of insanity, but Riel repeatedly asserted his sanity and refused to allow the plea to be carried on. On July 31st, Riel addressed the jury at some length on the wrongs of the Half-breeds, again denied that he was insane and asserted his full confidence of an acquittal. On August 1st, Judge Richardson finished his charge to the jury, who retired at 2.15 p.m. They returned with a verdict of guilty in about half-an-hour. They recommended the prisoner to mercy. Riel was praying fervently in the box while the jury were returning the verdict. When asked if he had anything to say before the sentence should be passed upon him he addressed the Court for over an hour, stating that he was the prophet of the New World and that he would yet live to fulfil his mission. He was then sentenced to be hanged on the 18th of September, 1885. He heard the sentence with a smile on his lips.

Riel's friends in the Province of Quebec and elsewhere were loud in their expressions of dissatisfaction at the manner in which the trial was conducted. They alleged that he was tried before an incompetent tribunal, and that a magistrate liable to removal at the will of the Government should not have been appointed to try a prisoner charged with treason-felony ; that a grand jury should have been specially empanelled for that purpose. A meeting in Riel's behalf was held in Montreal on August 9—Dr. Lachapelle in the chair—when the Hon. R. Laflamme, ex-Minister of Justice, expressed the opinion that the fundamental principles of British justice had been ignored at the trial. Resolutions were passed unanimously, to petition both the Dominion and the Imperial Parliaments on behalf of the prisoner. Mr. Benoit, M.P., and Dr. Martel, M.P., were requested to take charge of the petitions. Similar meetings were held at Longueuil and other places. After some preliminary litigation the appeal from the decision of the Court at Regina came before the Court of Queen's Bench at Winnipeg on September 2. The prisoner was represented by Messrs. Fitzpatrick and Lemieux, of the Quebec bar, and J. S. Ewart, of the local bar. Messrs. C. Robinson, Q.C., and B. B. Osler, Q.C., of Toronto, appeared for the Crown. Counsel for prisoner contended that both Riel and the original record should be produced in Court. The Court decided that the point was well taken and adjournment was made till the 4th September. The further hearing of the case was resumed on that date; but the prisoner was not produced, the Crown declining to bring him to Winnipeg. Mr. Fitzpatrick, for the prisoner, stated that as the papers asked for had arrived from Regina, they would proceed with the argument. Mr. Lemieux raised the old plea of the informality of the trial at Regina, and contended that the stipendiary magistrate was incompetent to try the case. He also urged the insanity plea. Mr. Fitzpatrick followed. He held that the Treason-Felony Act was one of Imperial jurisdiction, and he questioned if it had delegated any power to Colonial authorities to legislate away any rights enjoyed by subjects of the British Empire. Mr. Ewart spoke on behalf of the prisoner and contended that the presiding justice should have taken notes. He strongly questioned the jurisdiction of the Court at Regina. Mr. C. Robin-

CHARLES FITZPATRICK. M.A.

son, Q.C., on behalf of the Crown, in an able address combated the idea that the Court at Regina was not legally constituted. Messrs. Osler, Q.C., and Aikens supported the arguments of the senior counsel for the Crown. An adjournment was made till the following day, September 5, when the Court (after hearing the reply of Mr. Fitzpatrick on behalf of the prisoner) confirmed the jurisdiction and finding of the Regina tribunal. A Cabinet Council was held at Ottawa on the 10th September, when the question of how to dispose of Riel was discussed by Sir John A. Macdonald and other members of the Government, and it was decided to respite the condemned man till an appeal could be argued before the Imperial Privy Council. In the meantime the trials of rebels of less note were being proceeded with.

On the same day, September 10, the trial of Scott, of Prince Albert, charged with complicity in the rebellion, was concluded at Regina—B. B. Osler, Q.C., for the Crown, and Henry J. Clark, Q.C., for the prisoner. The case was a very exciting one, with several lively passages at arms between the counsel. The jury in twenty minutes returned with a verdict of not guilty. Lean Man (Indian), pleaded not guilty, and was released on his own recognizance to appear for sentence when asked. Other Half-breed prisoners were let off in the same way.

The Cree Chief, Poundmaker, was arraigned before Judge Richardson and Dodds, J.P., at Regina, on August 17, on the charge of treason-felony, in making war at Cut Knife Creek, on May 20, and capturing a provision train at Eagle Hills. After hearing the evidence of Colonel Herchmer, N.-W.M.P., Robert Jefferson, the Chief's son-in-law, and others who swore that they saw Poundmaker at Cut Knife during the fight, the jury retired for half an hour, and then returned with a verdict of guilty. Poundmaker when asked what he had to say why sentence should not be passed, replied:—"I was good all summer; people told lies. I saved lot bloodshed. I can't understand how it is that after saving so many lives I am brought here." Then, waving his hand majestically, he said with a smile, "I am a man, do as you like. I am in your power; I gave myself up; you did not catch me."

Judge Richardson sentenced him to three years in the penitentiary. When he heard the sentence he asked that he be hanged right off as he preferred that to imprisonment.

Big Bear, the Indian Chief who led the volunteers such a wild-goose chase, through the Beard Mission Country, was sentenced on September 27 to three years in the penitentiary. The old warrior stood calmly waiting his doom and only evinced his displeasure at the sentence by a prolonged grunt. Two and Two and others

JUDGE RICHARDSON.

of Big Bear's band got two years, and Red Eagle and four Sioux braves were sentenced to three years' imprisoment.

On September 22 Wandering (or "Travelling") Spirit (see picture, page 99) appeared before Judge Rouleau, at Battleford, and pleaded guilty to killing Thomas Quinn, Indian Agent, at the Frog Lake massacre. Two days later Judge Rouleau sentenced the prisoner to death, and in doing so addressed him as follows:—"If a white man murders an Indian he must hang, and so must an Indian if he kills a white man. The sentence of the Court is that you, Wandering Spirit, be taken back to gaol till Friday, the 27th day of November, and then taken to the scaffold and there hanged by the neck until you are dead; and may God have mercy on your soul."

Little Runner, Lazy Man, The Gopher, Straight Man, Old Man, Little Wolf, Calling Bull and Fair Sky Thunder were sent to prison for terms varying from two to fourteen years. The undermentioned Half-breeds have been sentenced by the Court held at Regina to the following terms of imprisonment:—Maxime Lepine, Philip Guardupuy, Baptiste Vandale, seven years each; Pierre Guardupuy, Alexander Fisher, Baptiste Rochlat, Patrick Fourand, Ignace Poitras, three years each. Adolphe Nolin turned Queen's evidence and was acquitted.

On Wednesday, October 21, it was announced that the application of Louis Riel for leave to appeal from the Court at Regina was refused by the Judicial Committee of the Privy Council, and their Lordships did not consider it necessary to call upon the Attorney-General to show cause why leave to appeal was not granted. They affirmed that the Court at Regina had jurisdiction of treason; that six jurymen were sufficient; that shorthand notes were lawful reports of proceedings; and that substantial justice had been done to Riel.

At a Cabinet meeting held at Ottawa, on October 22nd, it was decided to postpone the execution of Riel until November 11th.

On October 30th, the Peace Society of London, Eng., presented a memorial to the Queen, praying for the commutation of the death sentence passed on Riel. Her Majesty declined to interfere, stating that the pardoning power had been fully delegated to the Governor-General of Canada, and that the Home Government could not interfere in Riel's behalf.

EXTRACTS FROM A PETITION

Drawn up by the friends of the Half-breed Prisoners confined in gaol.

The humble petition of the prisoners condemned to death or imprisonment respectfully sheweth:—That, having inherited the spirit of adventure and energy of the discoverers and first settlers of the country, they left the valleys of the St. Lawrence half a century ago to go and settle two thousand miles away on the banks of the Saskatchewan, where they have succeeded, after long and faithful work, to create on this hitherto unknown corner of the country prosperous establishments. . . . . That the opening of the Canadian Pacific attracted around them a foreign population, and the wealth of the primitive establishments founded by the Metis soon excited the envy of an army of speculators from the older Provinces of Canada. . . . . They, who had always lived peaceably and free on their vast prairies, were astonished to learn that the Government of Canada wanted to cut up their farms: more than this, they witnessed whole townships conceded to political speculators. . . . . At the cost of tremendous sacrifices they sent, on numerous occasions, their missionaries to the capital to demand justice; each appeal for justice was followed by a fresh reinforcement of troops to intimidate them. . . . . Yes, we fought, and we do not blush to avow it before the whole country. We would have died on the spot had it not been for the sake of our poor wives and our dear children, who had sought the shelter of the forests from the cannons of the Government troops. . . . . Our homes were sought out. Everything that hands could be laid on was carried away. What our women attempted to protect was torn away from them. . . . . Our unfortunate spouses and our poor children! On the prairie they wandered for a long time, half-clad, dying of hunger and misery, weeping for their husbands, for their fathers, their brothers, who had died shot through the heart, or who had been made prisoners and loaded with irons. After having killed and wounded the men; insulted the helpless women and children; after having plundered our fields, driven away our cattle, pillaged our modest habitations, fire was put to our homes—and we lost all. Are we not sufficiently punished? Humanity now demands its rights. Will its penetrating voice find an echo in your hearts? . . . .

RIEL'S EXECUTION.

On the 9th of November Riel received a further respite until the 16th. A. P. Sherwood, Chief of the Dominion Police, reached Regina on the evening of the 15th bearing the order of the Governor-General for the execution to take place at eight o'clock on the following morning. Every preparation had been made for the execution. The scaffold was extended from the rear of the south end of the guard-room. The mounted patrol were kept on duty by day and sentries posted all round the barracks by night. When Sheriff Chapleau and Colonel Irvine waited on Riel to convey the intelligence of his doom, he said: "Well, you have come with the great announcement." The Sheriff replied that the death warrant had come. Riel said: "I am glad that at last I am to be relieved from my sufferings." He thanked the Sheriff for his personal considerations, and requested that his body be given to his friends to be buried in St. Boniface.

After the Sheriff had read the warrant for his execution, Père André entered the doomed man's cell, and up to the hour of death was never absent from his side. Together they prayed the whole night long, Riel being most fervent. Toward 3 a.m. he dozed, and finally slept soundly. Père André watched him as he slept. Shortly after six o'clock Riel awoke, and from that time until eight o'clock, when the fatal bell began to toll, he prayed without ceasing.

At 8.15 Riel was escorted to the scaffold by the hangman, Jack Henderson, who had been Riel's prisoner at Fort Garry, and Deputy-Sheriff Gibson, attended by Père André and Rev. William McWilliams. He wore a loose woollen surtout, gray trousers, a woollen shirt, and moccasins. He walked firmly to the scaffold, repeating "In God do I put my trust." As he spoke this prayerful exclamation a smile lit up his face. Descending the few steps of the scaffold he stood on the drop with his face turned northward.

Père André and Father McWilliams continued to

pray, and Riel said: "I do ask the forgiveness of all men, and forgive all my enemies." At times his words were inaudible, but ever and again his deep and earnest prayer could be plainly distinguished above the subdued and gentle voices of the priests. At 8.18 the executioner pinioned his arms behind him; the white cap was drawn over his head; both priests holding lighted candles and repeating the prayers for the dying. As Riel stood there uttering the words "Jesu, Marie, assistez moi," the bolt was drawn. The length of the drop was eight feet. At the first moment of the fall the body remained still; then the knees drew up violently; three or four times the body swayed to and fro quivering, and then Louis "David" Riel was no more. The suspense had been long, but the agony was short. The hangman did his work well. There could have been no pain whatever. The circulation ceased in four minutes, an unusually short time. No death could be more merciful.

During his last moments Riel's behaviour excited the pity and admiration of all.

In a few minutes Dr. Dodd, the attending surgeon, pronounced life extinct, and the body was cut down. The usual inquest was held in the gaol, and the following verdict rendered:—

"That the body is that of Louis Riel, convicted of high treason, and sentenced to death; that the judgment of death was duly executed upon the body of the said Louis Riel on this 16th day of November, 1885, and that death was caused by hanging at the police barracks, near Regina, N. W. T., as directed by the Court. (Signed) H. Dodds, M.D., Coroner; Fred Champness, Foreman; William P. McCormick, John Dawson, William D. Firstbrook, David H. Gillespie, W. B. Jones, jurymen."

The coffin was then nailed up, to be temporarily placed in the burying-ground attached to the barracks, pending the relatives obtaining permission to carry it to St. Boniface.

THE TROOPS IN THE FIELD.

STAFF.

Major-General F. D. Middleton, C.B., General Commanding; Lord Melgund, Hon. Maurice Gifford, Hon. C. Freer, Capt. Wise and Lieut. Doucet, A.D.C.; Major Buchan, Acting Field-Adjutant.

REGIMENT OF CANADIAN ARTILLERY.—"A" BATTERY.

Lieut.-Col. Montizambert in Command; 115 men, 4 officers, 2 guns, 1 gatling; Major C. J. Short and Capt. C. W. Drury in Charge of the Battery; Capt. J. Peters in Command of the Battalion; Lieutenants, J. A. G. Hudon and V. B. Rivers, with Lieut. O. C. Pelletier, of 9th Battalion, attached, Capt. A. A. Farley, with Lieut. Power attached, Lieut. Imlah, with Lieut. Cimon attached; Lieut. W. H. Disbrowe, of the Winnipeg Cavalry, Supernumerary; Acting Surgeon, J. A. Grant.

"B" Battery, stationed at Kingston, 8 officers, 104 men, 2 guns, 1 gatling; Major Short; Captains Farley, Rutherford; Lieutenants Imlah, Chinic, Power, Pelletier, Attached; Supply Officer Lieut.-Col. Forrest.

TORONTO EXPEDITIONARY FORCE.

Lieut.-Col. W. D. Otter, Commanding; Lieut.-Col. E. Lamontagne, Supply Officer, Dep. Adj. Gen. of the Ottawa Military District, No. 4.

"C" Company Toronto Infantry School.—85 Men and 4 Officers.

Major, Henry Smith; Lieuts., J. W. Sears and R. L. Wadmore; Surgeon, F. W. Strange.

2nd Battalion, Queen's Own Rifles.—257 Men and 18 Officers.

Lieut.-Col., A. A. Miller; Major, D. H. Allan; Adjutant, Capt. J. M. Delamere; Quartermaster, James Heakes; Surgeons, Jos. W. Leslie and W. Nattress; Capts., T. Brown, H. E. Kersteman, J. C. Magee, W. C. Macdonald; Lieuts., P. D. Hughes, W. G. Mutton, H. Brock, R. S. Cassels, E. F. Gunther; 2nd Lieuts., A. Y. Scott, A. B. Lee, J. George.

10th Battalion, Royal Grenadiers.—250 Men and 17 Officers.

Lieut.-Col., H. J. Grasett; Major, G. D. Dawson; Adjt., Capt. F. F. Manley; Paymaster and Acting Quartermaster, Lieut. W. S. Lowe; Surgeon, Dr. G. S. Ryerson; Capts., F. A. Caston, Jas. Mason, O. L. Leigh Spencer, C. Greville Harston; Lieuts., D. M. Howard and Irving, G. P. Eliot, Forbes Michie, W. C. Fitch; 2nd Lieuts., Jno. Morrow, J. D. Hay, A. C. Gibson.

Governor-General's Body Guard.—80 Officers and Men, and 74 Horses.

Major Commanding, Lieut.-Col. G. T. Denison; Major, Orlando Dunn; Acting Adjt., W. H. Merritt; Acting Quartermaster, Chas. Mair; Lieuts., F. A. Fleming and T. B. Browning; Capt., C. A. K. Denison; Surgeon, J. B. Baldwin.

GOVERNOR-GENERAL'S FOOT GUARDS —48 men, 3 officers; Capt. Todd; Lieuts. Gray and Todd.

MIDLAND BATTALION.—342 MEN AND 34 OFFICERS.

Lieut.-Col. A. T. H. Williams, Commanding; Majors, H. R. Smith and Lieut.-Col. James Deacon; Adjt. E. G. Ponton; Paymaster, Capt. J. Leystock Reid; Quartermaster, Lieut. J. P. Clemes; Surgeons, Horsey and Jas. Might. 15th.—Capt. and Adjt., T. C. Lazier; Lieuts., J. E. Helliwell and C. G. E. Kenney. 40th.—Capts., R. H. Bonnycastle and Lieut. J. E. Givan. 45th.—Capts., John Hughes and J. C. Grace. 46th.—Capts., R. Dingwall and C. H. Winslow; Lieuts., R. W. Smart and J. V. Preston. 47th.—Capt., T. Kelly; Lieuts. Sharp and Hubbell. 49th.—Capt., E. Harrison; Lieuts., H. A. Yeomans and R. J. Bell. 57th.—Capts., J. A. Howard and Thos. Burke; Lieuts., F. H. Brennan and J. L. Weller. R.M.C.—2nd Lieuts., R. J. Cartwright, C. E. Cartwright, G. E. Laidlaw, H. C. Ponton, A. T. Tomlinson and D. C. F. Bliss.

YORK AND SIMCOE BATTALION.—342 MEN AND 34 OFFICERS.

Lieut.-Col. W. E. O'Brien, M.P., Commanding; Majors, Lieut.-Col. R. Tyrwhitt and Lieut.-Col. A. Wyndham; Adjt., Major Jas. Ward; Paymaster, Capt. Wm. Hunter; Quartermaster, Lieut. Lionel F. Smith; Supply Officer, Lieut. G. H. Bate, G. G. F. G.; Surgeon, John L. G. McCarthy; Capts., Major W. J. Graham, Peter Burnet, Allison Leadley, R. G. Campbell, John T. Thompson, Geo. H. C. Brooke and Jos. F. Smith; Lieuts. Capt. Jno. Landrigan, Thos. H. Drinkwater, Chas. S. F. Spry, Geo. Vennell, Jno. T. Symonds, Thos. Booth, Jno. K. Leslie, S L. Shannon; 2nd Lieuts., Thos. H. Banting, K. L. Burnet, I. T. Lennon, R. D. Ramsey, Wm. J. Fleury and Jno. A. W. Allan.

7TH BATTALION "FUSILIERS," LONDON.—237 MEN, 20 OFFICERS.

Lieut.-Col., W. D. Williams; Majors, A. M. Smith and W. M. Gartshore; Adjutant, Capt. Geo. M. Reid; Quartermaster, Capt. J. B. Smyth; Paymaster, Major D. McMillan; Surgeons, J. M. Fraser and J. S. Niven; Capts., Thos. Beattie, E. Mackenzie, F. H. Butler, T. H. Tracey, R. Dillon and S. F. Peters; Lieuts., H. Bapty, C. B. Bazea, A. G. Chisholm, W. Grieg, C. F. Cox, H. Payne, Jas. Hesketh, C. S. Jones and J. H. Pope.

65TH MOUNT ROYAL RIFLES, MONTREAL.—317 MEN, 23 OFFICERS.

Lieut.-Col., J. A. Ouimet; Majors, G. A. Hughes and C. A. Dugas; Paymaster, C. L. Bossé; Adjutant, J. C. Robert; Quartermaster, A. La Rocque; Surgeon, L. A. Pasé; Asst.-Surgeon, F. Simard; Capts. Ostell, Des Trois Maisons, Bauset, Roy, Villeneuve, Giroux, Prevost, Ethier; Lieuts. Plinquet, Des Georges, Starnes, Villeneuve, Lafontaine, Robert, Doherty and Normandin.

MONTREAL GARRISON ARTILLERY.—250 MEN AND OFFICERS.

Lieut.-Col., W. R. Oswald; Majors, W. H. Laurie and E. A. Baynes; Paymaster, W. Macrae; Adjutant, T. W. Atkinson; Quartermaster, J. A. Finlayson; Surgeon, C. E. Cameron; Assist.-Surgeon, J. M. Elder; Chaplain, Rev. J. Barclay; Capts., W. C. Trotter, F. Brush, C. Laurie, F. W. Cole, D. Stevenson, C. H. Levin; Lieuts., W. H. Lulham, J. D. Roche, G. C. Patton, F. W. Chalmers, H. T. Wilgres, J. K. Bruce and B. Billings (acting).

CAVALRY SCHOOL CORPS, QUEBEC.—30 MEN, 3 OFFICERS, 33 HORSES.

Commandant, Lieut.-Col. Jas. F. Turnbull; Lieuts., E. H. T. Heward and F. L. Lessard.

THE TROOPS IN THE FIELD.

9TH BATTALION RIFLES, "VOLTIGEURS," QUEBEC.—204 MEN, 28 OFFICERS.

Lieut.-Col. Amyot ; Majors, Roy and Evanturel ; Paymaster, Major Dugal ; Quartermaster, A. Talbot ; Adjutant, Casgrain Pelletier ; Supply Officer, M. Wolseley ; Surgeon, A. Dublois ; Asst.-Surgeon, M. Waters ; Capts. Frenette, Chouinard, Drolet, Garneau, Pennee, Fages, Pinault, Fiset and Lavasseur ; Lieuts. Hamel, Baillairgé, Labranche, Depuis, Casgrain, De St. Maurice, Dion, Shehy, Pelletier, Routhier, Larue and Beique.

THE HALIFAX PROVISIONAL BATTALION.—348 MEN, 30 OFFICERS.

Lieut.-Col., J. J. Bremner ; Majors, C. J. Macdonald and T. J. Welsh ; Paymaster, W. H. Garrison ; Adjutant, E. G. Kenny ; Quartermaster, Capt. J. G. Gorbin ; Asst.-Surgeon, D. Harrington. No. 1 Co.—Capt. J. E. Curren ; Lieut., J. P. Fairbanks ; 2nd Lieut., A. Anderson. No. 2 Co. —Capt., J. McCrow ; Lieut., W. L. Kane ; 2nd Lieut., R. H. Skimmings. No. 3 Co.—Capt., B. A. Weston ; Lieut., A. Whitman ; 2nd Lieut., H. A. Hensley. No. 4 Co.—Capt., R. H. Humphrey ; Lieut., B. Boggs ; 2nd Lieut., C. E. Cartwright. No. 5 Co.—Capt., C. H. MacKinlay ; Lieut., J. A Bremner ; 2nd Lieut., J. McCarthy. No. 6 Co.—Capt., H. Hechler ; Lieut., H. St. C. Silver ; 2nd Lieut., T. C. James. No. 7 Co.—Capt., A. G. Cunningham ; Lieut., J. T. Twining ; 2nd Lieut., C. R. Fletcher. No. 8 Co.—Capt., J. Fortune ; Lieut., C. J. McKie ; 2nd Lieut., C. K. Fiske.

90TH WINNIPEG BATTALION OF RIFLES.—334 MEN AND OFFICERS.

Lieut.-Col., Alfred McKeand, Commanding ; Majors, Chas. M. Boswell and Lawrence Buchan ; Paymaster, A. H. Witcher ; Quartermaster, H. Swinford ; Surgeon, Geo. T. Orton ; Asst.-Surgeon, J. W. Whiteford ; Capts., C. F. Forrest, H. N. Ruttan, W. A. Wilkes, C. A. Worsnop, R. G. Whitla, Wm. Clark ; Lieuts., H. J. Macdonald, G. W. Stewart, H. Bolster, Zach. Woods, E. G. Piche, F. L. Campbell ; 2nd Lieuts., R. L. Sewell, J. G. Healy, C. Swinford, H. M. Arnold, A. E. McPhillips and R. C. Laurie.

91ST BATTALION, WINNIPEG.

Lieut.-Col., Thos. Scott, M.P., Commanding ; Majors, D. H. McMillan and Stuart Mulvey ; Adjutant, Capt. W. C. Copeland ; Quartermaster, Capt. W. H. Bruce ; Surgeon, Maurice M. Seymour ; Asst.-Surgeon, Frank Keele ; Inspector of Musketry, A. W. Lawe ; Capts., J. A. McD. Rowe, Thos. Wastie, Wm. Sheppard, S. J. Jackson, J. H. Kennedy, J. C. Waugh, R. W. A. Rolph, Jno. Crawford ; Lieuts., F. I. Bamford, E. C. Smith, R. C. Brown, J. B. Rutherford, Major A. Cotes, Geo. A. Glinn, A. Monkman, A. P. Cameron ; 2nd Lieuts., W. H. Saunders, R. Hunter, G. R. Reid, T. Lusted, H. W. Chambre, H. McKay, F. R. Glover, T. B. Brondgeest, Ed. Ellis and F. V. Young.

92ND WINNIPEG LIGHT INFANTRY.

* Lieut.-Col. W. Osborne Smith, C.M.G., in command ; Majors, John Lewis and W. B. Thibadeau ; Adjutant, Capt. Chas. Constantine ; Paymaster, E. P. Leacock ; Quartermaster, R. La Touche Tupper ; Surgeon, J. P. Pennefather ; Asst.-Surgeon, S. T. Macadam ; Capts., W. R. Pilsworth, W. B. Canavan, F. J. Clarke, Dudley Smithe, T. A. Wade, T. P. Vallancy, D. F. McIntosh ; Lieuts., D. G. Sutherland, G. B. Brooks, T. G. Alexander, J. W. N. Caruthers, Augustus Mills, N. Caswell, T. Gray ; 2nd Lieuts., R. G. MacBeth, J. A. Thirkell, W. R. Currie, F. T. Currie, Thos. Norquay, Thos. D. Deegan.

WINNIPEG FIELD ARTILLERY.

Major, E. W. Jarvis; Capt., L. W. Coutlee; Lieut., G. H. Young; 2nd Lieut., G. H. Ogilvie.

WINNIPEG TROOP, CAVALRY.

Capt. C. Knight; 2nd Lieut. H. J. Shelton.

THE NORTH-WEST MOUNTED POLICE.

Commissioner A. G. Irvine in command; "A" Division, officers and men, 47; "B" Division, officers and men, 132; "C" Division, officers and men, 73; "D" Division, officers and men, 199; "E" Division, officers and men, 111.—Total, 562.

BOULTON'S SCOUTS—80 men, 5 officers.
FRENCH'S SCOUTS—25 men.
DENNIS' SURVEYORS' SCOUTS—50 men, 3 officers.
MOOSE MOUNTAIN SCOUTS—51 men, 3 officers.
STUART'S RANGERS—150 men, 4 officers.
ALBERTA MOUNTED INFANTRY—50 men, 3 officers.
BATTLEFORD INFANTRY—40 men, 3 officers.
REGINA HOME GUARDS—40 men, 3 officers.
BIRTLE HOME GUARDS—40 men, 3 officers.
CALGARY HOME GUARDS—50 men, 1 officer.
YORKTOWN HOME GUARDS—50 men, 3 officers.
QU'APPELLE HOME GUARDS—40 men, 3 officers.

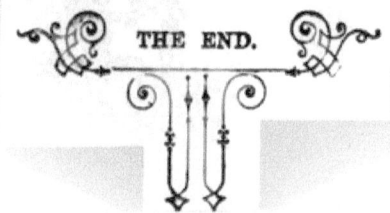

THE END.

www.ingramcontent.com/pod-product-compliance
Lightning Source LLC
Chambersburg PA
CBHW051728300426
44115CB00007B/514